American Colossus

AMERICAN COLOSSUS

Big Bill Tilden and the
Creation of Modern Tennis

ALLEN M. HORNBLUM

Foreword by John Newcombe

University of Nebraska Press | Lincoln and London

Library of Congress Cataloging-in-Publication Data
Names: Hornblum, Allen M., author.
Title: American Colossus: Big Bill Tilden
and the creation of modern tennis /
Allen M. Hornblum; foreword by John Newcombe.
Description: Lincoln: University of Nebraska Press, [2018] |
Includes bibliographical references and index.
Identifiers: LCCN 2017037675
ISBN 9780803288119 (cloth: alk. paper)
ISBN 9781496204318 (epub)
ISBN 9781496204325 (mobi)
ISBN 9781496204332 (pdf)
Subjects: LCSH: Tilden, William T. (William Tatem), 1893–1953. |
Tennis players—United States—Biography. | Tennis—History.
Classification: LCC GV994.T5 H67 2018 |
DDC 796.342092 [B]—dc23 LC record available at
https://lccn.loc.gov/2017037675

Set in Charter ITC Pro by Mikala R Kolander.
Designed by L. Auten.

To Richard Hillway, who follows Bud Collins and
Frank Phelps in maintaining the highest standards
of scholarship and respect for the history of tennis

When nature removes a great man, people explore
the horizon for a successor; but none comes, and
none will. His class is extinguished with him.

—RALPH WALDO EMERSON

Genius . . . is the capacity to see ten things where
the ordinary man sees one, and where the man of
talent sees two or three, plus the ability to register
that multiple perception in the material of his art.

—EZRA POUND

Contents

Foreword

JOHN NEWCOMBE

I decided at ten years of age that I wanted to play at Wimbledon and represent Australia in Davis Cup competition. This was 1954, television had not quite arrived in Australia, and events like Wimbledon were listened to on the radio or read about the next day in the newspapers.

At twelve I was selected by Tennis Australia, along with seven other boys, in an elite training camp for three hours each Saturday morning lasting eight weeks. Our coach, Dave Thompson, was very tough on us over a three-hour period each morning and allowed us only one drink break.

Dave told us if we wanted to make tennis an important part of our lives, we needed to understand the history of tennis and who our great champions had been. He said that Bill Tilden was maybe the greatest player ever and had written an excellent book on tennis titled *Tennis A–Z*. I believe it has come out under other titles as well. I had my parents acquire the book and read it cover to cover. The chapter that really got my attention was "Match Play and Tennis Psychology."

By the time my own career was over, I was known as a player who had some major weapons, one of which was my strong mental approach and self-belief. Two things Tilden said in that chapter: First, there are two ways to break down an opponent's game—attack his weakness and go after his strength and break it; the second one has more risk, but if it works it will destroy him. Second, to be a champion you must have very strong self-belief; however, if the self-belief drifts into conceit, you will be in trouble, as conceit is very brittle.

I delved into Tilden's life and loved reading about his challenges with other greats of his time, particularly the Four French Musketeers, Lacoste, Brungon, Cochet, and Borotra. As a founding father of today's Association of Tennis Professionals and a hater of amateur bureaucracy in sport, I was fascinated with Tilden's constant challenges with the U.S. Tennis Association. He was the greatest player of his decade, a forerunner of professional tennis, a great athlete, and in my book one of the top eight players of all time. Who can say who is the greatest? All a player can do is be the best in the world over a long period of time. Tilden certainly achieved that.

I am so happy that Allen Hornblum has taken on the task of writing about Bill Tilden. I believe it will be a book that every young tennis player who dreams of greatness should read. I wonder how many pros on the circuit today know about Tilden, Little Bill Johnston, the Four Musketeers, Perry, Budge, Brookes, Wilding, and countless others who were pre–World War II or for that matter the champions of 1945–68.

Acknowledgments

As someone who has played everything from football, baseball, and basketball to cycling, tennis, and track and field, with a few other sports thrown in for good measure, I think I understand the physical demands as well as the technical skill each sport requires. And though I have broken my share of bones and spilled enough blood on athletic fields over the years to qualify as a legitimate sports nut, playing the game often and passionately does not equate to knowing its history. Regrettably, this lack of historical knowledge is particularly true for those who play the great game of tennis and is most egregious for the pre–Open Era.

An outlier in this regard is Richard Hillway. A former Big Eight tennis champion at the University of Colorado, Hillway would not only spend his life playing and teaching the game, but also become a voracious student of the sport's origin, early years, and popular evolution. Today he is one of the world's leading authorities on the history of tennis. It would be my good fortune to be introduced to Hillway early on in my quest to learn about Bill Tilden and even greater luck for Hillway to sign on as my personal tour guide of sports' golden age and Big Bill's monumental contributions to the game. As I gathered documents and newspaper clippings and then went to work writing chapters, Hillway and I talked daily—sometimes several times a day—about my discoveries and how it squared with his knowledge of the man and his unparalleled role in the game. Big Bill's slow but inexorable climb to the top and his indelible impact were always at the heart of our discussions. Debates and disagreements over aspects of Bill's life and career, his battles with the United States Lawn Tennis Association (USLTA), and the reasons for his arrest and waning from public memory were frequent. Hillway's help and enthusiasm—as well as his wealth of historical material—were invaluable in capturing the real Bill Tilden story.

Ken Benner, a tennis aficionado in his own right and one of America's leading sports memorabilia collectors, would allow me to select a number of photographs from his fine collection of Tilden material for display in the book. It was Ken who also introduced me to Hillway and then directed me to Jean Park and Sibby Brasler at the Legacy Tennis and Education Center in Philadelphia. Access to Legacy's Clothier Tennis Library and their collection of *American Lawn Tennis* (ALT) magazines—the bible of the game's day-to-day development during the first half of the twentieth century—was indispensable in tracking the sport's evolution from a sedate leisure activity of the well-to-do to a true athletic contest of wide popular appeal.

The Free Library of Philadelphia's periodical section proved a home away from home on all too many occasions as I scanned a daily retinue of century-old newspapers in tracking the Tilden family's history and Bill's emergence as a topflight tennis player. In addition to staff at their main library, Frank Peterson and Rekha Wadhera at the Northeast Regional Library were particularly helpful with my seemingly endless microfilm requests. Kelly Conn at the Los Angeles Library was also extremely kind in fulfilling my request for relevant newspaper articles. Dr. Mark Rabuck at Germantown Academy was very helpful in illuminating for me Bill's and his brother Herbert's academic and athletic careers at the school. His discovery of century-old photographs of the Tilden brothers is also much appreciated. Of similar assistance were Nancy Miller, Mark Frazier Lloyd, and Timothy Horning at the Archives of the University of Pennsylvania, which supplied valuable information concerning Bill's activities as a college student and athlete. Bart Everts proved equally helpful in regard to Bill's rather short career at Pierce Business College. I would also like to thank the staff at Temple University's Urban Archives for their assistance with newspaper clippings and their extensive collection of photographs involving Bill's myriad pursuits. I would also like to thank Jim Munday and his staff at the Union League of Philadelphia's Heritage Center as well as the staff of the Pennsylvania Historical Society.

I also owe a debt of gratitude to a number of former players who knew Tilden and patiently answered my questions, including Vic Seixas, Dick Savitt, Gardnar Mulloy, and Angela Buxton. Seven-time Grand Slam winner John Newcombe also deserves my thanks for readily agreeing to write his fine preface to this book. Finally, I would also like to thank Dr. Bill Rosenberg, Dr. Judy Newman, Dr. Vincent McNally, and Alan Holman for their thoughts and assistance on various aspects of this project.

Introduction

Bud Collins, the noted *Boston Globe* journalist and television sports commentator, convincingly argued some time ago when reflecting on the historical arc of his favorite sport, "If a player's value is measured by the dominance and influence he exercises over a sport, then William Tatem 'Big Bill' Tilden II could be considered the greatest player in the history of tennis." That succinct but weighty assessment remains as true today as it was when it was made well over a generation ago. Though great players with highly identifiable names such as Connors, McEnroe, Borg, Edberg, Lendl, Becker, Agassi, and Sampras have filled stadiums and thrilled audiences around the world with their exceptional play, their impact on the game of tennis remains infinitesimal compared to the court leviathan of sports' golden age. Even today's most accomplished and inspiring racket wielders such as Novak Djokovic, Rafael Nadal, and Roger Federer pale in comparison to the influence and power Tilden had over the game.

Though some current tennis fans may argue that Stefan Edberg was more dignified, Andre Agassi better liked, John McEnroe more entertaining, and Roger Federer a winner of more majors, Tilden is still their superior. Not only did he dominate every aspect of the sport, but he also transformed it from a leisure activity of the WASP upper class to a popular sport of mass appeal and in so doing enabled tennis to challenge baseball, boxing, and football for space on the sports pages of the nation's broadsheets and tabloids. Additionally, there is more than enough evidence to argue that by the mid-1920s, Big Bill had become the best-known and most followed athlete on the face of the planet. As was often said of him by the game's keenest observers the world over, "He is in a class by himself, I do not expect to see Tilden's like again!" and "He is the greatest of the great—the superman of tennis."

Tilden was certainly unique. Driven, flamboyant, contentious, melodramatic, creative, egotistical, egalitarian, thoughtful, and opinionated, the "autocrat of the courts" transcended his sport as much as, if not more than, any athlete in history, including Babe Ruth, Jack Dempsey, Red Grange, and Bobby Jones—all great athletes with whom he shared the headlines during what has been called the most colorful era in American sports.

Born in the last decade of the nineteenth century, Tilden was a good athlete, but there was nothing to suggest his future prominence. In fact, it might be fair to say he was rather shy, retiring, and even sickly as a youth. Like most children he played various sports, but he took a particular interest in the relatively new game of lawn tennis. Demanding athleticism and a high degree of skill, the game would become a lifelong passion. Our numerical vocabulary seems too limited to accurately quantify—much less describe— the commitment and number of hours Tilden spent hitting balls against the walls of his home or on the courts of the nearby cricket club. With his older brother's ancient wooden bat strung with fraying lamb gut, Tilden spent countless hours practicing, impersonating past stars, his fascination with tennis growing as strong as any sport ever had on a child's imagination.

His obsession, however, did not translate into early success. In fact, his high school and college play was of no great distinction, and he readily admitted to often having considered giving up the game. But his love and perseverance were eventually rewarded. By his midtwenties, the once gangling youth had matured, become less erratic, less prone to tactical blunders. He began displaying clear signs of mastering the art of hitting the ball where and how he wanted. The emergence of a strategic sensibility and an unrivaled mastery of the game's key strokes would become emblematic of his long reign as the sport's greatest player. He could pulverize the ball and blast opponents off the court or tap delicate drop shots that left adversaries stunned and in a state of paralysis. His knowledge and use of spin were unprecedented. Chop shots, slices, topspins, sidespins, and underspins flew back at opponents in a barrage of dizzying trajectories and speeds that underscored his incredible racket control and impressive armory of court weaponry. Add to his myriad ground strokes an arsenal of heavy artillery—his serves—including the most feared weapon in the game, his "cannonball" that shot by amazed players like a bullet. Many opponents pondered how anyone was expected to defeat him. In actuality, few did;

his dominance stamped him as a grass-court assassin and a certified icon of the sports world. *Genius* and *colossus* were terms that were regularly associated with him.

Tilden's impact was transformative; he almost single-handedly revolutionized the Victorian game from its effeminate image as a sissy activity for the wealthy at sedate garden parties to a real man's game that appealed to masculine, red-blooded Americans. No one who witnessed the tall Philadelphian rip off howitzer-like forehands and backhands—one almost imagined the whiff of gunpowder in the air—could think anything other than this was no longer a placid outdoor distraction for genteel aristocrats.

Adding to the macho image were Tilden's size and athleticism. At six-foot-two and 155 pounds, he was taller than most, with a raven-like wingspan and shanks that allowed him to reach any ball by covering vast acreage in just a few turf-gulping strides. His cheetah-like speed was augmented by unlimited stamina. Blessed with grace, power, and endurance, to a thoroughly overmatched opponent Tilden could well have been reimagined as a lethal avatar packing the punch of Jack Dempsey, the intricate footwork of Vaslav Nijinsky, and the longevity of a California redwood.

More impressive yet was Tilden's cerebral approach to the game. Not just a contest of physicality, a match with Big Bill was an IQ test where everyone but him proved intellectually deficient. Very few, indeed, were capable of galloping across a lawn while wielding a racket in a skillful manner, and playing a high-level chess match, simultaneously. The results were boringly predictable. As newspaper headlines regularly recounted, "Tilden Wins Again" became a familiar refrain. A rare loss precipitated much speculation, but as one savvy opponent opined, "Even when beaten, Tilden leaves the impression with onlookers that he is better than the victor."

The numbers confirm his supremacy. As an amateur, he won 138 of 192 tournaments and 907 of 967 matches for an astounding .938 average. Between 1920 and 1930 he won three British (he was the first American-born player to win the Wimbledon title) and seven American titles. The ten major titles would not be eclipsed until decades later and not by an American until the end of the century. From 1920 to 1925 he won every major singles tournament he entered. His Davis Cup record of seven consecutive team titles was equally formidable and still unmatched. Once he jettisoned his amateur status for the professional ranks, he would go on to do the heavy lifting during the height of the Great Depression to turn pro tennis into a popular and commercially sound economic enterprise.

That biographical snapshot alone would solidify Bill Tilden as one of the athletic greats, but he was so much more than just a successful jock. Tilden not only taught and lectured about the nuances of the game like a grass-court pied piper, but also wrote books—well over two dozen fiction and nonfiction titles—and hundreds of articles for newspapers and magazines. Several of his how-to tennis books are considered classics and still widely read. His love of the written word extended to drama and the stage. He performed on Broadway, wrote stage plays, funded several theatrical productions, and appeared onstage in theaters around the country. He even acted in several silent films at the height of his celebrity during the Jazz Age. Though many would argue his best dramatic performances were on the athletic pitch and not the stage, his appreciation of the dramatic arts and occasional on court histrionics led some newspaper reporters to refer to him as "the John Barrymore of the courts." In addition, he was known to be a bridge player of some consequence and a serious collector of opera and classical music. Can it be of any wonder then that Tilden aficionados are convinced if he wasn't a twentieth-century Renaissance man, he was pretty darn close? In fact, Italian author Luca Battozzi was so impressed with Tilden's accomplishments that he referred to him as "the Leonardo da Vinci of tennis" in his recent book on Tilden.

Other serious students of tennis and sports in general, such as Richard Hillway and Larry Lawrence, believe Tilden to be exceptional for a couple of additional reasons. Tilden, they argue, is the most forgotten member of America's pantheon of great athletes. Not only that, but he also may be the greatest athlete the upper classes ever produced. One could add that he just may be the greatest gay male athlete produced in America. Such claims are of course debatable, and the controversy surrounding Tilden's fall from grace and absence from popular memory can be the subject of endless speculation and argument. But sports fans are, if nothing else, passionate and argumentative, characteristics to which Big Bill was certainly no stranger. I would be only too happy if this book would spark such a discussion and thereby remind sports fans of one of the greatest and most interesting athletes to ever traverse the world's athletic fields.

American Colossus

Part 1

The Struggle for the Top

1

"A Game of Society"

There is no sensation in the sporting
world so thoroughly enjoyable to me as that
when I meet a tennis ball just right in the
very middle of my racquet and smack it.

—WILLIAM T. TILDEN 2ND

The "bombshell announcement on the morning of July 19, 1928," hit the sporting world with the force of a tropical typhoon. In addition to millions of flabbergasted sports fans around the globe, "the people of Paris and France" were particularly hard hit; they were said to be in a "state of shock." As one exasperated observer recounted, "Without warning, without an intimation of any kind, the elaborate structure built by the French Federation . . . was wreaked as if hit by a cyclone."[1]

Recriminations and statements of befuddlement and outrage were echoed in far-flung capitals from Brisbane and Tokyo to Stockholm and London. "Incomprehensible," "ridiculous," "utter folly," "beyond understanding" were just a few of the reactions by stunned sports and editorial writers trying to make sense of it all. It was inexplicable that the greatest player in the history of tennis would be prevented from playing in the Davis Cup challenge round against France, the champion nation. And to have such mischief perpetrated by one's own nation was truly mind-boggling.

Newspaper headlines and controversy were certainly no stranger to "Big Bill" Tilden, an iconic figure of the "golden age of sports" and the first American-born player to win the Wimbledon trophy. A transformational figure who popularized the sport, helped propel lawn tennis from exclusive country clubs to public playgrounds, and would one day professionalize the game, he was also a multitalented connoisseur of theatrical drama and classical music, an author of more than two dozen books and hundreds of magazine articles, and a bridge-playing enthusiast of championship caliber.

Granted, he could be petulant, tiresomely difficult, and as demanding as an Indian prince, but he was also an athletic talent of Herculean proportions. Now he was being sanctioned for writing articles about what he was best known for and what he knew best. The entire episode was bizarre, but one thing was clear: the old-line oligarchs of the American amateur tennis federation were out to finally level him.

Tilden's greatness, his exceptional prowess at lawn tennis, was universally recognized as the stuff of "genius." Columnists and respected athletic authorities regularly referred to him as "the king of them all," the "absolute monarch of the courts,"[2] the "Napoleon of lawn tennis."[3] Only Babe Ruth rivaled him for sheer star power. But the Babe's mythic stature was confined to American shores; Tilden's was international.

Members of the American Davis Cup team practicing in Paris were devastated by the news and spoiling for a fight. Tilden was their hero, their leader; they began to organize a strike. They would refuse to play the host nation.

The French were even more chagrined. Their displeasure quickly escalated to indignation; they had been preparing to defend the Cup—the most cherished team trophy in the world of athletics and the first time a non-English team was defending the trophy—before the earth they stood on was cut out from under them. They had constructed an expensive new tennis stadium—Roland Garros—to show off their team, the pride of France. Now the biggest name in the game was precluded from playing; the financial loss would be tremendous. French players were equally peeved. Defeating the American team without Tilden was no victory at all; where was the honor?

Even some United States Lawn Tennis Association officials were caught off guard and embarrassed by the decision. The sanction and how it was secretly orchestrated offended their sense of fair play and due process. "I hereby tender my resignation as Chairman of the Davis Cup Committee to take effect immediately," said one disgruntled American official.[4]

Unwilling to take a financial bath, not to mention a loss of prestige by hosting a topflight international encounter without the game's greatest player, the French initiated a last-gasp diplomatic offensive. They began to lobby the American ambassador to France for relief. If necessary, they would even go to the White House.

It was all too much for most observers to make sense of. One of the decade's greatest athletes being penalized for writing newspaper articles, tennis players going on strike, high-ranking officials abruptly quitting, diplomatic channels being pursued, and confusion and turmoil seemingly everywhere—one would be hard-pressed to come across another instance of an athlete precipitating such controversy and all-out mayhem. But William T. Tilden 2nd was no run-of-the-mill sportsman. "The Everest of the lawn tennis Himalayas," he was a once-in-a-century athletic wonder who captivated the sports world as assuredly as he dictated his dominance to those who had the audacity to step across the net from him.[5]

Once the broad-shouldered and reed-thin Philadelphian walked on a tennis court and took hold of his weapon of choice, it was as if Merlin's magic wand had been transformed into a racket containing a devilish array of drives, spins, lobs, chops, and drop shots in its arsenal. No one prior to Tilden had ever attempted, much less mastered, such an imposing array of shots. Such athletic excellence and technical superiority were thought by some to be divined by the gods or at the very least fashioned in Dr. Frankenstein's laboratory. But the truth was far more mundane and conventional. As with other great champions, it starts with a child mesmerized by a particular athletic item emblematic of the game. It was no different for young Tilden.

More like an oddly configured snowshoe than the superlight, aerodynamic tennis rackets of today, the Victorian-era "Pim" captivated "Junior" Tilden like few other objects during his childhood. Though in appearance rather unremarkable and strung with a thick-gauge gut that resembled frayed string, the ancient tennis racket quickly became an item of desire for the youngest member of the Tilden household.[6] Despite its weighing in at nearly sixteen ounces and possessing a swollen, ax-like handle that a child's hand could barely grip, young Tilden fantasized about the wooden contraption the way most children daydreamed about King Arthur's Excalibur. As he would admit many years later of his unrelenting desire, "I coveted it with all my six-year-old soul."

Regrettably, the hefty, unadorned racket belonged to his brother, Herbert, who was seven years older and just beginning to make a name for himself in local lawn tennis circles. Junior could only imagine the joy of one day possessing it. When his father brought home a new model, a "Hackett and

Alexander," for his oldest son, Junior pounced on the ragged but beloved Pim. "I snitched it," confessed Tilden unabashedly. "Let me admit the truth. I swiped it without a qualm of conscience, and grabbing my one soiled, corroded and definitely dead tennis ball, strode forth."[7]

The "pinched racket" was the start of a lifelong love affair between a man and his sport. The unlikely marriage of a molly-coddled child and a shabby racket would eventually result in enthusiastic crowds at packed stadiums, front-page newspaper headlines, and friendships with some of the world's most famous celebrities. The union would also culminate in the making of athletic history, as well as the indelible image of one of the most iconic figures in the annals of sport.

The youngest Tilden's stealth attack on his brother's property would be committed at the family's country cottage in the Catskill Mountains. Onteora, New York, was a fashionable mountain retreat for the well-to-do from large northeastern cities desiring a relaxing sanctuary from the sweltering midsummer heat. Until the theft of the racket, Junior Tilden had shown interest only in "artistic things," a creative sensibility "inherited from [his] mother" and one that was "never quite understood by [his] father."[8] A turn-of-the-century art colony approximately three dozen miles south of Albany and about a dozen or so west of the Hudson, Onteora (an Indian word for "mountain of the sky"), according to Tilden, "was a place that stimulated the imagination and spurred love of beauty in one who had any artistic leanings."[9] The upscale, arty atmosphere became a magnet for a host of celebrated writers, actors, musicians, and other artistic performers.

The chic mountain colony was home to Maude Adams of *Peter Pan* fame and thought to be the highest-paid stage performer in America at the dawn of the twentieth century; Madame Louise Homer of the Metropolitan Opera; John Alexander, the portrait painter; Mary Knight Wood, the songwriter; Ruth McHenry Stuart, the author; and General Custer's widow. Mark Twain was often a guest at Onteora. It was not unusual for Junior Tilden to be playing with other children or off on a solitary hike up Onteora Mountain and come upon some celebrated artist painting a bucolic scene of rich "reds, browns, and golds of autumn leaves just coming from the green summer foliage" or hear the "deep rich contralto" of a prominent opera performer practicing her vocal exercises.

The summer colony was abundant with creative talent. And Tilden, like most children, was encouraged to partake of Onteora Club's many artistic endeavors. He would make his "first dramatic experience" in *Buttons*, an amateur play directed by the great Maude Adams.[10] But much to his family's surprise and occasional consternation, their youngest son's interest soon centered on an old racket and several oxygen-depleted tennis balls.

To his parents' dismay, their six-year-old had discovered the walls of the family's mountain house were a perfect surface for imitating the strokes of the great tennis players of the day. A long porch on one side and a "driveway, large, level, and with a nice shale surface, provided an excellent court," Tilden would one day write. And the side of the house presented "a wonderful backboard for practice."

And so began a great player's athletic calling, though, as Tilden would later lament, his "tennis career almost ended at the start." Some of his overly enthusiastic swipes at the ball had more pace than accuracy, and very early on "one beautiful shot," he came to admit, "went speeding directly at the window of my father's den." The result, according to the remorseful perpetrator, was "a wealth of shattered window pane over my father as he lay enjoying his afternoon siesta." A terrible "moment of awful hush" followed, something like the silence that "precedes an earthquake or the braking of a monsoon." He looked for a place to hide, but the expansive driveway allowed for none.

His father's cry of "Junior"—a familial but disliked moniker he would grow to detest—rang down like thunder from the heavens, a clear sign the gods had taken a disapproving stance on his latest passion. Painfully recalling the incident many years later, Tilden soberly wrote, "I came, he saw, and he conquered."[11]

Junior was given a stern lecture, the offending instrument confiscated, and he was forbidden from playing the game ever again. More than a month would pass before an alliance with his mother garnered enough family clout for him "to once more reach the driveway and the side of the house with racket in hand." During the coming days, months, and years, young Tilden would spend countless hours banging tennis balls off the wall of his mountain home or any other flat surface he came upon in hopes of emulating his older brother's skill and success. Many windowpanes were smashed in the process—Tilden called "practicing strokes and breaking windows a delightful pastime"—but it was the cost of learning the game. "Out of the maze of shattered windows and stern rebukes," he would one day proudly write, "emerged what later became my Cannonball and American Twist serves," not to mention a half-dozen other strokes that Tilden mastered.[12]

Progress was noted early on. At the tender age of seven Tilden won the 1901 fifteen-and-under Junior Boys Championship at Onteora. His competitors were several years older and no slouches on the court. In fact, Tilden was down 6–1, 5–0 in the final before pulling off a remarkable comeback, a dramatic ashes-to-garland turnaround he would go on to perfect and repeatedly demonstrate throughout his amateur and professional career. Though rather modest in stature, the two-inch pewter cup with the inscription "Onteora Club, Boys Singles, 1901" was as cherished as if it was the Wimbledon Championship Trophy.

His older brother, Herbert, however, was unimpressed. "Aw yer yellow," barked his brother. "You never ought to have come close to gettin' licked." At the time Junior was wounded by his brother's sneering wisecrack and thought him cruel, but would later admit, "He pricked the bubble of my swelled head." The brotherly scolding "gave me the chance to be a real tennis player."[13]

There is no record of his parents' thoughts on their youngest son's first athletic triumph. No doubt they were proud of his success, but they also may have been a bit surprised. Junior had never shown a propensity for great physical achievement. Moreover, any indication of grit and fortitude was an unexpected blessing. The Tilden family had already been severely scarred; just the act of surviving childhood was a notable accomplishment in the Tilden household.

As the Tilden family gathered around the table for their Thanksgiving meal in 1884, they had much to give thanks for. They were healthy, increasingly prosperous, and growing in number. It was a joyful and optimistic time. Despite this comforting family portrait, however, it would be their last Thanksgiving together. In fact, the majority of them would not make it to Christmas. A shadow had fallen over the Tilden home. Death would strike quickly.

Just a few days after the holiday Willamina Tatem Tilden, the youngest of William and Selina Tilden's three children, and not yet a year and a half old, died. Several days later Elizabeth, the oldest, came down with a terrible headache, sore throat, swollen neck, and escalating fever—once again the dreaded signs of diphtheria. By the ninth of December Elizabeth, who had just turned four, was dead. On the fifteenth, less than a week later, Harry Bower, not yet three and the Tildens' only son, would be claimed by the same infectious disease that was infamous for aggressively steamrollering through homes with young children. Philadelphia, like New York, Boston, Baltimore, and other big cities before the discovery of an effective antitoxin, was ripe for recurring waves of diphtheria. Deadly epidemics had become commonplace; even upscale families like the Tildens were impacted. Ironically, it would be a Philadelphia company in the mid-1890s that would manufacture the first antitoxin in the United States. But it would arrive too late for the three Tilden children. Their parents would escape the carnage—at least physically—but their three beautiful and joyous children now resided in a quickly growing family plot at Ivy Hill Cemetery.

It is difficult to imagine the psychological trauma visited upon William and Selina Tilden after losing three precious children in little more than a fortnight. The pain, the indescribable loneliness, the deathly silence in a household that once bubbled with laughter and joy . . . but the Tildens—certainly Mr. Tilden—were made of sterner stuff and persevered. In fact, one could even argue the suddenly childless couple flourished as they struggled to rebuild their shattered lives.

Said to have a "commanding appearance" and an assured, competent manner, William Tatem Tilden was born in St. George, Delaware, a small town nestled along the banks of the Delaware River and the Delaware and Chesapeake Canal in 1855. His father, Edwin Marmaduke Tilden, was a prominent New Castle County physician and could trace his lineage back to the Middle Ages and British nobility. Tyldens were said to be friends of Henry II, and at least one, Sir Richard Tylden, was "Seneschal to Hugh de Lacy, Constable of Chester . . . and afterwards accompanied Coeur de

Lion to the Holy Land and fought under him at Ascalon in A.D. 1190."[14] The large Tylden clan held manors in a half-dozen English towns and were especially prominent in Kent. The first member of the family to set foot in the New World was Nathaniel Tilden in 1634. A former mayor of Tenterden, England, he decided to move his large brood, including a wife and seven children plus an equal number of servants, to the new Massachusetts Bay Colony. They eventually settled in Scituate. It was also about this time that the change from y to i in the family name was made.

Over the years the Tilden clan gravitated to different parts of North America. One branch fled to Canada during the war for independence and ultimately became the equivalent of Hertz in the rent-a-car business north of the border. Another branch settled in New York and produced Samuel Tilden, a prosperous lawyer, Tammany Hall corruption fighter, and well-thought-of governor. Best known for being cheated out of the 1876 presidential election, Tilden settled quietly in his Greystone Estate in Yonkers and left a good part of his personal fortune to the construction of New York City's impressive free public library on Fifth Avenue.

The Tilden line that ventured farthest south settled in the Middle Atlantic region around Delaware and Maryland. After the sudden death of Dr. Edwin Marmaduke Tilden, his wife, Wilhelmina Tatem, relocated to Philadelphia, where young William was educated at a series of public and private schools and eventually graduated from the city's well-respected Central High School in 1872.[15] His first job was with the Philadelphia and Reading Railroad as a clerk in the passenger department, but he left after six years for a job with the shipping firm Peter Wright & Sons, where he remained for two years. At some point during the late 1870s, Tilden entered the wool business and specialized in raw materials used by manufacturers of blankets, carpets, and plush carriage robes.

It was through this line of work that good fortune smiled on Tilden, as it enabled him to meet his future wife, Selina G. Hey. Miss Hey was the daughter of David Hey, a well-known businessman who was head of a successful wool and hair enterprise. Coming from good Quaker stock on her mother's side, refined, and with a definite propensity for the arts, she was also quite attractive. Naturally, she caught the eye of the equally handsome William Tilden. Their marriage on November 6, 1879, led directly to William's rapid rise up the corporate ladder. Taken into a partnership with his father-in-law, he would assume the mantle of ownership with his father-in-law's retirement. Soon after, the firm changed its official name to the William T. Tilden Company.

Fortunately, William and Selina were able to partially temper the soul-searing tragedies of late 1884 by the birth of another child, their son Herbert Marmaduke, on November 2, 1885. Through keen parental concern and careful oversight, he would grow up strong and remain healthy and active through his childhood. A little more than seven years later, on February 10, 1893, another son, William Tatem Tilden Jr., would be born at 209 West Chelten Avenue in Germantown.[16] Though "Junior" was named after his father and would exhibit a striking physical resemblance to the family patriarch—the lantern jaw and long face being the most prominent features of the Tilden family—it would be his mother who would have the greatest impact on his development and sensibilities. A woman of culture, and an accomplished pianist with a profound love of classical music, she would impart her artistic tastes on her youngest child far beyond anyone's normal expectations. Though his father was increasingly ensconced in business and political activities—predilections that would be passed on in part to his older brother, Herbert—"Junior" would show little interest in commerce. Encouraged by his father to follow in his footsteps and learn the rudiments of business, young Tilden would repeatedly reject such entreaties. He would remain his mother's child and wedded to literature, theatrical fare, and music throughout his life.

Around the time of their youngest son's birth, the Tilden family moved to an upscale section of Germantown, where they built a large Tudor-like mansion they called Overleigh. Once an independent town approximately six miles northwest of Philadelphia, Germantown was first settled by Quaker and Mennonite families in the 1680s. Incorporated into the city's new and extended boundaries in 1854, Germantown became home to a rather affluent class of residents during the last decades of the nineteenth century. Located at 5015 McKean Avenue—practically a country lane at the time—Overleigh was an impressive structure and was often said to be "one of the handsomest residences in the district of Germantown" and its owners some of the "happiest." The many-roomed mansion was emblematic of Mr. Tilden's rising status in both the business world and the civic life of the city.

At the end of the street—and literally just a stone's throw from the Tilden family's front door—were the expansive and manicured grounds of "Manheim," or what would become known as the Germantown Cricket Club (GCC). Destined to be one of the world's great cathedrals of lawn tennis, the clubhouse and surrounding grounds were already recognized as one of America's elite social and athletic institutions.

Though there are various accounts regarding the origin of Manheim—both the street and the section of Germantown—the most reliable may be that the name "honors the home of Baron Heinrich Wilhelm von Stiegel, who upon his arrival in America from Manheim, Germany, in 1761, purchased considerable land in Germantown."[17] Alternative theories include a tract of land stretching from Germantown Avenue to the Schuylkill River being purchased by the Fraley family from Joseph Shippen around the turn of the nineteenth century. "On a portion of the tract [was] laid out a square . . . with Manheim Street running through the center." The tract was to be divided into fifty building lots and styled as part of "the village of Manheim." Though some of the lots were sold and eventually developed, a good portion of the project was labeled a "complete failure."[18]

Whatever the true origin, the acreage bordering Manheim Street became known to one and all as Manheim and would remain so until World War I.[19] It was also there that a collection of young men—athletic rivals initially—agreed to establish a cricket grounds. Brought across the Atlantic by English mill hands during the nineteenth century, the game of cricket picked up American admirers, who began to form their own teams. William Rotch Wister was one of "the first Americans to have noticed the points of play" and encouraged a group of Germantown men to form their own team and "measure their strength" with both homegrown and foreign teams throughout the Philadelphia area. The result was the Germantown Cricket Club, which was formed in 1854. The game's popularity grew quickly, and a rival group—some of the members being younger siblings of the Germantown squad—formed their own team and gave themselves the name Young America Club. Both teams had prominent sponsors, the older squad having the support of the Wister family and the younger team led by the large and enthusiastic Newhall family.[20]

Apparently, "so rapid was the growth of cricket that after six years there were reported to be no less than thirty clubs in the neighborhood of Philadelphia," with the Germantown clubs having the largest and "most enthusiastic supporters." Women were increasingly drawn to the spectacle, and their attendance was said to have added a festive atmosphere to contests and "zest to the game."[21]

Not surprisingly, the game's popularity declined during the Civil War, as many players were off serving in the military and a more serious mood pervaded the nation, but cricket witnessed a resurgence and even became fashionable in some locales once the conflict ended. Philadelphia was such an area. English mill hands from Kensington, students from Main Line colleges, and well-bred Anglophiles displayed an enthusiasm that attracted teams from abroad. The matches drew decent-size crowds—some as large as twenty thousand—necessitating the construction of a grandstand. Prominent personages would occasionally attend. In fact, General George Meade, the victor at Gettysburg, was the guest of honor when the Germantown Cricket Club opened its new cricket grounds in the Nicetown section of Philadelphia on October 17, 1866, with a match against the St. George's Club of New York. The hometown team developed a reputation, and word went out that Philadelphia was the only city in America where British and colonial teams could find a real challenge. Squads from England, Ireland, Canada, and Australia paid regular visits. The "Gentlemen of Philadelphia" returned the favor and occasionally traveled to England for a series of amateur matches. The international competitions did much to solidify the area's reputation as a hotbed of cricket.

By the late 1880s, however, economic constraints forced a consolidation of the two clubs, with Germantown becoming the team's official name and the blue and white of Young America the squad's colors. It was also decided that they would purchase their own pitch rather than continuing the expensive practice of renting playing fields in Stenton and Nicetown.

In 1889 the club purchased a piece of land made up of the former Littell and Price estates bordering Manheim Street.[22] The combined acreage eventually became "one of the best appointed cricket grounds in the world." Known locally as "Manheim," the Germantown Cricket Club was its official name.[23] The proud members assured themselves that "no field surpasses Manheim" in quality.[24] The following year a contract was signed with Charles McKim, of the architectural firm McKim, Mead, and White, for the construction of a clubhouse on the grounds.

The new club's members had decided to spare no expense; they wanted to make a statement. As sociologist E. Digby Baltzell has aptly written of this era, "Social Darwinism provided the ideological rationale for the Anglo-American gentlemen's right to rule, the *club*—both urban and suburban, and around the world from Calcutta, Kimberley, and London to New York, Boston, and Philadelphia—was becoming a major factor in creating and preserving class mores and class exclusiveness."[25] Less than a decade earlier Boston's elite had founded the Country Club in the suburb of Brookline, Massachusetts. Its impact was immediate; the well-heeled throughout the Northeast took notice and wanted to establish their own replicas of "the great country houses of rural England, so the families of the American business gentry could spend their leisure hours" in similar comfort.

McKim, Mead, and White quickly became the architectural firm of choice for such symbolic retreats. Their first great project was the Newport Casino in Rhode Island, to be followed by similar structures in Narragansett Pier and at Rhinebeck, New York. Like their wealthy New England and New York cousins, the social and economic elite of Philadelphia desired their own temple of leisure during what would become known as the "great age of elegance." The finished product—the Germantown Cricket Club in Philadelphia—according to Baltzell, was "surely the finest tennis club building after the [Newport] Casino." The members were pleased; the structure was as exquisite a specimen of modern colonial architecture to be found anywhere. The new edifice was worthy of its title as being one of the oldest athletic organizations in this country.[26]

The new clubhouse, a smaller women's clubhouse, an Italian garden, and cricket grounds were showcased with a highly publicized match against Lord Hawke's English cricketeers before a crowd of forty thousand that attended the six-day affair. A large grandstand that could seat several thousand patrons had been erected at the southern end of the grounds. The structure walled off another recent British import—lawn tennis courts—from the more favored cricket grounds. The cricket field would also be used for a host of sporting and nonsporting events over the years, including parades, summer musical concerts, various dramatic performances, soccer matches, and even some early Penn-Princeton football games before the universities decided to invest in their own athletic stadiums. It would not be long, however, before a gradual shift in club members' passion necessitated a dramatic reordering of athletic priorities. Manheim, like most other posh country clubs, was about to undergo a radical shift in the leisure priorities of the sporting set.

What became the new game of interest was created by Major Walter Clopton Wingfield, a retired British cavalry officer, in 1874. The former Welsh officer called his creation "lawn tennis" or "sphairistike," but "lawn tennis" was the more enunciation-friendly appellation it came to be known by. To everyone's surprise, except maybe Wingfield's, the game caught on with an upper class that was growing in wealth and free time and in search of ways to exploit both. Almost immediately, England's aristocracy took to it. Everyone from the Prince of Wales, the Crown Prince of Prussia, and the Duke of Edinburgh to the Marquis of Exeter, Earl of Leicester, and the Earl of Salisbury went out and purchased the necessary items to play the game. In fact, just about every duke, earl, viscount, and marquis in the expanding British realm seems to have taken note.[27] Nonroyals were not to be denied; they were similarly enthusiastic, and the game spread rapidly.

No one is quite sure who first brought the game of tennis to American shores, but one oft-told tale is that while vacationing in one of those far-flung British outposts, Miss Mary Outerbridge saw the game and apparently thought it would be equally popular back home. On her return from Bermuda, she brought a lawn tennis set back with her, and with the assistance of her brother, A. Emilius Outerbridge, laid out a court on the grounds of the Staten Island Cricket and Baseball Club. Her intuition proved accurate, as the game became quite popular. Similar stories were being played out at other East Coast sites of studied leisure. By the late 1890s clubs and groups from Massachusetts to Arizona had established their own lawn tennis courts.

Back in England the new game was quickly outstripping other Victorian-era outdoor pastimes like croquet, archery, and badminton. Desiring something more vigorous and challenging, British men and women increasingly found Wingfield's new diversion of lawn tennis "the ideal game . . . and it would soon drive both croquet and badminton off the velvet lawns of the stately homes of England." Nothing may illuminate the game's growing popularity more than the fact that in 1877, just three years after Wingfield placed a patent on a portable tennis court and published a rule book for the game, the All England Croquet Club formally changed its name to the All England Lawn Tennis & Croquet Club and immediately set about to organize the first National Championship at Wimbledon.

A somewhat similar scenario was being played out in Boston. A group of cricket players looking for a greater athletic challenge laid out a lawn tennis court in Brookline on the old Sears estate and named the site Longwood. Within a decade cricket at the club was practically mothballed, and Longwood would become synonymous with top-caliber tennis in New England.

With tennis becoming known as "a game of society," upper-class Americans were charmed by its simplicity, emphasis on skillful technique, and physical difficulty. The game's other accouterments, unfortunately, "had a kind of cultured atmosphere which did not endear it to the general public."[28] Regardless, by 1880 lawn tennis was being played at nearly three dozen clubs, mostly on the East Coast, but also as far west and south as San Francisco and New Orleans.

By the turn of the century the pattern was clear: cricket was in decline, and the popularity of lawn tennis was growing rapidly. According to an item in the Germantown Cricket Club annual report for 1900, "The increased interest in the game of lawn tennis, which was so decided last year, continued all through the past season on the courts to such an extent that, on a number of occasions the facilities of the club were taxed to the utmost, and players had to yield their courts to those awaiting their time to play."[29] The upshot: lawn tennis had taken hold and become the new country-club passion.

Like his older brother before him, young Bill would be homeschooled, a practice his overprotective mother adopted to ensure germs and other noxious elements were kept at a safe distance. She and a team of private tutors would provide his first years of formal education. Consistent with their stature in the community, both boys would eventually be sent to Germantown Academy, one of the finest schools in all of Pennsylvania and well on its way to becoming the oldest nonsectarian school in the nation. Established during the Revolutionary War, the school was known for a rigorous curriculum, its excellent reputation, and a clientele that included some of Philadelphia's most respected families. George Washington, in fact, would send his adopted son there.[30]

Herbert Tilden started at Germantown Academy in 1896 when he entered fourth grade. He would flourish both academically and athletically at the small select school, participating in a number of clubs, running the gamut from the Belfry (drama) and Mock Trial clubs to Philo (academic honors and community service) and the Invitation Committee (annual senior dance). No slouch in the classroom, Herbert's real leadership was displayed on the school's athletic fields, where he was a key member of the baseball, football, cricket, and bowling teams. Herbert would graduate Germantown Academy in 1904 and matriculate at the University of Pennsylvania later that year.

Junior Tilden was homeschooled for a longer period than his older brother. According to Germantown Academy records, William T. Tilden Jr. was first registered as a student at the school in 1905, when he would have been twelve years old. Whether the delay was due to his mother's extreme caution regarding her son mixing with other children, her suspicion that something was amiss regarding his development, or young Bill's dread of formal schooling is open to speculation. There is no doubt that Bill, who admitted to being "not a particularly nice child . . . detested school and avoided it" with a passion.[31] As he would frankly admit in his autobiographies, "There was one thing as a child at which I drew the line, and that was school. It seemed to me then that it was always in the way of so many other more interesting and important things I wanted to do." Tilden went on to confess, "By dint of much propaganda work with my mother, a few well-placed headaches when needed, and some unintentional but none the less serious illnesses, I managed to substitute a series of alleged tutors for school. Somehow," Tilden proudly admitted, "I managed to escape school until I was fifteen."[32]

Germantown Academy's thin collection of student records from that time and Tilden's faulty memory regarding his initial introduction to Germantown Academy are puzzling. It is quite possible Mrs. Tilden registered her son for the 1905–6 school years but quickly withdrew him. According to the Dr. Mark Rabuck, the school archivist, there is no further record of his activities or participation during those years.[33] It is possible that after years of homeschooling, an attempt was made to have their youngest child attend a well-respected brick-and-mortar school in the neighborhood, but the effort proved unsuccessful. Junior would continue to be homeschooled for several more years until a severe family illness necessitated some dramatic changes in the family's living arrangements as well as Junior's education.

Their youngest son's protracted transition from his mother's side to an actual educational institution seems to have had little impact on the Tilden household. Older brother Herbert had easily adapted to the rigors and demands of Germantown Academy, and Mrs. Tilden did not seem particularly troubled that "Junior" remained at home and by her side throughout the day. By all accounts mother and son were devoted to each other and no doubt spent a good deal of time in discussion about the arts, and she encouraged her son's appreciation of good music.

If the head of the household had any concerns about the situation, there appears to be no record of it. Part of the reason may be due to his increasing involvement in the political and civic life of the city. William T. Tilden was becoming a pillar of society and a force to be reckoned with. Philadelphia was an ever-growing economic powerhouse—"an industrial giant" that was often compared to "Liverpool-Birmingham or perhaps Essen-Dusseldorf"— and Tilden was riding the crest of the city's increasing importance.[34]

A vibrant commerce and manufacturing center during the last decades of the nineteenth century, Philadelphia was a recognized production hub for everything from steamships and locomotives to cigars and ice cream. And though thousands of skilled and unskilled laborers worked at impressive production sites like Cramp's Shipyard and the Baldwin Locomotive Works, those employment numbers may have paled in comparison to the vast numbers who were employed in the city's textile industry. By the turn of the century approximately 20 percent of Philadelphia's seventy-one hundred manufacturers were textile plants, employing around 35 percent of the city's quarter-million workers.[35] Mills making everything from clothing and carpets to hats and tapestries stretched from Kensington to Manayunk, and although the William T. Tilden Company did not rival the output of larger textile plants like Keystone Knitting Mills, John B. Stetson, and John Bromley and Sons, the owner and chief operating officer of the smaller Tilden operation was making quite a name for himself.

Though he was putting many hours in his office located at 254 North Front Street near the Delaware waterfront directing the affairs of his wool and hair business, Tilden was contributing many additional hours during the late 1880s and '90s as an active member of various financial, political, and civic institutions in the city. He had become a board member of the Manufacturers Club of Philadelphia as well as the National Association of Manufacturers, an officer of the Sons of Delaware, Philadelphia's prestigious Union League, the Historical Society of Pennsylvania, the Board of Trade of Philadelphia, the Presbyterian Church, the Young Men's Republican Club of the Twenty-Second Ward, and the Philadelphia Bourse, among a host of other well-known commercial, social, and political organizations.[36]

Tall, with a strong jaw, graying hair, and prominent mustache, the striking merchant with a fresh carnation in his lapel was a popular after-dinner speaker and widely viewed as a natural leader. A tireless workhorse and prudent decision maker, it was said that "he possessed a most agreeable personality and genial manner, and his honest methods gained him a large and ever-increasing circle of friends."[37] Philadelphia's political leaders were quick to take note and speculated on his electoral potential. But they were mistaken if they thought he was someone who would take orders and do their bidding. Tilden was not out to build a résumé or attain a cushy job; he was not just another affluent but bored businessman with political aspirations.

Successful in business, Republican in philosophy, and conservative in taste, he was a man of some standing, but he was not opposed to change. In fact, Tilden was developing a reputation as a reformer, and not all of his initiatives won the support of the city's conservative business establishment. As the *Journal of Commerce* said of him in the early years of the new century:

> He is not a faddist nor possessed of utopian ideas of obtaining perfection. He approaches this subject with that same practical business sense which he applies to the conduct of his own business. He demands that public servants be chosen for their peculiar fitness for their duties they have to perform; that they give to the city or state the same faithful and unselfish service that they would be expected to give to a private employer; that elections be honestly conducted and the will of the people obeyed and that the business interests of the city be entirely divorced from the machinations and intrigues of politics.[38]

Not surprisingly, such a man is often sought out for board membership in civic groups or positions of leadership in political organizations. The Philadelphia Public School System invited him to join their board in 1899 and not long after appointed him head of their important Property Committee, and the Union League—the citadel of Republicanism—made him a director in 1901 and followed that with his election as a vice president. At least a half-dozen other organizations from banking to fire prevention had him somewhere on their organizational mastheads. Tilden was circulating in rarefied air, but he was no party hack or corporate flunky. He knew right from wrong and did not mind mixing it up if he thought something of importance was at stake.

Casting caution aside, he took on entrenched political powers when he supported businessman John Wanamaker over powerful party boss Matthew Quay for U.S. senator from Pennsylvania in 1896. Just a few years later he was chairman of the Businessman's League supporting McKinley for president. And soon after, he ruffled the feathers of fellow Republicans by becoming chairman of the city committee of the City Party, which dealt a stinging defeat to the Republican organization in the reform wave of 1905. Such efforts contributed to Tilden's growing reputation as an "uncompromising fighter" and a principled "independent."[39] It also repeatedly placed him on the short list of prospective mayoral candidates, an honor he seemed to have little interest in pursuing.

By the early years of the twentieth century William Tatem Tilden was someone of stature and a recognized leader in the nation's third-largest city. No surprise then that he could comfortably mix with other prominent movers and shakers in the business and civic arena such as William Elkins, Thomas Stokes, Henry Pepper Vaux, A. W. Biddle, Cortwright Wetherill, Owen Wister, Joseph Drexel, John Strawbridge, and John Wanamaker, all esteemed members of the Germantown Cricket Club.[40]

For the young and impressionable Tilden boys, however, the names they were most captivated by were those of Frederick B. Alexander, William A. Larned, William J. Clothier, Beals C. Wright, and Holcombe Ward, American tennis champions who regularly competed on Manheim's grass courts, courts that Junior could easily spy from his bedroom window. Between watching matches there, scampering about as an occasional ball boy, and daydreaming about one day playing important matches on Manheim's pristine grass courts, Tilden was not joking when he said, "I was practically born into the Germantown Cricket Club."

Much like his older brother, who might have been a better all-around athlete, Junior prided himself on being competitive—he called it possessing a "game sense"—and playing "all games naturally well." He was tall for his age, lithe, and fleet-footed, physical attributes useful in a range of sports, but instead of lugging a football on a gridiron or catching fly balls on a baseball diamond, he became fixated on the grass tennis courts just beyond Manheim Street. The newest British import was gradually overtaking cricket as the sport of choice of Philadelphia's leisure set, and young Tilden had become enthralled by the athleticism and adroit racket skill displayed by the game's top players. Even decades later he could still fondly recall Bill Larned's "machine-like, sweeping ground strokes . . . the peculiar accurate underhand poke drive of Bill Clothier, hit as if he were in slow motion," and Ward's "unorthodox high twist serve."[41] Just the mention of great foreign stars like the Doherty brothers of England, Norman Brookes of Australia, and Anthony Wilding of New Zealand caused him to "breathe with awe."

It was more than the players' athleticism or skillful strokes, however. Tilden was drawn to the overall atmosphere. The chivalry and daring of the competitors "seemed to reflect the glamour of romance in the spirit of sportsmanship that was ever present on the courts and the genial good fellowship that existed among its players," he would one day write.[42]

Indeed, for one of Tilden's social class, sport was drenched in the tradition of the gentleman amateur. Winning was almost secondary to how one played the game; sportsmanship was the centerpiece of the entire exercise. As Baltzell would write in his fine account of the game's English heritage, "Along with toughened character, the code of good sportsmanship stressed the amateur values of the all-rounder, and winning as less important than playing hard and fairly."[43] Young men of this class were judged on their knowledge of the classics, what schools they went to, and their ability at games. Athletics were considered a training ground for one's moral development. In fact, many a headmaster at elite institutions such as Andover, Groton, Choate, and Germantown Academy must have viewed the pitch on their campus as a moral platform for a lad's later life. Cricket was imbued with this ethic, and the game's introduction in the colonies—including America—helped foster a gentlemanly spirit and class consciousness in a host of leisure activities. Lawn tennis would be ingrained with this same tradition and sporting ethic.

As the stars of the game competed just a few yards from his home, Tilden's admiration and flights of fancy grew increasingly strong. The close proximity encouraged idol worship. The players' generous spirit and display of grace under pressure impressed him. "Gee!" he would say to himself. "These chaps must be regular fellows. I wish I knew them all."

He certainly knew one of them—his brother, Herbert. Building a reputation as a top local player, Herbert had led his high school team, was now doing the same at the University of Pennsylvania, and was well on the way to establishing himself as Germantown Cricket Club's best tennis player. Young Bill learned the game's rudiments from his brother, but Herbert could be highly critical and occasionally condescending. "Herbert regarded me pretty much as a total loss," Bill sadly admitted, "and seemed to think I was rather a blot on the family."

The criticism stung, but Bill was determined to be a tennis player, and his brother's sniping comments were not going to deter him. He practiced religiously and carefully observed the strokes of his brother and the international stars like Frederick B. Alexander at Manheim and the Onteora Club in the Catskills during the summer. "I was fascinated by the contortions of his service, the grace and speed of his drive," wrote Tilden years later. "I determined to be another Fred Alexander."[44]

Young Tilden's life was progressing quite nicely. Unlike his older brother, who was known for a sturdier constitution, Junior lobbied his mother and complained of headaches, and "some unintentional but nonetheless serious although helpful illnesses," to escape that dreaded institution known as school. Granted, he had to contend with what he called "a series of alleged tutors," but it was a small price to pay for the additional free time. He was by his doting mother's side throughout most of day, except for when he ventured off to the nearby tennis club to watch matches or work on his own strokes. For a fifteen-year-old, it was quite a good life, stress-free and with the freedom to pursue everything from Frank Merriwell novels and listening to recordings of his favorite composers to long neighborhood hikes in the summer and ice skating in the winter. But a cruel turn was in store for both Junior and his family. On a trip to Atlantic City with Bill in 1908, Selina Hey Tilden would be stricken with a painful paralytic attack that would leave her incapacitated and bedridden. Young Bill's comfortable, anxiety-free lifestyle would now take a dramatic turn.

2

"A Useless Kid Who Would Never Be Worth Anything"

I began to study tennis from the
standpoint of geometry and physics.

—WILLIAM T. TILDEN 2ND

The doctors' verdict was Bright's disease, a severe kidney condition associated with extreme lower-back pain, high fever, and nausea. Selina Hey Tilden had been struck with a particularly virulent form of the disease, known
today as acute or chronic nephritis, leaving her partially paralyzed and,
in her son's words, a "complete invalid." She would now require constant
care, presuming she survived. The attack had come so unexpectedly and
with such devastating results that she was unable to immediately return
from the Jersey Shore to Philadelphia. In fact, many months would pass
before she was able to come home.

Sudden and overwhelming illness was no stranger to Mr. and Mrs. Tilden,
but it was to their youngest child. Not yet alive to experience the devastating
loss of his three older siblings in 1884, he referred to his mother's health
problem as "the first blow to our family and the beginning of the chain
of events that absolutely changed my whole mode of living."[1] Junior was
naturally shaken. He would later admit to being "shocked" and "terribly"
depressed by the event, for he and his mother were inseparable and "great
pals." After being raised virtually at her side, he was now confronted with
the realization she might not survive. That lingering threat and the inability
to see her for extended periods of time must have been agonizing.

Her tenuous state and her inability to return home threw the Tilden
household into disruption. Overleigh was no longer the smooth-running
operation it had once been. Besides directing the affairs of the family business, William T. Tilden Sr. was deeply involved in various civic initiatives,
including the construction of new schools for an ever-growing Philadelphia
public school system, and the manager of an expansive new addition to the

Union League's property that would extend it the entire block from Broad to Fifteenth Streets. Both projects, not to mention his many other duties, had him spending less and less time at Overleigh. To better oversee those duties, he had taken an apartment at the Union League. His wife's illness could not have come at a worse time.

Herbert was in his last year at Penn and was being encouraged to follow in his father's footsteps and join the family's wool business. He had also fallen in love and was considering marriage. The Tilden family's "disorganized" state in the aftermath of Selina's health crisis impacted everyone, and it was not long before it was thought best to relocate the youngest member of the family. Junior was sent a couple blocks away to live with his mother's unmarried sister and cousin, Miss Mary Elizabeth Hey and Miss Selena G. Hey, who lived at 519 Hansberry Street. Literally just on the other side of the expansive grounds belonging to the Germantown Cricket Club, the semidetached three-story house was a considerable comedown in size and luxury from his family's McKean Avenue mansion, but the loss of comfort and familiarity was just one of many adjustments Junior had to contend with.

As Mary Elizabeth, his mother's sister, took it upon herself to spend an inordinate amount of time nursing her at the Jersey shore, Junior was left in the capable hands of his cousin Selena. Fifteen years older than her pampered cousin, she proved quite adept, but she thought it wise considering the circumstances—if not long overdue—that Junior finally acclimate himself to a regular school environment. "I could not work the tutor game long on her," admitted Tilden regretfully, and he soon found himself "shoved into Germantown Academy."

No doubt the adjustments to a new home and his first school experience, plus the very real prospect that his mother might die, were difficult, but young Tilden survived the ordeal. Apparently, his mother's guidance and his various tutors over the years had sufficiently prepared him for Germantown Academy, where he would begin eleventh grade in 1908. The experience did little to change his opinion of school; he "disliked study intensely" and "avoided as much of it as [he] could and still get by in class." Subjects like "Latin, German, and Geometry" would have been a lost cause if it were not for young Bill's "very useful memory," which repeatedly "pulled [him] through his final examinations."[2]

His athletic career at Germantown Academy was not much more impressive. Some at the school still remembered Herbert, Junior Tilden's older brother, who graduated in 1904 and had gone off to Penn, where he had become captain of the tennis team and won the intercollegiate doubles title in 1908. The younger Tilden was less outgoing than Herbert and took part in fewer school activities. Tall, thin, and not nearly as sturdily built as his brother, he focused his energies on one sport, tennis, and made the school team.[3] By 1910, his senior year, Junior Tilden was captain of Germantown Academy's tennis team and its number-one player, but his game was lacking. For some reason it had fallen apart, or undergone a "complete collapse," in Tilden's overly critical opinion. "I became one of the almost group," he would write in an autobiography. "I almost won every match, but never landed a single one." It was perplexing because Tilden believed he was "quite good" between the ages of seven to thirteen, but by the time he turned fourteen his game was on a downward trajectory. He idolized his brother but feared Herbert considered him "a total loss" and a "useless kid who would never be worth anything." He would just grow up to be a "blot on the family honor, and a serious drawback to the game of tennis."[4]

We do not have any of Herbert's own papers or documents that would confirm this low opinion of his brother's tennis ability. Maybe he drove him with critical remarks just to try to get the best out of him. But an examination of their tournament play during their high school and college years illuminates the fact that the Tilden brothers played surprisingly little doubles together. This may indicate, as young Bill would one day write, "My brother . . . looked on me as a distinct handicap on any tennis court, particularly as a doubles partner."[5]

Though he is mostly disparaging of his two-year stint at Germantown Academy, Tilden must have done reasonably well scholastically, as he was named the "class poet" at the 1910 graduation ceremony. One of only nine orators for the event, he may have had the longest and most humorous presentation, his rhyme-filled recollections of classmates and teachers covering twenty-two stanzas and one hundred lines. Included in *Ye Primer*, the graduation yearbook, are a number of interesting items and photographs that further illuminate Tilden's two years at Germantown Academy. At the time of his graduation he was five foot ten tall and 128 pounds. His most obvious characteristic was "Thinness," his ambition "to be a clown," and his favorite expression "Curses." Curiously, for favorite place, he answered, "With girls who are easily entertained."[6] Photos from the yearbook show a long-faced, serious young man who more often than not was formally attired in a long, narrow tie. Even his tennis-team photos show Tilden, racket in hand, the only member of the seven-man squad wearing a necktie. As a team captain Tilden should have been part of another school photograph honoring the captains of Germantown Academy's football, baseball, cricket, bowling, and tennis teams. For some unknown reason Tilden did not make that session.

Like his older brother, he would go on to enter the University of Pennsylvania in early October 1910. And like Herbert, Junior was expected to major in business and commerce at the Wharton School of Business, though he had little to no interest in such subjects. His academic record at Penn is "rather confused" and discloses numerous instances of "withdrawals" and "cancelled" classes. Not surprisingly, he passed courses such as Constitutional Law and American Social Problems but did not pass Political Economy and Business Law. Apparently, he was encouraged and dutifully did repeat his freshman year. Part of this may have been due to a "leave of absence" he was granted from March 6 to April 7, 1911, that was said to be due to "illness."[7]

That period also corresponds to his mother's rapid decline and eventual death in May 1911. Although he had been living close by on Hansberry Street with his aunt and cousin, he visited his mother often and was clearly aware of her deterioration. Until her illness—and what some believe culminated in a stroke—she had cared for her son with uncompromising love and devotion and had passed on to him her great affection for the arts, music, and drama. He was her child, and he would never forget it. While his father would continue to take on additional civic challenges and become a political force who entertained Presidents McKinley, Roosevelt, and Taft at his McKean Street mansion and the Union League, young Junior Tilden would now live with and be cared for by two spinster relatives. And although they would dote on him and make his life as comfortable as possible, the loss of his mother must have made his college years at the very least problematic, or, as he described it, "very broken."

The pall cast over this period due to his mother's ill health and eventual death caused him to be more reclusive and "avoid several scholastic activities" he would have "enjoyed but for which at the time [he] had no heart." These included the dramatic organizations, the Belfry Club at Germantown Academy, and the Mask and Wig at Penn. "Probably I could not have made either organization," Tilden modestly admitted, "but my tremendous love for the stage would have been partially satisfied."

No doubt a college highlight—and maybe the only one—was earning a spot on the Penn tennis team. This is especially significant since there is so much misinformation on Tilden in the public arena, some of it arguing that Tilden was not good enough to make his college squad and that he actually graduated. In fact, both are untrue. He did play on the team and is seen proudly wearing his college sweater in team photos. It is also true, however, that he did not set the tennis world on fire with his sparkling play. "During my school and college career," he would one day write, "I engaged in countless tournaments, of which I won none. I battled through scores of team matches, but never beat anybody."[8] These were lean years in Tilden's mind, and despite loving all aspects of the sport, he admits to having his periodic doubts. "Between the ages of twelve and twenty," he would write, "I gave up the game, on average, about once a week."[9]

The loss of matches and occasional qualms about his lack of progress did not cool his ardor for the sport, as he began to teach tennis to whoever displayed an interest in learning the game. By 1912 he was traveling to schools and playgrounds throughout the Philadelphia area with Paul W. Gibbons, another area tennis buff, in an effort to spark interest in the sport. Gibbons was the president of the Philadelphia and District Tennis Association and greatly interested in promoting junior tennis in the region. Having a college player like Tilden was a godsend in that it was rare to find a young man willing to give up his time, travel the city, and provide free instruction to neophytes.

"Our system was not difficult nor elaborate," said Tilden, "but it proved effective." Each weekday afternoon they would go out together or apart and visit different schools for an hour or so after the school day. "We would meet all boys interested in tennis and give an illustrated talk on strokes, ending by allowing the boys to ask questions they wished, which we answered to the best of our ability." From that group they would choose two or four of the better boys for "a personally coached team or squad, which we would meet on Saturday. These boys were taught not only strokes but were coached in tactics and strategy." Tilden believed the scheme "created tremendous interest in the schools in Philadelphia, while among the boys themselves the rivalry to make the personally coached squad was tremendous."

Gibbons was thirteen years older than Tilden and was quickly making his way up the administrative ladder. He had organized the Philadelphia Tennis Association and would be critical to just about every tennis initiative in the area over the next three decades, including organizing the Cynwyd Club and the Penn Athletic Club and providing leadership to the Middle States Lawn Tennis Association. In the latter capacity he would prove an adroit and steadfast supporter of Tilden's during the player's many squabbles with members of the national tennis association.[10]

As Tilden's academic career limped along with a series of uninspiring chemistry, economics, political science, and business courses, the high point of each day may well have been listening to his growing record collection or more likely tennis related—either playing for his college team and local country clubs or teaching the nuances of the game to Philadelphia-area high school students. The year 1915, however, would prove as difficult a year as he had yet endured and culminate with the end of his association with the University of Pennsylvania and the dreaded business career his father had planned for him.

On January 25 of that year a "testimonial dinner" was held in honor of his father at the Union League. A large crowd of league members had turned out on a cold, wintry night "to honor the big brother who went out into the world and did us honor, discharged every task that was laid upon him with credit to himself and to the family, and had done credit to the bringing up of this Union League household." William T. Tilden that night was often described as the "big brother [who] rang true every time he was tested. He was never known to fail in the slightest iota, in duty to a friend."

Several speakers that evening would offer further testament to Tilden's stellar leadership, sound judgment, and overall excellence. He had been elected to lead the Union League for three successive terms, 1912, 1913, and 1914, and had diligently carried out his duties with honesty, integrity, and incredible selflessness. Though he had first been elected vice president of the league with a smattering of resistance due to his history of independence and reform-minded political proclivities, he had eventually won the respect and loyalty of the entire membership. No one had ever doubted his patriotism and love of country.

His crowning achievement in the eyes of many league members may well have been his astute leadership of the half-million-dollar expansion of the league's clubhouse. The $527,600 project that would consume an entire center city block between Broad and Fifteenth and Sansom and Moravian Streets was an extravagant undertaking at the time and "expected to surpass in completeness of equipment any similar building in the country." The six-story structure of Indiana limestone was a difficult, all-consuming project, but the membership had selected the right man for the job. Tilden's experience as the chairman of the public school system's Property Committee had prepared him well. He was more than equipped for the challenge. At the 1909 ceremony laying the new building's cornerstone, Tilden diplomatically shunned congratulatory applause. "It gives us great pleasure to take part in these ceremonies, and realize through the laying of this corner-stone that part at least of their work has been accomplished," said Tilden, "but we still have our armor on. When this building has been successfully completed and we have laid our armor off, will be a better time than now, for us to celebrate."[11] Commitment to the project at hand and lack of interest in any form of self-aggrandizement: it was a typical Tilden performance.

At the January banquet the embarrassed honoree would conclude the evening by thanking the membership for the dinner and warm statements. "I guess I am a sentimental sort of a cuss," said Tilden, "but I do thank you. I care little about the dinner. I love the flowers—and I don't like the word *love* between men—but I am pretty fond of you and this gem which you have given me, I hope will never disgrace."[12]

For the hundreds who attended the banquet—and the many thousands throughout the region who knew of his many and varied contributions—Tilden's death barely six months later would prove a stunning loss. He was universally respected, and most believed he could have won election as the city's mayor if he had shown a semblance of interest in holding public office. Tilden had turned sixty in March, appeared in good health, and continued his busy schedule of business and civic engagement, but a particularly hot spell during midsummer had affected him. He was forced "to take to his bed in his apartment at the Union League."

Though weak and in considerable discomfort, Tilden left his sickbed for a late-July meeting of the Philadelphia School Board, the last one before the summer recess. Of his many associations his position as chairman of the school system's Property Committee was arguably the one closest to his heart. Dedicated to advancing public education, Tilden had overseen the construction of twenty-six elementary schools and three high schools at a cost of $10 million. It was a tremendous undertaking that was widely admired for its competence and attention to detail. His leadership during one of the system's largest construction booms had resulted in Tilden earning the sobriquet as "the Father of Fireproof Schoolhouses" in Philadelphia.[13]

Several in attendance at the meeting made comment on Tilden's condition, but he "waved their protests aside and said he felt it his duty to be present at the last meeting of the session."[14] The next day, July 21, his health rapidly declining, Tilden was taken to the hospital near his home. Doctors at the "German Hospital" seemed unable to successfully treat the "complication of diseases," and Tilden's condition quickly worsened. Early the next morning Dr. George A. Cameron and Dr. Henry F. Page, the attending physicians, notified Tilden's sons they should come immediately to the hospital. His boys, Herbert M. Tilden and William T. Tilden Jr., now in their twenties, were at his bedside when the end came at eight in the morning.[15] Death was caused by "pulmonary edema, a swelling of the muscles around the heart." The body was removed to Overleigh, where services were held, and the body was prepared for burial on Monday afternoon.

When news of Mr. Tilden's death reached the Union League, expressions of sincere regret were heard on every hand. The flag on the roof was immediately placed at half-mast, and a portrait of the former president was moved to the front of the main lobby and draped in black. It was said members wore a sober expression and spoke in hushed tones for many days in respect to their former leader's passing. "Mr. Tilden's death is a great loss to the city of Philadelphia," said Henry R. Edmunds, president of the Philadelphia Board of Education. "He was one of the best, if not the best chairman of the Property Committee the Board has ever had. Diligent in attending all meetings, alert, quick to grasp any proposition presented to him, he had ever the courage of his convictions and would never do a thing he did not think was right no matter how much his friends urged him to take a certain course of action." It was then ordered that all flags on city schools be placed at half-staff.

The Reverend Charles H. Dodd, pastor of the Second Baptist Church, conducted the service, and the twelve honorary pallbearers included some of Philadelphia's most respected business, political, and civic leaders, including John Gribbel, president of the Union League; Judge Dimner Beeber; and famed merchant John Wanamaker. "Scores of handsome floral tributes" surrounded the walls of the Tilden estate. One wreath from his brothers at the Union League was more than fifty inches in diameter. "Employees of the league, with whom Mr. Tilden was very popular, sent as a mark of their respect a panel six feet high made up of orchids, white carnations, and lilies of the valley."[16]

"From office boy in a shipping firm to one of the city's most progressive and widely known citizens" became a common refrain in Tilden's many lengthy newspaper obituaries. It was roundly agreed that hundreds of average citizens and "scores of acquaintances were mourning his death." In tribute to his belief in public education and work on behalf of the public school system, the Philadelphia Board of Education would vote to name a new school in southwestern Philadelphia after him.

His obituaries usually closed with mention of Herbert Marmaduke and William Tatem Jr., Tilden's sons. Some even noted that the younger son was a rising tennis player.[17] Junior, or Bill as he preferred to be called, was in no mood to appreciate the compliment. Both his mother and his father had now joined the three siblings he never knew at Ivy Hill. Granted, he was being well taken care of by his aunt and older cousin, and Herbert was still alive, but his brother was now married with two children. He had his own life. Feelings of loss and isolation were most prevalent.

Ironically, just a couple weeks earlier, Bill had been riding a wave of optimism and sense of accomplishment, as his tennis game was showing another glimmer of improvement. In what the newspapers described as "a big upset" and "remarkably fine tennis," young Tilden had won both the singles and the doubles titles at the Schuylkill Valley Tournament at the Plymouth Country Club in Norristown, Pennsylvania. Playing for Germantown Cricket,

Tilden won the Philadelphia title when he defeated fellow club member Stanley W. Pearson in singles, 1–6, 6–4, 6–4, and, more impressively, he and his partner, Roy R. Coffin, defeated what was thought to be the more formidable team of Wallace F. Johnson and Joseph J. Armstrong in doubles, 2–6, 6–4, 6–1.[18]

It was a decided turnaround in the Tilden household; Junior was now garnering the headlines and the competitive trophies, and Herbert was taking a backseat to the kid brother he once considered a handicap. While Junior was in high school, his older brother had been winning honors at Penn and the Germantown Cricket Club for his exceptional tennis play. He had won the intercollegiate doubles title (with Alex Thayer) in 1908 and was being written about as a "young player with considerable promise." His play was described as being "of the sensational order."[19] Junior could not help but admire his brother's accomplishments, his recognition and reputation as one of the best players in the area. Herbert was a definite role model.

Herbert and Alex Thayer, a member of the Penn football and baseball teams, continued to win local tournaments and rise in the national rankings, but success was not guaranteed. Stumbles occurred along the way. In the 1910 Pennsylvania State Championship, for example, "a decided upset" occurred when Herbert, "picked as the most likely winner of the meet, succumbs to the prowess" of another local player.[20] He was good but certainly not unbeatable.

The period from 1910 to 1914 was a time of transition for the Tilden boys. Herbert, now in his midtwenties, married, and approaching fatherhood, won some local tournaments, lost others, and made modest gains in the national rankings, usually falling somewhere between thirty-one and fifty-five in singles and slightly better in doubles. His younger brother, now in his late teens, rarely won anything, but keen observers were beginning to take notice. The young man occasionally displayed flashes of real ability, sometimes brilliance.

At the 1912 Pennsylvania State Championship, for example, both brothers went down to defeat early, but the younger Tilden was now the one drawing praise for his fine play. As *American Lawn Tennis*, the official chronicler of lawn tennis throughout the world at this time, said of Junior's game, "Young Tilden has a service almost as terrific" as the tournament's eventual winner, "and earned nearly as many aces with it. Tilden has improved tremendously since last year and will undoubtedly be heard from later."[21]

In one of his very few tournament victories, Tilden—whose early claim to fame was being the "younger brother of Herbert M. Tilden"—was accorded considerable acclaim.

> He is tall, full of energy and quite spectacular. His shots have plenty of pace and his volleying at times is severe and decisive, but he is apt to be wild and to depend too much on pure speed instead of going in for direction as well. His judgment is far from being uniformly good in going to the net. . . . There is good material in the youngster, but he needs experience and poise. His shots have enough direction to save him from being termed a swatter, but his escape from the charge is a narrow one.[22]

Yes, a hint of criticism, but praise all the same. Not bad for a young player, but not all reviews were so positive. Most received no comment at all.

In truth, he seemed to disappear in some matches. For example, during his college career his play never drew a whisper. This has led some to incorrectly argue he never made his college squad. He did but with lackluster results. Individual and team victories went unheralded. When Penn defeated a series of teams, including Johns Hopkins, Georgetown, Pittsburgh, and Lehigh, Tilden garnered no attention.[23] As Tilden later admitted of this time, "I usually followed a good performance with one that was so bad it more than counteracted the victory." He recalled how "elated" he was in his four-set triumph over Stanley Pearson in the final of one 1914 tournament only for it to be followed by a humiliating first-round defeat at Utica for the New York State title. The lack of consistency frustrated Tilden. "I gave up tennis regularly about six times or more a year following these ridiculous defeats by men I should have beaten easily," said Tilden, "only to change my decision by the following morning. The only sort of recognition I received was the universal agreement that I was a typical dub, just a hopeless idiot who could never get anywhere in tennis."[24]

Such up-and-down, patchy play is not uncommon among average players with middling racket skill. Most can be accurately labeled unpredictable, inconsistent, and erratic. "Tilden was definitely erratic," argues Richard Hillway, the nation's preeminent tennis historian of the game's early years. "To begin with Tilden was a late bloomer," argues Hillway, and his early years were influenced by his admiration for the aggressive, serve and volley style of American champion, Maury McLoughlin, a national phenomenon at the time. His brother Herbert, like many others, had also adopted the frenetic, net-rushing style of play. One's ability to rush the net and close off points quickly was wildly popular then, but such a style of play did not foster a sound, all-court game. Young Tilden hit much harder than most players and went for his shots rather than attempting to keep the ball in play. The result alternated between gorgeous shots and wild misses. In other words, he could be both spectacular and dreadful at nearly the same time.[25]

Tilden was in agreement. His play during his late teens and early twenties, he would one day write, ran the gamut from "brilliant to . . . lousy." Moreover, he had the quixotic notion that "one man could learn every shot known in tennis, a distinctly revolutionary idea in that day. The concept then," according to Tilden, "was that every player had to be definitely a driver or clubber or volleyer, and nothing else. My brother, who was a marvelous volleyer, but whose groundstrokes were practically non-existent, called me a crazy kid in about seventeen different and lurid ways. I was generally referred to as promising but erratic."[26]

The upside of Junior Tilden's game, as Hillway notes, is that sometimes he could be quite remarkable. Inexperienced observers took notice. Even at this early stage the athleticism and beautiful shot making were occasionally jaw-dropping. Those with a more sophisticated eye saw the potential and might even have asked to partner with him in a game of doubles. And that is just what occurred in July 1913 when reigning national women's champion Mary K. Browne asked the tall, gangly twenty-year-old if he would like to be her partner in the mixed-doubles competition currently being held at the Germantown Cricket Club. Flattered that a current national champion would make such a request, he quickly signed on, and the rest is tennis history. The Browne-Tilden duo won the championship trophy; it would be Tilden's first National Championship. And though mixed doubles was not the popular rage, it was a significant accomplishment for a young man whose love of tennis was matched only by his rather erratic play and mediocre record. Comment on his tennis prowess at the event was decidedly favorable. As one reviewer wrote, Tilden was "one of a number of young players whom Quaker City followers of the game expect to go very far."[27] The unlikely duo would repeat the triumph the following year.

The next two years would bring more of the same slow progress, with those nagging potholes of questionable play and resignation all along the route. In 1913, for example, Bill was awarded a Class 3 (31–40) national ranking but went unranked the following year. He would jokingly refer to himself during this period as a "member of the young Pete Swattems, young Pete being the type of player who wallops every shot," most of the balls going into the net or the backstop. A hard-serving net rusher at this time, he was so anxious to get to the net that he often footfaulted. On one embarrassing occasion he footfaulted seven times in one game. According to Arthur Voss, Bill also earned the nickname "one-round Tilden" for his early exit from tournaments.[28]

Wins and losses accumulated, but Junior Tilden gradually worked his way up the Philadelphia-area country club–circuit mountaintop. By the spring of 1915 Junior was playing number-one singles at the Germantown Cricket Club; his brother, the former champ, was now relegated to playing doubles. On May 10 Bill lost a three-set match to Wallace Johnson, one of the area's best players, in a match against the Merion Cricket Club. Three days later he defeated E. B. Dewhurst of the Huntingdon Valley Country Club in straight sets. Comments on Tilden's singles and doubles play at the time accurately captured him as a work in progress. In losing a mixed-doubles match to former national champion Bill Clothier, Tilden was described as "wild at times, and netting sitters and driving out of court." In defeating Craig Biddle in a four-set match, he was viewed as "alternating very good and very bad, but his speed, both of foot and shots, and his long reach, gave him a superiority that Biddle could not overcome."[29]

Some defeats proved as noteworthy as victories. In a loss to a top national opponent, Tilden was described as a "new star of remarkable brilliance" and the overhyped "savior of American tennis." Such glowing praise, Tilden admitted, resulted in "one of the most overgrown domes you could ask for." Just five days later, however, a "steady reliable old war horse of no great ability" soundly beat him. "The bubble was pricked," said Tilden. "My head came down to normal size, and to all and sundry I was once more just a dub."[30] And like an athletic metronome, one day he would be very good and the next day not so much. When Junior lost in the semifinal of the 1915 Pennsylvania State Championship to Wallace Johnson (who once played in the final of the National Championship) in a hard-fought 7–5, 8–6 affair, it

was written that "Tilden's service and volleying brought him within striking distance of victory, but his unsteadiness at critical times was fatal."[31]

The criticism's unusual lethal reference would prove prophetic, as later
that summer his father, William Tatem Tilden, would suddenly take ill and
perish soon after. Though much closer to his mother, his father's passing
must have been an emotional jolt. With the loss of the undisputed head
of the Tilden clan as well as an accomplished entrepreneur and civic powerhouse, for the Tilden brothers the specter of filling the old man's shoes
must have been daunting, particularly so for Herbert, who was most like
his father and employed as secretary-treasurer of the family business.
Incredibly, however, the tragic drama of losing a close relative would repeat
itself all too soon.

Herbert and his young wife had taken their two young children to Cape
May, a fashionable resort area on the South Jersey shore in late September.
While swimming in the ocean one afternoon, Herbert apparently caught a
mild cold. His resistance low and his spirits equally so with the recent passing of his father, Herbert's sniffles and cough quickly escalated into pneumo-
nia. As opposed to his mother's experience seven years earlier, Herbert and
his family managed to make it back from their weekend seaside excursion
to Overleigh, but the die was cast: by Wednesday, September 22, Herbert
would be dead. Once again Junior would be part of an early-morning vigil
and witness the death of a loved one. Herbert, just twenty-nine, the older
brother he looked up to, the all-around athlete who starred at Penn and
Germantown Cricket, and the one who taught him the rudiments of the
game he loved so much, was now gone. He had joined his parents and his
other siblings buried at Ivy Hill Cemetery.

Remembered in tennis obituaries as "a former Pennsylvania and Delaware
doubles title holder and one of the best known players in the Philadelphia
district," he was renowned for his "attacking ferocity" and "fierce rushes to
the net and incessant activity." His playing style was "marked by extreme
brilliance and erraticness [sic], as he always strove to get to the net, his back
court game being only fair." The stylistic assessment could have applied
equally well to his younger brother.[32]

Though the last of his family, twenty-two-year-old William T. Tilden Jr. had the good fortune to have a loving aunt and cousin anchor his life and care for him. He also had a modest inheritance that allowed him to do as he wished without concern of financial matters hanging over him like a dark cloud. Interestingly, his father had never written a will, leaving a more complicated legal matter for various municipal offices to navigate. Dimner Beeber, a trusted friend of Mr. Tilden's and a prominent lawyer who had served on the Pennsylvania Superior Court, served as the administrator regarding the letters of administration.

According to legal documents filed with the Orphan's Court, "the said intestate was possessed of Goods, Chattels, Rights and Credits" to the value of $100,000 and of real estate to the value of $20,000. An extensive itemized list of possessions at Overleigh included dining room furniture, china, and glassware estimated at $445; living room furniture, bookcases, pictures, lamps, and a clock at $375; and other items, from children's chest of drawers to bathroom linens running from $5 to $100. Several accounts at Penn Mutual, New York Life, Equitable Life, and others held savings between $10,000 and $25,000. Mr. Tilden's "Locomobile car" was appraised at $3,600.[33]

The death of his father also allowed Bill to spread his wings for the first time. Long thwarted in asserting himself by a domineering father, Tilden was intent on some immediate changes. One of the first was his decision to change his name and official designation. Known by most family members and friends as "Junior," he had early on developed a distinct distaste for the nickname. It grated on him, and he always promised himself that at the first opportunity he would jettison the loathed moniker. That occasion having arrived with his father's passing, he immediately informed one and all that he should now and forevermore be referred to as William Tatem Tilden 2nd. No longer would he tolerate being called "Junior," "June," or any other variation of the name.

Evidence of this can be plainly seen on the letters of administration regarding appraisal of the family possessions, the official court and register of wills documents filed in Philadelphia's city hall after his father's death. Both of the deceased sons were required to sign their signatures on the documents. The signatures read "Herbert M. Tilden" and "William T. Tilden 2nd."[34] It would take at least a year or two for news of the name change to properly circulate. Even late into 1917 and 1918 there would still be mention of William T. Tilden Jr. entered as a tennis tournament participant at different venues around the country. No doubt Bill set them straight at every opportunity.

Tilden has written that "between the age of fifteen and the time I left college during my senior year . . . I lost my mother, father, and brother. Tennis, along with almost everything else in life, lost flavor and I tossed them all into the discard."[35] He would further write, "My college career ended in 1915, my senior year, when my brother's death necessitated my considering something more practical than studies." Actually, there was no need, practical or otherwise, for Tilden to drop out of school. He had financial security and a place to live with loving relatives, and he could see completion of his college degree in the not too distant future. But Tilden did not enjoy school—certainly not the business program at Wharton he was enrolled in—and was desperate for new challenges and adventures.

In fact, evidence suggests he very likely left college months before his father died. According to an entry on his college transcript, Tilden "withdrew" from school on "2/3/15." Moreover, and adding further credence to such speculation, there appears to be no academic activity during that year, at least not at Penn. If that is the case, it would mean Tilden quit school five months before his father's and seven months before his brother's deaths.[36]

Regardless of the specific date, Tilden dropped out of the University of Pennsylvania sometime during 1915 and fell back on what he most enjoyed and what he did best. "I agreed to go back and help coach the team at Germantown Academy," he would write in *My Story*. He emphasized, "There would be no money involved . . . all completely amateur and in the spirit of the old school."

Curiously, in none of Tilden's three autobiographies—or in any of his many newspaper and magazine articles—does he mention his time at Pierce Business College. According to school records, "William T. Tilden 2nd" was a student at the school in 1915.[37] Known as the Pierce School of Business

Administration at the time, the school was originally designed as a business training school for returning Civil War soldiers, and the institution had just moved into a new seven-story building located at 1420 Pine Street. There was one particular feature of the structure that no doubt caught Tilden's eye: in addition to a panoramic view of Center City Philadelphia, the fenced-in roof contained a regulation-size tennis court. Tilden never received a degree from the institution, and school officials are not even sure how many courses he may have taken, leading the more skeptical observer to believe he probably spent more time on the roof playing tennis than studying in the school library.

Far better documented is Tilden's time as volunteer tennis coach at Germantown Academy. Apparently, the high school team was lacking guidance and direction, and he generously decided to assist them in whatever way he could. He was already doing much the same for interested young members of the Cynwyd Club, just outside Philadelphia. As it would turn out, Tilden might have been the "real beneficiary" of the decision to teach tennis to young people. The students' many questions—"How do you hit a service to make it bounce high (or low)?" "How do you hold the racket for the backhand?" "How?" "Why?" on technique, tactics, and psychology—spurred him to consider the game in greater depth than he had ever done previously. He may have been a college dropout, but he was about to become a serious graduate student regarding the art, mechanics, and psychology of tennis.

As he would ashamedly admit regarding the students many questions, "My ignorance annoyed me and I made up my mind I'd really get to know the answers. I began to study tennis from the standpoint of geometry and physics, began to work out carefully a strategic and psychological approach to the game. Thus my first real pupil, and my most successful, was myself."[38] Tilden would forever maintain that his extraordinary success at tennis was "directly traceable to the pains I took in learning enough to teach my old school team."

By teaching high school students tennis and immersing himself in the finer points of the game, Tilden said he began to "recover slightly from the blows of the recent deaths of my immediate family. . . . I took up life again." Tilden rather quickly reacquainted himself with what he enjoyed most in life. He fell back on what he considered his "favorite things, tennis, music, drama, movies, and literature."

41

He also acquired his first paying job. He took a position with a local newspaper, the *Philadelphia Evening Ledger*. It is most likely his hire had nothing to do with his athletic prowess and rising tennis prominence, but more so his connection to the famous family name and his knowledge of drama and the arts. The newspaper appointment as a "general assistant" to various departmental editors would place him under two of the newspaper's rising stars. As an assistant to Kenneth MacGowan, the drama critic, and Gilbert Seldes, the music editor and social critic, Tilden was learning reporting, wordsmithery, and social and artistic commentary from two of the best young minds in the business. MacGowan was in his late twenties, a fountain of knowledge about the dramatic arts, a director of the Provincetown Playhouse, and destined to make a name for himself as a Hollywood producer of such fine films as *Young Mr. Lincoln* (with Henry Fonda), Fritz Lang's *Man Hunt*, and *Jane Eyre*. Gilbert Seldes was just a month older than his young assistant, but a Harvard grad, with a passion for artistic and social commentary and an appreciation for a vast array of creative work, from comics and jazz to vaudeville and film. His love of aesthetic culture and desire to democratize the arts no doubt had a significant impact on Tilden's concepts of high- and lowbrow art and Broadway drama.

In his autobiographies Tilden expressed pride that his "newspaper schooling" was put in such "capable hands." MacGowan and Seldes took their passion, the arts, as seriously as Tilden was about to take his. There can be little doubt that he probably enjoyed his journalistic education more under their tutelage at the *Evening Ledger* than he did his commerce courses under the stodgy professors at Penn. Much of his time, apparently, was pleasurably spent "viewing the pictures of Paramount, Fox, and Metro" before they were shown in public movie theaters and distorted by Philly's local "board of censors." Tilden was perpetually aghast at "the deletions ordered by this high-minded board of old fogies." Their conservative taste, he would repeatedly find, was "incredible and passeth all understanding."[39]

Now that he had a real job earning a legitimate salary and no longer wasting time in college classes he had little interest in, he could turn to his true delight: studying and playing the sport that had so captivated him and passing that knowledge on to young people with a similar zest for the game.

Though he may have claimed that "everything else in life lost flavor" after the unexpected deaths of his father and brother in the summer of 1915, in fact he barely missed a beat in his campaign to develop young tennis enthusiasts in the Philadelphia area. In October, just a couple of weeks after burying his brother, Bill Tilden was teaching the game to aspiring players.

One witness to this unusual and selfless educational contribution was Carl Fischer, a precocious fourteen-year-old suburban youth who was attracted to the offer of free tennis classes being conducted at Cynwyd, a newly formed tennis club on the western border of Philadelphia. At about the halfway point between the older and more famous Merion and Germantown Cricket Clubs, Fischer and a dozen other youngsters were introduced to a tall, long-limbed college player by Paul Gibbons and told there would be a class each week at Cynwyd for those serious about learning lawn tennis. All of the boys found the offer particularly appealing. Tennis instruction was rare at this time, especially so when it was being provided without charge.

The tennis player's attire struck the boys immediately; it was obvious he had just lost a close member of his family. "He was wearing a black tie, had a black arm band on his suit coat, and was wearing a silk shirt with broad black and white stripes," recalled Fischer. "These were considered proper mourning apparel at that time."

> We met at the end of an empty ballroom which we had to ourselves at that hour with a single tennis racket as the sum total of our equipment. We talked for perhaps twenty minutes outlining in sequence exactly how he felt he should proceed in teaching us. He implied that we would all be teaching each other and thereby teaching ourselves. And after this first session we all knew what he meant. We started with what is generally considered the most important single stroke, the forehand drive. First he showed us the basic grip, the several slight variations and the significance of each. Then the footwork and the body movement, the backswing and the follow-through.[40]

The boys, all junior members of the Cynwyd Club, were transfixed; it was increasingly apparent that their instructor knew what he was talking about. He underscored the game's difficulty, emphasized that it required a high level of both athletic ability and technical skill, and had a psychological dimension that most players overlooked. "Tennis is a very complicated game," Tilden told the boys, "and it's much easier to do everything wrong than everything right. If one does one thing wrong, the stroke—the shot—won't turn out properly. So we are here to learn each and every stroke and learn to execute it properly."

"Tennis is a game of movement," he told them, "so footwork is vital. Following the ball on to your racket, swinging fully and freely on your groundstrokes, service, overhead smash, and half volley are all basic rules. Do not crowd the ball except perhaps on the volley, which one blocks." Each aspect of the game, each stroke, was broken down into its component parts and explained. Footwork, for example, which most of the boys had never given any serious thought to, was repeatedly stressed. Their young instructor said it was difficult, if not impossible, to make contact with a ball properly if one's feet were slow to set up or misaligned. A player's arms, shoulders, torso, legs, and feet had to move as one fluid unit.

"One should move into the ball," Tilden repeatedly demonstrated, "and turn sideways as one hits it whenever possible, thus obtaining maximum power and control of the shot. Power of the shot," he argued, "came from the body weight moving into the ball. One should not attempt to get power by swinging the racket through rapidly. In fact, carrying the ball on the racket, so to speak, is very desirable and gives additional control."

Tilden then gave each boy a turn at swinging the racket. It must not have been a pretty sight. "Boy, did we look bad," recalled Fischer, "and he let us know it." But through constant correction and "repeating the process over and over," the boys improved, some quite markedly. "We couldn't help but realize that if we didn't swing properly without having to adjust to a ball in flight, how could we expect to make good shots." Such lessons graphically illustrated to the boys one of Tilden's key principles: more points are lost through errors than won by good play, especially by average players.

By combining his knowledge of the game with his notion of the most effective teaching techniques, Tilden structured his sessions so that each student would get the most out of the class. "Each of us was called upon to tell what was right and what was wrong with each swing," said Fischer. "You really had to observe carefully and think. Did the pupil move properly into the ball, bend his knees for the low ones, and keep his racket head up on each swing, giving better control than when dropping the head?"

Fischer and the other boys soaked up as much information as they could. No one had ever bothered to teach them the fundamentals of the game.

In fact, there were few who knew the nuances of lawn tennis at this time who bothered to pass that knowledge on to others. The students may have been impressed with their new instructor, but Tilden—unbeknownst to them—was occasionally baffled. Many of their questions were beyond his expertise.

"I knew little if any, more than the boys themselves," an overly modest Tilden would later admit, "but they didn't know that and I took great pains not to let them get wise. Unfortunately, they were an inquisitive group and kept asking me questions I had trouble to answer. 'Why does the ball slide off the racket if you step away from it?' or, 'Why must you watch the ball?' or 'Which is better, a chop or a drive?' and endless other queries pounded in my ears. I didn't know any sound reasons," Tilden admitted, "but I made up my mind I would learn. So in my rash attempt to teach what I really didn't know, I began to study the science of tennis." According to tennis historian Rich Hillway, "Tilden had never thought this deeply about each aspect of the game. In teaching the young kids he became his own best teacher. The guy had a brilliant mind and managed to figure out what was important to produce each shot. He then passed that on to the kids."[41]

Through the youngsters at the Cynwyd Club and those on the tennis team at Germantown Academy, Tilden was forced to refine his knowledge of the game. Pace, velocity, spin, game tactics, overall strategy, and the mental component of breaking down an opponent's game were all examined now in the minutest detail and then reexamined. That intensive investigation combined with his ultimate goal of mastering every stroke known to the tennis-playing world was his personal quest. Most accomplished players thought such a mission an outlandish goal—even his brother, Herbert, considered him a "silly kid" for such contemplations—but Tilden, now in his early twenties, was obsessed. Was it possible to create an omnicompetent tennis player? Could a superplayer be developed, someone who had command of every known stroke in the game?

By the end of that first instructional session at the Cynwyd Club, the boys were swimming in information, and their practice strokes had shown definite improvement. "After the first session," said Fischer, "all of us were really moving into the shot for the first time in our lives. By persistent repetition that first day, hopefully a habit pattern was being established. Two hours had gone by and it seemed more like twenty minutes."[42]

In successive weeks new strokes were introduced to the students. Tilden opened with the forehand drive and discussed the basic variations—the classic flat drive used to pass an opponent at the net and the topspin cross-court passing shot used to pull your opponent off the court. "Tilden could thread a needle with the former," said Fischer, and all the students practiced the shot, envisioning themselves with their instructor's peerless command.

The lesson on the serve was a course in itself, said Fischer, "because never to my knowledge has any other player even attempted to develop and perfect four effective services. His cannon ball was greatly publicized. It was hit absolutely flat, the ball thrown to the top of his reach but no higher. He gave no indication he was going to use it. Actually he delighted in hitting it by you before you realized he was serving, thus enhancing its effectiveness. His height, long arms, and perfect timing were helpful factors. More often than not the opponent's racket did not touch the ball."

In addition to the speedy cannonball, Tilden also showed them "his heavily sliced service which stayed low and skidded quite a bit in to the opponent's body . . . his routine American twist service which did the reverse . . . and a fourth which had far more body weight and less wrist twist to it." He told them when to use each type of serve and how game situations dictated what serves were most appropriate. Fischer said Tilden stressed tennis as a thinking man's game, and one should always be contemplating how to break down an opponent's game. "He told us to find our opponent's weakness," said Fischer, "and play to it. Never change a winning game. Always change a losing game."[43]

Carl Fischer learned his tennis lessons well. The first of Tilden's many protégés, he would go on to have a first-rate tennis career and win the national intercollegiate tennis championship. As stated earlier, however, it may have been Tilden himself who benefited the most from those early tennis classes. As E. Digby Baltzell points out in his excellent history of tennis in America, the decisions Tilden made in the aftermath of losing his father and brother in 1915 and taking on the teaching assignments at Cynwyd and Germantown Academy "marked vital turning points in Tilden's tennis career." Baltzell referred to those twin mentoring assignments as the "intellectual spark, which led him to become one of the keener students of the game of tennis who ever lived." As he thoughtfully added, "Perhaps a genius is someone who is never satisfied with traditional answers but rather is driven to take infinite pains to get to the very roots of his art or science."[44]

That dedication was rewarded as the genius factor crystallized in coming years. Tilden pondered the game's complexities, worked to unlock its many riddles, and strove to incorporate the answers in his game. It had not been quick or easy, it would never be, and there would be no overnight revelations. Years of intense thought and endless hours of practice were involved, but Tilden was not averse to hard work; he was up for the challenge.

3

"Always Keep Mentally Alert"

Remember that 80% of all points in tennis as a whole
are lost by errors, not won by earned points.

—WILLIAM T. TILDEN 2ND

In mid-March 1916 Philadelphia held its first open indoor-tennis tournament. Sparing no expense in this first-of-its-kind late-winter indoor event, organizers laid a heavy canvas covering with appropriately marked lines inside the city's First Regiment Armory, only to discover the canvas would not take hold. Slippage was apparent, and so were the potential dangers. By waxing the floor the day before in preparation of a ritzy society ball, they had unintentionally sabotaged the athletic contest scheduled for the following day. A mad dash quickly commenced to take up the rug, wash and scrape the floor, and then replace the canvas cover. Armory workmen may well have been more exhausted than the contestants.

Despite the last-minute adjustments, the overall play was said to be "brilliant and Tilden from the first service until his final terrific placement ace delivered a series of brilliant shots which have seldom been equaled in Philadelphia tennis competition." The reporter for *American Lawn Tennis* observed that by the time young Tilden's more experienced and higher-ranked opponent woke up and began to play, it was "too late." He found himself facing "a super Tilden. There was no stopping the young champion, who was spanking every drive, service and volley with all the force he could bear. The two sets took less than thirty minutes when Tilden left the court with the victory 6–1, 6–0." Regarding Tilden's play, "it was agreed by almost everyone who saw the match, that no player in the world could have, on that occasion, stood up under his wonderful attack. It was superlative tennis, an exhibition that will live forever in the memories of those fortunate in seeing it."[1] Not surprisingly, Tilden would lose a four-set match in the tournament final to a relatively undistinguished player, 4–6, 6–3, 6–4, 6–4.

Critics sneered that it was a familiar script for "one-round Tilden," one day great, the next day quite ordinary and error prone. But despite the result progress was clearly evident. There were more victories now and fewer defeats, and early-round losses were increasingly rare. And then there was the stellar shot making; even novices recognized there was something special about Tilden's strokes and court coverage. Tilden was working his way up the rankings and developing a reputation in local tennis circles. In June he would play in the Keystone State Championship and lose a tightly fought battle in the final, 3–6, 6–3, 13–11. His play was described as "fast-paced," "very impressive," and exhibiting "great form." And yes, some still considered his play "erratic."[2]

At this time the top Philadelphia-area tennis players included William Clothier and R. N. Williams, both former national champions, and Craig Biddle, J. J. Armstrong, Wallace Johnson, Stanley Pearson, P. B. Hawk, and Norman W. Swayne, among other talented racket men. When Tilden defeated Biddle and a seasoned Boston player at a tournament in Philadelphia, the United States National Lawn Tennis Association (USNLTA) took notice and invited him to a well-known North Jersey summer tournament at Seabright. Tilden defeated one promising Californian and took another, R. Lindley Murray, to a grueling 15–13 third set before losing. His performance garnered him another invitation, this one to play in the National Singles Championship at Forest Hills. It was a major breakthrough and the honor exhilarating, but he lost in the first round to Harold A. Throckmorton. Downcast by his early exit, he feared he would once again be considered "just a dub."[3]

There was no quit in Tilden, however, and he continued to work on his game. He replayed in his mind the unforced errors, the tactical miscues, and what he could have done differently to defeat his opponent. Should I have hit with more pace, or should I have relied more on spin? Should I have played more from the baseline or continued to rush the net? Every game, every point, was reexamined. He was also forced to confront a disturbing realization: younger players were winning national titles, while he labored for victories in smaller, less prestigious tournaments. William M. Johnston of California, for example, won the American title in 1915 as a twenty-year-old. Dick Williams won the intercollegiate title in 1913 at twenty-two and the American title the following year. Tilden, now twenty-four, had never even won a round in the national tournament and wondered if he ever would.

He labored on, however. When not at the *Evening Ledger* writing drama or entertainment articles or teaching tennis at Cynwyd and Germantown Academy, he could usually be found hitting balls—one after another, hour after hour—always in pursuit of improving a certain stroke, learning another, or mastering an additional tactical weapon. When there was no partner to hit with, he fell back on a long-established ritual: hitting balls against a wall, backboard, or anything else that would allow him to test various grips, footwork, and swipes at the ball. As Carl Fischer observed of his mentor, "He worked harder and spent more hours practicing against a backboard than anyone I have ever known. He totally dedicated himself to tennis."[4]

Despite his less than impressive debut at the National Championship, he continued to compete and play smaller tournaments closer to home. His effort and dedication were rewarded at the end of 1916 when he earned a place in Class I—those ranking between 11 and 20—of America's top tennis players. By early 1917 Tilden was ranked number 2 in the Philadelphia area, ahead of such formidable players as Wallace Johnson, Bill Clothier, and Craig Biddle.[5]

Tilden also added some new titles after his name in 1916. He became a publisher and editor, the vehicle a new tennis magazine. In a project he probably never would have been able to initiate if his father had still been alive, he continued to demonstrate his love of the sport by not only teaching it but also writing about it. Along with Paul Gibbons he established a magazine called *Racquet*. Combining their love and knowledge of the game— and their desire to propagate its expansion beyond country clubs and the affluent that were its most devoted practitioners—they produced articles that incorporated player profiles, instructional tips, match summaries, and upcoming tournaments. Between his competitive play, his teaching, and the pithy articles on the game he now wrote, it is unlikely that anyone in America was more consumed by the sport of tennis.

Much of his success climbing up the tennis rankings was based on an indefatigable work ethic and unceasing on-court activity, but some success was also due to the growing conflict in Europe. The world was at war, and a number of top American players were either already involved in the fight or soon would be. They included the many-time American champ W. A. Larned, who was in the Flying Corps; William M. Johnston, who was stationed near the equator; and Frank Hunter, who was serving in the North Atlantic.[6] Philadelphia-area players such as Lieutenant Richard Norris Williams, Lieutenant Dean Mathey, Major B. S. Prentice, J. J. Armstrong, and Willis E. Davis were all fighting in France.[7] In fact, some of the greatest names in the game's history were placing their lives on the line. The great Australian player Norman Brookes was in Mesopotamia, the fine French player André Gobert was flying planes across the German border, and Kenneth Powell of Britain was fighting in France.

World War I, an unrelenting and unforgiving human threshing machine, would extinguish millions of lives. Ill-conceived and horrific battles at places like Ypres, Verdun, and Passchendaele result in horrendous carnage. The many sea battles were only slightly less costly. Accomplished and occasionally celebrated tennis players were among the dead and wounded.

One of the game's most iconic figures, the dashing Tony Wilding, a four-time Wimbledon champion, was killed not far from Flanders Field. A New Zealand native who perfected his game at Cambridge, Wilding was tall, athletic, and a natural leader. Possessing classic strokes, he could hit with pace and spin and was equally comfortable playing offense or defense. He regularly defeated America's best and helped Australia accrue several Davis Cup victories, but battlefield combat in the early years of the war proved too daunting. "At the age of 31, on May 9, 1915, he was killed in action at Neuve Chapelle, France."[8]

Wilding would not be the only champion to lose his life. Australian champions Ernie Parker and Arthur O'Hara Wood would be killed in battle as well. North American players were not excluded from the human devastation. The fine Canadian player Robert B. Powell, a three-time Wimbledon quarterfinalist, was cut down on the very same battlefield as Wilding, and Philip Lighthill, former captain of the Syracuse University tennis team, was killed when a German torpedo sank his ship. Tony hotbeds of privilege and tennis, even those in America, did not go unaffected by the European conflict. Some of Tilden's favorite sites were greatly impacted by the war. Two tennis players from the Cynwyd Club, seven players from the Germantown Cricket Club, and sixteen members of the Merion Cricket Club were killed in action.[9]

Tilden was much affected by the heroism demonstrated by his tennis-playing compatriots and after the war would often comment on their selfless acts and "magnificent page in the history of the World War. No branch of sport sent more men to the colours from every country in the world than tennis, and these men returned with glory or paid the supreme sacrifice on the field of honour."[10]

Brought up in a home that stressed patriotism, love of country, and civic participation, Tilden wanted to do his part once the United States entered the war. Like other top players willing to put their careers—tennis or otherwise—on hold in order to perform their patriotic duty, Tilden enlisted in the Radio Signal Corps and was "sent out to Carnegie Tech (now Carnegie Mellon University) for training; but on arrival it was discovered [he had] first degree flat feet."[11] His medical rejection proved serendipitous, for instead of being precluded from participating in the war effort or possibly losing his life, Tilden caught an unusual and "lucky break." As he would self-deprecatingly write of his unexpected good fortune, he would not only fight "the World War in Pittsburgh," but also be given the opportunity to become "a first-class tennis player."[12]

Few learning the story miss the irony of someone just a few years off from being placed alongside Ruth, Dempsey, and Grange—and proclaimed one of the great athletes of the twentieth century—being rejected for military service. Fortunately, Tilden had a guardian angel looking over him, one that would ensure he would get the chance to serve his country as well as boost his "growing tennis intelligence" quotient. His angel would come in the form of a brusque army officer. Colonel John C. W. Brookes was the commanding officer of the Pittsburgh military district, and he was also a tennis enthusiast. Tilden referred to him as a "tennis nut of purest water," and the colonel knew of Tilden and his surprising medical dismissal. He immediately sent for Tilden and glared at the just-rejected recruit.

"'Tilden,' he said grimly. 'I understand you are about to be rejected for flat feet.'

"'Yes, sir,' murmured Tilden.

"'Well, I think I can get you transferred into the Medical Corps—that is, if you want to stay in the service?'

"'I'd like to stay in,' said Tilden.

"'Very well. Report back here in two hours. That's all.'"[13]

"Naturally, I was delighted," said Tilden, "and through the kindness of Col. Brookes I became the world's worst soldier in the Medical Corps."[14] He would be stationed at the little hospital in Pittsburgh throughout the war, but in fact spent a good deal of his time doing what he enjoyed most, playing tennis. Tilden had many friends and contacts in Pittsburgh who graciously allowed him "club courtesies" whenever he had the time. Better yet, Colonel Brookes waived both rule and custom, thereby allowing Tilden to play tennis with the base officers who appreciated his play and incisive tips for improving their respective games. It came as no surprise to anyone when Tilden and the colonel soon "established themselves as doubles champions of the military district."[15]

All of this obviously contributed to what Tilden called his "poor" showing as a soldier. This too can be credited to Colonel Brookes, for he began to take an increasing interest in his flat-footed soldier's athletic career. "He held to the belief," Tilden would one day write, "that I could do more good raising money for the Red Cross and War Funds than completing my training a few weeks earlier, and he used to send me to tournaments and matches of the U.S.N.L.T.A., which was donating all gate receipts to these great causes."

"The result," according to Tilden, "was that, due in a great measure to Col. Brookes, in 1917 and '18 saw my tennis make a great stride forward at a time when most players were going back." Tilden was the first to admit his "future success was due to his opportunity to continually play tennis throughout the war."[16] Even when Bill was a college-age tennis player, Tilden's father insisted he forego tennis competitions and join the family at their Onteora mountain retreat. The lack of freedom and tournament play during the summer always irked; now he was encouraged to participate in matches around the state and country.

America's entry in the war would have a definite impact on tennis play on the home front. Lawn tennis, and tournament tennis in particular, "was at a very low ebb during the 1917 season. The National Lawn Tennis Association decided that the sanctioned tournaments should be held without championships or prizes and they should be called Patriotic Tournaments, the proceeds of any to be contributed to the Red Cross."[17] There were not only fewer tournaments with less fanfare and quality participants, but also fewer balls. Tennis balls were increasingly in short supply, and what few they had were going up in price.[18]

In April 1918 Tilden would win the national clay-court singles title in Chicago. The tennis cognoscenti were impressed. "Tilden's service was a deadly weapon," wrote one *American Lawn Tennis* reviewer. "The ball was coming over like a flash of lightning and sometimes defying return; and some of his other shots were quite unplayable." There were favorable comments about Tilden's ability to track balls down and "return them with terrific speed and splendid direction." His doubles play was also praised, one reviewer calling his performance "scintillating."[19]

Just a few weeks later Tilden performed another unique tennis feat: he sponsored "a party of New York youngsters to play their Philadelphia counterparts in a series of matches at Germantown Cricket Club and the Cynwyd Club." In what may have been an unprecedented initiative by an American tennis player, Tilden and his organizational partner, Paul Gibbons, spread the gospel of tennis and furthered the game's growth by encouraging youngsters to partake of its many attributes. The New York contingent left Penn Station early on a Saturday morning and was met by Tilden and Gibbons at the North Philadelphia Station, where they were whisked off to Manheim for a series of matches. That night the players were taken to the Forrest Theater for a comedy review and were back on court on Sunday and Monday before returning to New York. It is unlikely that any other top American players were contemplating, much less coordinating, such an investment of time, money, and energy on behalf of young tennis players.[20]

During the coming weeks as the summer tennis season heated up, Tilden played in a series of competitions running the gamut from the Church Cup, which was an annual event between Boston, New York, and Philadelphia, and tournaments in Harlem and Pennsylvania. At the Church Cup matches held at the Merion Cricket Club in early June, Tilden was described as "right on the edge, full of pep and snap." His serve, always a crowd pleaser, was said to be "so fast," his opponent "could not connect with it." It was reported that "his first serve came over at a terrific speed and the second was slow and heavily topped with a nasty break to it." Most of his matches were "one-sided" and showcased the Philadelphian at his best, "his brilliance being sustained and his mistakes being very few." Area observers, who knew his play best, thought "his tactics were better than usual" and that "he made very few of the bonehead plays that often mar his game."[21]

Just days later Tilden was up in New York at the Pelham Country Club, winning the Harlem Tennis Tournament. His play was once again described as both "brilliant and erratic." Taking a humorous poke at Tilden's propensity to push aside and dominate his doubles partner, one reviewer said Tilden played "mixed singles . . . but for once was able to carry it off."[22]

In July Tilden "outclassed the field" in the Pennsylvania Championship held at Merion. It was said he "played at a very high order," and for all the other contestants "nothing could be availed to stop him." Tilden won both the singles and the doubles. His partner in the latter was Carl Fischer, three years removed from having Tilden place a racket in his hand and showing him how to use it. The youngster was a good student and now demonstrated he knew what to do with it.[23]

At the South Side Tennis Club in Chicago in late June for the Clay Court Championship, Tilden put on quite a show and "easily [became] the feature of the tournament." Many of the nation's better players were off fighting in the war, but there was a "large turnout of competitors" hoping to take their place in the tennis firmament. Some experts argued it was impossible to predict a winner, but Tilden quickly cast his shadow over the competition. Though Tilden injured his foot in a recent event, he was said to have given "one of the greatest exhibitions of speed, skill, and judgment ever seen in Chicago." As one reporter gushingly commented, "We have had Wilding, Brookes, McLoughlin, Larned, Johnson, Williams, Bundy, and in fact almost every player of note, with their varied styles of strokes and serves, but never have we had one man who possessed such an assortment as Tilden. He seemed to have them all."[24] We can only imagine what Tilden thought when he read such comments, but there must have been a sense of satisfaction; his long-sought goal of creating a superplayer who mastered all the strokes might be coming to fruition.

Just a few weeks later he would follow that up with the national doubles title at the Longwood Cricket Club in Boston. Tilden's choosing to partner with a fifteen-year-old tennis prodigy named Vincent Richards made the achievement all the more noteworthy. Vinnie, as he was known, was the two-time national boys champion and would become national junior champion at sixteen. Tilden had been mentoring the young Yonkers, New York, athlete for several years and had no hesitation in teaming up with him for a major competitive event. The youngster was a natural athlete and a wildly successful volleyer. Just as he had done with Carl Fischer, Tilden had no compunction about competing for a title with an inexperienced but talented novice. He knew the boys, he taught them, and he believed he could win with them. It was a unique trait Tilden would practice repeatedly over the years. He enjoyed the company of young people and the satisfaction of defeating more experienced teams, and he was much invested in developing the court skills and futures of young American players.

Tilden's heroics had been fostered by Colonel Brooke's granting him a month's leave. It followed a request to the War Department by the USNLTA "to release ten players . . . to compete" in upcoming national tournaments. Proceeds of the events were to be contributed to the Red Cross. When bureaucratic lethargy held up Tilden's paperwork, Brookes called Washington and demanded to know "why the devil the leaves of all these men hadn't been granted."

Being close and of value to the commanding officer had its advantages. Tilden often found himself the colonel's driver when the need arose to escort dignitaries to area military hospitals and army installations, especially during the influenza epidemic. "Here was I," said Tilden, "a lowly lousy private, seldom in the company of anyone less than a Major, and scared to death all the time." Fortunately, his benefactor was neither intimidated nor absent of ideas of what to do with the visiting War Department officials. "We would meet the delegation at the [train] station," wrote Tilden in his autobiography, "drive them to the Pittsburgh Athletic Club for breakfast and then, without time to rest, rush them to the tennis courts where he and I would exhaust them until they were putty in his hands."[25]

In August 1918 the National Championship returned to the West Side Tennis Club at Forest Hills. The singles competition drew an entry list of nearly ninety players, with William T. Tilden Jr. and R. L. Murray considered "most likely to win." Soldiers just back from the war and pleased to exchange their rifles for tennis rackets included Lieutenant S. Howard Voshell and Lieutenant Craig Biddle.

Tilden's semifinal match against Ichiya Kumagae, a top Japanese player, illustrated why many tennis savants expected Tilden to win the national title. In what was described as "a marvelous exhibition," Tilden "literally blew [Kumagae] off the court 6–2, 6–2, 6–0." Kumagae was said to be "very good . . . but he could scarcely have stood up against the unexampled fury of Tilden's attack and the skill of his masterful racket work."[26] For a Labor Day crowd of more than two thousand, it was an athletic display that "has seldom been seen. It was a super-Tilden revealed for once in a complete match." No one who witnessed Tilden that day contemplated the word *erratic*, and there were quite a few who saw the tall Philadelphian as the "favorite for the title."

As most keen observers predicted, Tilden would meet R. Lindley Murray in the final. A well-built six-foot-two lefty out of California, Murray was four months older than Tilden, and though he wasn't consumed by the game like Tilden, he was accustomed to a bit more success. Currently ranked number one in the United States, he had lost in the semifinals of the 1916 championship but won the "Patriotic Tournament" title the following year. A Stanford grad with a degree in chemical engineering, he was kept Stateside by the military during the war to design new types of explosives. Like Tilden, he had entered the 1917 "Patriotic" tourney to raise money for the Red Cross. The only tournament he played that summer, he won.

Though Tilden was thought to have more racket control and shot-making ability, Murray was a fine athlete and a noted Stanford trackman with an aggressive style of play. "My strong points," said Murray, "were a vicious serve, a quick dash to the net and the ability to volley decisively anything that came near me."[27]

Tilden was confident. He had beaten Murray on two occasions earlier in the season, but victory was not to be. Murray played his hard-hitting attacking game—powerful serves followed by an all-out rush to the net to close out points—that kept Tilden on his heels. Seemingly unable to get out of first gear, Tilden, to the surprise of many, lost in straight sets, 6–3, 6–1, 7–5. "It was Murray's day," said Tilden graciously, "and I am perfectly satisfied. Only sorry that I could not utterly hide the leg."

Not intended as an excuse for his less than stellar play, Tilden was hampered by a painful boil on his foot that impacted both his mobility and his ability to assume a proper stance to strike balls. According to S. Wallis Merrihew, the editor of *American Lawn Tennis*, Tilden told him that "the injured leg cost him a few games and possibly a set, but it had little effect on the outcome of the match." It would not be the last time a health issue surfaced to impair Tilden's quality of play.

Despite the unexpected loss Tilden did not hold a grudge. In fact, he displayed a chivalrous spirit by being one of the first to argue Murray deserved to be voted the number-one American player of 1918, even though Tilden had more than sufficient credentials to assume the title himself. He had won seven tournaments during the year, including the National Doubles Championship, and defeated Murray twice.

The controversy as to who should be number one was due to a USNLTA rule, which stated that a player had to be in at least three tournaments during the year to be ranked. But tradition also dictated that the winner of the National Championship earned the number-one ranking. Murray had participated in only two tournaments the entire year. In addition, Tilden had not only played in five times as many tournaments and accumulated an impressive won-loss record, but also defeated Murray in one tournament and one exhibition match during the year. The upshot was a genuine year-end tennis controversy and a healthy contingent of supporters in each camp.

Hoping to resolve the matter in a gentlemanly fashion, Tilden argued, "Some people feel that my record entitles me to No. 1 this year, but in my opinion the National Champion should be No. 1 no matter if he had not played in another tournament all the year; or if he had several defeats against him. I don't want you to think that any such reports as my believing that I deserve No.1 are true, for they are not."[28]

Others were not so magnanimous. For them, Tilden was surely the better choice. Paul Gibbons, for example, urged the USNLTA in "A Minority Report" to examine the record; it "clearly entitled him to be placed at the

No. 1 position." Gibbons stressed Tilden's greater body of work: "Mr. Tilden's record," he pointed out, "was 39–1 while Murray's was 10–1." Moreover, he went on to argue:

> Mr. Tilden went into the match with . . . a foot that was already showing signs of dangerous infection. On the morning of the match he could hardly walk, his foot being dressed by H. W. Hanna, a reputable chiropodist operating in Philadelphia. Mr. Hanna warned Mr. Tilden that he was doing so at great risk as he dressed his wound he could not stand even the slightest pressure on any part of his leg. The wisdom of this warning was borne out by the fact that immediately after the National Championship, Mr. Tilden was taken to the hospital with an infected leg.[29]

The Gibbons report included a letter from Homer W. Hanna stating that when he was called to Tilden's Vanderbilt Hotel room in Manhattan, he discovered "an abscess" on his "heel and on the direct line with the tendon Achilles. There was a localized collection of pus some of which was discharged from an outlet at the apex. The condition caused considerable swelling, accompanied with inflammation extending from the heel to the knee, giving the patient great pain under pressure of standing." Hanna's recommendation was simple: "The man, in my opinion, should then have been declared physically unfit to compete as he was absolutely incapacitated. This I did tell him, but he said he thought he would try and play through."[30]

Tilden did play through. Loathing the prospect of defaulting—something no self-respecting player would do at the time—he chose to compete and lost. The decision not only cost him the number-one ranking, but also necessitated a trip to Germantown Hospital in Philadelphia for an infected leg that required surgery.

Once released from the hospital Tilden returned to his army unit in Pittsburgh. But there would be one more hospitalization before year's end. In November Tilden would have his appendix removed. It was the height of the flu epidemic, and hospital wards were busy. He would survive the ordeal but find himself "flat on [his] back" on November 11, 1918, and in no condition to celebrate with other Americans the Armistice that ended World War I. From his hospital-room window all he could see were the bodies of flu victims being buried in the adjoining cemetery. On a more positive note Colonel Brookes once again interceded and hastened Tilden's discharge from the United States Army. On the last day of the year Tilden was back home in Philadelphia and a civilian again.

The new year would witness Tilden's ongoing quest to scale the top of the tennis-establishment mountain. The years 1919 and 1920, according to Tilden's autobiography, would be his final step "to assuming the role of World's Champion. Still trying to consolidate my all-court game, still having my troubles with it, nevertheless I could feel that the pieces were slowly falling into place."[31] Tilden was number two in the United States and a much-respected competitor now, but it was not enough; he wanted to be the best, number one.

Preoccupied with mastering every stroke and every variation of each stroke for every occasion, Tilden practiced continually in hope that a newly learned offensive shot or wily defensive tactic would be the final piece of the puzzle. His rising status as a top-tier player afforded him some new opportunities and greater visibility in newspaper and magazine sports sections. A magazine advertisement for Bancroft racquets, for example, showcased Tilden as a national doubles champion. Relatively harmless by today's standards—the personal endorsement of Bancroft's "Winner" model racket—but such notoriety and commercial associations a hundred years ago could easily draw the disapproving eye of the USNLTA.[32]

Another unprecedented opportunity came in the form of a request by S. Wallis Merrihew, the editor of *American Lawn Tennis*, to write a guest column on any tennis-related subject he desired. No doubt aware of Tilden's experience as a journalist for both a Philadelphia broadsheet and his own tennis magazine, Merrihew still may not have expected such a substantive and much-talked-about submission.

Tilden's March 15, 1919, article, "Variety Is Essential for Tennis," was a serious examination of tennis and a blueprint on how the game should be played. Opening with a quote by William Shakespeare on the importance of variety in life, Tilden advised readers, "Variety or versatility is the . . . essence and cardinal principle of tennis success."[33] All the great players, he argued, were examples of versatility. The onetime devout serve and volleyer was now recommending a more nuanced all-around game that contained a full armamentarium of weaponry and defensive ability. One or two potent strokes were insufficient for the modern game, especially against topflight competition.

He encouraged all young players to maintain form at all cost. "The great mistake made by many novices," wrote Tilden, "is to forsake form the moment they start to lose." Consistent with that was the first order of business, laying a proper "foundation." The drive—both forehand and backhand—were "the foundation of every tennis game." They should be learned first and then the service, volley, smash, and chop in that order. Most important, "practice should be a careful plugging away at a single shot until that shot is learned thoroughly."[34] Tilden preached "four fundamentals" in mastering each stroke: "1) Keep your eye on the ball. 2) The body must be at right angles to the net when striking the ball. 3) The weight must always travel into the stroke from the back to the front foot. 4) The shot must never be hurried or cramped."

The lengthy two-page article would go on to articulate a number of Tilden's bedrock beliefs. "Remember," he cautioned readers, "80% of all points in tennis as a whole are lost by errors, not won by earned points." "The two greatest things in match play are to put the ball in play and never give the other man the shot he likes to play." "Never change your style when ahead. Do not take chances when winning. The time to take chances is when you are losing." "The whole secret of tennis success outside of actual stroke perfection (which anyone can learn in time) is to always keep mentally alert. Use the bean at all times and under all conditions."[35]

Tilden's how-to manifesto was an intellectual tour de force and may have been a first by one of the nation's up-and-coming tennis players. Tennis historian Richard Hillway believes many of the points in the article had been trotted out before by players, but Tilden "unified" them into a "coherent philosophy" that was far advanced for its time. "By working with the Germantown Academy boys and giving great thought to how the game should be played," said Hillway, "Tilden developed his own philosophy of the sport. By 1919 his strategy and philosophy were fully developed; now he just had to marshal his ability to orchestrate it."

Hillway believes Tilden was "unique" as a thinker, writer, and player. Others had written books about the game after becoming champions, but Tilden was still on his way up—he hadn't won the major outdoor National Singles Championship yet—but his analysis of the game was clearly more sophisticated than that of anyone else at the time. That was illustrated in his style of play; he had evolved from a frantic net rusher to a clever, crafty baseliner. "He took the game to the next level," argues Hillway. "It wasn't just winning points and games to him; it was the interplay of stroke and counterstroke. It was the cat-and-mouse strategy that piqued his intellectual curiosity. He savored the game's complexity and appreciated players who were thoughtful and challenged him intellectually."[36]

Like a chess master articulating a new tactical approach, the article stimulated a good bit of debate in tennis circles. Tilden was now seen as more than just another good up-and-coming player; his thoughtful approach to the game sparked a number of rejoinders that were printed in forthcoming issues of *American Lawn Tennis*.[37] The ALT editor and several top players entered the fray. Some quibbled over minor aspects, such as the importance of the chop stroke and Tilden's too fine a distinction between "pace" and "speed," while others addressed more central questions. Regardless, Tilden was now being viewed as a serious thinker and writer on the game of tennis.

Tilden's rising status afforded him the opportunity to initiate his own tennis tournaments. Some were quite unique, such as the matches he held on the roof of the John Wanamaker building in Center City Philadelphia. His celebrity helped attract "a classy entry list" that included quality players such as Wallace Johnson, Frederick Alexander, Ichiya Kumagae, Howard Voshell, and young Vinnie Richards. In his ongoing effort to promote young players—Tilden was the first one to suggest the USNLTA begin a ranking system of top junior players—he ensured that the rooftop tournaments had a junior competition that attracted the top teenage players from the middle-Atlantic states and New England.[38] Tilden also arranged that his Wanamaker rooftop tournaments were free to the public. The "no admission fee" fan-friendly gesture was an outgrowth of two Tilden concerns: to enhance the sport's growth and open it up to the public at large. He was forever troubled that the sport he loved so much was often perceived as a leisure activity of the rich and famous.[39]

After a snowstorm brought a halt to the open-air event, matches were reconvened, and the tournament's chief organizer proved triumphant. In a hard-fought final against Vinnie Richards, more than fifteen hundred people watched Tilden come back from a 5–1 deficit in the fifth set to escape with the victory and championship trophy. The rooftop event was so successful that a second was held a month later.[40]

As opposed to his mentor, young Richards was a true prodigy who took to the game like few before or since. Just a couple of weeks after losing the rooftop match to Tilden, the youngster defeated him at the Seventh Regiment Armory in New York City for the national indoor title. For a sixteen-year-old it was an astonishing victory and an "embarrassing loss for the now number two ranking player," who was up two sets to one before faltering in the final.

Bill and Vinnie continued to play as a doubles team and won the national title, but as Arthur Voss states, "For a time it appeared that Bill might have to find another partner for the 1919 season when Richards was suspended by the USNLTA in May for allegedly violating a provision of the amateur rule which permitted a player to be employed by a store carrying sporting goods but not primarily to sell tennis equipment."

Richards, who came from modest circumstances, was hired by the Alex Taylor Company as a salesman despite his youth. Suspicion increased when the company began an advertising campaign with the sentence "Vincent Richards will select your Taylor racket for you."[41] Ever vigilant for creeping professionalism in the amateur ranks, the USNLTA "almost like a bolt from the blue" suspended young Richards from further tournament play and pointed to section 4 of article 2 of the association's bylaws. The provision read, "A person shall cease to be an amateur by committing any of the following acts: By permitting or sanctioning the use of his name to advertise or promote the sale of tennis goods for pecuniary profit, or by permitting his name to be advertised or published as the author of books or articles on tennis of which he is not actually the author."[42]

According to Voss, the USNLTA began an investigation to determine "whether other players might be benefiting improperly from their tennis reputations." Member clubs were sent questionnaires concerning expense money, travel fare, housing expenses, and any other perks and inducements offered to players to attend tournaments. "The findings of this survey," according to Voss, "were never made public."[43] To the more skeptical observer the decision should have come as no surprise. The USNLTA had been gradually losing ground on the amateur-versus-professional question for some time. A number of players—including Tilden in the Bancroft ads— were taking part in commercial advertisements, but sanctions, reprimands, and penalties seemed to be applied selectively. There is no denying, though, that the old-line oligarchs of the tennis establishment were fighting a vigorous rearguard action against the encroaching threat of commercialism and professionalism. Wedded to their increasingly outdated notion of amateur play, USNLTA officials would bully players for many years to come in their quixotic effort to keep tennis simon-pure and an amateur sport, despite all the seedy evidence to the contrary.

The Richards matter was resolved and his suspension lifted when the Taylor Company dropped the young player's name from the advertising campaign. Tilden was mostly a bystander at the time and silent on the issue, but he was destined to become a painful thorn in the organization's side regarding the increasingly problematic fiction that tennis was, and would be forevermore, an amateur endeavor.[44] He had seen what the association had done several years earlier to one of his tennis heroes, Maurice Evans McLoughlin, when it was discovered he had a connection to a sporting-goods firm.

Better known as "the California Comet" or "Red Mac," McLoughlin in the minds of many revolutionized the game of tennis in the early years of the century with his pizzazz and energetic style of play that emphasized "storm the net at all costs."[45] Born in 1890 and a product of Northern California public courts, McLoughlin "came out of the West with a cannonball service, spectacular volleys and overhead smashes."[46] Admittedly, Tilden was "just a kid of seventeen but a confirmed tennis nut" when he first saw Red Mac play his exciting game at Manheim in 1909 on one of his rare trips east, but he became an overnight convert of the aggressive net-rushing style of play.[47] Though he never won a Wimbledon trophy, McLoughlin captured two straight U.S. Championships before the war, was a key member of several American Davis Cup teams, and sparked a radical reassessment for those practicing a sedate backcourt style of play.

A heroic figure to many a tennis enthusiast, he "incurred the wrath" of the USNLTA, which "believed he had smirched the fair name of tennis . . . by having a connection with a sporting goods house." The old guard vigorously argued that if this "awful example of dire commercialism" were not quickly stamped out, it would inevitably "ruin the game itself." Mystified by the hubbub at the time, Tilden "never dreamed" he would one day "play the role of McLoughlin" in a series of troubling rifts with the game's elders. Their "zealous, some times over-zealous . . . desire to protect the lily-white amateur game of tennis from the smirching feet of filthy lucre" would become an increasingly bitter point of contention between player and tennis association.[48]

There is some reason to believe, however, that Tilden as well had appeared on the USNTLA's improprieties radar screen. According to Robert T. Paul, a reporter for the *Philadelphia Evening Public Ledger*, Bill had been accused in early 1919 of breaching amateur regulations and was "soon to be declared a professional and barred from amateur ranks" for selling tennis rackets at a large Philadelphia department store. It was Paul's belief that the allegation was designed to damage a rising Philadelphia athlete who was increasingly defeating the best tennis players from New York City. It was Paul's argument that "petty jealousy" existed between New York and Philadelphia, and "natives of the Big Town had an ill feeling toward the athletic stars of this city."[49] According to Paul's investigation, Tilden was employed at the John Wanamaker department store, but he served in a managerial capacity and was not primarily selling tennis rackets in the store's sporting-goods department. In other words, he was not trading on his celebrity as a tennis star and in no way violating any USNLTA regulations. In time such skirmishes would grow in both frequency and severity between athlete and athletic association.

With the passage of winter and the arrival of spring, the 1919 outdoor season began to heat up. Tilden would not only pursue the American title and defend his number-two ranking, but have to do it against some of the greatest players of the last decade who were now returning from war. Delighted to be able to lay down their weapons in exchange for less lethal sporting equipment, the former athletes were anxious to reclaim their rightful position at the top of the tennis pyramid. Two men in particular, Richard Norris Williams II and William M. Johnston, were accorded special concern.

Two years older than Tilden but of the same upper-class social strata, Williams was born in Geneva, Switzerland, to a wealthy American who had taken residence in the mountainous country for health reasons. A serious connoisseur of tennis, he provided his son with professional lessons from an early age and was rewarded with young Dick winning tournaments before reaching his teenage years and eventually winning both the National Singles and Doubles Championships of Switzerland. In 1912 and now of college age, Mr. Williams was bringing Dick back to America to matriculate at Harvard College.

In one of life's cruel ironies, father and son eagerly booked passage on the maiden voyage of a British luxury liner, the *Titanic*. Despite its grandeur, notable passenger list, and auspicious launch from Southampton, England, the impressive oceangoing vessel was no match for an iceberg, and fairly quickly hundreds of well-heeled passengers found themselves desperately swimming for their lives in frigid North Atlantic waters. When he was pulled onto a life raft after considerable time in the water, young Williams was barely alive and his frozen legs of particular concern. His father was less fortunate and one of more than fifteen hundred people who went down with the ship.

Williams would overcome that tragic high-seas event in gallant style. As a Harvard student he would win the intercollegiate championship in 1913 and again in 1915. Between those triumphs he would walk off with the 1914 National Championship, an extraordinary feat for a young man still in college. A stylish, "risk-taking shot maker," according to Bud Collins, Williams played an aggressive, go-for-broke game that shunned caution in favor of outright winners. He used a continental grip that allowed him to "take the ball so much on the rise," says Voss, "that they were virtually half volleys, and he disdained to give himself any margin of safety or to play defensively when he was not at his best."[50] He was capable of spectacular streaks of play, but he could also be quite error prone and erratic. On one of his good days, however, he was practically unbeatable. In addition, he was now coming back a decorated hero, wearing the French Croix de Guerre on his chest.

Equally impressive was William M. Johnston, a miniature howitzer out of San Francisco who quickly became a fan favorite due to his small stature, bludgeoning forehand, and unrivaled fighting spirit. At first blush one could not help but view the "slight, sandy-haired, anemic-looking man . . . as less the great champion" than a potential hospital patient. But "by virtue of a lion heart, a matchless forehand drive and magnificent volleying, and an undying will to win," Bill Johnston, according to Tilden, should be considered among "the all-time greats."[51]

No more than five feet, seven inches in height and a svelte 120 pounds in weight, the public-court product appeared frail and timid, but woe the imprudent opponent who stepped on a court with him. Like McLoughlin a few years before, Johnston utilized "a Western grip, his palm almost underneath the racket handle and the wrist well behind it. Johnston put all his weight into the shot as he met the ball well out in front of him at the top of the bound, usually coming up and over it to achieve heavy topspin."[52] All opponents saw were a series of speedy missiles coming at them from a wiry little man whom they had once dismissively considered an impostor. His serve and backhand were adequate and his volleying excellent, but it was his pulverizing forehand drive that sent chills through his opponents. Though Johnston was slight in stature, everyone feared getting on a court with him.

A year younger than Tilden but much quicker to achieve success, Johnston had defeated both Williams and McLoughlin on his way to winning the National Championship in 1915. Learning of the little Californian winning the most important singles title in the land at such a young age could only have further dampened the spirits of someone who often considered himself a dub on the court. And the timing could not have been worse: Tilden had just dropped out of school and lost both his father and his brother to sudden illness.

By midsummer of 1919 most of the "returning warriors" had regained their prewar form. In fact, Johnston had recently defeated Tilden at the National Clay Court Championship. That was as it should be, according to most tennis fanatics. Johnston, a fan favorite, was the living embodiment—especially when compared to the much taller Tilden—of the David and Goliath fable. At six feet, one and a half inches and 165 pounds, Tilden towered over the rather small but stouthearted former champion. As Al Laney, a longtime *New York Herald-Tribune* sports reporter, described Tilden, "He had unusually long legs, slim hips, a narrow waist and somewhat hunched shoulders from which extended long prehensile arms. His face, too, was long, with a lantern jaw, long nose and high forehead."[53] This "Ichabod Crane" physique may have appeared peculiar to some, but it was gradually proving ideal for top-tier tennis play.

But it was more than the size disparity or the little Californian's fighting spirit that won the hearts of ardent tennis fans over his taller competitor. In reality more than a few fans were put off by Tilden's unusual idiosyncrasies and strange personality; they enjoyed seeing him cut down to size. "More than a few fans," as Voss has written, "were antagonized by Bill's unpleasant mannerisms and seeming arrogance, and wanted to see him beaten." Though a spectacular shot maker and brilliant tactician, his court decorum was horrid. It was not unusual to witness Tilden pout or lambaste a linesman for a bad call or insult a ball boy for taking his time to retrieve an errant ball. Know-nothing umpires came under particular scorn. As Al Laney has noted, up until Tilden, it was rare for a top player—particularly one emanating from one of America's elite country clubs—to exhibit such "mercurial" and "irascible" behavior. Initially "repelled" by such embarrassing and regrettable episodes, Laney found himself increasingly "fascinated by Tilden's personality."[54] Others—mostly serious students of the game—would similarly ponder Tilden's strange quirks and torrid blasts of ill temper, but for the most part the average fan found him a talented bore and delighted in seeing him defeated. That was especially the case when he met Johnston in the final of the 1919 National Lawn Tennis Championship.

During the two-week tournament Tilden knocked off an impressive list of top tennis talent on his way to the championship round. The defeated included Craig Biddle, Ichiya Kumagae, Norman F. Brookes, and Richard N. Williams 2nd. Many thought the Brookes match was the best of the tournament. Just over forty but still capable of formidable play, the legendary "Wizard" was a two-time Wimbledon winner. Playing his normal aggressive game, he rushed the net repeatedly, but Tilden controlled play from the baseline. An endless succession of lobs finally wore the tough Australian down. Tilden's victorious performance was described as "the perfect combination of strategy and tactics."[55]

In the semifinal round against Williams, Tilden played a similarly heady game. Known as a risk taker, Williams could not resist going hard for the lines. Tilden allowed his opponent to self-destruct by feeding him a series of soft balls that threw off Williams's rhythm and encouraged him to hit out in an attempt to pull off winning shots. The unforced errors piled up. Tilden employed only pace to finish off a point. The strategy worked exquisitely, and more than a few observers were of the belief that Tilden was playing the finest tennis of his career.

When he took the court against Johnston in the final, Tilden was considered the "prime favorite." The little man from California was no shrinking violet, however. He was a remarkable fighter, and his confidence was high; he had just defeated Tilden a month earlier for a major clay-court title. They might have appeared like Mutt and Jeff in physical stature as they shook hands at the net, but there was no difference in the size of their hearts or their desire to win.

It was not long after the first ball was struck that perceptive tennis observers recognized this would not be Tilden's day to shine. In what would prove to be one of Bill Johnston's most impressive displays of consistency and power tennis, he defeated Tilden decisively, 6–4, 6–4, 6–3. As reporters would gush, "It was impossible to overpraise Johnston for his straight set defeat of Tilden. From start to finish he was the better man. He had Tilden utterly at his mercy throughout the contest. Tilden was made to look like a novice."[56]

"It was a most satisfying experience," according to reporter Al Laney. Upset that Tilden had beaten Williams in the semifinal, he was now delighted in seeing tiny David slay mighty Goliath. The little man had "hurled his projectiles into Tilden's court, pounding his backhand to a pulp, and he served, smashed, and volleyed decisively, controlling the game at will." Laney wrote that the popular decision "was beautiful and the cheering was thunderous."[57]

Ever gracious in defeat as usual, the tall Philadelphian—the once projected winner—must have been heartbroken. He had been so close to achieving his long-sought goal, winning the National Championship. Though the result pleased tennis fans, the startling turnabout generated much comment and speculation. Up until the final Tilden had looked unbeatable; he was playing some of the best tennis of his life. "That he should go down in straight sets," according to one perplexed scribe, "was unthinkable." "What happened?" was the general question of the day.

Connoisseurs of the game recognized that "Johnston did the thing that Tilden did not believe was possible—he kept the ball in play until he had an opportunity to kill." Normally a savvy baseliner with a variety of potent strokes that enabled him to control play, Tilden was thought to be "below form" in the final, inexplicably unable to lob, and unwise in committing such a "great blunder" as to stay back and play Johnston from the backcourt. Others gave full credit to Johnston's aggressiveness, his lack of errors, and his surprising ability to return "every shot that Tilden sent over."[58]

Although speculation over the surprising outcome would continue for some time, Tilden—always a thoughtful tactician—knew immediately what had sealed his doom. Johnston had relentlessly smashed shots to his backhand. The balls came with such pace and regularity that Tilden grew insecure and resorted to an "undercut backhand slice" that kept the ball in play but proved deficient at keeping his opponent at bay. With each weak slice return, Johnston hit with more aggression and took control of the net until he closed out the point. What Bill needed to do, according to Voss, "was to turn his backhand drive into a consistently strong, forceful shot, similar to his Eastern forehand drive, that he could hit flat or with topspin, and enable him both to pass Johnston at the net and to take the offensive away from him in backcourt exchanges."[59]

Bill Johnston—the little man with the most potent forehand in the game—would finish 1919 ranked number one among American players. Tilden, once again, would be ranked second. A fundamentally sound backcourt player who was known as "wonderfully steady" with "an extraordinary service," as well as "practically every stroke known to tennis," Tilden had established himself as one of the world's best players. But he was not content with that. There was more to learn, more to prove, more to accomplish. He now set out to do just that.

Part 2

A Champion's Reign

4

"A Year of Living Triumphantly"

Champions are not born. They are made. They emerge
from a long, hard school of defeat, discouragement,
and mediocrity, not because they are born tennis
players, but because they are endowed with a force that
transcends discouragement and cries "I will succeed."

—WILLIAM T. TILDEN 2ND

Despondent over his decisive defeat in the 1919 National Championship, but excited by the prospect of being named to America's Davis Cup team, Tilden decided his game—stroke by stroke—needed to be reexamined. This was especially true of his ineffective backhand; it needed a complete overhaul. The battering he took from the anemic-looking Bill Johnston was particularly troubling. Like a pebble in his shoe he couldn't remove, the painful recollection of his subpar play exasperated him. The meek replies from his off wing were embarrassing; the feeble stroke had to be rectified, immediately. "The many errors off my backhand," he would one day write of that Johnston match, "lived clearly in my memory, and when the announcement of the challenge for the Davis Cup was made public, and it was intimated to me that I might go abroad with the team, I determined that if I went I would leave my old backhand in the United States and take a new one with me."[1]

With the onset of fall and the cold winter months to follow, Tilden took the unusual step of relocating to New England. No, he would not jettison his racket for ski poles; he was not one for throwing in the towel, even for a brief respite. Long committed to mastering each and every shot known to the game—and some that weren't—Tilden focused on developing an offensive backhand, a shot that would not only defend against net rushers like Richards and hard-hitting thumpers like Johnston, but truly be a weapon in its own right, a shot that would zoom past aggressive net men as well as create problems for more defensive-minded baseline players.

The reason for the move to New England was the fact that Providence, Rhode Island, was home to one of the nation's few indoor tennis courts at this time, and it was owned by J. D. E. Jones, a prominent life-insurance executive. Jones had been a competitive player in the early years of the century and offered Bill use of the facility if he would provide some coaching tips to his son, Arnold, who was equally enthralled with the game and beginning to be recognized as one of the nation's top young players. While working to improve young Arnold's ground strokes—which had already won him the 1919 national boys championship—and occasionally selling an insurance policy, Tilden devoted himself to the reconstruction of his unimposing backhand.[2] As Tilden would one day write of this remarkable bit of athletic surgery:

> It is no easy job to learn a new stroke in three or four months, particularly when it is a new trick for an old dog, yet it had to be done. My first step was to work out a sound grip, swing and footwork, not a very difficult thing to do in theory and, once worked out, to put it in practice. There came the amusement for every one but me. Four times a week, sometimes more often, Mr. Jones or Arnold and I would do battle in the indoor court. . . .
>
> I set out to learn a backhand and every shot I could play backhand I played. I intended to learn a drive, and drive I did. Only the walls or the net could stop my efforts during the first weeks. Far and wide went my shots, yet even at the darkest moments, when I was ready to burn my racquets and quit the game—and these moments were not infrequent—I would make one beautiful shot once in a while that gave me courage to go on. It would prove by its very effectiveness that I was on the right road, and that only the mastery of the mechanics of the stroke stood between me and my new backhand. Week by week I saw my backhand grow. Sometimes I would think I had lost it; the touch would go off for days at a time and I could not hit the ball in the court; then back it would come again, better than before.
>
> Over these weeks my pride suffered many a humiliation. It is not particularly enjoyable to a Davis Cup candidate to be repeatedly defeated by either a junior or a veteran who had virtually retired from active tennis some years before. Many a defeat at the hands of both I swallowed and laid them, often not too silently, on the altar of my backhand drive. Gradually the turn came. I began to gain control of the new shot. It seemed to me that, in a period of about ten

days, the work of the whole winter crystalized and my game jumped ahead a full class. I played better tennis, in certain ways, than I had ever played before in all my life.˙

One cannot work consistently on anything without obtaining definite and interesting results. The only drawback is the length of time it takes to show these results. Most players are not willing to devote more than a week or two at the most to the mastery of a stroke. If they have not the desired result then they usually let it go with a shrug. "What is the use?" they say. Well, possibly they are right; yet it seems a shame to me to pass up the ability to do anything well, simply because the effort seems tedious. Strokes cannot be learned in months, and actual progress in years.

I have never regretted the hours, days and weeks that I spent to acquire my backhand drive, for to it, and it primarily, I lay my United States and World's Championship titles. I am convinced that had I not done the work necessary to the mastery of that stroke, Johnston would have continued to defeat me just as decisively after 1919 as he did that year.[3]

In retrospect, it is quite rare, especially today, for an established player to relocate himself for a period of time in the hope of totally revamping or learning a new tennis stroke. Those who achieve success, win tournaments, and attain a high ranking but subsequently lose a significant match are more likely to blame the loss on poor conditioning or an injury, or just chalk it up to a bad day at the office. Few, if any, march off to some secluded training site to relearn a stroke and remain in isolation until the assignment is complete. Tilden, however, was not your typical tennis player. With a keen mind for athletic mechanics and tactical play, he realized he would always be vulnerable to a player like Johnston with a potent forehand drive if he just walked on a court with his current complement of strokes. His decision was especially uncommon considering he was normally praised for his shot making and impressive collection of strokes. But Tilden was a perfectionist; he knew his arsenal had a fatal weakness that needed to be corrected.

The winter pilgrimage of 1919–20 would also underscore another critical feature of Tilden's training regimen: "intensive practice." As he would repeatedly tell his students and write in his how-to tennis manuals, "Practice may not make perfect, but believe me it has made many a good tennis player.

I am a great believer in practice. My idea of intensive practice is to pick out one stroke and hammer away at that shot until it is completely mastered."[4]

Tilden's impressive array of knee-buckling serves is a perfect example of intensive practice. "I spent hours in serving alone, trying to disguise the twist and pace of the ball," Bill admitted. "I would take a dozen balls and serve them to No. 1 court with one style of delivery. Then I'd cross over and hit them back with another type of service. Next, I'd try the left court front both sides. My next move would be to pick out a certain section of the service court and aim for that until I could put the ball just where I wanted it. Finally, I'd strive to put the ball there with tremendous speed."[5] That single-minded dedication paid off. Tilden's potent complement of serves went beyond what any other player at the time had mastered, and more than one opponent swore the lanky Philadelphian could pick off a beetle walking across the top of the net with one of his feared cannonballs from twenty yards away.

Tilden's work ethic was nothing short of extraordinary. Many observers and admirers would comment over the decades regarding his willingness to practice until he had achieved his goal. In one well-known account, Grantland Rice, the famous sportswriter, and Ty Cobb, of baseball fame, were staying at the Augusta Country Club in 1930. Tilden was also there participating in a tournament and was on the court practicing a particular stroke. Under a hot Georgia sun, Rice and Cobb took a seat and watched Tilden for more than an hour. Hitting ball after ball in an effort to nail the stroke down, Tilden never varied his workout. It was an incredible exhibition of single-mindedness, an athlete in the form of a human metronome. Cobb, a great but grim athlete who admired grit and determination, turned to Rice and said, "He's quite something. He's not afraid of work."[6]

For E. Digby Baltzell, such displays of commitment—whether in seclusion or at a public event—"illustrated the very essence of [Tilden's] genius and rage for perfection." How different, he would go on to muse, such an attitude was from more recent generations of players. "The pattern of play today," he would quote tennis great Fred Perry, was so "boringly predictable. They were never troubled to learn anything new." Their game was always the same. Tilden, on the other hand, "was never the same player two days in a row."[7]

Contrary to numerous, but inaccurate, accounts, the new shot did not make an immediate impact. Tilden was in no way an instantaneous or overnight sensation. Controlling and perfecting the new backhand was more a slow slog through a clay or grass quagmire than a high-speed spin around the Indianapolis raceway. In fact, one is hard-pressed to discover any mention or news account of the new stroke in newspapers during most of 1920. Its impact was much more subtle.

In those early months the hard-driving backhand he had been trying to gain command of was still a work in progress; he was smart enough to realize he did not want to be overly aggressive and shoehorn it in with his other complement of near-perfect strokes. He knew it would take time and an incredible amount of practice. Favorable comment regarding Bill's game was already established at this point. Both sportswriters and players admired his ground-stroke arsenal. Even top foreign players like Norman E. Brookes, who was not shy about criticizing Bill's odd idiosyncrasies and general "lack of temperament," admitted that Tilden "played more strokes well than any man he had ever met," hefty praise from someone known as a tennis "wizard" and a former Wimbledon champ.[8]

Even given Tilden's many athletic gifts and keen mind for muscular mechanics, incorporating a new stroke into his already formidable collection of match weaponry was not a guarantee for quick success. In one of his first matches of 1920, for example, he lost. The late-February battle in Providence proved disappointing, as Tilden went down to defeat against Richard Harte of Boston, 6–3, 6–1, 5–7, 9–7. Harte, an intercollegiate champ, was no ordinary club player, but neither was he Dick Williams or Bill Johnston.[9] There was satisfaction, however, in one of the earlier matches. He had defeated R. Lindley Murray, the former West Coast trackman who had beaten him for the national title in 1918.[10] The loss to Harte, though, rankled him. Additional practice sessions were usually the doctor's prescription for such unforeseen setbacks. Rich Hillway also points out that Tilden often used matches as practice sessions. In other words, he was less interested in winning points and games than experimenting with new shots and different technique.

Quickly regaining his old form, Tilden won the singles and doubles competitions at the "Twenty-First Indoor Championship" in New York City in

March and a month later won the singles and doubles titles at the North & South Championship in North Carolina. Another impressive double would come at the Church Cup Tournament between Boston, New York, and Philadelphia. He was not unbeatable, however. Later that month in Philadelphia Tilden would lose a five-setter to local chop-stroke artist Wallace Johnson. Interestingly, none of the sports reporters covering these matches along the Eastern Seaboard made mention of Tilden's revitalized backhand.

April was also the month when he was named to the U.S. Davis Cup team. It was an honor he always dreamed of, representing his country in international competition. And even though he was slotted behind Bill Johnston and Dick Williams—both former national champions—and Charles Garland, the young intercollegiate champ from Yale, Tilden was delighted. If the script went as team leaders proposed at this early date, Johnston and Williams would play the singles matches, and Williams and Garland would be America's doubles entry. Tilden would be held in reserve in case of injury to one of the stars.

The team appeared strong on paper. But other American squads over the years had as well, with disastrous results. Australians had claimed ownership of the Cup in 1914 and showed no signs of relinquishing it. The history of the Wimbledon Championships was even more disconcerting. No American had ever won the gentlemen's singles title, certainly a major embarrassment for American tennis. As great as they were, top-notch American talent like Richard Sears, Oliver Campbell, William Larned, Maurice Evans McLoughlin, and Dick Williams had never won the cherished title of "world champion" on England's revered grass lawns. In fact, only one player, McLoughlin, had even managed to make it to the championship round. More than four dozen American players—eight of them national champions—had entered the All England Lawn Tennis & Croquet Club championship over the years without a singles title to show for it. Wimbledon, the holy grail of racket sports, was a bright but elusive goal.[11]

After delays caused the American Davis Cup team to miss their cruise-line departure, Secretary of War Newton D. Baker—a "keen tennis enthusiast"— assisted them by providing passage on the *Northern Pacific*, a U.S. Army transport ship.[12] His first trip abroad, Tilden was often seen with a camera in one hand and a handful of rackets in the other. On his return he would be able to officially declare himself an "internationalist," a term reserved for the game's best players who participate in elite international tournaments.

The team's first competition at Queen's Club in mid-June confirmed the American squad's potential. Tilden defeated Brian I. C. Norton of South Africa and Zenzo Shimidzu of Japan, but lost in the final to Johnston, 4–6, 6–2, 6–4. Johnston's victory and that of Williams and Garland in the doubles competition was a positive omen on the eve of the Wimbledon Championships. But even the staunchest supporter of the Stars and Stripes could not afford to be overly optimistic; the history of the event for American contestants was far too disheartening.

It was while preparing for Wimbledon to commence that Tilden established friendships with two of America's foremost celebrities. Returning to his hotel from practice one day, he "found traffic on the Strand at a complete standstill and a mob of people jamming the streets for two blocks from the Savoy entrance." Tilden immediately assumed the king and queen or some other members of the royal family were at the hotel. He proceeded to battle his way into the lobby and the front desk, when he was "suddenly face to face with a short, dark, striking-looking man and with him a most beautiful little woman who looked almost like a child." Turns out they were royals, all right, but the branch known as Hollywood royalty. It was Douglas Fairbanks and Mary Pickford, and they were under siege by "a ring of cameras and jabbering reporters." On their honeymoon and with tours of London and Paris on the schedule, Fairbanks and Pickford were known as the most popular couple in the Hollywood film colony and destined for even greater celebrity in coming years. The commotion by legions of fans at the Savoy Hotel documented their popularity overseas. Deciding to assert himself, Tilden grabbed the sleeve of the famous motion-picture actor and shouted, "Mr. Fairbanks, I'm Bill Tilden of the United States Davis Cup team. It's swell to see you."

Nearly breaking the player's hand—Fairbanks was an athlete in his own right with a gymnast's grip—and flashing his "famous Robin Hood grin," the actor said that he and Mary "were just wondering where you boys were staying. We want to go out and see you play. Come along and let me introduce you to Mary."[13]

And so began Bill's friendship with the wildly popular movie actors. He would come to spend many an enjoyable day at Pickfair and thereby come in contact and form friendships with an array of top theatrical talent. One of the most famous and personally supportive would be Charles Spencer Chaplin. Like many at the time, Tilden considered Charlie Chaplin "the greatest genius of the screen and the most brilliant comedy brain in the world." Over the years Tilden would be the recipient "of many instances of Charlie's generosity" and given wide latitude in the use of the actor's private tennis court. It just so happened that Chaplin was "an ardent tennis fan," who played "the game remarkably well" and possessed an especially potent forehand. Tilden would come to believe that the little comedian was "never more happy than when playing a warmly contested doubles match with friends on his own court." Over the next decade or two Chaplin would make a concerted effort to catch Tilden's athletic performances on both sides of the Atlantic.

On the Worple Road tennis complex better known as Wimbledon, a familiar and disappointing script seemed to be playing out once again when Johnston—America's best hope—was defeated in a second-round match by the fine Irish Davis Cup player J. C. Parke. Tilden watched the match and took mental note of the victor's strengths and weaknesses. He was quick to realize Parke was at his best taking the ball on the run, hitting out while scampering from sideline to sideline. To beat Johnston one had to be very good, and Parke was all that and more. It was a shocking setback for the U.S. team, but there were other results that were equally surprising and far more upbeat. Other members of the American team—specifically Tilden in singles and Williams and Garland in doubles—were still in play.

In the third round Tilden knocked off Parke in what most observers considered an extraordinary display of shot making and tactical tennis. Reporters commented on Tilden's "amazing variety of shots and the unerring headwork." One could not help but admire the tall Philadelphian's "mix of drop shots, hurricane drives, clever lobs and volleys," along with his "frequent changes in pace and remarkable accuracy." Parke, an outstanding player, was said to be "constantly in a quandary."[14] Added another knowledgeable observer of the match, Tilden "fed the Irishman the strokes he did not like, cramped his mobility, and won easily."[15] The victory must have had added import for Tilden, as he had been a ball boy for Parke when the Irish star had visited the Germantown Cricket Club more than a decade earlier.[16]

Tilden's fourth-round match with British star A. R. F. Kingscote was far more challenging, as he lost serve seven times and was pressed repeatedly before winning the fifth set, 6–3. His fifth-round match against Australian Randoph Lycett was only slightly less difficult, as he won 7–5, 4–6, 6–4, 7–5. His next match, against fellow American Chuck Garland, was a three-set breeze compared to the difficulty he would face against Japanese star Zenzo Shimidzu in the seventh round. Tilden won the match in straight sets, 6–4, 6–4, 13–11, but an old knee injury had been aggravated when he had tried to retrieve a deep lob. For the rest of the match he played with a pronounced limp that hampered his mobility and affected his play. The long and difficult last set only further aggravated the injury.

Despite the physical setback, Tilden was now in rarefied air. Only one other American—Maurice "the California Comet" McLoughlin—had ever made it to the challenge round of Wimbledon, and that was seven years earlier. Tilden would now play the defending champion, Gerald Patterson. A powerful, broad-chested six-footer with a lethal serve and intimidating forehand, the Australian was an explosive athlete, an experienced internationalist, and a war hero to boot. As the "standing out" 1919 Wimbledon champion, he could leisurely sit and observe the aspiring pretenders to his throne. His opponent in the challenge round would have to run the gauntlet of seven strenuous matches just to earn the privilege of playing him. Exhaustion was a key factor; physical injury was another. Tilden might have qualified on both counts.

Though he dismissed concern in his public comments, Tilden's injury was obvious in his doubles play. The leg wrapped and his mobility compromised, Tilden was forced to discard the support bandage in an effort to gain additional quickness and improve his labored play. He would never admit it, but the injury may have contributed to the spanking he and Johnston were handed by Williams and Garland. Newspapers speculated on the severity of his physical infirmity, and headlines such as "Net Title Hinges on Tilden's Knee" became commonplace on both sides of the Atlantic.[17]

Samuel Hardy, the American team captain, considered holding Tilden out of the Wimbledon final so he would have time to heal and compete in the upcoming Davis Cup matches, but Tilden reassured Hardy and everyone else he was fine. He was prepared to play the "best game of my life," Tilden informed the press. He told reporters he had "unquestionably found his top American form in England" and had never played better than when he had defeated J. C. Parke the previous week.[18] The day off before the challenge match with Patterson, Tilden argued, would be enough time for his injured knee to repair itself. Hardy remained unconvinced. As he pessimistically cabled back to his USLTA superiors in New York, "Tilden's knee wrenched. May default Saturday."[19]

Never one to succumb to an injury and constitutionally opposed to the concept of an athlete defaulting, Tilden took to the pitch. When the combatants met at center court, Patterson was the picture of health and confidence. The much-respected defending champion was surely the crowd favorite. But Tilden, too, had more than his fair share of supporters. As opposed to American audiences British sports fans were much taken with the tall, rail-thin Philadelphian. His odd habits, verbal expressions, and idiosyncrasies caught their fancy; they enjoyed someone with personality. They found humor in his "bearskin," the fuzzy wool blue sweater he wore onto the court, and his assured manner as he cradled an assortment of rackets in his arms.[20] As one British writer commented on his attire and general appearance, Tilden wore "a long-haired fur sweater which reached half-way down to his knees, which gave him the appearance in the distance of a huge gorilla." That combined with his being "very tall, very long-armed and long-legged, very broad-shouldered, a chin like the Rock of Gibraltar, and an attractive mocking grin, instantly made him the personality of the 1920 Wimbledon meeting." So much so it would seem that "during the first week everyone was asking, 'Have you seen Tilden play?'"[21]

His disdain for linesmen and habit of crying "peach" at an opponent's winning shot also tickled them. But more than the verbal pyrotechnics and unusual attire were the ballet-like athleticism and exquisite shot making. His ability to return what most considered unhittable balls, and his devilish firepower—from paralyzing and unexpected drop shots to overpowering drives—all contributed to a growing aura of admiration, if not endearment. Clearly, "Big Bill"—as the British tabloids distinguished him from "Little Bill" Johnston—was truly something special.

The first set was a decisive victory for the reigning champ. Patterson's powerful serve, overhead, and forehand drives repeatedly made their mark. But Tilden, ever the thinker and tactical analyst, was not dismayed by the 6–2 score; he was measuring his opponent. It was not unusual for him to mentally evaluate his competition early in a match. Some of his shots were designed not to win points but to test his opponent's mobility and reply. Consistent with that goal came a flurry of bullet serves, deft spins, delicate drop shots, and point-ending volleys that tested Patterson and kept him on the move. That first set was intended to catalog Patterson's strengths and weaknesses on a mental spreadsheet in preparation of orchestrating his own game plan. Central to that athletic assessment was Tilden's realization that for all Patterson's skill and power, the big Australian worked hard to conceal his Achilles' heel: a weak backhand.

From the second set on Tilden pounded balls to the champion's backhand. It was a replay of the 1919 American championship, only this time Tilden was the ruthless predator savaging the chink in his opponent's armor. Due to a relentless onslaught of shots, the tide turned immediately, and Tilden won the second set, 6–3. The third and fourth sets were much the same, Tilden winning easily, 6–2, 6–4.

News reporters at the scene were duly impressed. Some would paint the contest as a battle between brains and brawn and attribute "Tilden's win . . . largely to superior headwork." The tennis in that second set, they would proclaim, "has seldom been equaled at Wimbledon. Mixing his strokes, but never ceasing to pound away at Patterson's vulnerable spot, his backhand, Tilden seemed to amaze his opponent by the superlative qualities of his play."[22] British newspapers were abuzz with startling, almost tragic, news. "Thousands had thought Patterson unbeatable," mourned the London Times the next day. "What happened in full view of Their Majesties will rank with such debacles as Hastings Field and Bunker Hill."[23] The London Morning Post referred to the first American-born Wimbledon champion as "super

Tilden" and an "irresistible force" in every instant when "he most needed to step up his game."[24]

As front-page newspaper headlines proclaimed "Tilden Is World Tennis Champion," much ink was spent trying to explain the dramatic upset. No longer the "dub," the "erratic" tennis fanatic who tried to be too "fancy" and master too many strokes, Tilden had triumphantly scaled the tallest of lawn tennis mountains. At twenty-seven—a comparatively late age for one's first major tournament victory—he was now world champion.

Long-frustrated American sportswriters waiting for a homegrown player to capture the Wimbledon title were beside themselves with joy. "The Wimbledon turf was trod by the giants of all lawn tennis–playing nations," wrote an ecstatic S. Wallis Merrihew. For almost forty years, "the best of our American players competed with England's leading exponents only to find the latter always superior." With the passage of years, "additional nations joined the competition and we essayed vainly to scale the Olympic heights of lawn tennis fame, always falling before British Isles and later Australasia."

Merrihew would go on to name "Dwight, Sears, the Clarks, Campbell, Larned, Wright, Ward, Alexander, Behr, and many others"—the cream of American tennis—who "could not do in nearly forty years of striving what has now been accomplished by William T. Tilden 2nd. He has won the premier title of the lawn tennis world." From an error-prone, late-blooming local player of no great distinction, Tilden molded himself into a thoughtful, hardworking connoisseur of the game. Some admirers were now talking of his "unlimited" potential.

As Merrihew gushingly stated of the new champ, "No man could be a keener follower of the game or closer student of its every aspect. As a theorist, Tilden tops Tilden as a player. To strokes of transcendent merit the Philadelphian adds a profound knowledge of grand strategy and tactics that enable him to plan a match as a master of chess arranges his campaign in advance. No one player in the history of the game has had as extensive a repertoire of shots as the new champion."[25] And to accomplish such a feat on one's maiden steps on the hallowed grounds of the All England Lawn Tennis & Croquet Club is "glory enough for Tilden, for his fellow members of our Davis Cup team, and for the country which is proud to have given him birth."

Most American newspapers gave Tilden's unprecedented triumph extensive coverage; that was especially so in his hometown. The July 4 *Philadelphia Public Ledger*, for example, devoted considerable space on the front
page and the sports section to accounts of the victory and the praise the
hometown boy was now receiving from both players and news reporters
around the world. There was also a large photo of Tilden with racket in
hand and wearing one of his quirky woolen pullover sweaters. One article
described the new champion's game as "the soundest and brainiest ever
seen on English courts," so varied in skill, and thought many of the finer
points of his "technique and cleverness beyond the comprehension of the
average spectator."[26]

An increasingly avid supporter of Tilden and now completely won over
by his Wimbledon triumph, Merrihew underscored for his readers the
salience of Tilden's earlier *ALT* article that extolled the virtues of an all-
court multistroke game. He called Tilden "the premier player of the world"
and took pleasure in watching "the all-court game carried to its ultimate."
The Philadelphian has "absolute command of every possible stroke," said
Merrihew, and such technical proficiency "was the highest example of the
[game's] art."[27]

No doubt lost in the rapture and commotion of an American finally winning the Gentlemen's Championship at Wimbledon was news that the
USLTA planned "serving notice on players that it proposes to amend its
rules so that no man's name shall be immortalized by having a tennis
racquet named after him."[28] Though some sports commentators openly
conjectured such an initiative was more than a "coincidence" after one
of the greatest accomplishments in American athletic history, there was
reason for concern regarding commercialism encroaching on amateur
sports. "Tennis as a sport, diversion, and exercise is expanding by leaps
and bounds," wrote one sports editor. "The governing body is right in
surrounding it with every safeguard. The small boy with the undeveloped
mind cannot always grasp the rigid rules, which do and should govern
amateur sports. If, however, he should ever rise to the distinction of winning a national tennis title, his years of association with real men who
love sport for sport's sake will have taught him to honor all the ideals of

the game." That storybook portrayal was now bumping up against the real world.

The game of tennis, according to most knowledgeable observers, "ranks with the cleanest of all sports." However, it was increasingly apparent that sport and commercial opportunity were rapidly developing a symbiotic relationship that purists and tradition-bound sportsmen found abhorrent. Was this as troubling a development as the USLTA seemed to believe? And what could prevent such mutual attraction? "Can a man who wins distinction in the athletic world help it," asked one columnist, "if some enterprising industrial concern should name its product after him?"[29]

The question had more than hypothetical importance and would become a point of increasing tension between successful athletes and the high priests of the USLTA. In mid-July, just as the association's conservative leadership feared, an eye-catching two-page advertisement for Bancroft tennis rackets showcased the company's newest model. Emblazoned on the racket's wooden handle were the words *The Tilden Winner*.[30]

Back in England the new world champion became focused on another campaign. Rather than taking some time off to physically recuperate and bask in the joy of unprecedented success, Tilden locked himself in his hotel room and concentrated on a new challenge—writing a book. Approached by a British publisher Methuen and Company—no doubt hoping to take advantage of the new champion's popularity—Tilden was offered the opportunity to write his own book about the game of tennis.

Jumping at the prospect, he set down his racket, picked up a pen and typewriter, and spent the bulk of the next two weeks putting on paper his thoughts on everything from stroke technique and game strategy to aspects of his personal history and sober reflections on the game's top players. No novice when it came to shoving a noun and verb together and crafting a well-told story, Tilden did not need a ghostwriter. He knew what he wanted to say. He also knew what tennis students needed to learn.

Beginning with the line "Tennis is at once an art and a science," Tilden set down in four parts and seventeen chapters an informative and entertaining primer on the sport he loved and had devoted so much time to. Admitting that "I began tennis wrong. My strokes were wrong and my viewpoint clouded," Tilden launched into his own struggles as a young player, his many years of meager results, and the slow but inexorable climb up the ladder of respectability.[31] Almost every page was graced with a humorous gem or literary flourish: "The service is the opening guns" of the match; "one fault is a mistake, but two faults are a crime"; and "the net attack is the heavy artillery" of a tennis match.

His many pearls of wisdom were learned through his own mistakes, or from his more rewarding experience instructing the boys on the Germantown Academy tennis team. He emphasized the game's fundamentals, advising readers: "tennis is played with the mind," "keep your eye on the ball," "never allow your opponent to play a shot he likes if you can possibly force him to one he dislikes," "practice is played with the racquet, matches are won by the mind," and "the first and most important point in match play is to know how to lose. Lose cheerfully, generously, and like a sportsman."[32] The sportsmanship theme was a critical piece of Tilden's philosophy of life and would be stressed in his many future fiction and nonfiction books and publications.

An added bonus was Tilden's frank assessment of his fellow players. Arranged according to country, he described the style of play of each nation's top players, their strengths and weaknesses, and their prospects for future success. He would not be accused of sugarcoating his opinions or boring his readers. R. L. Murray, for instance, was called a "terrifically hard worker" who possessed a "very fast forehand drive," but "his footwork is very poor" and his "forehand drive exceedingly erratic. His is not a great game," wrote Tilden. "It is a case of a great athlete making a second-class game first class."[33] In all Tilden evaluated more than thirty-five players from ten countries. He did the same for the world's best women players.

Incisive, engaging, and almost every page of interest, *The Art of Lawn Tennis* appeared in London bookstores in October 1920 and in America a year later. In 1922 an "American publisher brought out a second edition, revised and enlarged" by the author. "The book went through eight editions by 1927 and ten all told by 1935, undoubtedly an all-time record for a tennis instruction book."[34] In less than a month's time Tilden had won a world championship and written a successful book. And the glorious summer of 1920 was still far from over.

Two weeks after his stellar Wimbledon performance and just a day or two after completing his first book, Tilden jettisoned his writing paraphernalia and reclaimed his trusty Bancroft tennis racket. He was now back on the court with the rest of the American Davis Cup team, doing what they had originally come to Europe for, namely, to defeat the French and English squads and thereby qualify for the Davis Cup challenge against Australia. No longer slotted as a subordinate member or replacement player, Tilden, along with Bill Johnston, was assigned to play singles and doubles. The decision proved wise, as the two Americans easily defeated the best France and England had to offer. Tilden beat William Laurentz in four sets, and Johnston defeated André Gobert in straight sets. The two Americans then took the French doubles team in straight sets. The last two singles matches were canceled due to rain. Against the English team at Wimbledon the Americans proved equally formidable, as they defeated J. C. Parke and A. R. F. Kingscote in both singles and doubles. Just as they throttled the French, the English team was unable to win one match. In so doing Tilden proved his great Wimbledon victory against Patterson was no fluke, and it also confirmed the American Davis Cup team's court prowess. Some began to suggest they were quite possibly unbeatable and one of the best national squads ever assembled.

Before traveling off to distant Australia to take on the Davis Cup champions at the end of the year, there would be other matches to play. Back in the States for the summer tennis season, Tilden was the main item of discussion at country-club events across the country. With Tilden the first American-born player to hold the grand Wimbledon trophy, tournament organizers worked frantically to ensure the new world champion would appear in their event. Some, including the famous Newport, Rhode Island, competition, would be disappointed. "Although Tilden was the man whose appearance had been awaited most eagerly," recounted one news article, "Newport tennis enthusiasts soon resigned themselves to his absence and settled down to the enjoyment" of other members of the formidable Davis Cup team in attendance.[35] Tilden must have been surely struck by the odd turnabout; dismissed by many early on and a late bloomer as far as top-flight competition was concerned, he was now being written about when he was not even a tournament participant. Tilden was now the hottest thing in tennis.

There was one competition, however, that Tilden would definitely not miss: the American lawn tennis championship. Tilden had come exceedingly close the previous two years but had been defeated in the final match by R. Lindley Murray in 1918 and "Little Bill" Johnston in 1919. They were frustrating losses to be sure, but Tilden had worked tirelessly to improve his game. His Wimbledon triumph had confirmed his progress. But there were skeptics who thought that unexpected success on the outskirts of London an instance of extreme luck. Even a hometown newspaper that applauded Tilden's "scintillating brilliance" at Wimbledon wondered if his "stroke of fortune" could be replicated on this side of the Atlantic.[36] Moreover, he had still not defeated "Little Bill"—the game's most popular player with American audiences—in a major final. As a proud American, he desperately wanted the national title.

Like most eastern elite country clubs at the time that hosted major events, the West Side Tennis Club in Forest Hills erected a temporary grandstand that could hold in the neighborhood of ten thousand paying customers. Seating was expected to be at a premium if expectations for a Johnston-versus-Tilden final held true. Each player would have to survive six matches just to reach the final. Both men would face a challenging array of players, including the likes of Vince Richards, Wallace Johnson, Bill Clothier, Nat Niles, Dick Williams, and Watson Washburn, among others. Expectations were high that the two big guns—the national champions of America and England—would survive the early-round skirmishes and square off to settle the debate as to who was the world's greatest lawn tennis player. As stated in a balanced *New York Times* commentary:

> There are many who will argue that William M. Johnston, America's national champion, is still Tilden's superior, having defeated him decisively in the final round at Forest Hills last summer, and since then taken two out of three sets from him in the finals of the London championship. But the fact remains that Johnston was put out of the world's most important tournament by the veteran J. C. Parke, who later lost in one-sided fashion to Tilden. . . . There can be no question to the merit of Tilden's victory. Tilden at present looks like the best tennis player in the world, actually as well as technically.[37]

Despite the *Times* opinion piece, Bill Johnston was the clear crowd favorite. Many were like *New York Herald Tribune* reporter Al Laney, who admitted he "fell in love with Little Bill instantly, completely, and without reservation," and were loath to respect a gifted but strange interloper. Tennis fans could not comprehend such a frail-looking body producing such powerful shots, especially the forehand drive, which "hurled projectiles" at incredible speed. How could such a small, sickly-looking man, many pondered, create such pace on the ball? Moreover, this tiny David who regularly slayed giant Goliaths was not only the definitive model of "grit and courage" but also the poster boy for proper decorum. His demeanor alone won adherents. The same could not be said for the new British titleholder. As Laney would later comment in his book *Covering the Court* about his initial observations of Tilden, "I never had seen such arrogance and such distasteful mannerisms. No expression of humility seemed possible. . . . [T]here seemed to be a conscious feeling of superiority."[38]

Curiously, what the people of Great Britain loved about Big Bill—in addition to his athleticism and technical skill—Americans hated. Obviously, national preferences on the subject of personality took very divergent paths on opposite sides of the ocean. What London tabloids found humorous and appealing, America judged "supercilious, arrogant, disputatious, quarrelsome, opinionated, and dogmatic."[39] Such behavior did not engender respect, much less affection, at least not initially. More than a few who traveled to Forest Hills for the fortnight of athletic combat came with the clear expectation, or at least desire, that Little Bill would give Big Bill a severe thumping, just as he had the year before.

When the nation's biggest tournament began on August 30, fans were anxious to examine the form of the two champions. In the first round Tilden took out Lawrence Rice of Boston in straight sets, utilizing an array of hard baseline drives and soft spin shots to confound his opponent. Johnston did close to the same to Carl Fischer, a Tilden protégé and University of Pennsylvania freshman, although the final set, at 10–8, proved a struggle for Little Bill.[40]

Both men faced significant fourth-round challenges: Vinnie Richards for Tilden and Dick Williams for Johnston. Young Richards, with his energetic net game and superb volleying, was capable of defeating anyone. Though he tried mightily and displayed both "sharp angled volleys" and "sensational" returns, the seventeen-year-old youngster did not have the firepower to knock off a committed Tilden in a major tournament. He won one set at

6–3, but Tilden's "superior speed" along with his ability to serve and drive with "exceptional power" proved too difficult to overcome.[41]

The Johnston-Williams match was the much-anticipated "magnet" that packed the stadium, as both men had won two legs of the national trophy and one more meant the prestigious piece of polished hardware belonged to the victor. Both men had served overseas in the military during the war, but Johnston was quicker to recapture his former court skills. Through "dogged determination" and his "ability to rise to the occasion," Little Bill "clung to his control and out-steadied" Williams, who was forced to play on a weakened ankle he had turned early in the second set. The straight-set score of 6–3, 6–4, 7–5 did not accurately indicate the quality of spirited play or the crowd's respect for both former champions.

Tilden and Johnston would successfully move through their next two matches and win their semifinal bouts, Big Bill defeating chop-stroke specialist Wallace Johnson in straight sets and Little Bill taking three out of four sets from former Harvard star George Caner. Passionate tennis fans now had what they had been yearning for, a rematch between the two biggest names and the two biggest games in the sport. Would the physically slight but stouthearted Californian reclaim his much-deserved national title, or would the long-limbed, multitalented Philadelphian, now proudly bearing Wimbledon fame, take the American crown, too?

The championship match and its literally earth-shattering side attraction would long stamp the event as truly something extraordinary. From the outset the overflowing crowd of twelve thousand realized this would not be a replay of the previous year's final. Playing aggressive, error-free tennis, Tilden won the first set decisively. The 6–1 score must have come as a shock to Little Bill's loyal supporters. The feeble backhand that Little Bill had repeatedly pummeled just twelve months earlier was nowhere to be found; it had been replaced with a potent backhand drive that shot balls through the court like bullets. Johnston had not played poorly, but Tilden was on his game. Consistent with Johnston's well-earned reputation as a fighter, however, he would raise his game and come back to take the second set, also at 6–1. After two sets and fourteen games the score was tied.

With the skies growing more ominous and the threat of rain increasing, some sharp-eyed patrons in the crowd noticed a distant speck among the darkening clouds, an airplane as it turned out, coming toward the stadium just as Tilden opened the important third set with his powerful cannon-ball serves. As the plane grew closer and the noise from its engine louder, many in the stadium watched it make a series of dives and climbs, as it was clearly focused on the sports spectacle occurring hundreds of feet below.

Lieutenant James Murray Grier of Philadelphia, an experienced navy man who had flown with the famous Lafayette Escadrille during the recent war, piloted the plane, a JN-Curtiss that had taken off from nearby Mitchell Field. Also on board was Sergeant Joseph Peter Saxe, one of the military's most experienced photographers who had captured the horrors of battlefield combat in the Philippines, China, Cuba, and Germany. Their assignment that afternoon "was to get photographs of the tennis play—to get them from as near as possible—for use in connection with army recruiting."[42]

Each time the plane swooped near the stadium and the motor roared, angry spectators turned their gaze from on-court action below to the noisy distraction above. On several low-flying passes, spectators could clearly "distinguish Saxe bending over the side of the cockpit snapping pictures of the players and the crowd." Some of these dives from an altitude of eight hundred feet were as low as two and three hundred feet, and more than one tennis fan felt if he stood "on tiptoe one might almost touch it." The plane's ever-lower descents "started a flurry among the watching throng," and "half-checked cries from all parts of the two stands" could clearly be heard.[43] Many, no doubt, feared the specter of a tragic accident.

On the pilot's fourth ascent and dramatic dive the aircraft came within a couple hundred feet of the grandstand, and spectators could clearly see Grier directing the plane and just a few feet back Saxe straining out the side of the cockpit to capture close-ups of the famous racket men, who continued to play despite the aeronautical distraction. Lieutenant Grier was giving the aged plane a workout, something he had been cautioned not to do, as "the old type motor . . . might cause trouble."[44]

It was not long after that the irritating engine noise stopped. The sudden silence caused many in the grandstand to look upward, only to see the plane stall, appear motionless for a second, and then dive to earth. Even the two athletic contestants locked in physical and psychological combat could not help but peer skyward at the deadly drama unfolding above them. Tilden, holding a 3–1 lead in the third set, was about to serve and toss the ball in the air when the engine "roar stopped entirely. Instinctively, I looked up," Tilden would write years later, "and was horrified to see the plane wobble and plunge downward. It missed the west stand with five thousand spectators by less than five hundred feet, and hit the ground so hard that we not only heard the crash but felt the shock through the earth. There was no doubt in anyone's mind as to the fate of the occupants. A murmur swept the crowd, and then a nervous movement. Johnston and I stood stunned on the court."

The plane had crashed less than "two hundred feet from the stands, the impact of the blow driving the motor three feet into the soil and shrouding the two mangled forms in sagging wreckage."[45] The umpire, according to Tilden, "realized that unless something were done quickly the crowd would stampede. He knew that Johnston and I were unnerved by the accident. Yet only by the immediate resumption of play could he hold the crowd and stave off a panic. He turned to Billy.

"'Can you go on?' he asked quietly. Billy walked to the receiving position. 'Yes,' he said.

"'How about you, Bill?'

"'I'm ready,' I said and asked the ball boy for the balls to serve.

"'Play,' cried the umpire, with all his authority."

The match resumed, and the "tenseness" of the high-quality play "caught and held the crowd." According to Tilden's recollection, only "fifty people from the more than ten thousand around the court left to see the wreck of the plane," but in actuality probably many more than that ran to see the lethal carnage. Tilden would later admit he knew "two men had gone to their deaths just over the fence and here we were starting to play a game. It seemed heartless, almost indecent." Some, no doubt, were disturbed play continued, but others felt the match's continuation "might have [prevented] a panic which would have injured thousands."[46]

Regardless, play continued, and Tilden won a hard-fought and event-filled third set at 7–5. Late in the fourth set the skies would present another distracting challenge: rain. Dark cumulous clouds covered Forest Hills all day. A slight drizzle caused a periodic nuisance, but with the Wimbledon champion up two sets to one and 5–4 in games, "the rain suddenly came down violently." According to Tilden's recollection, "The entire crowd rose, pulling on raincoats and lifting umbrellas, and started for the exits and shelter." Believing the conditions "impossible," Tilden asked the umpire for a let—a stoppage of play—just as he returned a Johnston serve. The let or stoppage was granted as Little Bill volleyed back Bill's reply. Just as the players realigned themselves to replay the point, "the voice of George T. Adee, the referee of the tournament, rang out over the stadium": "As referee of this tournament, I rule that the point is Johnston's."

The referee's highly unusual intrusion into what is normally the umpire's call set off a tense meeting between the two tournament officials. Neither seemed willing to budge. Tilden, the injured party, managed to control his infamous temper and quietly await the decision as to which official had jurisdiction. When the umpire, E. C. Conlon, returned, he informed Tilden that Adee "refuses to change his decision, and the point stands now to Johnston." Sympathetic, he went on to tell Tilden if he cared to protest to the USLTA, "I will fight for you from the floor." Tilden was beside himself with disbelief, and Johnston appeared too embarrassed to accept the point, but the referee's decision was final. "When play resumed a few minutes later . . . Bill was so upset that he served three double faults to lose the game, and Johnston held serve to win the set."[47] Tilden would later admit, "The incident did upset me enough to make me throw the fourth set after holding a good lead."[48]

The match for the American championship—which included a fatal plane crash, a drenching downpour, and a strange bureaucratic brouhaha—was tied. After four sets and thirty-eight games, the match was dead even. Both men prepared themselves for the decisive fifth set, the winner to be proclaimed the national champion for 1920. Johnston, hoping his opponent was exhausted from the mentally and physically taxing match, decided to assume all-out aggression and rushed the net at every opportunity. He would challenge Tilden's ground strokes and force him to come up with winners, an unlikely prospect after several hours of on- and off-court turbulence. He broke Tilden's service twice and took a 3–2 lead and began to pound his opponent's backhand as he did the year before. But this was 1920, and that lame wing was now a weapon. Stroking the ball with uncommon pace and accuracy, Tilden ripped off four straight games to win the match.

As the newspapers would recount for those unable to be present for the much-anticipated title match, "Johnston's daring proved his undoing. He rushed the net persistently intent upon blocking Tilden's forehanders and backhanders and while he did volley many of them back for earned points, Tilden passed him more frequently and ended the match in convincing style." The last set would be Tilden's at 6–3. Both men were spent, but the national title now belonged to Tilden.[49]

As *American Lawn Tennis* would capture the final moment, "After [Tilden] had gone through nerve-wracking and courage testing vicissitudes, and had several times been within a stroke of the match only to be denied, the realization came that here was a great genius of the game, a player whose mastery of nearly every stroke was greater than that of any of his predecessors, whose gameness was not to be denied, whose ability to rise to greater and yet greater heights when the need came was little short of phenomenal. This match was the acid test. From it the tall Philadelphian emerged triumphantly, mint-stamped sterling."[50]

The 6–1, 1–6, 7–5, 5–7, 6–3 triumph once again propelled Tilden onto the front page and the lead sports headlines across the country. In what newspaper accounts described "as sensational a match as had been played in a title tournament," the new champion was hailed for his "dazzling speed and strokes" and his ability to "sweep away all before him," as he had done at Wimbledon. Many articles paid homage to the "little Californian"—the defending champion and prematch favorite—for his plucky, "tenacious" effort, but then added that the little man faced an impossible assignment. "In defeat there was glory aplenty" for Johnston, lamented the *Philadelphia Public Ledger*. "He went down striving his utmost to turn the tide in his favor. He played well and daringly and probably it was the best tennis he has shown this season, but his best was not good enough to beat the super tennis that his rival played on the other side of the net."[51] Despite "some superb volleying" and "swift drives for the corners or along the side lines that kept Tilden running all over the court," Johnston found the ball repeatedly coming back to him. This confounding dilemma had no satisfactory answer. His opponent had no obvious weakness.

Some would attribute the impressive victory to the challenger's greater stamina, his vast array of court weaponry, and his mental toughness. Others attributed it to Tilden's "bullet-like service" that "whizzed across with incredible speed," leaving Johnston helpless. The new champion had nearly two dozen aces; Johnston had none. Surprisingly, there would be little to no mention of the new champion's secret weapon—a reconstructed backhand. Tilden, however, knew immediately what aspect of his tennis arsenal deserved credit for the victory and his first National Championship. "I have never regretted the hours, days and weeks that I spent to acquire my backhand drive, for to it, and it primarily, I lay my United States and World's Championship titles," Tilden would write in his classic work *Match Play and Spin of the Ball.* "I am convinced that had I not done the work necessary to the mastery of that stroke, Johnston would have continued to defeat me just as decisively after 1919 as he did that year."[52]

With the victory it was difficult not to accord Tilden the title "the man of the year." The unprecedented Wimbledon triumph combined with the American title left no room for debate. "Always known as a great stroke-maker, Tilden dispelled whatever doubt may have existed as to his match-playing temperament." Possessing "the highest quality of gameness," an incomparable array of shots, and shrewd court tactics, "all glory," swooned one newspaper, "to the illustrious son of Philadelphia."[53]

If any further confirmation of his general court prowess and superiority over Little Bill was needed, it occurred a few days later in Philadelphia, when the Germantown Cricket Club hosted the annual East versus West Tournament, a major athletic event at the time. It was most evident to everyone at Manheim by this point that the club's future rested with its tennis portfolio. The GCC was originally established as a cricket club, but "interest in cricket," according to a board-meeting entry, "had dropped almost to the point of extinction." Practically all were in agreement: there was "little hope of reviving interest."[54] Tennis was now the game that attracted dues-paying members and ticket-paying spectators. And Tilden was the biggest thing on the planet.

Though there were many attractive matches on the docket, the eight thousand paying customers were there for another Tilden-Johnston battle. Both competitors "received a big ovation" from the appreciative "capacity crowd" when they stepped on Manheim's lush green courts. In what would be described as a "brilliant encounter that fairly scintillated with magnificent shots," Tilden won the contest, winning three out of four sets.[55]

The East-West event afforded Bill's home club an opportunity to fete the onetime neighborhood ball boy who had made good. Nearly two hundred tennis enthusiasts turned out for a banquet in Tilden's honor. He was presented with a diamond-and-sapphire stickpin, much good humor, and a round of highly congratulatory speeches. His Davis Cup team compatriots delivered some of the most noteworthy lines. Little Bill, always a model of chivalry, "went flatly on the record to the effect that Tilden was the greatest tennis player in the world." Not to be outdone, Sam Hardy, team captain, called Bill "the greatest player the world had ever known and that he believed that in a few years Tilden would be even better than he is today."[56] Time would prove that prediction quite accurate.

The Davis Cup scrap Down Under at year's end was still the biggest item on the calendar, but until then there were other state and regional tournaments on Bill's schedule. In October, for example, he would win events in Virginia and Rhode Island. At the latter tournament in Providence, he would team with young Arnold W. Jones to win the doubles championship as well. In addition to his many on-court performances, he also continued to write newspaper and magazine articles such as the one he did for *American Lawn Tennis* on the career of former American champion Bill Clothier.[57] That issue would also prominently display the Tilden image and name in a large two-page Bancroft racket advertisement, a commercial promotion that must have caused discomfort to purists wedded to outdated and strict amateur guidelines.[58]

After an exhausting five-day cross-country train ride—with stops in fifteen cities to put on tennis demonstrations and give public lectures—Tilden arrived in San Francisco for the American Davis Cup team's long overseas voyage to Australia.[59] Hundreds gathered at the waterfront ferry depot on Saturday, November 6, for an impromptu tennis exhibition by departing team members. Most had come to see the "tall, dark, springy young man wearing a cap, khaki mackinaw coat, an armful of rackets, and a suitcase." Those fearing a "lame exhibition" due to the champion's long, challenging year of play and lengthy train ride were excited to see snappy play, wonderful shot making, and an upbeat spirit. Never one to disappoint an audience, Tilden was said to have made a "wonderful impression."[60]

Though he loved to drive—the longer, the better, it would seem—Tilden was much less comfortable on board an airplane or oceangoing vessel. These travel preferences and aversions would be lifelong, and some would be established on this trip. The rough seas caused Tilden to be seasick for much of the trip's first leg to Hawaii. Once the team docked, many in the travel party toured the islands and area around Honolulu. Tilden recuperated in his room and came out only for a "large beef dinner."[61] Tall but trim, Tilden could eat, even when he had not played a match or was not feeling well. Now fortified and on dry land, he and Little Bill put on an exhibition for the many residents and fans who came out to wish the players well in their campaign to regain the Cup. The team then boarded their ship for the very long voyage to the South Pacific.

Though just twenty years old, the Davis Cup tournament had arguably become the world's greatest athletic competition. The Cup itself was an ornately decorated foot-high sterling bowl that was donated by Dwight Filley Davis, a young Harvard grad and top tennis player at the turn of the century. It was his hope to spark an international competition to determine the nation with the strongest tennis team.[62] The International Lawn Tennis Challenge Trophy—soon to be known as the Davis Cup—would go to the national four-man team that won three out of five matches consisting of four singles and one doubles match.

With Malcolm Whitman and Holcombe Ward as his teammates, Davis and the United States won that first international tennis scrum over Great Britain in 1900 at the Longwood Cricket Club in Boston. The initial Davis Cup matches went to America. As the years passed additional nations joined the competition, but very quickly the United States—despite its wealth of tennis talent—was pushed aside, and both Great Britain and Australasia (New Zealand was combined with Australia for the new designation) came to dominate the annual tournament. A team from the United States had won the trophy only three times in the competition's twenty-year history, the last being in 1913. That undistinguished record became a sore point for most believers of American athletic superiority.

During the twentieth century Australia was much taken by the game and quickly produced a bevy of top talent. Their current stars were Norman Brookes, a small, wiry left-hander from Melbourne, and Gerald Patterson, the tall, broad-shouldered power hitter who had just months earlier lost his Wimbledon crown to Tilden. Though Brookes, a two-time Wimbledon champion, known as "the wizard" for his ability to return the most difficult shots, was getting on in years and Patterson had just relinquished his title as "world lawn tennis champion," they were formidable players with impressive résumés. And they were committed to preserving their nation's lawn tennis dominance. It would take nothing less than a superteam to defeat them.

In honor of Anthony Wilding, the great New Zealand player and four-time Wimbledon champion who was killed on the bloody fields of Flanders during the war, the challenge match was scheduled for the Domain Cricket Club in Auckland on December 30. The American squad arrived almost three weeks early in order to regain their form after the long journey and adapt to the antipodes' extreme summer heat. The long hours of daily practice Tilden and Johnston put in would pay off handsomely, as the valiant but outgunned Aussies did not win a match.

Brookes fought gloriously, but at forty-three the odds of him defeating Tilden were slim. One of Tilden's heroes as a youth, Brookes, he believed, "had everything—charm, color, individuality and an intelligence that impressed you the moment you met him."[63] But time does not stand still, and Tilden was no longer the young lad harboring "secret hero worship for the World's Champion from down under." The tall, lanky Philadelphian was now a champion in his own right, and he was quick to prove it. After having a 5–3 lead in the first set, Brookes would eventually lose it at 10–8. Tilden won the second set as well at 6–4, before Brookes finally took the third at 6–1. After the walkabout Tilden regained his interest and won the final set at 6–4. Patterson had much the same difficulty with Johnston, winning the first set and losing the next three. The doubles match would prove equally dissatisfying for the reigning champions, as the Americans won three of four sets. On the first day of the new year and final day of singles competition, Big and Little Bill allowed their opponents just two of the eight sets played. It was a decisive 5–0 victory, a devastating clean sweep. After a six-year drought the United States reclaimed possession of the Davis Cup.

Trumpeting the American team's capturing "the blue ribbon of the lawn tennis world," headlines across the globe carried news of the convincing triumph. "Tennis Lovers Hail Return of Davis Cup" was the headline that greeted readers of the New York Times, thereby making for "a spectacularly happy New Year's." "The famous emblem of international supremacy in lawn tennis," the paper proudly crowed, "is thus returned to American possession for the first time since 1913." Aussie journalists were in agreement. "The United States," wrote Major R. M. Kidston of the one-sided victory, "is the rightful owner of the Davis Cup."[64] Moreover, the play of Tilden and Johnston, Kidston would go on to write, "was so convincing, their speed so commanding, that nobody, least of all Brookes and Patterson, has anything but words of praise, not only for their victory, but for their manner of winning."

"Few international sporting events," it was said at the time, "have attracted more attention or been followed with greater interest."[65] Julian S. "Mike" Myrick, president of the USLTA, called the victory "a fitting climax to what should doubtless be regarded as the most successful season in the history of American tennis." Not to be outdone, S. Wallis Merrihew, the dedicated American Lawn Tennis publisher, emotionally admitted, "No words can describe adequately the deep felt thankfulness, the unalloyed joy" that came with regaining the Davis Cup. It was an accomplishment that he and other patriotic Americans "could scarcely cease to wonder at."[66]

For William T. Tilden 2nd, the Davis Cup blowout was the culmination of a glorious and most incredible year. All the work, all the effort, had finally come to fruition. To win the Wimbledon Championship on his first attempt, the U.S. National Championship after years of disappointment, and the prestigious Davis Cup in one year was nothing short of mind-boggling. Add to that the publication of his critically acclaimed first book. Longtime connoisseurs of the game scratched their heads and wondered if there was anything that compared to such singular achievement.

Dismissed as a "dub" for many years, thought "silly" for attempting to learn and perfect so many strokes, and saddled with the label "erratic" for much of his career, Junior Tilden, the pampered child who rarely drifted from his mother's skirt, was now sharing headlines with such fearsome athletic warriors as Ty Cobb, Jim Thorpe, and Jack Dempsey. As one amazed supporter would write of Tilden, "He is a triumph of personality, of intellect, of consummate court craft, and unique mastery of stroke."[67]

For the young boy at Onteora who secretly cherished his older brother's ancient racket and fantasized about playing and beating the world's greatest tennis players, the dream had come true.

5

"You Hit Too Hard"

Tilden had now perfected the full gamut of
his strokes. He was already the most complete
lawn tennis player who ever trod a court.

—E. C. POTTER JR.

What a difference a year makes. However trite that familiar expression, it accurately captures Tilden's history-making transformation from an often-dismissed journeyman player on the country-club tennis circuit to one of the greatest and most creative to ever swing a racket. Just twelve months earlier, in January 1920, he was toiling away in a cold barnlike structure in New England, trying to revamp a weak backhand with seemingly little progress to show for it. Now, a year later, he was king of the hill—the winner of the British, American, and Davis Cup Championships—and celebrated on each of the major continents as an athletic marvel and crafty racket man who was, according to many, remaking the game.

On the day after the Davis Cup exchanged hands, Tilden was anointed "monarch" of America's lawn tennis fraternity; he had been ranked number one by the USLTA. It could have also been argued, as it was by the *New York Times*, that "Tilden is in name as well as in fact the world's champion, for his victory last summer at Wimbledon in the All England tournament, carried the larger title with it as well."[1] One month short of his twenty-eighth birthday—an age when most top players were already on the downside of their athletic careers—Tilden had finally achieved the pinnacle of success, America's top-ranked player. As king of the mountain in these early days of 1921, he must have had few regrets, though one of them might have been that his father and brother had not lived to witness his rise to international stardom. His love of the game and devotion to mastering every aspect and stroke had not been for naught. Although it had taken many years, his single-minded resolve had been rewarded.

Tilden's selection as the nation's best tennis player must have been particularly gratifying for one member of the USLTA's selection committee, Paul W. Gibbons.[2] It is safe to assume Gibbons never suspected that the earnest young man assisting him less than a decade earlier in spreading the gospel of tennis to local high school students would one day be a Wimbledon champion and the nation's highest-ranked player. Back in 1913 young Junior Tilden, as he was then known, was an unexceptional college student and player of no great distinction whose only outstanding features were a love for the game and willingness to talk up its attributes to boys at area schools and community playgrounds. That unimposing Penn net man was now the greatest player in the world.

Even foreign ranking services placed Tilden at the top the world's first ten. A. E. Crawley, for example, an English player and writer who regularly compared players' records for his rankings, put four Americans in the world's first ten, and Tilden was at the top.[3] It was hard to argue with his impressive accomplishments over the past year.

Interestingly, in addition to coverage of Tilden's and Johnston's great play Down Under, and the former's well-earned number-one ranking, there were other news articles related to tennis on the home front. One of them dealt with the need for an open tennis championship for the nation's best young players. The author was none other than "William T. Tilden."[4]

In a continuation of his long interest in building and supporting boys' tennis programs, Tilden was encouraging the USLTA to throw more resources and organizational thought into boys' tennis programs. "Progress necessitates change," he argued, and due to "phenomenal" growth in the "spread of tennis among schoolboys of America," additional opportunities for advancement were necessary. One of these was "the crying need" for "an open junior championship" that would be held annually in big cities such as Chicago, New York, Philadelphia, and Boston.[5] "I believe that an open tournament for juniors and boys is absolutely necessary," Tilden preached, "for it seems to me that any boy who is anxious enough to compete in the event that he will journey to the city where it is held deserves the opportunity to play."

Though there may have been others who thought the notion reasonable and worthy of support considering the public's growing interest in tennis, it was Tilden who championed the cause. Passionate about the sport and as comfortable stroking a keypad as a tennis ball, Tilden had signed a contract with the *Philadelphia Evening Bulletin* to write a series of articles for the Saturday edition on developments in the game. One cannot be sure, but he either wrote the series before departing with the Davis Cup team for the South Pacific or wrote them in New Zealand while preparing for the match. Regardless, it was an expenditure of time and effort that few, if any other top players, were willing to commit.

Before returning home and what was expected to be a grand celebration, the American team remained Down Under and played in New Zealand's championships, followed by a series of exhibition matches in Sydney and Melbourne. The Australian competitions included the nation's best players. Continuing his excellent form, Tilden would be the only one of the many competitors for both countries to go undefeated in all of his matches.

When the victorious Davis Cup team arrived back in the States on February 17, hundreds of people flocked to greet the S.S. *Ventura* at the pier in San Francisco Harbor. A regimental parade band; speeches by Mayor James Rolph Jr., W. B. Alexander of the Chamber of Commerce, and other dignitaries; and adoring tennis fans were all part of the reception and general festivities.[6] Tilden told the enthusiastic audience that the American squad was so powerful, "the United States will be able to keep the Davis Cup for some time." The boastful prediction generated much applause and patriotic cheers among the appreciative fans. After the event Little Bill said his good-byes and went home with his wife. Big Bill, a cross-country journey ahead of him, first stopped at the St. Francis Hotel, where it was observed "his appetite had lost nothing by the sea voyage, and the way he attacked his luncheon left no doubt in the minds of his companions as to his fitness."[7]

Bill arrived back in his hometown on the morning of the twenty-first of February and was greeted by the mayor and other Philadelphia dignitaries when his train pulled into the station. Paul W. Gibbons, who knew "the superman of tennis" better than most, was one of them. Going immediately to his Germantown home on Hansberry Street, Bill said hello to his aunt and cousin, uttered a few pleasantries, and was quickly off to a series of congratulatory receptions in his honor, including a luncheon at the Manufacturers' Club and a similar event at the Post Office Building. "It's great to be back," Bill informed one audience. "It was a wonderful trip and left no doubt in the minds of the Australians that the United States is the champion tennis nation today. Our stay in Australia was one round of pleasure. We started right by taking all five matches in the Davis Cup struggle and of course that put us in the best humor possible. I doubt if anything could have spoiled the trip after that."[8]

Mayor J. Hampton Moore told one excited audience that Tilden's "feats on the tennis court" were more than just athletic accomplishments, but "beams in the halo of Philadelphia's glory." Tilden's achievements, added Moore, "cause Philadelphia universal satisfaction . . . and aroused the keenest sense of pride in our fellow citizen. Now that you are back," he told Tilden, "the very least we can do is give you a warm, hearty Quaker City greeting and welcome and tell you that Philadelphia is proud of her son."[9]

Obviously enjoying the moment, Bill thanked all those who took time to greet him and told the assembled he saw great things in the future for American tennis. "Billy Johnston could drop out. Norris Williams, Wallace Johnson, myself and all the rest of the players the public now knows could disappear," said Bill, "but so long as we continue the development of our youngsters on the present scale we are sure to remain supreme. There is nobody to seriously threaten us. I have not seen any comparison in all the countries I have visited." The statement was met with enthusiastic whoops and cheers. Newspapers carried glowing accounts of the many honors and receptions given the man who was said to have withstood "the most strenuous lawn tennis schedule during the last nine months of any player that ever represented this country."[10] At a subsequent gala in Tilden's honor at the Bellevue-Stratford Hotel, more than four hundred attendees heard Mayor Moore and Olympic rower John B. Kelly give rousing speeches about Bill's athletic contributions, his place in history, and the city's eternal indebtedness to him.

In one long article in the *Philadelphia Inquirer* concerning Bill's much-ballyhooed arrival back home, mention was made of William T. Tilden, the player's father, "who was for many years active in our municipal affairs and took a deep interest in our national affairs." It was plainly wondered "what William T. Tilden, who was accustomed to so many honors himself, would think if he could have known of the world triumphs of his son and could be here to greet him."[11]

During the winter and early spring Tilden continued to work on his game, write articles, and plan his summer tennis schedule. Attending banquets, receptions, and dinners in his honor had now become an ever-increasing part of his itinerary. When he attended a meeting at his own club, board members of the Germantown Cricket Club gave him a standing ovation with "prolonged applause followed by three cheers."[12] What could be more glorious than a neighborhood boy who had grown up on Manheim's grass courts, gone abroad, and returned a national hero?

Unmentioned at the time—and for obvious reasons—was the embarrassing fact that Big Bill's club dues were in arrears. Diplomatic messages—both verbal and in writing—would be sent making note of their illustrious member's mounting debt without resolution. Apparently, the world's top player "had been in arrears for both dues and house charges for some time and the treasurer of the Club had been unable to collect them." All were in agreement: it was a delicate issue concerning a celebrated American athlete. The sensitive matter required some diplomacy; neither player nor club needed an unflattering news story. At a subsequent monthly board meeting Samuel H. Collum, chairman of the club's tennis committee, happily informed his colleagues he had finally "succeeded in collecting the delinquent account of Mr. William T. Tilden 2nd." That embarrassing financial conundrum may have been remedied permanently when the club decided to make both Big Bill and Little Bill "honorary members."[13]

Manheim's decision was not unique; many of the nation's top country clubs were doing the same. Tilden was now a star attraction, and every group, organization, and club wanted a part of him. His participation at tournaments was widely considered the yardstick for measuring financial success. Those events without Tilden were automatically lackluster and of lesser stature in the public's mind. His absence translated into reduced interest, fewer patrons, and modest gate receipts.

That unattractive scenario was glaringly proved the previous summer after the Davis Cup team returned from Europe and Tilden along with them as America's first-ever men's Wimbledon champion. The team was expected to immediately travel to Rhode Island to take part in Newport's prestigious and tradition-rich tennis tournament. Tilden, however, had other plans and "threw the fashionable Newport colony into a state of bewilderment by refusing to play in the tournament."[14] When confronted by alarmed tournament officials and surprised journalists, Tilden stood his ground and said, "No, I'm not going to Newport. I have a date for next Thursday to play at Fairmount Park in Philadelphia. I want to help the young players as much as I can."

Shock would be a most appropriate term to describe the reaction of those well-to-do throughout New England who were looking forward to the new world champion's appearance. It was the first time anyone could recall a prominent American player turning down the famed Newport Casino for a tutoring session with children, and at a public city park, no less. Government leaders were enlisted in the campaign to change Tilden's mind, but to no avail. After several insistent telegrams from Governor Robert Livingston Beeckman of Rhode Island, "urging him to play at Newport," Tilden diplomatically refused the invitation. He kept his engagement at Fairmount Park in Philadelphia, "where 5,000 enthusiasts turned out to see him play and give an open-air lecture on lawn tennis."[15]

The Newport snub was another unmistakable indication that an array of majestic strokes was not the only revolutionary thing about this new champion. He most definitely had different priorities as well as a different understanding of his social obligations. The incident also underscored why he became a heroic figure to thousands of middle- and working-class children around the country and a source of periodic consternation to the affluent country-club types who looked with disfavor on anyone cavalier enough to abandon his own kind for what some considered common riffraff.

And just as his absence at an event caused collective dismay among society types, his celebrity also meant that whatever he chose to orchestrate or involve himself with had a good chance of success. That included his rather dubious winter rooftop tournament twelve stories above Market Street in Philadelphia. Learning from the previous winter's rooftop debacle at Wanamaker's department store, Tilden moved the event back to April to lessen the chance of the event being impacted by a snowstorm. Once again more than fifteen hundred tennis lovers attended the elevated competition and watched the hometown boy defeat a very respectable field that included the likes of Wallace Johnson, Watson Washburn, and Vince Richards.

It was at this time that *The Art of Lawn Tennis* entered American bookstores for two dollars a copy. Called "unique in both style and content," the book was thought "very aptly captioned for it reveals the artistic, inspired, soul-stirring element of the sport as no other book has ever succeeded in doing." Calling Tilden's use of language "appropriate," his expression "succinct yet vivid, and his diction at all times fluent and forceful," the reviewer was obviously impressed. He would go on to comment that Tilden was well known for "his immense variety of strokes" that "have distinguished him from practically all the players of the age," but now he had "disclosed himself a pen-artist of the first flight" as well.[16]

Though the book reviews were positive, it was still Tilden's tennis game that was drawing the most comment. Many considered it revolutionary and the height of athletic artistry. Tennis pundits wasted no opportunity to write articles about the champion's finely crafted strokes, psychological approach, and overall court generalship. S. Wallis Merrihew, for example, a longtime connoisseur of lawn tennis, could wax eloquent on any single aspect of the champion's game, and often did. On his potent first serve, for instance, Merrihew wrote that he had long believed no stroke or service had yet been devised "that cannot be countered." However, Tilden "has evolved a service that is so new it has not yet been countered. It is the most effective form it can be, and usually is, made by standing flat footed and hurling over at terrific speed a straight hit ball. Its pace, aided by judicious placing, make it the lethal weapon it undoubtedly is." Yet Tilden, Merrihew would go on to explain, "does not win by serve alone. His armory contains other equally potent weapons, and his skill in selecting them is the chief factor in his success."[17]

Such glowing assessments had become commonplace by now and attending laudatory dinners a regular part of the schedule. One of the larger was the USLTA's banquet honoring the victorious Davis Cup team. Though a sparkling success—and attended by some of the game's greatest champions—it hid a disturbing point of contention between the tennis association and the game's most important player.

In Tilden's opinion the unexpected financial disagreement was the opening salvo of his long and fractious relationship with the high priests of the USLTA. It began in earnest in the spring of 1921 as he planned his forthcoming defense of his Wimbledon title. When the organization expressed their desire that Tilden go abroad "some weeks earlier and play for the championship of France," Tilden was agreeable. But the tennis association's "parsimonious attitude," in Tilden's opinion, "led to the first serious dispute" between America's top player and the game's corporate overseers.[18] In short the issue was money; specifically, who would pay for the champion's lengthy trip abroad?

As Tilden described the incident in *My Story*, "Figuring that I had an income of my own, the Association decided not to take care of my living and traveling expenses completely on this trip." The American champion was greatly offended. As he went on to argue, "When they extended the invitation to lead an American group abroad, they informed me that I would be graciously allowed one thousand dollars. Out of that enormous sum I was supposed to pay my boat fare over and back, live three weeks in Paris—and then four weeks in London." Tilden thought such a schedule a financial impossibility, even maintaining the tightest of budgets. "Besides," he went on to write, "I felt it beneath the dignity of the United States to have its champion travel in any way except first class. I so notified the Association, and told them unless they were willing to pay my complete expenses, both traveling and living, I had no intention of going abroad."[19] His decision was more than a warning shot across the bow of the USLTA.

"A complete impasse," in Tilden's mind, the situation was truly grave, but resolution would come from an unexpected source. In April the U.S. Davis Cup team received an invitation from the president of the United States, Warren G. Harding, to visit the White House on May 6 and put on a tennis exhibition for him and the Washington media. Bill was delighted by the invitation, but prior to the event five days of hard rain had turned the White House court into a sea of mud. Undeterred, Tilden encouraged the White House to do whatever they could; the exhibition should not be canceled. Groundskeepers came up with an ingenious solution: they dried the court out by burning two hundred gallons of gasoline on it.[20]

Prior to the tennis demonstration, President Harding invited the team into his office. After a few brief remarks and opportunities for photographs, the president took Bill aside as the group was leaving for the court.

"I hear you are not planning to go to Europe to defend at Wimbledon," said Mr. Harding.

"That's true, Mr. President," Bill replied.

"I have no desire to intrude into your private affairs or to influence you against your will, but we at the head of the Government feel that international sports are more valuable than diplomacy in obtaining friendship and understanding among nations. We hope that any American champions who hold titles abroad will defend them if possible, and will use all their influence to bring our foreign friends to our shores. If you can see your way to reconsidering, I would appreciate it."[21]

Patriotic, and already a firm believer in the goodwill spurred by international sport, Tilden admitted, "That ended that. Naturally I changed my mind on the spot and agreed to go to Europe."

Pleased by Tilden's decision, the president proceeded to inquire what had caused the champion to take such a surprising stance in the first place. "With pleasure," replied Tilden, and when he had explained what had transpired, "Mr. Harding expressed himself to the effect that it was a damned disgrace" for a national champion to be treated so shabbily.

As Tilden would recount the incident years later in *My Story*, one can infer that President Harding may have spoken to officers of the USLTA, since "forty-eight hours later [Tilden] received word that they would pay [his] complete expenses."[22] No doubt Bill relished his victory over the USLTA. The incident only added to his already firm conviction that as an international sports celebrity, he was entitled to a lifestyle "befitting a champion."

"For the rest of his life," Arthur Voss would write, "Bill continued to hold to the philosophy that he was entitled to go first class at the expense of the USLTA and tournament committees, and powerful gate attraction that he was, he almost always had their full cooperation in this regard." As Al Laney would write of the champion's attraction to first-class travel and posh hotels, Bill "traveled like a goddamn Indian prince." Cross-country train excursions were often taken in a large, comfortable compartment car, and chauffeur-driven autos were placed at his beck and call on his arrival. George Lott, a young tennis compatriot of Tilden in later years, told Voss, "Tilden was the man who set the precedent for tennis players to live in a style to which they were not accustomed."[23]

The crisis resolved, Bill and the other members of the team sailed off for Europe in mid-May. The World Hard Court Championships at St. Cloud on the outskirts of Paris and the fortieth anniversary of the famed Wimbledon tournament in London awaited them. Almost immediately, however, a new problem would emerge. Tilden's health was in a state of decline, and a long voyage followed by a series of difficult athletic challenges was not what a prudent doctor would prescribe. As Bill frankly admitted, "A long, hard winter of play had left me very much run down. Almost the first thing I did on arriving in France was to pick up an infection which resulted in a series of serious boils."[24] In addition to being overtennised, too many banquets, and in need of some rest, Bill would blame his medical dilemma on the general lack of sanitation in postwar France, particularly with regard to their "bathing facilities." He would forever remain assured that it was there that he "picked up the germ that almost cost [him] both the French and British titles."

Tennis historian Rich Hillway believes, "Tilden's immune system was always in a compromised state. He was often sickly as a youth and missed a lot of school. As a child and even in college, he was often sick. Though a fine athlete and willing to put in the hard work to make himself a champion, he really wasn't a healthy kid. He was easily infected with whatever was going around."[25] These periodic health conundrums would eventually dissipate, but not before he had suffered some serious physical ailments.

Though increasingly listless and on the verge of a blood infection, Bill was still strong enough to do battle with some of Europe's top players as well as another court icon of the era. "Champion of champions, the queen of queens," Suzanne Lenglen was probably the only other lawn tennis star of the early 1920s who rivaled Tilden for athleticism, racket wizardry, and shear star power. Never defeated in her own country after the age of fifteen, a French national hero, and an athletic prodigy with perfect technique and an unsurpassed will to win, Lenglen was a performer of practically unrivaled glamour and accomplishment.

Trained at an early age by her father to be a lawn tennis warrior, she could perform physical feats on a court no other woman had ever attempted. Equal part sprinter, gymnast, and ballet dancer, Lenglen was a bandeau-wearing, racket-swinging wunderkind who took France—and then the

Continent—by storm. Seemingly invincible against other women players during the postwar period, her legend quickly grew. Even American sports aficionados followed her triumphs and anticipated her appearance on this side of the Atlantic. Her fame was so great that Al Laney admits his "first glimpse of Suzanne was disappointing after the buildup" she had received. He saw "a plain girl with dull, almost sallow colorless skin and strong irregular teeth. She had large hands and feet for so slim a person, and her face in repose had a strong melancholy cast."

But get her on a court, and almost "at once she was all animation and vivacity. How sudden the change and how immediate the effect," Laney would exclaim. After watching her practice on the French Riviera in 1919, he would write that her technique and athleticism were a "revelation. Here was a girl with as much skill as, and a greater variety of strokes and greater ease of execution than, any man I had encountered. And with it a natural grace of movement I had never seen equaled on a tennis court."[26] Over the next few years Lenglen would do more for women's tennis than any female who had ever picked up a racket. A woman stepping on a tennis court was now not only acceptable but fashionable. And her impact on hairstyle, women's athletic attire, and female physicality in general became more than tolerable; it was trendy and chic. As Laney summed up her popularity that stretched from New York to London and Paris to Berlin and Monte Carlo, "she became the rage, almost a cult."[27]

Very few artists, entertainers, or athletes enjoyed such public adulation and widespread print coverage, but Bill Tilden was one of them, and, not surprisingly, the king and queen of lawn tennis eyed each other suspiciously and jealously guarded their reputations. In fact, one could safely argue they detested each other. Thin-skinned, protective of their image, and sensitive to criticism, the two prima donnas lost no opportunity to take verbal swipes at each other. Incidents that would embarrass the other were cultivated as well.

On one famous occasion shortly after Bill arrived in Paris, Lenglen spotted her American nemesis practicing on the slow red-clay courts of Stade Français in St. Cloud, the site of the forthcoming World Hard Court Championship. Tilden was hitting with Molla Bjurstedt Mallory, a transplanted Lapp who had found fame and a wealthy Wall Street husband in the United States. A former national tennis champion of Norway, she had won the American championship five times and was a good friend of Bill's. Lenglen, taking in the scene, strolled down to the court to watch the two American champions practice. She was not impressed, but that was Tilden's plan. He knew she would not waste an opportunity to embarrass him and heighten her own stature. As he would one day write of the infamous incident, "I was hitting rather badly and the thought came to me that if I looked enough off my game Suzanne might ask me to play her." The expectation of the two tennis rivals going at it on court was not as far-fetched as one might think; there was much talk at the time that Mademoiselle Lenglen could hold her own with the top male players. Tilden, of course, considered the suggestion absurd. There was no way a woman—even one of championship caliber—could beat a man of equal athletic pedigree. Such a notion was just "amazing and ridiculous" to Tilden, and he decided on the spot to prove it.[27] The trap had been set. "I proceeded to be really lousy," Bill recalled, "and sure enough Suzanne called to me. 'Will you play a set?'"

Bill agreed, and the trap was sprung. Within seconds word got around the tennis complex like wildfire that Tilden and Lenglen, the greatest male and female players of the age, were about to do battle. Reporters dropped their present assignments and scampered over to watch the much-anticipated contest. The match was short but far from painless; Tilden quickly ran off six straight games to win 6–0.

Enjoying the quick, one-sided contest, Tilden coyly asked, "Will you play another?"

"No," replied Suzanne, "you hit too hard."

As reporters flooded the court seeking the players' comments, Tilden was amazed to hear Lenglen disingenuously remark, "Yes, Mr. Tilden and I played, but whether he won six games or I did, I really don't know."[28]

Tennis historian Richard Hillway adds a little-known but interesting aspect about the match. So convinced was Tilden that the Frenchwoman presented little challenge to him that he allowed Suzanne to take a 40-love lead in every game, before he really started to play his serious brand of tennis. To be so close to winning a game and then lose is terribly frustrating. To have it done to you a half-dozen times in a row is maddening. But that was Bill's way of showing the French wunderkind there was a pecking order to the sport and she was not yet at the top.

Soon after, however, Tilden would be beset with a nasty, debilitating health malady—Bill would refer to the entire episode as a "nightmare"—that would challenge his will and quality of play as never before. While he was feeling worse by the day and his interest and ability to play tennis were declining, the most visible sign of illness was the appearance of boils and other painful skin eruptions. "The boils got me down," Bill admitted, "and the only times I could pry myself out of bed were when I had to play." He would become so sick that the experience would leave a rather sour impression of the City of Light, something that most people would find hard to fathom.

Though he found taking the court increasingly difficult—just getting out of bed had become an effort—Tilden was the class of the World Hard Court Championship field. Upsets claimed some of the better players, such as André Gobert of France and Manuel Alonso of Spain, making Tilden's road to the final somewhat easier. By the time he went through his preliminary matches, losing only three sets in the process, and faced Belgian Jean Washer in the final, he was obviously ill and the abscesses ever more problematic, especially those around his feet and ankles. For someone expected to perform athletically for two or three strenuous hours, it was a significant challenge. Reporters were diplomatic in their assessments and used terms like *fatigued* to describe his appearance, but even when impaired Tilden was capable of extraordinary things.[29]

Washer was a fine European player and left-handed; Tilden was never keen on playing lefties. On more than one occasion over the years he was heard to say he would prefer to play a very good right-hander than a moderately good lefty. And though Washer would play "gamely" and "showed great speed in covering the court," there were only a few instances when his potent forehand drives placed Tilden on the defensive. From the first set, according to most accounts, he was completely "outclassed." Tilden just had too many shots and too much athletic ability for the gutsy but underequipped Belgian. The 6–3, 6–3, 6–3 victory did not truly capture Tilden's superiority. When the champion hit a perfect drive down the line and out of the reach of Washer to win the match, "the immense crowd . . . cheered for fully five minutes." It was said that no tennis player in France had ever received such a long and enthusiastic ovation.[30] Tilden appreciated the crowd's approval but was more focused on getting off his feet and back into bed as quickly as possible.[31]

American tennis fans following Tilden's European triumphs got their first inkling of the champion's precarious state of health when they read headlines in their local newspapers that Tilden had been hospitalized on his arrival in London. Some like the *New York Times* tried to downplay the severity of the crisis with a headline that read, "Tilden Enters Hospital for Rest; Condition Not Serious," but the patient was certainly in no shape to pick up a racket against the world's best players.[32] His condition was so serious, in fact, that two tournaments prior to Wimbledon that he was scheduled to play in—Beckenham and Roehampton—were dropped.

If there was anything fortunate about Tilden's current predicament, it was the fact that in the 1921 Wimbledon Championships—the last to be played at the old tennis grounds on Worple Road—the past year's titleholder stood out in wait of a worthy challenger. Tilden had requested he be allowed to play through, but the All England Club was not quite prepared to break with tradition. That would come the following year. Fortunately for Tilden, if he would have had to play through as is done today, the defense of his crown would have been impossible—he was too ill and confined to his bed in an English nursing facility for ten days.

Though convalescing and under doctors' orders to rest and not exercise, Tilden was still able to write, and that he did. Feeling in need of fulfilling his contract for a series of articles for the *Philadelphia Evening Bulletin*, Tilden continued to put pen to paper and draft informative pieces on the latest developments on the European tennis circuit. For example, just after leaving Paris he submitted a piece on a rising young star from Spain. Manuel Alonso was described as "an all court player" with potent "ground strokes, both fore and backhand," and "volleying that is remarkable for its angles." Equally important, as far as Tilden was concerned, young Alonso was "a sportsman of the highest type as he is as modest in victory as he is generous in defeat."[33] Probably most remarkable about the article is the restraint of the author. Tilden made no mention that he had won the World Hard Court Championship or that he was writing the article from a hospital ward.

Tilden was not allowed to leave his London "hospital until the day that Wimbledon started, and could only begin practice on the second Monday following." This provided him only a few days to prepare for the winner of the all-comers in the challenge round. When he stepped on Center Court he was greeted with a rousing ovation from a packed grandstand. "Many," it was reported, "had arrived outside the gates by 3 o'clock in the morning, while play did not begin until 2 in the afternoon. Hundreds sat around all day to be sure of their places and not a single inch of room was vacant when the players took the court." Rarely, if ever, it was said, had lawn tennis "been at such white heat" over a championship match.[34]

For those at courtside, however, it was obvious the champion was not well; he appeared visibly pale, wan, and sickly. One American admirer said Tilden "looked yellow and far from fit." Tilden admitted to him that "he had not got his stamina and will back yet," and it was showing. He said he was "playing like a fish."[35] Some tennis pundits were already preparing their obituary-like assessments.

> Tilden, the great Tilden of 1920, was but a shadow of his true self. Over a year of incessant competitive tennis, culminated in an operation and sojourn in a nursing home had taken its inevitable toll. Tilden, the supreme artist, lives on his nerves. His wonderful game is the product, not of a nerveless machine, but of a sensitive instrument strung to its highest pitch by the calls of the great event. But when the events succeed each other with breathless rapidity, as in the past year, the finest instrument loses its tone. Tilden during the past fortnight showed all too evident signs of a loss of stamina and keenness.[36]

His opponent, on the other hand, was the picture of health and youthful exuberance. Brian Norton, a twenty-one-year-old South African star, had already developed a reputation for being "completely irresponsible" and "bubbling over with high spirits and the joy of life." Known for his quickness and court coverage, he was "always on his toes and bouncing about as light as a feather" and reminded British tennis authority John Olliff of "a Ping-Pong ball bouncing up and down on top of a stream of water."[37] The good-looking lad with wavy hair, pug nose, and what was described as a "wicked enchanting smile" was a "mirthful mischief maker," but a talented one. And it would be this fireball of energy and enthusiasm that Tilden—just out of a sickbed after a ten-day stint as a patient—would be confronted with before thousands of expectant tennis fans.

Norton had defeated American Frank Hunter in a hard-fought five-set semifinal match and squeezed by rising Spanish star Manuel Alonso in another difficult five-setter, thereby earning the right to take on the Wimbledon champion in the challenge round. For hospital physicians, the prospect of a weakened, recently released patient picking up a racket—much less playing an exhausting world-class match—was the height of lunacy. But for Tilden, champions had an obligation to perform.

His level of performance early on, unsurprisingly, was described as "pathetic." According to one critic, "he could do nothing right" and lost the first two sets 6–4, 6–2, in less than thirty minutes.[38] What happened next in what Tilden himself would refer to as a "screwball match" would be debated for years to come.

Inexplicably, Norton, up two sets to none, appeared to let down. For even those new to the sport, Norton "very obviously eased up" and allowed Tilden back in the match. In fact, the youthful challenger seemed so uninterested or upset at times that he won only one of the next thirteen games. Norton's up-and-down play during the match would only underscore his reputation for childish behavior and inability to take "anything in life seriously." "Boy" or "Babe" Norton, as he was often called, was acting once again "like a naughty little schoolboy."[39]

Tilden, however, saw the sudden turnabout as an inexperienced challenger becoming overconfident. He liked Norton and considered him a "close personal friend." They were staying at the same hotel, and Tilden would subsequently write that Norton, "almost better than anyone else, knew how ill I had been and in what precarious shape I was for a challenge round."[40]

While Norton steamrollered through the first two sets, Tilden tried to regain some semblance of form and make a match out of it. Between looking awful and playing worse, it came as no surprise to Tilden to see his young opponent get cocky. "He was so certain that I could not last the match," Tilden would write, "that he became overconfident and quite careless. Even though playing badly I was benefiting by the exercise in the first two sets, which Norton did not realize."

By the start of the third set Tilden recognized he had to shift gears, adopt a different strategy, and utilize some other strokes. Nobody, of course, could do this better than Tilden. His complement of offensive and defensive weaponry dwarfed what any other player had in his arsenal. Hoping to disrupt Norton's solid play as they began the third set, Tilden began to employ a series of drop shots. The strategy worked; Norton, though fleet-footed, was unable to reach balls that died like shot quails after passing over the net. The specter of "Norton standing helpless without getting the ball" so angered "ignorant sections of the crowd" that many began to yell derogatory comments in Tilden's direction. One outraged fan shouted, "Play the game, Tilden." With Tilden a fan favorite just a year earlier, many paying customers no longer seemed entranced by the tall American's woolly-bear sweaters, unusual court commentary, and distinctive personality. They were not happy with his shot selection, and they let him know it.

Though Tilden was known for being easily unnerved by bad calls, lazy ball boys, and obnoxious crowd behavior, he seemed to have been less affected by the Wimbledon version of the Bronx cheer than his opponent. The whistles and personal epithets cascading from the gallery visibly irritated Norton. He appealed to the umpire that he would quit if "the spectators continued to annoy Tilden." This forced "the umpire to admonish those in the stands several times" for their rude behavior. Norton was obviously bothered that the crowd would react in such an unsportsmanlike fashion toward a great athlete who was clearly unwell. Tilden's game definitely improved in the third and fourth sets, but many who observed the match would remain firm in their belief that Norton threw both sets. The entire scenario was considered "a most extraordinary happening."[41]

Viewing his critics as "British both in nationality and sentiment," Tilden believed the stadium hecklers generating most of the "boos and catcalls" had never seen a drop shot. "For some strange reason [they] decided it wasn't cricket."[42] He played on seemingly unperturbed or already too pre-occupied with his painful boils, lousy play, and a troublesome opponent to pay attention. After four sets of wildly uneven tennis, the score stood at 6–4, 6–2, 1–6, 0–6. Those last two sets, especially the fourth, reenergized Tilden's supporters in the grandstand. The American champion "played the fourth set," it would be written, "as if he meant it to be a one man show. He sent over whiz-bang services and steadied himself beautifully. He played hurricane shots all around the court and captured a love set."[43]

Once again, it seemed to many, Tilden was playing to form, pulling out a glorious victory from the firm grasp of defeat. Tilden believed Norton had become arrogant; the kid was "convinced" he could win the match at any time. In Norton's mind Tilden was just too ill to endure a long match, so he gave minimal effort in the third and fourth sets. Never did he expect Tilden to survive a fifth set.

But withstand it he did, and both players offered some of their best form of the day. Tilden's play was still uneven, but his moments of sheer brilliance were delivered more frequently. And no longer did Norton seem to throw points; he was now committed to winning the championship. Both men wanted the title and fought hard. Norton surged ahead and took a 5–3 lead, but had difficulty closing out the match. Needing but one point for victory on two separate occasions, he was thwarted on the first when Tilden fired off one of his unhittable cannonball serves. And a "most remarkable psychological break" intruded on the second. The latter came after a long baseline rally when Tilden hit a ball he thought was long and approached the net to congratulate the new champion. To his amazement the ball fell good on the line, and Norton, seeing his opponent come to the net, presumably to volley, attempted a difficult passing shot—which he missed. "Had he realized it," wrote Tilden afterward, "hitting the ball back anywhere at all in my court would have been enough because I had already passed up the match."[44]

Norton's error brought the score to deuce; the defending champion was still alive. Calling upon his "last bit of reserve," Tilden "ran out the set 7–5 with the best tennis played that day." Gratified the battle was over, but physically and mentally depleted, Tilden would write of that final moment, "I remember little of the end of the match or how I got back to the clubhouse. Once there, for the first time and last time in my tournament career I fainted dead away."

Although his quality of play was clearly inferior to that displayed the previous year, Big Bill was able to repeat as Wimbledon champion. Most connoisseurs of the game recognized that "Tilden triumphed more over physical conditions than by superlative merit," and few doubted—including Babe Norton—that Norton would have had little, if any, chance of winning if the defending champion had been in good health.[45]

Not surprisingly, newspapers around the world trumpeted Tilden's "superb uphill struggle" and his all-around greatness, and, as the *New York Times* would maintain, "his record is matchless in the history of the game." Though Jack Dempsey's decisive victory over French boxer Georges Carpentier would dominate the sports pages at this time, those who followed lawn tennis had much to savor in accounts of the recent Wimbledon Championships. And like the big heavyweight prizefighter, Tilden was solidifying his place in sports history. Many newspapers echoed the sentiment of the *Philadelphia Inquirer* when it proudly proclaimed "America's superiority" across the globe both in the ring and on the court.[46]

Tennis chroniclers of the day had much to chew on; the champion provided a wealth of journalistic story lines. "While his game is . . . the all court game," wrote S. Wallis Merrihew in an *American Lawn Tennis* editorial, "it is the most versatile and unorthodox of any game yet displayed by a champion. It is hopeless to copy it. It may be said, as Tilden remarks, that a player should be possessed of all the strokes. This is true. But not one player in one hundred thousand could even hope to play these strokes as Tilden plays them. In him we have a lawn tennis genius, at whom we can marvel; but we cannot hope to emulate him, or any considerable part of him."[47]

Others would write of his confounding tricks with the ball, his impressive versatility, his jaw-dropping athleticism, and his almost unnatural ability to hit so many shots. News articles would refer to him as "the master," a "unique genius," a genuine "colossus," and "the American Mountain." His play—even when physically impaired—left people in a state of wonderment.

As to the final men's singles match of the 1921 Wimbledon tournament, it would remain for the ages one of "the great enigmas of lawn tennis." Bizarre: most certainly. Inexplicable, that too, but many still tried. How does one explain the unexplainable? A wounded and ineffectual champion down two sets to love comes back to triumph: highly improbable. But it happened.

Most fans of the game knew of Tilden's penchant for the dramatic. He loved crowds, and he loved to perform. Coming back from certain defeat was part of the show, but his match with Norton was different. For years—decades, in fact—tennis aficionados would forever after trot out theories to explain the incredible turnabout. Most would buy into the theory that "with victory in sight the haggard appearance of his adversary was too much for Norton's nerves. He was touched with pity. What a shame that a great champion should lose his title without even a set to his credit. He eased up . . . and gave Tilden balls he could not help put away."[48]

At least one former player who remained close to the game suggested a provocative sexual angle as the cause to one of the game's stranger incidents. Ted Tinling was a bald-headed six-foot, seven-inch player of middling talent in the 1920s who developed a lifelong association with tennis as both match official and fashion couturier. He nurtured a strong friendship with Suzanne Lenglen and other top players and would one day write a memoir of his six-decade association with the game. In it he would argue, "I have known several connoisseurs who were present [at the Tilden-Norton match] and all accepted the fact that a psychological, probably homosexual, relationship affected the result." Tinling believed young Norton was smitten with the older, more accomplished player and "could never bring himself to defeat Tilden."[49]

Richard Hillway puts little stock in the theory. The Colorado tennis historian says, "Tinling was hardly an objective observer" and quite protective of Lenglen's reputation. Moreover, he believes Tinling was guilty of "subjective fantasy," as there is no proof to support such an inflammatory theory. Tinling was gay himself and reading more into the incident than is necessary. Norton was young, impetuous, and prone to careless, unthinking play. He had also been worn down by a series of five-set matches and troubled by the gallery's verbal abuse of Tilden, someone he admired and considered the game's greatest player. Mental and physical errors, according to Hillway, began to characterize Norton's play. And that could prove fatal against Tilden, for even a weakened Tilden was still a pretty good tennis player.

A perfectionist, Tilden knew his Wimbledon exhibition was below par and publicly apologized to British sportsmen for his victorious but underwhelming performance as he was about to set sail for America. It was a gracious gesture by a proud athlete and theater lover who believed in giving the paying customer a good show. He regretted he had not given a typical Tildenesque performance. He would conclude his apology with kind words of praise for two of the game's young players—Babe Norton and Manuel Alonso—for both of whom he predicted great things in coming years.[50]

By mid-July Bill was back on native soil, but he was still feeling the effects of his illness and chose to withdraw from some grass-court tournaments, no doubt to the chagrin of event organizers. Few knew at the time that Tilden had retreated to a cool corner of New England's picturesque White Mountains to fully recuperate. Short hikes in pastoral woodlands, listening to classical recordings, games of bridge, and some serious reading would now occupy his time. But there was pressure to pick up a racket again; he was world champion and a much-desired commodity.

Consistent with not pushing his luck health-wise as he rounded back into shape, he jettisoned more physically demanding singles competition for some less strenuous doubles action. At Longwood in Boston, ironically, he would find himself in a battle royal. He and Vinnie Richards defeated R. Norris Williams and Watson Washburn, an excellent doubles team who had just won tournaments in Newport and Seabright, but it would be far from the light workout he had expected. The hard-fought 13–11, 12–10, 6–1 battle, which Tilden called "nerve-racking tennis" and "the most bitterly contested struggle of my life," entitled him and eighteen-year-old Richards to once again call themselves the national lawn tennis doubles champions.[51] At crucial moments of the match Bill could be heard saying, "Now, kid, let's go." At others he sacrificed words for action.

In his account of the match in his weekly newspaper article, Tilden gave all the credit for the victory to his young partner, the "tow-headed junior champion" whose "astonishing shots rained off his racquet" like recurring mortar shells. Williams and Washburn, America's Davis Cup doubles team, wrote Tilden, "made the tactical error of concentrating its attack on Richards when the boy was playing so well." Not once did Tilden make mention of his own extraordinary play in the grueling match. He had done the same when journalists asked for a postmatch comment. "Vinnie did it," Tilden told them. "I only kept the ball in play."[52]

Next up was defense of the Davis Cup against an unexpected adversary—Japan. England, France, Denmark, Belgium, Spain, and several other nations had competed for the right to play America, but they had fallen by the wayside. Though the Japanese victory over Australia was generally perceived as a startling upset, knowledgeable fans of the game knew the Japanese had developed some fine net men and had fielded a most worthy team. Those underestimating the Asian contingent ended up like the Australians, defeated and watching the Davis Cup challenge round from the stands. Tilden, a keen judge of talent, predicted early in the year that Japan would be America's opponent in the challenge round. He was well aware that Japan had cultivated "a small group of remarkable tennis players," particularly Ichiya Kumagae and Zenzo Shimidzu.

Kumagae was a lefty who played a baseline game and possessed a potent forehand drive that "spreads destruction among his opponents." Murray, Voshell, Richards, and Tilden were among his victims. Shimidzu was also a baseliner with a strong backhand, excellent volleying skills, and a quick learner. In addition to both men being "marvelous court coverers" and "absolutely untiring" in their pursuit of victory, Tilden considered them excellent "sportsmen and delightful opponents."[53]

By late August Bill was telling the press he was "fully recovered" from his "recent illness and full of pep," but this may have been happy talk or just plain wishful thinking.[54] In any event it was not great news for the Japanese Davis Cup team, who knew they would be playing not only the world's best at Forest Hills, but arguably the greatest Davis Cup team ever assembled. For the first defense of the Cup in many a year on home soil, public interest was great. Even veteran news reporters got carried away with patriotic imagery.

> Circling over the humanity-laden stands of the West Side Tennis Club here today, with a whirl of wings that could be heard around the sporting world, the American eagle suddenly swooped to the emerald turf carpeting the pit whose sides belched forth encouragement—screeched, screeched again—and then winged its way hence, clutching in either talon a sprig of crushed cherry blossoms of Japan.
>
> The strength of one talon was the skill, the agility, the art and the overwhelming power of William T. Tilden, 2nd of Philadelphia; the weight of the other, the brilliance, the indomitable courage and the cool. But dynamite fighting qualities of William M. Johnston of California.[55]

On a scorching-hot September day more than fifteen thousand fans filled the stadium to see what an "Oriental team"—a novelty at the time—could do against the world champions. Johnston made quick work of Kumagae, dispatching him by a tidy 6–2, 6–4, 6–2 score. Tilden, however, had his hands full. Shimidzu was putting on quite an athletic performance. "Dashing from one side of the court," one reporter would write, "then into the net after a soft one, back again after a lob, and then into position once more went that little Japanese citizen. Try as he would, Tilden with his dazzling assortment of shots, could not keep the ball away from his lightning-like opponent."[56]

Despite some extraordinary shot making, Tilden found himself down 7–5, 6–4 after two sets. To make matters worse Tilden was looking "perceptively weaker with every game." By the third set he seemed to many to be "fairly staggering around the blazing sun-baked court, a pallid, pathetic figure, a mere shadow of his own great self."

With Shimidzu seemingly unaffected by the heat and serving for the set and match at 5–4, something astonishing happened. As an exhausted Tilden took his place on the baseline to receive serve, the crowd rose as one and gave their exhausted champion a rousing and sustained ovation. "With his ears ringing with the applause of his countrymen," a reporter would write, "Tilden harkened to their pleas to stop the Japanese tornado. Up came his head, he spurred his tortured muscles to action and went in to win."[57]

With "spectators aroused to a frenzy and shouting encouragement," a fierce battle ensued. Like Prometheus rising from the ashes, Tilden halted the onslaught and eventually claimed victory. Astoundingly, he would win fifteen of the next eighteen games, taking the last three sets at 7–5, 6–2, 6–1. It was a typical Tilden performance: incredible athleticism, jaw-dropping skill, and heart-pounding drama. Sports pundits and tennis fans would point to a now classic bit of Tilden theatrics in describing the dramatic comeback, but there was far more to the story.

Decades later Tilden would explain what really happened. He would write in *My Story* that he was tactically prepared for Shimidzu, but not fully recovered from his recent illness and found himself poorly equipped to handle New York City's brutal summer heat and humidity after "reveling in the cool air" of New Hampshire's tranquil mountains for two weeks. Moreover, Shimidzu played far better than expected, returned everything hit to him, and kept Tilden on the run throughout the first two sets. "Suddenly," admitted Tilden, "the heat got to me. I felt as if someone had hit me over the head with a club."[58]

"With defeat staring me in the face," Tilden would write, and the fear of costing his country the Cup, "I shot the works." Committing whatever little energy he had left and knowing that a ten-minute rest break was in order if he won the third set, Tilden adopted a "furious net attack." The plan worked, and Tilden—"playing inspired tennis"—finally won a set. The score was now 5–7, 4–6, 7–5. "How I dragged myself up the stairs to the shower-room, I'll never know," Bill would later write. With his sweaty clothes still on, he turned on the cold water and collapsed on the shower floor. With the aid of Sam Hardy, the Davis Cup captain, Tilden undressed and remained under the refreshing cascade for nearly the entire ten-minute break. Hardy laid out a new set of clothes, and Bill quickly dressed and "returned to the court feeling human for the first time" since he was overcome by the heat.[59]

Shimidzu, however, "made the mistake," according to Bill, "of resting on the clubhouse porch." It was a costly decision, as it wasn't long into the fourth set when he could see his fearless Japanese opponent begin to tighten up and lose his amazing speed and mobility. His muscles had begun to cramp, his movement faltered, and his defense crumpled. Tilden would win the last two sets 6–2, 6–1. At the time, however, most believed it was another example of Tilden's theatrical bent—as well as his "peculiar genius." He liked to put on a show for the audience. "Tilden scored more important victories after seeming to be beaten," Al Laney has written, "than any other champion."[60] Little did they know how truly dire was the situation.

According to Laney, there is even more to the story. He has written that Tilden never really recovered his health and was still suffering with ugly, painful boils. One "ripe carbuncle" cropped up on the instep of his right foot just in time for the Shimidzu match. With Tilden in extreme pain and his movement hampered, relief did not arrive until intermission after the third set when a doctor lanced the boil and drained the pus. On Tilden's return the foot was tightly bandaged, and Bill could once more play his game. Tilden, according to Laney, never mentioned the handicap because he did not want to take any credit away from his opponent. He said, "It would have been unfair to Shimidzu, who played magnificently."[61]

The next day Williams and Washburn would win the doubles competition and thereby ensure the Davis Cup remained on American soil. Big and Little Bills followed up with decisive victories in the final singles matches, Tilden defeating Kumagae 9–7, 6–4, 6–1 and Johnston taking down Shimidzu 6–3, 5–7, 6–2, 6–4. The 1921 Davis Cup tournament concluded as it had the year before, in a 5–0 wipeout. Japan has never again reached the final round of the Davis Cup.

Next on the docket was a ninety-mile ride south to Philadelphia and the Germantown Cricket Club for the Men's National Singles Championship. As a first-time host of the men's championship—and the proud home club of the two-time Wimbledon and defending national champion—Manheim pulled out all the stops to ensure a successful tournament. They had repeatedly boasted that the meet would be the greatest assemblage of tennis talent in the nearly fifty-year history of the game. Players from seven nations were scheduled to compete.

From the city's public transit system and police department to the construction of a stadium with all the proper amenities on club grounds, everything was examined, reconfigured, and spruced up in order to facilitate what was expected to be an unprecedented demand for tickets. The club's eating rooms were expanded, nursing stations were established for emergencies, new parking lots were created, and all vehicles were cleared from nearby streets. Even the Pennsylvania Railroad was altering schedules and adding trains to transport the expected surge in patronage.

On the eve of the tournament's start Bill let it be known that much good work had been done, but a critical feature necessary for the success of the event had been overlooked. As the sports editor of the *Philadelphia Public Ledger* disapprovingly wrote in his column, "Just when the greatest array of champion tennis players, representatives of many nations, are in one tournament, the process of making the draw has been attacked. It is alluded to as the 'blind draw,' and no less a personage than William T. Tilden, 2nd, the world's champion, opposes it and suggests it be abolished."[62]

A newspaperman wedded to tradition and comfortable with institutional authority, William H. Rocap took the side of "the officials of the United States Lawn Tennis Association," whom he referred to as "men who have given the sport a life study," and concluded that the draw for such events was fine as it was, no meddlesome tinkering need be encouraged. As Rocap adamantly argued, "No plan has proved better than the present, otherwise the USLTA officials would have adopted it."[63]

Not easily intimidated, open to new ideas, and keen on improving the game for both players and fans, Tilden saw the need for a seeding system. As currently practiced under a blind draw, championship matches were often anticlimactic, as the tournament's top players frequently met in the early rounds. Tilden and other reformers were calling for a seeding system predicated on ranking players according to ability. That would foster a scenario where the best players met not in the early rounds but in a tournament's final rounds. The ticket-paying public deserved to see the athletic drama build: top players should fight it out at the end, not the beginning, of a tournament.

Traditionalists—as well as Mr. Rocap—were not quite ready to make a change. The result was predictable: Tilden, Bill Johnston, and Vinnie Richards—three of the nation's best players—along with Shimidzu and R. Lindley Murray were in the same quarter of the draw. If it turned out as expected, a somewhat premature confrontation between the tournament's two best players—Big Bill Tilden and Little Bill Johnston—would occur in the fourth round.[64]

Interestingly, there was an undercurrent of suspicion that the tide was turning; some whispered Tilden may be in decline. His recent struggles on court made for good theater, but could it be the champion was on his way down? "It is the pace that kills in lawn tennis," theorized the *Philadelphia Inquirer*'s Perry Lewis, "and there is the impression that the hero of Wimbledon, the first American to carry off the much-prized British honors, is displaying his last flashes."[65] Few knew what was really ailing the talented player from Philadelphia; Bill never spoke of his injuries or health maladies. He always tried to play through them. But there were enough good players entered in the National Championship for some to believe the defending champion could be taken out.

In actuality, Tilden was finally rounding into shape. From all indications his health appeared significantly improved. Irving C. Wright certainly thought so. Wright had the misfortune of drawing Big Bill in the first round. The Boston native's visit to Manheim ended in record time after being throttled 6–0, 6–0, 6–1.

Little Bill, on the other hand, was now the one with health concerns. While in New York for the Davis Cup contest, he came down with a case of ptomaine poisoning that left him weak and ill suited for a series of tough athletic contests. His prospects for repeating as national champion—he had won the title in 1915 and 1919—were further diminished by having to play energetic and dangerous Vinnie Richards in the third round. If he survived that encounter, his major nemesis, the supertalented Tilden, was his opponent in the very next round. Always a crowd favorite, Johnston "was unexpectantly [sic] extended" in his first-round match against a relatively unknown player. Reporters were kind. Little Bill was said to be "slightly indisposed and lacked his customary punch."[66]

As expected, spectators saw some tremendous tennis in the early rounds. Philadelphia chop-stroke artist Wallace F. Johnson defeated Davis Cup member Watson Washburn in five well-played sets. Former national champion Dick Williams lost to J. O. Anderson of Australia in another entertaining five-setter. And Vinnie Richards, anxious to avenge a recent loss to Johnston at Seabright, set his sights on taking Little Bill out of the tournament.

Almost in the blink of an eye Vinnie went on the attack and had a two-set lead before Johnston could get his wits about him and play some decent tennis. Knowing the loss of another set would send him unceremoniously back to California, Little Bill fought hard and took the third set at 6–3. Needing just one more set, Richards aggressively went at his opponent once more, but the ten-minute rest break helped rejuvenate Johnston and he fought back valiantly. Young Vinnie was now the one showing fatigue and fighting for his life. A long and exhausting fourth set eventually went to Johnston at 9–7. The tide had turned, and Richards had little left; he would lose the fifth and final set 6–2. Once again Little Bill's stout heart and fighting spirit had pulled him through.

His reward was the much-anticipated match with the world champion the very next day. Tilden, the great tactician, had soundly defeated Shimidzu in straight sets—a bad sign for Johnston supporters—and "set out from the first point to run Little Bill the greatest possible distance on every shot" in order to tire him.[67] The quality of play throughout the match was very high and every point bitterly contested. Johnston won the first set, Tilden the second, and "the gallery sat entranced, engrossed, conscious that it was seeing one of the game's great matches," wrote one observer. "Two masters were performing before them, and thrill followed thrill in rapid succession."[68] But it was becoming increasingly evident to those with a keen eye that Little Bill was tiring and having difficulty keeping up with Tilden's broad array of court weaponry. Both men went after each other vigorously in an effort to win the crucial third set, but Little Bill's early 4–2 lead slipped away, and Tilden won four games in a row to close out the set.

After the ten-minute intermission it was apparent to many that "nothing but a miracle could save Johnston, who was plainly showing the effects of his long, drawn out match against Richards."[69]

The fourth set proved a kaleidoscope of "whirlwind attacks" by both players, but Johnston could not maintain a lead and "tired fast from his tremendous exertions in court covering." Tilden's level of play would continue to improve as the match went on, and he would run his worthy opponent until exhaustion finally claimed him. For the second straight year, stouthearted Little Bill proved unable to unseat Tilden as the American champion. He would go down to defeat 4–6, 7–5, 6–4, 6–3. As Johnston netted the last shot, Tilden sighed with relief as the "pleasure at winning" mingled with "regret at [Johnston's] elimination" from the tournament. As always, Tilden would later write, "Johnston proved himself a great player and fine sportsman."[70]

The battle between Big and Little Bills would be described in front-page news articles as "the greatest match of the greatest year lawn tennis has ever known now belongs to athletic history, and the Tilden dynasty still rules the world of the racquet and net." Before what was described as "the largest crowd that ever witnessed a tennis match in this or any other country . . . the ruling monarch of the courts, once more conquered the most formidable pretender to his throne."[71]

The tournament's final match would be "more or less a family party," in the words of Tilden, as his opponent, Wallace Johnson, and most of the fourteen thousand in attendance were Philadelphians. The title bout began under a dark, ominous sky with light rain an occasional obstacle. The damp ground would prove perfectly suited for Johnson's deft armada of undercut drop shots. Balls barely bounced, and Tilden had difficulty getting to and returning shots. The players traded service games with what Tilden called "monotonous regularity," until the drizzle increased in frequency and force, making playing conditions both dangerous for the combatants and uncomfortable for stadium patrons. As spectators scampered for cover, match officials finally decided to halt the contest at eight-all.

When play resumed two days later under a hot sun with another packed gallery and a firmer playing surface, Tilden had a decisive advantage. All agreed they should start from scratch, and Tilden made short work of the challenger. Johnson, no longer able to win points on a waterlogged court, was beaten 6–1, 6–3, 6–1 in a quick forty-five minutes. Big Bill had now won the British and American men's singles titles two years in a row, the World Hard Court Championship in France, two Davis Cup titles, and just about every other tournament title of significance in which he participated.

Once again the name Tilden dominated newspaper sports sections like few other athletes. Only the great Jack Dempsey rivaled Big Bill for sheer star power across the globe. For tennis enthusiasts there was no argument: Tilden was tennis. "Of Tilden and his play there is nothing to do but to accord praise," stated an appreciative *American Lawn Tennis* editorial. The piece would go on to mention Johnson, Shimidzu, Johnston, and several other top players as the "scalps that dangle at his belt. And against all he was convincingly superior. His transcendent skill stands out above all, and enables him to sit enthroned on an eminence Himalayan in its altitude." Tilden, the piece glowingly concluded, is "the greatest master of the racket the game has yet produced."[72] Incredibly, William T. Tilden 2nd had not even begun to play his best tennis.

6

"No Ordinary Man"

His like has never before been seen on a court, and
probably will not be for many years to come.
He is the daddy of them all—a real tennis genius.

—PERRY LEWIS, *Philadelphia Inquirer*

William T. Tilden 2nd began 1922 just as he had the previous year: he was
the world's number-one-ranked tennis player. Other top net men from
around the globe such as Johnston (America), Shimidzu (Japan), Patterson
(Australia), Norton (South Africa), Alonso (Spain), and Gobert (France)
were all swallowed in his wake.[1] The newspaper headlines, the full-page
advertisements, the glowing editorials all underscored Tilden's stature as
an athlete par excellence. Corporations pushing commercial products from
tennis rackets to cigarettes were actively engaged in acquiring the champion's endorsement and having Big Bill pictured alongside their merchan-
dise. Newspaper columnists were equally enamored and quite comfortable
admitting it. "This man Tilden is a champion after a newspaperman's own
heart," crowed Cullen Cain of the *Philadelphia Public Ledger*.[2]

"A rare and radiant type" of athlete and individual with a unique personality that kept providing writers an endless stream of provocative story
lines, he was like a gift that just kept on giving. The reigning titan of his
sport—he was even compared to a big jungle cat that "flattens the greatest
of contenders with his paw"—Tilden was discussed and dissected by an
army of captivated reporters who were much taken by his perceived invincibility, his propensity for the dramatic comebacks, and his brazen on-court
demeanor that annoyed as many spectators as it charmed.

Many wordsmiths from the sports pages to more serious journalistic
venues felt the need to take the man's full measure. A much-recurring
editorial theme was Tilden's historical import; where exactly did he rank
in the pantheon of the game's most admired players? "Is Bill Tilden the

greatest tennis player of all time?" was a frequent refrain of sportswriters from Albany to Aberdeen and Antwerp to Adelaide.[3] The answer was usually the same: yes, absolutely. "His record in the last twenty months gives him standing in any debate on this subject of that there can be no doubt," argued one scribe. "And since the world loves a vivid and flashing performer best, it may well be that this will be the Philadelphian's proud place in the history of the game."

Such words of praise seemed universal. "Tilden proved conclusively," stated the editor of *American Lawn Tennis*, "that given health and heart, he is the master of any player now wielding a racket on any court of the world. His power of sustained aggression, his variety of stroke, his improved ground stroke equipment, above all his capacity for facing a crisis and surviving it, as much as by moral as by manual strength—these qualities, as well as his sound tactical skill, were revealed beyond cavil."[4]

Even those late to the Tilden bandwagon and begrudging in their praise were finally forced to admit that the tall, idiosyncratic racket wielder was the very best the sport had so far produced. Al Laney, for example, the longtime *New York Herald Tribune* journalist, conceded he had first idolized McLoughlin and then Johnston, but had always remained cool to Tilden. Even after the tall Philadelphian had gone "unbeaten in any important match for two seasons," Laney resisted the fawning praise that just about every other sportswriter was imparting in his columns. As Laney skeptically wrote of Tilden: "His forehand was thought to have neither the pace nor the accuracy of Johnston's, his slices no better than Wallace Johnson's, his volley inferior to Richards', his overhead less decisive than McLoughlin's, and the famous cannonball service not noticeably faster than Patterson's. As an all-court tactician Tilden was not rated with Brookes. He had not the wonderful touch, rhythm, and economy of movement of Williams, it was said, and Shimidzu made far fewer errors while being a much better retriever."[5]

Despite his strong affection for Little Bill and equally intense distaste for Big Bill's sometimes-imperious demeanor, Laney had to finally admit the obvious—Tilden was unbeatable. There was no sense denying it any longer: Tilden had repeatedly proved himself the best lawn tennis player in the world. Much of the credit for this in Laney's estimation was the champion's backhand; it was now a weapon of pulverizing import. "The acquisition of this flat backhand had changed everything," wrote Laney in *Covering the Court*, his account of the game's growth in popularity and Tilden's climb to tennis supremacy. "It was the shot that made it impossible to keep Tilden on the defensive for long or break down that defense. It was the one stroke that put him above the class of his contemporaries, and there is some ground for believing it the finest single stroke ever developed in tennis."[6]

Admiring words for sure, and from someone who was not a fawning groupie, at least not initially. But Laney, like many others with a keen eye for the game's nuances, readily recognized Tilden had transformed a weak stroke into a potent weapon. The once ineffectual backhand that could be easily exploited had become a frightening howitzer that fired shots like bullets. Opponents tried their best to stay away from it. Tilden's sabbatical during the winter of 1919–20 when he retreated to Providence to revamp a limp facet of his game had paid off handsomely. He had come back from New England with a stroke for the ages. Hit as "flat as it is possible to strike a tennis ball," in Laney's words, its pace exceeded that of any of the game's best forehands, including that of Laney's hero, Little Bill Johnston.

The stroke itself was a free-flowing swing of the arm and turn of the torso. Part balletic, part muscular torque, its whiplash action sent the ball flying at unprecedented speeds. As Laney described it, Tilden "could give it as much speed as he wanted from almost any position in the court, swinging it across court or down the line with undiminished pace as he pleased. In an exchange of backhands with this stroke, Johnston was cruelly handicapped, as were all other players of the day." As Laney would go on to write, Tilden was well on his way to becoming the "absolute monarch of the courts."[7]

No surprise then that Bill began 1922 on court, but the courts he was now playing on were squash courts. He had been encouraged to help out his Manheim team in some of their interleague contests. Though he would occasionally have "his hands full" returning the shots of more experienced squash players, he was a good-enough athlete and racket man to come out victorious.[8]

Just a few days after being mentioned in newspaper sports sections as an accomplished squash fill-in, Tilden was back in the papers as the new coach of the University of Pennsylvania's tennis team. Consistent with his many years of teaching tennis and fostering the game's growth with young people, Tilden had "volunteered his services" to coach his former college team. At least one sportswriter for the *Philadelphia Inquirer* thought this a brilliant administrative decision, as Tilden was viewed "as great a teacher as he is a player of tennis. The youngsters who learned the game under his watchful eye are fast forging their way to the front rank."[9] Tilden protégés such as Vinnie Richards, Carl Fischer, and Arnold Jones were mentioned in the article, as was a Tilden-inspired tennis exhibition to be held at Penn's Weightman Hall that would include three of four members of America's Davis Cup squad. A banquet was scheduled to follow that would honor Tilden, Wallace Johnson, and Paul Gibbons for fostering tennis both at the university and in the general Philadelphia community.[10] Though it is unlikely that Bill was any more than a part-time tennis consultant at Penn, for those who got the chance to hit with and receive nuggets of court wisdom from the game's greatest player, it was probably an unforgettable experience.

Though Bill's well-developed ego no doubt enjoyed the lionizing commentary regarding his athletic performances and community service, these first weeks of 1922 were preoccupied with another form of off-court dramatic art—the theatrical stage. An interest of long standing but never pursued, it was about to blossom into an artistic passion nearly rivaling his love of tennis.

Theater thrived in Philadelphia at this time, and there was no shortage of dramatic productions to choose from. During the last days of January, for example, a drama lover could have seen William Farnum appearing in *Perjury* at Fay's Theater, Billie Burke starring in *Intimate Strangers* at the Broad Theater, and Jane Gray in the lead role in *The Skin Game* at the Walnut Theater, but on the night of January 31 the hottest ticket in town just might have been for the ballroom of the elegant Bellevue-Stratford Hotel. It was there that Booth Tarkington's comedy hit *Clarence* was being presented with none other than Big Bill in the title role. Performed by the Belfry Club of Germantown Academy, the play was the drama club's twenty-ninth annual production and the school's major annual fund-raiser.

The club's presentation at Philadelphia's premier hotel was most unusual, "an achievement, which would have been scarcely possible without the aid of William T. Tilden."

Tarkington's eccentric 1919 comedy is about a recently discharged soldier who wanders into the suburban home of an affluent family and becomes the household's handyman and, soon after, the much-desired love interest of every woman in the vicinity. Characterized by an endless series of malapropisms and eccentric characters, the play was quite popular in postwar America. Tarkington, a two-time Pulitzer Prize winner, had his play's Broadway premier with Alfred Lunt and Helen Hayes in the starring roles. In Philadelphia its Bellevue-Stratford premier starred another world-class performer who was said to be "the attraction of the evening." Bill's portrayal of a former soldier fending off a hoard of infatuated women stirred much amusement and repeated "shouts of laughter from the audience." Photographs of various scenes that subsequently appeared in *Ye Primer*, the school's annual magazine, show Tilden looking quite handsome and the object of desire in his bold military-dress uniform. The play's last act, according to one review, solidified the tennis champion's reputation as a ladies' man and "heavy lover."[11]

As Germantown Academy was an all-male institution at the time, the entire cast, including "female parts," was played by boys, who were said to have done a "wonderful" job. The role of Cora, played by Alexander Wiener, "was one of the hits of the evening." In addition to his prowess as a budding thespian, Wiener was also a talented tennis player who would develop a strong friendship and tennis-playing partnership with Tilden.

The play was so successful that the Belfry troupe was encouraged to give additional performances, which were then quickly scheduled at the YMCA and the Germantown Boys Club. It is unlikely that anyone compared Tilden's performance to that of the accomplished thespian Alfred Lunt, but the experience did much to foster Bill's interest in the stage and a closer association with his former high school's drama department.

Bill had already been volunteering at his alma mater as the school's tennis coach, a relationship of which the institution was admittedly quite proud and "fortunate to secure." Few high schools, even those of a prestigious stripe as Germantown Academy, have a recognized world champion on staff.

The 1922 squad was expected to be a good one, and Tilden "cherished the hope of producing a championship" against the likes of Episcopal Academy, Central, Penn Charter, and Germantown High School.[12]

Like any youngster fortunate enough to meet a world-class athlete, Alexander "Sandy" Wiener would never forget his introduction to the local tennis icon. "It was in the fall of the year 1921 that I first met Bill Tilden," Wiener would recount for a youth magazine in the mid-1920s. "The meeting came about through a friend of both of us, and I never shall forget that day when I first grasped the hand of the greatest tennis player that ever lived."

The very next day, as it would turn out, Bill was scheduled to give a talk at Germantown Academy's chapel, and when the school day was over he asked the young man if he would like to join him and see a movie. "That afternoon was the beginning of our friendship," recalled Wiener. "He told me he had heard that I played a good game of tennis and that he would like to see me play. I had taken tennis lessons from William Hinchcliffe, the Yale coach and professional at the Skokie Country Club, Chicago, and those lessons had started me on my game; but it did not seem a game for the champion to bother about."[13]

Bill must have been impressed with what he saw of young Wiener on the court, for a couple of days later he showed up at Sandy's home in his car and took Sandy to the Germantown Cricket Club for a hitting session. There was another boy waiting for Bill, so all the pressure was not on Sandy. "I shall never forget the first ball he hit to me," Sandy recalled somewhat embarrassingly. "I made up my mind I was going to return it somehow; but in thinking this I forgot to get a good grip on my racket, and when the ball hit it the racket turned in my hand and fell to the court, while the ball rolled off to one side. Then Bill gave me my first advice in tennis: always have a tight grip on the racket when you hit the ball. Gradually fear left me, and I made a couple of fairly good shots; but most of them were poor. I was much too conscious of the fact that I was rallying with a great tennis player."

Just a week later Bill would be invited to the Wiener home for dinner. To the surprise of all at the dinner table, Bill asked, "Sandy, how would you like to play doubles in some tournaments with me next year?" Sandy was taken aback by the honor and momentarily speechless. Bill added that he liked Sandy's game, especially the earnestness with which he approached the sport. After dinner Bill had a long and more serious talk with Sandy's parents about his offer. It must have gone well, for, as Sandy would write, "When he left my home that night I was his new doubles partner."

Bill told Sandy he expected good things from the duo. He predicted they would reach the semifinals of every tournament in which they played. "As it turned out," Sandy recalled, "he was one hundred percent right, for we reached the semifinals in every tournament except two; one of those two we won, while in the other we were beaten in the round before the semifinals."[14]

All during the winter of 1921–22—when they weren't rehearsing their lines for Tarkington's *Clarence*—they practiced strokes in one of the squash courts at the Germantown Cricket Club. The almost daily lessons had Tilden stressing the importance of footwork, the proper grip for each stroke, standing at right angles to the net for backhand and forehand strokes, and a host of other principles that were central to one's success on the court. "Days and days we worked," Sandy admitted, "until one day Bill said, 'Sandy, do you want to be a great tennis player?' I answered 'Yes.' Then he told me I must give up football and baseball and concentrate on tennis." Sandy recoiled at the suggestion; he loved playing other sports at school, especially football, and the notion of giving them up appalled him. "I hated like poison to give football up," Sandy said, "and began to argue with Bill about why I should do so. He soon convinced me that I was wrong, saying among other things, that it is better to be a great star in one sport than a mediocre player in two or three."

The spring of 1922 would be young Wiener's trial by fire under the champion's tutelage. Sandy played number-four singles on the school team and won only three matches. But he was young, only a freshman. His potential was obvious, especially with Tilden guiding him. For Sandy, however, his disappointing season was "terribly discouraging." The lad was understandably depressed. Bill, however, cautioned him not to be so hard on himself. He counseled him that the learning process for a game as difficult and complicated as tennis could be challenging. Demanding athletic ability and great skill, tennis was one of the hardest sports to master; it required a tremendous work ethic and many years of dedication before excellence would be achieved.

He went on to tell Sandy why they had just practiced strokes during those cold winter months: they were the critical rudiments of the game. "Most of the boys I played were pat-ball players with no style at all," said Sandy. "I would try to make my shots in the correct manner, and my opponent would just push it back to me; so of course I was the first to miss. Bill told me that these pat-ballers would get no farther in their game, and that I would beat them in a few years. He was right. I have beaten every boy to whom I lost my first year on the school team. When you are playing a pat-baller, don't pat the ball with him, but practice and make your shots right."

Bill and Sandy's maiden voyage as a doubles team in the spring and summer of 1922 was fairly good and "fulfilled Bill's prophecy." They beat a few good teams, but also lost to some lesser-quality teams. At the end of the season Sandy entered the Boys National Championship in Boston. Bill was expecting good things from his latest protégé, but it was not to be. Sandy won his first match and appeared strong in his second as he took a 4–1 lead, but then grew overconfident, let up a bit, and ultimately lost. Sandy learned a painful lesson in that match, which Bill repeatedly reiterated: "Never let up when you are in the lead."

"During the winter of 1922–23 I practiced as much as I could," said Sandy, "playing in the indoor courts at Buffalo, Providence, Montreal, and Philadelphia. In the spring I went to Bermuda, where Bill and I played some matches. Then the school season came again, and this time there was a little improvement. I finished the season by winning about half my matches."

The following year the Tilden-Wiener doubles team would become a formidable unit, winning three titles and reaching the semifinals in all their other contests. It goes without saying that older, more experienced doubles competitors often outclassed Sandy on the court, but Tilden was the great equalizer. He usually dominated play regardless of who was on the court. As Wiener's game improved he began collecting various titles, but the Boys National Championship would prove once again to be a terrible disappointment. "I weakened," Sandy frankly admitted after being put out in the second round. "The reason I lost the match, according to Bill, was that I did not have enough competitive spirit." It would prove another painful lesson for Sandy. "Fight is just about as important in tennis as it is in football or boxing."

In coming years Sandy Wiener would continue to learn important lessons about tennis as well as life from Tilden. And as Wiener grew in height, strength, and ability, the Tilden-Wiener team would become more of a respected threat at tournaments than an object of curiosity or derision. They repeatedly knocked off quality teams with highly ranked players, and Sandy's singles record at Germantown Academy went unblemished: he would go undefeated during the 1924 season. Just as his instructor predicted, the long hours of practice were paying off.

Despite increased success and Wiener's maturation, and increasing independence and assertiveness, Big Bill continued to provide tennis tips and overall guidance. If he saw Sandy falter at either, Bill was quick to set him straight. Stay focused, keep your eye on the ball, concentrate on your footwork, and analyze your opponent's likes and dislikes were just a few of Bill's oft-repeated directives.

Keep your head in the game and always put forth your best effort were two key Tilden principles. Breaching either precipitated a fatherly lecture. Sandy admitted:

> I had a tendency to be a little lazy on the court, as I did not run after balls which I thought were out of my reach. When Bill made me chase shots I thought he was crazy, because it seemed foolish to waste one's energy. I soon saw I could get to shots which I never dreamed I could make, but it was not until 1925, in a match in Chicago in which I played Berkley Bell, Junior Champion of Texas, for the Illinois State Junior Championship, that it was fully impressed on my mind. As I went on the court Bill said to me, "Chase every shot until you can't stand up." I carried out these orders, and it won the match for me. I put back shots which Berkeley thought he had "put away," and they so surprised him that he'd miss his shots.

Entering competitions from coast to coast, Wiener saw a good bit of the country as well as life. Most of it would have been sheer fantasy for the average schoolboy, especially the socializing with famous members of the Hollywood film community. Tournaments in Southern California resulted in as much fraternizing with film stars as court play. As Sandy readily admitted, "We spent most of our time exploring the wilds of Hollywood. We met Douglas Fairbanks, Mary Pickford, Charles Chaplin, Harold Lloyd, Jackie Coogan and many others. We saw all kinds of scenes being filmed and had the time of our lives." No doubt the film stars did as well. Big Bill was every bit their equal as an international celebrity. They congregated around him the way film buffs flocked to Fairbanks and Chaplin.

During the midtwenties the Tilden-Wiener team took some serious scalps, such as their victory over the quality team of George Lott and Emmett Pare and their near victory over the far more seasoned duo of R. N. Williams and Watson Washburn in a close five-setter in the National Championships. Their record earned them a top-ten ranking as a doubles team. Not bad for a youngster still in high school.

Not surprisingly, Wiener's singles game witnessed progress as well, and he began to knock off some of the game's more respected names, such as José Alonso of Spain and Takeichi "Tackie" Harada of Japan. "I began to taste blood," Sandy proudly boasted of his accomplishment, but this elevated air of self-importance annoyed his mentor and led to their temporary breakup.

> It was at the Palm Beach tournament that Bill and I had our only disagreement. He thought I had a slight inclination to self-satisfaction after beating Harada that caused me to not try my hardest. In the finals of the men's doubles we were playing Howard Voshell and Manual Alonso. We had them two sets to one, and at the beginning of the fourth set we began to fight about shots, about where I should play and numerous other things. We lost that set and the next in a very short time. After the match we had a talk. Bill would not agree with me on certain points in tennis, and I would not agree with him on others. When we left Palm Beach we were no longer a doubles team. We had broken up and did not expect to play together again. This break lasted for two months, until my father brought us together. We thrashed things out, and when Bill left we were good friends again and resolved to continue with our doubles combination.[15]

The recemented union proved not only durable but increasingly vexing to opposing teams. Tilden and Wiener defeated a host of imposing doubles teams at top tournaments, making for what Sandy said was "the best season we ever had." They claimed the Rhode Island State Championship in taking down Howard Voshell and A. H. Chapin, finalists at the National Clay Court in St. Louis, defeating the Kinsey brothers in the process, followed by a Chicago tournament that claimed victories over a number of top teams before losing to the likes of Little Bill Johnston and Clarence "Peck" Griffin. After defeating a couple of fine teams in the national doubles competition, they lost to Johnston and Griffin after having a two-set-to-one lead. Bill's arm tightened up, and he could no longer strike the ball cleanly. But the setback was temporary, as they came back to beat significant teams, including foreign squads like the imposing French team of Max Decugis and Jacques Brugnon. It was all pretty heady stuff, and only a very few lucky boys in the entire world experienced it: those selected by Bill Tilden.

For Vinnie Richards, Carl Fischer, Arnold Jones, Sandy Wiener, and those fortunate few who would follow as Tilden protégés, the formation of a close relationship with an international icon was nothing short of extraordinary. The vast majority of top players at this time—or at any other time, for that matter—would never have entertained the silly notion of teaming up with a young player to compete in major doubles tournaments. Competitive players normally seek out the strongest player to partner with to ensure maximum return on their effort.

Tilden, apparently, was dismissive of this commonly accepted practice. Though his doubles play was excellent and his results quite respectable, his reputation as a doubles player is underwhelming compared to his tremendous singles record. Even Bill referred to himself as "the world's worst doubles player."[16] But imagine what that record would have looked like if he had chosen only to partner with the likes of Bill Johnston or Dick Williams. The accumulation of court triumphs, however, was not the only thing that stirred Tilden. He gained greater satisfaction taking on young partners, teaching them the game's finer points, and then defeating older, more experienced teams. How does one then explain a series of such unusual friendships, friendships that for most lasted a lifetime and endured through good times and bad?

Richard Hillway believes Tilden suffered from some sort of arrested stage of development, an emotional attachment and interest in young people, particularly teenage boys, whom he enjoyed being around and sharing his love of tennis, music, and the dramatic arts. He just simply enjoyed their company as well as being in charge.

John Olliff, a well-respected tennis authority from Britain and longtime correspondent for the *Daily Telegraph*, had similar thoughts on the issue.

Like many others, Tilden fascinated him. It was not just Tilden's exceptional athletic ability and nonpareil tennis skill, but also his truly unique personality. As he would write of the champion, "Bill Tilden was no ordinary man." Olliff believed that at a very early age, Bill "developed strong likes and dislikes for people and things, and just as strongly was he himself liked and disliked by others. He was a youth with a powerful character and an impelling personality."[17]

Olliff was not oblivious of the strange behavioral patterns exhibited by this incredibly gifted athlete. Yes, there were the superficial aspects: the woolly-bear sweaters, the odd on-court remarks, and the embarrassing displays of emotion at bad line calls, but his attraction to teenagers was more mystifying. "His habit after winning a championship," as Olliff points out, "of dining with three or four boys of fourteen or fifteen years of age was considered unnatural, when so many of his tennis-playing friends and officials would have been so honoured to dine and spend the evening with him." This was a central quandary of the Tilden puzzle.

After considerable thought Olliff came to believe Tilden

> had a strong hero-complex, and he always wanted to be the hero of everything in which he took part. For this reason he was always interested in youth, for youths are far more enthusiastic hero-worshippers than grown-ups. He was always surrounded by a group of boys usually about fourteen to sixteen years of age. He thought more of taking in hand a promising young player, coaching him and playing with him in doubles than he did of improving his own game. Tilden's prodigies appeared annually, one after another. They were all going to be future champions, but they met with very varying degrees of success, and some with no success at all.[18]

Not all, as Olliff points out, became as accomplished as his first protégé, Vinnie Richards.

Most important, not one ever accused Tilden of any tawdry, salacious, or scandalous piece of mischief. Apparently, Bill was always the model of decorum and constantly looking out for the boys' interest. He was unquestionably a formative and unforgettable influence in their lives. Many, in fact, would subsequently donate significant financial scholarships in his honor at various educational institutions.

Tilden's interest in young people was further amplified in 1922 with the publication of his first piece of fiction. Entitled *It's All in the Game*, the collection of fifteen short stories, each approximately fifteen pages in length, was Tilden's attempt to fill a void in the canon of sports literature. As the author frankly stated in the book's preface, "Every sport has its own literature. Baseball, Golf, Football, Track, Polo, Crew—each and every one has found a great reading public for the books of fact and fiction that have grown up around the sport. Tennis has had many incidents in books of facts, but thus far fiction has more or less escaped." Taking it upon himself to correct this sin of omission, Tilden reasoned, "There must always be a start and from a feeble beginning sometimes great things spring. So I dare to offer the feeble beginnings of tennis fiction . . . hoping that someone else will carry on the idea to bigger things."[19]

The title story concerned Robert Wallace Cotter, a sixteen-year-old boy known to all as Buddie, whose "two great passions were fighting and tennis." Though a tenacious competitor and dedicated to improving his game, he was unfortunately plagued with an uncontrollable temper that regularly intruded on a steady course of progress. It is at this time that Buddie comes in contact with Dick Thomas, the national champion, who appears a composite of Richard Norris Williams and Bill himself, as he "played tennis for amusement and the love of the game and held a keen interest in young players."

Thomas provides guidance and tennis tips to Buddie about the mechanics and nuances of the game as well as court etiquette, but the boy's temper tantrums are a recurring concern. At the National Championships for both the boys' and men's divisions, for example, their respective approaches to adversity are graphically highlighted. When Buddie receives what he perceives to be a bad line call at a crucial point in the match, Buddie fumes and loses focus, and very quickly "his whole game collapsed." He is left defeated, discouraged, and embarrassed. When a similar scenario befalls Thomas in his match, however, he goes about his business seemingly unperturbed and "walked quietly to position to receive" the next serve. There are no histrionics or emotional outbursts. Buddie is stunned by the champion's composure and subsequently watches his hero gain the upper hand and win the match. When Buddie asks, "How did you do it? How did you keep your temper in that fourth set?" the champion, with a knowing grin, replies, "All tennis players take what comes in a match, boy. It's all in the game."[20]

The irony, of course, is that any serious follower of Tilden's career knew he was not the model for this story. His match conduct was more often than not an object of unfavorable comment. His menacing glares and angry comments to umpires, linesmen, and ball boys were well known. For him to be writing stories about proper tennis decorum was absurd to some, but Tilden knew well the history of his sport, its esteemed lineage, and the principles that should be passed on to the game's neophytes. He did not encourage novices to act as he did, but urged them to follow in the footsteps of more worthy models of the game—even if some of them were fictional. The fourteen other stories in the book would stress similar themes of court deportment, clean living, generosity, honesty, and good sportsmanship.

Many of the stories, as Tilden admitted, "are based on true incidents," while the names of characters such as Bill Jolson, George Palmerson, Norman Brokaw, and Mr. Hydrock are easily recognizable—"very thinly camouflaged," in Bill's own words—for their flesh-and-blood inspirations. Many of the vignettes can be quickly identified with the author's life, such as in "Dick Takes the Chair," where the story opens with Buddie at the "advanced age of twenty-one," convinced his nickname "must go by the board." He is insistent that now and forevermore he be known as Robert Wallace Cotter.[21] Obviously, Bill's own disdain for the moniker "Junior"— his childhood nickname—was the genesis of the story line.

Though some literary critics at the time felt it necessary to remind the reading public that Bill's foray into the world of literature was not going to remind anyone of Theodore Dreiser or Sinclair Lewis, it should be remembered that his goal was never intended to produce a literary classic. As more fair and restrained reviewers noted, It's All in the Game was a "book for kids," though older readers may discover "something that makes you glad that you are still enough of a boy to enjoy a book like this."[22]

Crafted in a similar fashion to the popular Frank Merriwell novels that a generation or more of young American boys grew up reading, Tilden hoped to write a book about tennis that would educate and inspire youth just the way he had been when reading Merriwell's stories of heroic figures at the turn of the century. Tilden was intent on writing stories like Merriwell that portrayed individuals who were able to combine both brains and brawn in a positive light and thereby inspire America's young people to excel in athletics and the classroom and be a credit to their communities. He was in the hero-creation business or, at the very least, illuminating right from wrong and successfully grappling with life's many challenges.

The harsh reviews by those who considered it harmless fun to skewer a famous athlete with the temerity to write fiction did not bother Tilden. He was his own man and was not easily dissuaded from doing something he thought was right or had set his mind on doing. He did not suffer fools gladly, nor did he back down from bullies, regardless of their institutional credentials. It was just such an attitude that sparked his involvement with a campaign to assist the Committee to Aid Devastated France in the country's postwar recovery. After illness prevented Suzanne Lenglen in 1921 from participating in her fund-raising efforts in America, Bill jumped in and organized a group of top players to perform in a series of well-attended matches in New York and New Jersey. At the end of each contest Bill auctioned off all the balls, rackets, and garb used in the tournaments. Rackets went for sixty to seventy-five dollars apiece. The events raised more than ten thousand dollars, and Bill was "immensely gratified" by the result and his part in a worthy cause.[23]

Not so impressed, however, were Julian Myrick and the other members of the USLTA. Intent on maintaining a firm grip on every aspect of lawn tennis in America, the committee berated Bill for organizing and participating in an unsanctioned tennis event. Bill was dumbfounded by the group's chutzpah—especially considering the worthy cause at the center of the issue—and further argued that "he should be free to play for charity" whenever he chose. The USLTA, however, insisted such events were their call, and they were in a better position to determine which events unscrupulous promoters ran and who was profiting.[24] For years and decades to come, the association would prove a thorn in Tilden's side when he took to the court to benefit a charity or cause.

In February 1922 readers of newspaper sports sections across the country were stunned to see Big Bill had decided not defend his prestigious Wimbledon title. As one newspaper headlined the story, "Tilden to Play Only in American Matches." It was true, the "world's master of racquets and monarch of the domain of tennis," the articles explained, did "not intend to go abroad the coming summer and defend his British laurels." "I have decided not to go to England," Bill informed the press after a presentation at a Philadelphia-area school, "for the strain of defending the title abroad is too great. I shall limit my competition to the United States, and shall play at Germantown during the National Singles in September and in the Davis Cup matches."[25]

The surprising news was most likely due to a confluence of factors that included his personal health and the monetary expense of such a trip. Bill's precarious physical condition and the painful memory of his last trip to Europe had resulted in a lengthy hospital stay and an extended period of convalescence. Though the concern was legitimate, it may also have been sparked by the decision of the United States Lawn Tennis Association to "not send an American team to Europe to compete in the Wimbledon Championships." This was due, the association claimed, to the "heavy expenses from sending teams the last two years and partly because of the effects of such traveling upon the players themselves." The committee, under the direction of Julian Myrick, USLTA president, said it recognized "the great physical strain that such traveling involves and recalled in that connection Mr. Tilden's poor condition when he returned from his trip to Europe in 1921." Myrick went on to say that "with the United States facing the keenest competition in the Davis Cup contest of 1922, the committee felt that its first duty was to safeguard the tennis interests of the country."[26]

It should also be understood that at this time, the Davis Cup competition was a more important athletic competition than an individual singles title, even one as celebrated as Wimbledon. Nations could bask in the reflected glory of the Davis Cup trophy, and there was more economic potential with the Davis Cup than a lone singles champion abroad. It should also be recalled from an earlier financial skirmish with the USLTA that Bill had no intention of going abroad on his own dime. If the association would not pay the freight for its national champion to go abroad, he was not going. The actual cost of sending American players to Europe, however, was questioned by Arthur Voss. He discovered that the USLTA made a handsome profit from its 1921 Davis Cup and National Championships.[27] To this day, no one is absolutely sure if it was the financial cost, Tilden's health, or some other reason that kept the champion from defending his Wimbledon title.

As he informed newsmen after his lecture to Swarthmore Preparatory School students, Bill was comfortable with the decision, as the American Championship at Germantown Cricket in September would have "the presence of all the great players in every country." The Manheim event, he believed, would "in reality be an international affair, and the winner has every right to be considered the world's champion tennis player."

During the course of his talk at the school, Bill told the students that "international tennis matches had done more to cement peaceful relations between the various countries than had even been accomplished by the recent Disarmament Conference in Washington." Ever the tennis salesman, he boasted about the game's attributes and its growing popularity around the world. Backing up his statement with numbers, he told the audience, "There are three tennis players to every baseball player and nearly ten times as many tennis players as football players. This is because tennis is an international game played in England, France, Russia, Sweden, Australia, Japan, Tasmania, Argentina, and numerous other parts of the globe."[28] Moreover, he proudly bragged of "the physical advantages offered by participation in tennis," and as a game an individual could play, it could be enjoyed long after one's high school and college days were over. It was all true, but the press was just interested in the big story: Bill's decision to not go abroad and defend his Wimbledon title.

During the spring Tilden traveled to the West Coast to play in a series of California tournaments. In early May he lost to Johnston (2–6, 6–4, 7–5, 5–7, 6–3) in the East versus West Tournament, which was followed by another loss to Johnston a week later (7–5, 7–9, 6–1, 6–0) in the Pacific Coast Championship. Bill never gave excuses for his losses, and he would never admit it, but his subpar play might have been due to the late hours he was keeping with his celebrity friends in the Hollywood film community. A defeat at the hands of Johnston was certainly no embarrassment, but Tilden would rather have not sparked renewed claims by Little Bill supporters that he now had the upper hand on the big Philadelphian.

Back east for the summer tennis season, Bill won a series of tournaments in New England, the Midwest, and the mid-Atlantic states. At one tournament at the Philmont Country Club just north of Philadelphia, Bill defeated two protégés (Carl Fischer and Sandy Wiener) on the way to the title. Rainy weather played havoc with the schedule, and one day Bill was forced to play four different matches. Just thinking about such a physical workout is exhausting. Although he was on court many hours that day, observers believed he could have significantly cut his workload if he had only chosen not to "experiment with some fancy shots that were performed at his opponent's expense."[29] Whenever he was pressed, however, he was said to have "turned on the big guns" and blown away his opposition.

In late August Bill went up to Chestnut Hill, Massachusetts, and declared the Longwood Cricket Club his own private playground. With Vinnie Richards he won the doubles title for the second year in a row and then won the mixed doubles title alongside Molla Mallory. A week later he was to face Australia's best in the Davis Cup final at the West Side Tennis Club in New York City. Bill appeared ready.

The Australian team of Gerald Patterson, James O. Anderson, and Patrick O'Hara Wood was indeed a good one, but they were up against as formidable a unit as ever walked on a tennis court. Led by Tilden and Johnston, they were joined by Dick Williams, another two-time U.S. champion, and Vinnie Richards, who had the potential to be one.

Not surprisingly, the United States crushed the Australians, 4–1. It was a complete mismatch. As one journalist creatively phrased it, "America's supreme place in the tennis sun is assured for another two years," due to the "omnipotent racquets of two great Bills—Tilden of the East and Johnston of the West."[30] Johnston, "the tiny terror of the American courts," had smothered the broad-shouldered Patterson, the newly crowned Wimbledon champion, in less than fifty minutes. It was a devastating display of controlled aggression by "a mighty mite of an athlete." Patterson had to repeatedly fend off hammered shots to his vulnerable backhand from the little but hard-hitting Californian. Johnston was at his best, and the big Australian was completely humbled. It was a dreadfully quick turnaround after winning the British championship just a few months earlier.

Tilden, by comparison, was less impressive, less sharp. He made numerous errors and an unusual number of double faults, but he won out in five difficult sets against the six-foot, four-inch Anderson—who had won the Australian championship earlier in the year—due to his abundance of "reserve and gameness." Erratic throughout the competition, the world's greatest player was obviously off his game, but still good enough to win out. Neither Johnston nor Tilden lost a singles match to his Aussie opponents. America was still the greatest nation in the world of lawn tennis.

The following week the eyes of the tennis world moved to Philadelphia, as the National Championships were scheduled for the expansive and manicured green lawns of the Germantown Cricket Club. Billy Johnston's adoring fans were buoyed by his dominating play against the Aussies in New York. Better yet, Tilden looked rather pedestrian in his own Davis Cup matches. Excitement was building. This would be the year; this would be the tournament that would see their hero take down the tall, cocky Philadelphian. The planets would finally realign themselves, and everything would be right in the universe.

Granted, it was not just a two-man field; there were many accomplished challengers from around the country and throughout the world in the draw, all with the dream of winning the American championship. But Tilden and Johnston were the most feared players, the class of the field. And Little Bill was prepared; he thought this would be his time. Tilden was not oblivious to his greatest challenger's fondest ambition. The defending champion knew that "Billy wanted that cup more than anything in the world. If he won it he planned to retire from tennis. That cup was his dearest wish and most cherished goal," Tilden would one day write of what he would come to believe was the "greatest of all my matches with Johnston."

Much was being made of the fact that several entrants—Williams, Johnston, and Tilden, to be specific—had won the trophy twice. In a much-revered tradition at the time, one more victory, and it was the winner's to keep. As much as Johnston desired "the noblest trophy cup in the history of tennis," as Tilden would write, "he had nothing on me. I wanted it just as badly and maybe more so."

Big Bill left no doubt as to his intentions as he stridently moved from one round of battle to the next. As a reporter described the human carnage in the aftermath of myriad showdowns with the champ, "Tilden had come thundering down through the lower bracket of the draw, leaving in his boiling wake a writhing and conquered group of victims."[31] Pat O'Hara

Wood of Australia, Zenzo Shimidzu of Japan, and Gerald Patterson of Australia—all top players—were just a few of the players sliced, diced, and cannonballed off the courts. No one seemed capable of handling Tilden's wide and menacing array of powerful drives, delicate drop shots, back-breaking lobs, deft volleys, and indecent serves. Only Little Bill, according to his loyal supporters, had the heart and firepower to shackle and dethrone the reigning champion.

And that is what appeared to happen after the tennis world's two greatest players—Johnston, the tiny but mighty fan favorite, and Tilden, the American champion—walked on the court at 3:04 p.m. before fifteen thousand eager fans on that afternoon. The highly touted "court gladiators" were greeted with a huge ovation and waves of applause as numerous photographers scurried about taking pictures of the game's two greatest combatants. Having won the toss, Tilden began serving with the sun in his face. His serves—both the booming cannonballs as well as the heavy-topspin variety—were negated, and baseline drives quickly dominated play. There were a series of impressive shots, but also out balls and those that were netted. When Tilden hit a ball long to end the game, Johnston had broken serve and taken a 1–0 lead. Tilden supporters could not have been pleased. Their dismay would only grow, as Little Bill would continue to perform at a high level. His savvy and aggressive play enabled him to take a two-set-to-love lead.

Years later Tilden would write of the classic battle:

For two sets, Johnston played tennis so faultless I could do nothing to hold him. I felt I was playing well, very close to my best, but Johnston had swept through to win 6–3, 6–4. Early in the third set I gained a break and he practically tossed the set, wisely saving himself while attempting to tire me. It very nearly paid. Following the standard ten-minute intermission, Johnston started like a cyclone, rushed into a three to love lead. It was at this point that I once more met an example of the official feeling toward me that prevailed in the USLTA. Julian Myrick, president of the Association, was seated in a chair on the court beside the umpire's chair. He had no business there and so far as I could discover occupied the chair for no more important reason than the fact that his presence would annoy me. As Johnston and I crossed the court at three love to Johnston, Mike, with that cold smile that we all knew, said to me with emphasis on the word "been": "Well, Bill, it has been a great match.[32]

Seething, Tilden claimed he "saw red." He fought to control himself and respond civilly. "Yes, Mike, so far," Tilden replied. He then walked back to serve and swore to himself, "I would win that match or die on the court."

Tilden was about to lose his serve and another game when "Lady Luck" smiled on him. Johnston rushed the net at 30–40, and Tilden tried to lob over him. The lob was too low, and Little Bill was able to smash it at Tilden's feet for what should have been a clean winner. Big Bill, however, instinctively took a wild swipe at the ball with his racket, and the ball "miraculously" jumped back over Johnston's head. The ball fell inside the baseline to tie the game. The play was so quick, so incredible, that "the crowd went mad." Tilden recalled one startled spectator screaming at the top of his lungs, "He didn't make it. I tell you, Tilden didn't make it! No man could make that shot!"

That extraordinary play would prove "the turning point," according to Tilden. "I never looked back. I won the game as Johnston felt the tide of battle turning against him. For the first time he grew uncertain and tense, his control faltered and his attack collapsed. I ran six games to win the set and forged ahead."

Staggering and on the verge of collapse, Johnston showed his game heart and tried to make a comeback late in the final set, but "his exhausted body refused to further answer the call of that great will." Tilden won that set and the match, 4–6, 3–6, 6–2, 6–3, 6–4. The American singles title for 1922, once again, belonged to Tilden.

Back in the Germantown Cricket Club locker room, Big Bill showered, dressed, and tried to comfort his worthy challenger, who was still recovering and too exhausted to dress. "I was damned lucky to win today, Billy," said Tilden without a trace of arrogance or false modesty. Little Bill looked up at his conqueror and replied, "No, you weren't lucky, Bill. I played the best tennis of my life today and you beat it. You deserved to win. But watch out for me next year, you big stiff!"[33] It was typical Johnston, a fierce fighter and good sportsman to the very end. Exhausted and brokenhearted, Little Bill would tell close supporters, "I just can't beat the son of a bitch." For his part Big Bill would carry the gleaming trophy across the lawn of the Germantown Cricket Club to his aunt's house; it was now his.[34]

From the final handshake and for several days thereafter, accolades poured forth for the match, the contestants, and the game's sterling champion. Repeatedly referred to it as a "gargantuan conflict" and "titanic battle," journalists struck notes of awe and amazement on their typewriters. "It was a duel, grim, desperate, to the death," wrote one inspired observer.[35] "Its like has never been witnessed and probably nothing quite like it will be seen again." The victor, of course, garnered "the supreme honors of the lawn tennis world, honors won by a display of dazzling skill, of undaunted courage and never-dying hope of mental and physical stamina beyond all praise."[36] "Once again, let the world of sport salute the prince of all champions," wrote Perry Lewis in a front-page story, "the wonder man who rules his chosen realm of athletics with a hand of iron more relentless and gripping than that of any other title holder; for another year let the domain of tennis bend its head in submission to the magic racquet swayed as a scepter from a Philadelphia throne for two solid years; again let William T. Tilden, 2nd, be acclaimed tennis champion of the United States and monarch of the world's courts."[37] Granted a bit hyperbolic, but there were no doubters at this point. Tilden strode the earth like an athletic colossus.

Even Johnston's most loyal supporters had to admit the unchallengeable truth of the matter: Tilden was the greater player. How else does one explain their hero having a two-set lead and a 3–0 margin in the third set yet lose the match? "In those first two sets," as one reviewer commented, "Johnston was as formidable as he ever was in his life. His accuracy was uncanny, his judgment faultless." Many thought he was "Tilden's master, not only defeating the Philadelphian, but running him all over the court." By the third set, however, when Johnston was beginning to weaken and show the effects of the pressure and long rallies, "Tilden warm[ed] up to his work. Then, quick to see that his slight opponent was faltering and leg weary, he pressed his advantage, not only to win the set they were in, but to wear down the Californian for the sets to come."[38]

Championship tennis, at least as it was played at this level, was as much an endurance contest as it was a test of athleticism and stroking ability. And "so it proved, for all times in the fifth and last set, the powerful Tilden was in entire control of the situation. It was the consensus among experts . . . that Johnston is too frail to ever take the measure of Tilden in a five-set match."[39]

"In short," Perry Lewis of the *Philadelphia Inquirer*, would muse, "Tilden has everything and plenty of it. His versatility in stroking is the wonder of the tennis world; his court generalship unexcelled despite a disposition to loaf along at times and experiment: he is resourceful when driven into a corner; he is capable, under pressure, of raising his game to lofty levels undreamed of before he reached the zenith of his form; and last, but by no means least, he has the stamina, the endurance, the strength to stand up under the punishment of a long match."[40]

Like Lewis, many a columnist and athletic pundit would recount the great names in the history of the game—Larned, Doherty, Brookes, McLoughlin, and Johnston. But as great as they were, there was now agreement, "none were so great as the present champion—William T. Tilden of Philadelphia."

If his reputation was not cemented in stone, at least it was inscribed three times on the trophy sitting in a place of honor in his aunt's living room. The day after all the tumult and drama, Tilden did what only Big Bill would do after two grueling weeks of competitive tennis against the world's best: he played another five sets of tennis with fellow members of the Germantown Cricket Club. It should come as no surprise that he won all five sets, but it may provoke astonishment to learn that he "defeated four men simultaneously." With two opponents at the net and two at the baseline—presumably an impossible task—Tilden found "a vacant spot to slip in a passing shot about whenever he chose."[41] And it should be known the players were not dubs; all could play, and one was Roy R. Coffin, a fine athlete and tennis player in his own right.

There truly had never been another tennis player like Tilden. But the euphoria and comparisons to the greatest athletes of his age would end abruptly, as less than a month later the champion would suffer a minor mishap that would eventually threaten his career as well as his life.

7

"The Boss of All Tennis Players"

He towers above all opponents on the courts.
The one player who can do anything he wants
with a ball, and who can defeat any other player
in the world any time he wants to defeat him.

—*New York Times*

The October 7 exhibition at an off-the-beaten-path venue was like hundreds of others Bill had ventured to in the hope of convincing curious adults and eager youth that tennis was the greatest of athletic activities and worthy of their investment in time and interest. But this short day trip across the Delaware to a remote section of South Jersey would take on an ominous quality that would linger for months and propel a dreaded cloud that virtually hung over the champion for weeks and threatened him both life and limb.

Just a few days later on October 12 Bill crossed the same river, but this time into the plush environs of central New Jersey to put on a tennis exhibition at Princeton University. Joined by Frank Hunter, Zenzo Shimidzu, and former Princeton star Dean Mathey, the college students and well-heeled residents of Mercer County were delighted by the quartet's caliber of play and general enthusiasm. And to the organizer they were "unanimous in declaring Bill Tilden a real champion" for coordinating the event and his uncanny ability to repeatedly return the hardest shots directed at him.[1] The well-attended affair also ended on an upbeat note, as Tilden and Mathey defeated Hunter and Shimidzu, 6–3, 7–5, 7–5. For this grass-court pied piper, it was just another occasion for the game's greatest ambassador to win over American sportsmen and their nonathletic cousins.

At the time there was not the slightest inkling that the finger Tilden had injured less than a week earlier at the Cohanic Country Club was about to become a problem. There was certainly no indication that his rather minor collision with a tennis-court backstop could result in a career-ending injury, much less a life-threatening health dilemma.

It was on Saturday, October 7, that Tilden would leave his Germantown home for an exhibition in the Garden State. Chop-stroke artist Wallace Johnson would be his playing partner this time, and the destination would be Bridgeton, a small, rural community in South Jersey's agricultural heartland. Equidistant from Philadelphia; Wilmington, Delaware; and Atlantic City to the east, Cumberland County was neither a cultural destination nor a hotbed of tennis, but Tilden was prepared to go anywhere there were fans of the world's greatest sport. It would be at this rather insignificant stop on the ever-frenetic Tilden express that "an incident occurred," he would later write, "that looked for a time as if it would end my tennis for ever and indeed for a few days looked as if it would end my life."[2]

The champ would come to admit he was "very much run down physically" after an arduous season of competition topped off by some extremely taxing battles in both Davis Cup and national singles tournament action. Rather than take a well-deserved break to rest and regroup, however, he plowed ahead with a busy series of exhibitions in the Philadelphia area. Tilden loved the sport and appreciated those who shared his affection for the game. As the national champion and the sport's greatest emissary, he felt it his responsibility to make public appearances no matter how small the crowd or distant the engagement.

Along the Cohansey River near Delaware Bay, the small-town exhibition was like hundreds of others where he had showcased his athleticism, racket skills, and love of the game. Even smashing into a fence laced with chicken wire while chasing a beautiful lob hit by Johnson was no different from the scores of other fences and backstops he had collided with while chasing a well-struck ball. But this one was different; this one would necessitate his being hospitalized and place his life in jeopardy.

Although all news accounts at the time would mention a "slightly lacerated" wound to "the middle finger of his right hand," Tilden would subsequently claim the collision "did not break the skin" and the finger was just "badly bruised."[3] Initially, Tilden claimed he "paid no particular attention to the incident," but in subsequent days "the finger grew sorer day by day for nearly a week." Bill was well known for a stoic demeanor regarding injuries, predisposed to play through discomfort and pain, and loath to consult with physicians, but the digit, now increasing in size and tenderness, forced him to do something he normally shied away from. He inquired of a school physician (presumably Germantown Academy) what he should do and was told it was probably a "sensitive callous" that should be soaked in hot soda water. For the next three days, however, the finger grew in both pain and size.[4]

Frustrated and increasingly concerned, Bill went to Dr. Walter Andrews, who lanced the finger, believing it was a simple abscess.[5] Poultices and heat were applied for a couple days, and then the doctor lanced the finger a second time, but there was no drainage. Dr. Andrews was puzzled. The next day, with the pain increasing and Bill unable to sleep, Andrews recommended Bill see a surgeon.

As Bill would write years later of the frightening event, "After three more days of extreme pain, during which my finger swelled to three times its normal size, we called in a surgeon, Dr. Wm. Swartley, now chief of the Surgical Staff of the Germantown Hospital, who after a careful examination dragged me off to the hospital for immediate operation. The poison by now pretty well through my system, a *staphylococcic* [*sic*] infection that had been my old enemy in Paris and London in 1921, and Dr. Swartley had not only the finger to fight but a case of septicemia."[6]

Bill's rather tame, dispassionate account does not mention a few relevant items such as a fever that now gripped him, Dr. Swartley's increasing concern about his patient's overall well-being—a slight abrasion had developed into a dire health threat—and Bill's refusal to be hospitalized. In fact, despite Dr. Swartley's urging Bill to enter the hospital, he resisted, stayed home, and continued with the poultices and heat treatment. Even after being given morphine, Bill was unable to sleep, the pain was so great. At nine o'clock the next morning, Bill was admitted to Germantown Hospital. X-rays, blood tests, and other diagnostic tests were performed. Bill was then taken directly to the operating room. The surgical procedure began at 11:15 a.m. and ended forty-five minutes later.[7]

News accounts at the time said that Swartley decided "to operate after administering a general anesthetic. Five incisions were made by Dr. Swartley, two underneath, one on each side and one on top above the first joint, so that the finger nail could be removed."[8] It is probable Swartley took swift action due to what he initially suspected and confirmed while operating:

"The finger was three times its normal size and the tension was so great the finger suffered a pressure necrosis and as a result the tip was black and almost gangrenous." The incisions were deep and to the bone and were followed by hot salt and Dakin's solutions and vaccine inoculations for the infections that had spread to Tilden's arms and body.[9]

The following day Dr. Swartley attempted to put a good spin on things and gave newsmen an overly optimistic report. He had ordered further tests and a laboratory culture to determine if a bone infection had occurred. "Should it be found that Tilden is suffering a bone infection," said the surgeon, "it is possible that his finger would become stiff, which I am told, would seriously impair him in his tennis play. However, although the infection is very serious, I hardly believe the bone is infected."

"We are hopeful," Swartley informed the press, "the germ to be the staphylococcus, a skin infection that is not serious. There is a possibility, however, that streptococcus toxemia may have set in. In this event the patient must be ready for a hard battle."[10]

Speculation immediately grew in both the press and the general public as to how seriously an injured, uncooperative finger would impact a player of Tilden's caliber. A key pillar of a tennis player's success, as Bill often told his young charges, is one's ability to firmly grip the racket. During the course of a match a player may change grips a thousand times or more while hitting forehands, backhands, slices, drop shots, lobs, and serves. Tilden, especially, with his varied spins and unconventional shot selection, would have seemed much affected by a rigid, inflexible finger. Some conjectured that even with Bill's "long, slim, sinewy fingers of tremendous strength," it would be a problematic assignment at best and possibly terminate his career. "His loss to the game," observed one tennis fan, "would be a calamity, incalculable and complete." Another argued, "The right hand of Tilden, and almost equally, the most important finger of that hand, is as necessary to him as is the finger of the greatest violinist or the voice of the foremost singer or actor."[11] Others joked that the surgical removal of a finger would relegate Tilden to play like a normal human being.

All attempts at humor ended less than a week later when it was announced that Tilden's condition had worsened. His fever had climbed, boils once again beset him, and his finger had become "gangrenous." The infection had apparently taken over his entire system. It was also reported that a section of the poisoned finger was "about to fall off." "Tilden Will Lose Joint of Finger" was a *Philadelphia Inquirer* headline in early November that announced the champion's worsening condition. Similar alarming notices throughout the country informed newspaper readers of the situation's increasing gravity.[12] Some accounts related "another segment of the finger had been taken off," while others predicted additional operations were being scheduled.[13] At one point Swartley admitted that he had first considered amputation, but now believed it "unnecessary as nature herself will remove the infected area."

Tilden was said to be under "constant observation," and if there was any sign the infection moved up the finger, "the knife will again be resorted to." Swartley explained that there was a "line of demarcation of infection plainly visible" that made monitoring the infection fairly simple. More difficult, however, was just how to treat the fevered digit. So far it had resisted the surgeon's best attempts to rein in the stubborn infection. At one point the situation seemed to be changing hourly. In fact, on November 6 Swartley told the press he expected that "within a few hours the diseased tissue will fall off." He was referring to diseased bone and dead skin, and that was in addition to the nail and tip of the finger that had already disappeared. Just in case a more proactive course proved necessary, an assortment of sharp surgical knives were on call.

Wanting to alleviate public fears about the severity of the situation and growing rumors of an abrupt end to his career, Tilden informed the press that stories of a career-ending surgery and his possible demise were premature. But there were real obstacles, he admitted, ahead of him. "Undoubtedly, I will have to revolutionize my grip," he told reporters.

> My arm will be stiff and my hand will be unaccustomed to the racket, but with practice I believe I will be able to overcome the handicap. If I am playing tennis of a kind that warrants competing in the National championship whether as a serious contender or not, I will compete. It is my belief that each succeeding champion deserves the right to defeat his predecessor, rather than gain the title through the default or retirement of the previous title-holder.
>
> If I am able to play next season, which I believe is possible, I shall team up with A. L. "Sandy" Wiener and play the majority of the big tournaments throughout the East and the Middle West. Even if my playing days are over, I intend to continue my work with the junior players of America.[14]

Bill would eventually write of his surgeon's increasing concern and frustration at the lack of progress in controlling the infection.

> Finally one day Dr. Swartley came to me and said, "Bill, older and wiser men than I am in the medical profession are urging me to remove your finger at the base and get you out of the hospital. If I do that I can get you home in twenty-four hours, but it will absolutely end all chance of your playing tennis again for it will ruin your grip on your racquet. I believe I can save the second joint on your finger if you are willing to stand the pain and take the time. Which is it to be?"

"Naturally," Bill would write, he chose "as much of my finger as I could save. It was not a pretty thing at best, but I had it a good many years then and had a sentimental interest in it."

Humor aside, he and Dr. Swartley, he would write, "battled that infection . . . for three full months and finally won" the fight. Tilden's recollection of the time involved might be exaggerated, but Swartley—after taking another inch off Bill's finger with one of those knives—did manage to save that second joint and, with it, Big Bill's tennis career.

Bill was able to leave Germantown Hospital in mid-November and return home to be cared for by his aunt and cousin. Though the worst appeared over, the stump of his finger as well as his entire hand were heavily wrapped in bandages, gauze pads, and adhesive tape. Not surprisingly, there was little expectation of a triumphant return to the court. While recuperating on Hansberry Street, most of Bill's time would be spent reading and listening to his vast record collection of classical music and Italian opera. When not wondering what the removal of his bandages would bring, he studied the latest work of popular playwrights and spent time with Germantown Academy's drama club.

When reporters were granted an interview, Bill was not optimistic. He expressed "little hope that he w[ould] be successful in defending his championship." "The loss of this joint is bound to affect my future in tennis," said Tilden regretfully. "You see, I play all my shots off the ends of my fingers. Such an accident would not materially affect a player like Bill Johnston who handles the racquet gripped in the palm of the hand, but with my style it's different. I do not believe that the injury will destroy the fundamentals of my game, but I'm sure I shall lose the finesse of my play."[15]

Confidence, a quality Tilden once had in abundance, now seemed in retreat. "The psychology of the thing is this," Bill soberly told the reporters. "In the last five years I have never really lost confidence in my ability to return any ball I could reach. When I missed I was surprised. In the future I know this is going to be reversed."[16] It was a shockingly frank admission from a player who scampered about the court like a whippet and returned even the hardest-hit balls like a human backboard.

Bill tried to be honest in his assessment of what he would be able to do on a lawn tennis court once the medical tape came off. "I doubt that I will be able to retain the championship," he told newsmen with a wisp of disappointment in his voice. "But I don't intend to stop playing in tournaments. I probably will hang around the lower half or middle of the first ten, and I'll get just as much fun out of the competition. After all, what difference does it make anyway, whether I rank No. 1 in the tennis list or farther down. Yes, I'll keep playing just the same and helping the juniors in the game. It's the fun of the competition and not the title that's really worth while."[17]

With agreement increasing among the sport's cognoscenti that Tilden's extraordinary run had probably come to an end and he would be unable to retain his American tennis title, he was questioned as to whether he would even bother entering the national tournament. To that there was no question. "The man who wins it," he argued, "is entitled to the right to win it over the net." Anything less by a defending champion, he believed, was disrespectful and unsportsmanlike. A true champion, no matter his condition, owed it to the game and his successor to show up and play.

Practically conceding his decline as a top player, he went on to state that Bill Johnston was now the "greatest player in the country." Bill's victory over him just a few months earlier for the American championship was the most difficult challenge of his career. "Of all my matches that was the hardest," said Bill. His respect and admiration for the little Californian were evident. If he could no longer claim the title as America's best tennis player, then Little Bill deserved the honor.

Before leaving, reporters were able to get the champ to address other tennis-related subjects. When it was suggested he would have lost "dollars and cents" from his injury if he had been a professional, Bill scoffed at the notion. He admitted he had been approached "by promoters six times" over the past couple years to turn pro. One even offered him the handsome sum of "$25,000 a year," but he was not interested. He believed in amateur athletics. However, he seemed to leave the door open by stating, "If the National Association drives the players to it by restricting their activities as it is now doing . . ."[18] Bill went on to say that some of the USLTA's rules and regulations were "unfair and unreasonable." He specifically cited the prohibition against players participating in charitable causes, such as the recent fund-raiser to aid France in overcoming the devastation of war. "Such ridiculous rules," said Tilden emphatically, "should be changed."

The champ left the clear impression he was loath to turn pro, but the association's often-bizarre strictures, directives, and policies may force him and others to do so. But the first order of business while he was bathed in medical bandages was whether he would be able to grip and swing a racket at all once the wound healed and the bandages were removed. "But if he cannot," one reporter would write admiringly in his column, "he will have been beaten by a condition and not a competitor."

By Christmas 1922 the question was still unanswered, but Bill was definitely on the mend. The combination of Dr. Swartley's judicious surgeries, Germantown Hospital's prudent care, and the nurturing love of his aunt and cousin had the patient in far better shape than was initially expected. When the gauze and medical tape were removed at the hospital, Bill was left with an ugly wound. Swollen, discolored, and practically immobile, the unsightly stub of a middle finger would require considerable exercise and tender massage before it could be called upon to do the simplest of tasks.

Bill and his two family nurses worked to reduce the inflammation and stiffness, while Bill drew up mental plans for how to compensate on court with a compromised digit. Almost immediately, unsurprisingly, Tilden tried to hold a racket. "I found my task even greater than I feared," Tilden would one day write of his personal challenge. "My finger was naturally very sensitive and gave me great pain when my racquet turned in my hand, but that was the least of my troubles. I had to learn new grips on all my shots, to use my first and third finger to compensate for the missing second. The result was that I studied and worked harder on tennis than ever before in my life."[19]

The intense effort paid off; before the year was out Bill was back on court. That in itself many found amazing, but there was even better news: not only was he able to play, but he also found he could still wield a racket well enough to win points. An indoor exhibition was organized for the Second Regiment Armory. Tilden—along with two of his protégés, Carl Fischer and Sandy Wiener—took to the court. The result shocked disbelieving observers. Granted, the champ lost both sets, 10–8 and 6–2, but the sheer fact that he was on court with racket in hand was the day's big news. As newspaper headlines informed readers, "Tilden Encouraged at First Workout: Champion Not Handicapped by Recent Amputation as Much as He Feared"; the world's best lawn tennis player was not to be counted out.[20] Despite a missing finger on his racket hand, there was still fire in his belly and a desire to play. "I feel greatly encouraged after my first try-out," Tilden declared. "I can grip my racquet far better and hit with much more power and precision than I believed I could. . . . Of course it is going to take several weeks of practice for me to determine exactly how much I have lost and how much of my former stuff I will be able to regain, but I must say I am far more hopeful that I believed would be possible after the first day's play. I was gripping my racquet with the finger which was amputated and I think I did it very well."

As reporters commented the unexpected vision of seeing Tilden back on court was startling. The finger had "healed more rapidly" than anyone expected, including "attending physicians." No one, quite frankly, thought it was possible. "To see him shoot his famous back-hand, zipping an inch above the net into his opponent's court," wrote one impressed scribe, "one would never think he had either anything the matter with his hand or that he was the least out of practice.[21]

Initially, Tilden showed some concern that he was unable to properly hit "his terrific sweeping forehand drive, which has been the terror of net players for the past four years," but it would turn out to be the formation of an unrelated blister and not the surgically removed finger that was causing the problem.[22] Out of commission for a couple months, his calloused right hand had gone soft, and the sudden use of it had caused a blister to develop.

He also seemed to refrain from certain shots that put greater pressure on the wound. His cannonball and high-bounding serves, for example, were missing in action. Apparently, the pressure on the hand was just too great for Tilden to bear at this initial workout. His slice serve, however, was quite effective and seemingly pain free. So too was his ability to half volley. Volleys from midcourt did prove far more difficult due to his unique tendency to use the tips of his fingers for delicate maneuvering of the racket.

Sandy Wiener and other of Bill's close tennis friends pitched in to assist the champ in regaining his command of a game he once dominated. With no fear of hard work and a devotee of "intensive practice," Bill threw himself into remastering strokes he had once taken for granted. "I pounded away at my volley and overhead," Tilden would write of the tennis boot camp he forced on himself that spring. "Naturally, I found the loss of my finger had affected my grip on the racquet and that it turned in my hand quite often. This increased the need for a speedy win of a point. I could no longer rely on my ability to out steady my opponent. I must hit for a winner at once. Gradually my incessant punching of volleys and overheads began to pay dividends. I actually reached a point when I was reasonably certain of winning at the net. I gained confidence, and with my confidence grew my effectiveness."[23] Tilden would ultimately give credit for the improvement in his volley and overhead to Sandy Wiener and "the loss of my finger."

On January 5, 1923—and to everyone's amazement—Tilden showed up on a court in Chicago for an exhibition against Frank Hunter, a top American player and the national indoor titleholder. Incredibly, Tilden defeated Hunter, 3–6, 7–5, 6–4. Few at courtside, who could visibly see Bill was missing a key appendage, could believe their eyes. As the event was captured by reporters for *American Lawn Tennis*, "The eyes of the country and the world were upon, not the comeback, but whether or not the loss of a portion of a finger on the playing hand would set back the play of William T. Tilden to such an extent that the star would go glimmering beyond the horizon; or whether by his great resourcefulness, he would come back in a remade game and once more shine among the luminaries." Readers of the magazine were given a resounding thumbs-up; he had returned in all his majestic glory. "Tilden met the test," read one article, "and convinced close followers of the game that he is the same master of strokes."[24]

It was quite clear to all, however, that Tilden did not come through his recent ordeal unscathed. For those seated in the rafters and unable to get a good look at the champ's wounded hand, it was still apparent something was amiss. That was especially obvious on those occasions when the pain of striking the ball with the racket was just too great, forcing Tilden to drop the racket and shake his hand in an effort to relieve the pain.[25]

After the match Tilden was upbeat and fielded questions from reporters. He told them he was managing "very well" in gripping the racket and had surprised himself with how much power and how precisely he was hitting. He held up his racket at one point, wrapped his fingers around it—four of them, at least—and said, "See, I can grip the racket as of old."[26] Those at the arena that night had considerably less doubt that the champion was back.

Two days later Bill would once again be "ranked first among the tennis players of the country according to the ranking committee of the United States Lawn Tennis Association." Following him in order would be Bill Johnston, Vinnie Richards, R. Norris Williams, and Wallace Johnson. Tilden and Richards were ranked as the nation's best doubles team as well. As much as he appreciated their recognition of his play over the past year, he was probably prouder of the fact that a number of his young tennis students had earned a national ranking, including Richards, Carl Fischer, Arnold Jones, and Sandy Wiener.[27] It should not be forgotten that it was Tilden who had urged the USLTA to give young players their due and to start ranking those in junior and boys categories.

Just four days later, on January 12, a prominent photograph of Bill appeared in the *Philadelphia Inquirer*.[28] A photo of Bill in the newspapers was nothing new; sketches and photographs of the champion had become commonplace since his rise to fame in 1920. But this one was different, or at least its place in the newspaper was different. It was the Amusement & Entertainment section of the newspaper that showcased the latest Hollywood films and stage productions appearing in town.

Bill had shed his white-duck tennis garb for a handsome tuxedo to perform in *Dulcy*, a new play by George S. Kaufman and Marc Connelly. Once again the stately Bellevue-Stratford Hotel was the venue for the annual Germantown Academy fund-raiser. But there was one significant change for the 1923 event: Bill was not only a member of the Belfry Club cast, but also the director of the production. Though his physical health may have been imperiled in recent months, his mind was quite active, especially so regarding his increasing interest in drama and the stage. His lengthy hospitalization and subsequent recuperation on Hansberry Street enabled him to assess appropriate material for his alma mater's annual fund-raising gala.[29] The event was a financial, if not critical, success, and the school was delighted to have such a renowned celebrity involved with school activities. Bill was now both the tennis and the drama coach. And, it should be pointed out, he was unpaid in both roles.

Greater investment as the production's director increased his anxiety. He was also self-conscious about his appearance, particularly his mangled right hand. For most of his appearances onstage he kept his hand secured in his jacket pocket. Such a masquerade was not possible on a tennis court, however.

Desirous of maintaining his ranking despite the daunting challenge it presented, Tilden continued to push himself to overcome his handicap, learn new grips, and get himself back into playing shape. This allowed him to notice that "the long enforced rest and great care" he had received from hospital personnel and his family had "eliminated [his] old enemy, Mr. Staphylococcus," from his system. As tennis historian Rich Hillway argues:

> Bill had always been a somewhat sickly child. Even into adulthood there were these unexplained episodes of sudden fevers and boils that were quite debilitating, not to mention frustrating. The finger infection that resulted in his hospitalization and surgery was one of the worst instances of what was probably some form of blood disorder or disease that had lingered in his system for some time. His ability to withstand what could have easily resulted in his death and the subsequent amputation actually ended up cleansing his system. Never again would boils, sudden fevers, or infections plague him. His health witnessed a dramatic improvement.[30]

Sports columnists covering Bill's comeback were awestruck by his resilience, though some were quick to note "his failure to smother all opposition" and the lack of his former court "wizardry." Had surgeons, one journalist inquired, "saved an arm and ruined a great athlete"?[31] Yes, Tilden was back, but would he be the same indomitable force that laid waste to all pretenders to the throne? Many were predicting it would be sheer fantasy to expect Tilden to maintain his crown. He was lucky to be alive. Just hitting balls should be considered an accomplishment. Others were not so quick to write off the champ.

Robert Edgren, a columnist for the *Philadelphia Evening Bulletin*, wrote a piece on Tilden's challenge that focused on other handicapped athletes who managed to overcome significant physical obstacles. For Edgren it really was a case of mind over matter. "If he makes up his mind to it," wrote Edgren, Tilden could regain "the master's touch," and there was "no reason Tilden shouldn't be better than ever." Such bold talk was backed up with examples: a golfer who lost the use of an arm due to an automobile accident but played on with his one good arm, a once paralyzed youth who became an Olympic high jumper, and a one-eyed pugilist who defeated many a boxer with twenty-twenty vision.[32]

Though clearly in the minority, there were a number of Tilden supporters who had faith Big Bill had what it would take to overcome any physical impairment he may have confronted. "Those who jump at the conclusion that a new champion will be crowned this year simply because Big Bill doesn't look so good these days," cautioned *Philadelphia Inquirer* sportswriter Perry Lewis, "may have some recanting to do before 1923 departs." Lewis prided himself on a discerning eye when it came to athletic ability and personal character. He had always been struck by Tilden's knack for overcoming adversity. Tilden was never so great as when he was pressed, never so formidable as when he appeared on the ropes and about to hit the canvas. "The champion is a disconcerting person on the court," argued Lewis. "He seldom touches the crest of his form unless inspired by the opposition and the importance of the match in which he is engaged. Tilden tries to do his best always, generally speaking, but he simply can't bring off those marvelous strokes, which are his unless pushed to the limit."

"There have probably been titleholders who outclassed the field by a wider margin than the Philadelphian," Lewis would write, "but no monarch of sport ever had such narrow escapes and still maintained his supremacy—no champion ever came from behind oftener when all seemed lost, and invariably in important matches."

In conclusion Lewis warned Tilden skeptics that despite Bill's health concerns and missing digit, the big man should still be "recognized as the boss of all tennis players. The man who could rally in the face of defeat and hold a world's championship against a Norton; who could hover on the precipice of ruin and then flatten a Shimidzu in a Davis Cup match; who could rise from the ashes to turn back a Johnston with the United States championship at stake is dangerous as long as he has a finger."[33]

Rising to the challenge as few others have attempted, Bill drove himself to recapture his former net skills as quickly as possible. No tournament was too small or little known for him to take an interest and grab some playing time. He even showed up at events unannounced, as he did at the Heights Casino in Brooklyn in late January and inquired "if he could get a game up for practice." The casino was the home court of Dean Mathey, and the two played three sets, all won by the former Princeton Tiger. For those with the unexpected privilege of observing the sport's greatest player relearn facets of the game, there was an "apparent handicap, but it did not seem an insuperable one. Tilden was obviously short of practice and uncertain in making some of his shots." There was a "discernable weakness" on his backhand side when pressed, and he "constantly favored his right hand" when holding the racket and balls, but all in all he appeared well on his way to overcoming his recent malady.[34]

That optimistic assessment was confirmed less than two weeks later in mid-February when Bill traveled up to Buffalo to participate in the city's annual Lincoln's Birthday Tournament. Though most in attendance viewed the champ's participation as a practice session and an opportunity to "try out his finger," they were in for quite a surprise, as were some very accomplished players who were taken down by him. One of them was R. Lindley Murray, a fine all-around athlete, former national champion, and someone who retained all ten of his fingers. Murray was defeated in the semifinal in straight sets, 6–0, 6–4. Bill went on to win the tournament. One reporter wrote, "Tilden started out against Murray playing the most remarkable tennis any of the spectators had ever seen." And Bill Larned, a former seven-time American champion who was in the umpire's chair, was in agreement: "It was the finest tennis he had ever seen Tilden play." No shot seemed too difficult, and there were practically no errors. "His marvelous play," according to one observer, "left spectators gasping in astonishment."[35]

A greater challenge was presented on May 2 when he played a couple of one-set matches against Billy Johnston and Vinnie Richards in New York City's Central Park. It was estimated that somewhere between fourteen and twenty thousand people attended the free event, designed to increase the number of courts in the park. Johnston had stopped in the city before leaving for a series of European matches, including the World Hard Court and Wimbledon Championships. It is not known whether Johnston and Richards decided to take it easy on the champ, but both ended up losing by a score of 6–4.[36]

The next day Bill talked Johnston into traveling back to Philadelphia with him. He wanted Little Bill to address the students at Germantown Academy and give them some advice and a demonstration of his racket prowess. Johnston was nervous about his speech—he was much more comfortable on court—but he did a more than adequate job encouraging the boys to "start right by watching good players and getting their strokes going properly in the beginning." He also admitted, "I am trying to pick up something from Tilden on my backhand. I used to hit my backhand straight. Now I am trying to bring the face of my racquet over and get some top-spin on the ball."

When Tilden and Johnston took to the new courts on campus, Big Bill played a mostly backcourt game and won 5–7, 6–4, 6–3. His errors, many of which occurred at the net, were attributed to "his injured finger."[37] It was noted by a reporter who covered the school event that Johnston appeared to be practicing his backhand stroke. "Several times he let loose with a Tilden-like backhand, but he is not really sure of this stroke yet."[38]

S. Wallis Merrihew, a strong supporter of both players and the publisher of *American Lawn Tennis*, had joined the men on their journey to the private school in Philadelphia and umpired their match. He took a close look at Tilden's game and came away impressed. "Watching Tilden yesterday in New York and again this afternoon," said Merrihew after the match, "convinces me that he has lost nothing, absolutely nothing."[39]

Bill would be on court numerous times during the spring of '23, including one date at the White House. President Harding was neither a player nor a serious connoisseur of the game, but he enjoyed inviting famous sports figures to the White House. The president's invitation is thought to have contributed to tennis's rising popularity in the early twenties. Happy to oblige, Bill would bring Vinnie Richards, Sandy Wiener, and Manuel and José Alonso, along with several top Japanese players. The Spanish and Japanese ambassadors to America were also delighted to be part of the festivities.

Bill would also take to the pages of *American Lawn Tennis* in May, penning what would become a periodic column entitled "Passing Shots." In addition to discussing the attributes of top foreign players, the fierce interleague tennis battles of Philadelphia clubs, and Little Bill's prospects at Wimbledon in this first column, there was also comment on Sandy Wiener and Donald Strachan of Philadelphia, Lewis White of Texas, and several other young American players around the country with noticeable talent.[40] His commitment to establishing an ongoing cadre of young players to keep America the dominant tennis nation was unique among both players and tennis officials at the time and would remain a constant source of comment in his *American Lawn Tennis* columns.

It would be another Tilden entry in that issue, however, that would spark considerable debate and discussion among the nation's tennis players. Tilden, the master of the all-stroke game, had long advocated "variety" as the key element to a winning game. Others argued, "Speed, speed, and yet more speed" was the best strategy for a serious player to adopt. Yes, Big Bill replied, velocity was important, and it certainly had its place in competitive tennis, but the player with the greatest variety of strokes usually proved the victor.

Bill remained unmoved by the numbers who supported speed of shot as the cornerstone of successful tennis. Spin, in his mind, was just as important, if not more so. And the game's future development, Bill argued, "lies in the variety of strokes . . . and in the growing realization of the value of studying tennis psychology."[41] Knowing one's opponent and his likes and dislikes on court was a critical factor in a good player's approach to a match. As usual Bill was years ahead of the field.

Back on court Tilden was proving to doubters that the champion had regained his old form. In Philadelphia he captured the district-wide championship against local rival Wallace Johnson, in New York City he won a number of matches against top competitors in the Church Cup Competition, and he then went on to win the Great Lakes and New England Championships against some of the best domestic and foreign players.

If he did lose a rare match, as he did in the Illinois State Championship against Manuel Alonso, Spain's rising young star, he came back the very next week, as he did in the National Clay Court final at the Woodstock Country Club in Indianapolis, defeating Alonso. Though Bill "played listlessly" in the first set, in which he won only two games, he righted himself in the second and went on to take the last three, 8–6, 6–1, 7–5. Reports of the match said "Tilden adapted his usually aggressive game to Alonso's style," and "after discovering that smashing play at the net would avail him nothing . . . Tilden settled down . . . to chopping and stroking, but at all times running the Spaniard from one corner to the other while taking the game relatively easy himself." Like no one before or at the time, Big Bill could change strategy at the drop of a dime. A master of all strokes in the tennis armamentarium—and a deft tactician to boot—he could quickly shift from offense to defense, hard shots to soft, backcourt to net play, and drives to drop shots like no one else who had ever picked up a racket. For all of Manuel Alonso's grace, skill, and athleticism, he was clearly outgunned and outstrategized. As one reviewer of Tilden's tactics dryly commented, "A perceptible change of pace aided in throwing Alonso off his driving game."[42]

Superlative conditioning could have been an additional factor in Tilden's victory; he usually appeared in better shape than his opponent at the end of matches. At Indianapolis the players endured brutally hot conditions that debilitated both players. Tilden took a pitcher of water and completely doused himself at one point. Alonso appeared dead on his feet and had to be helped from the court at the match's conclusion. Tilden was that rare commodity, an athlete who could sprint like a cheetah and traverse long distances like a marathon runner.

If his athletic endeavors were not enough to spark admiration, Tilden added to his résumé as a burgeoning Renaissance man by continuing to write both fiction and nonfiction books. Readers of *American Lawn Tennis*, for example, anxious to devour articles on Bill's latest tournament conquests, came across half- and full-page advertisements for *It's All in the Game, and Other Tennis Tales*; *The Art of Lawn Tennis*; and *Singles and Doubles*.[43] It was quite clear, if Bill wasn't playing the game, he was writing about it.

To the dismay of tournament organizers such as those behind the famous Newport Casino event, Bill decided to take some time off from the tennis-cluttered midsummer schedule. He would fill his time reading, writing—both fiction and nonfiction—and listening to his ever-expanding record collection. His increasingly frequent "Passing Shots" articles would cover topics ranging from "promising" young players whom tennis aficionados should keep an eye on and the "importance of holding tennis exhibitions" for youngsters to perfect their skills to his recent West Coast swing that reintroduced him to members of the Hollywood film colony, including Douglas Fairbanks, Mary Pickford, and Charlie Chaplin.[44]

It was while Tilden was in Los Angeles that he began to get as much ink in the entertainment and gossip columns of West Coast newspapers as he did in the sports section. Though he had beaten Manuel Alonso in the singles championship of Southern California 9–7, 6–4, 6–2, it was his rumored association with a major film siren that caught the attention of Hollywood press agents. As one newspaper introduced the salacious story, "Has Bill Tilden of Germantown supplanted Charlie Chaplin in the affections of Pola Negri?"

Bill fended off waves of media questions linking him to the actress by stating it was all just a case of bad timing. He was in California just as Pola and Charlie were ending their relationship. "I think too much importance has been placed on the fact that Miss Negri and I have been seen together. But I don't wish to say any more than I consider her very charming."

Pola's response was equally curt, "I can say nothing except that I admire Mr. Tilden very much. You must not ask me more."[45]

But that was Hollywood, a fairy-tale land that thrived on yarns, tall tales, and dreams that might never be realized. For Big Bill the media attention about his "engagement" and romantic adventures with a Hollywood starlit may not have been entirely undesirable.

When he did return back east and to the court in late August for the big push in the season's most important tournaments in September, he proved for one and all that a spot of downtime was not detrimental to one's game, provided that game belonged to Big Bill Tilden. At the National Doubles Championships in 1923, Bill made the competition his own little playground by pairing with Babe Norton to win the men's doubles and joining with Molla Mallory to win the mixed-doubles title. Both victories were over top-caliber teams, including Dick Williams and Watson Washburn, a former victorious American Davis Cup duo, in the men's doubles. The five set result was 3–6, 6–2, 6–3, 5–7, 6–2.

Bill had every right to crow about his doubles victories, but he was actually more excited by the recent success of his former disciple; Carl Fischer had just won the National Intercollegiate Tennis Championship. Tilden, his longtime mentor, was delighted and said that Carl "deserves all the fame he wins." In a "Passing Shots" column Bill recalled meeting Carl eight years earlier, "a little lad in knickers, just learning the game. The patience, study, and earnest effort of his boyhood, in which he thoroughly mastered the fundamentals of the game are standing him in good stead now and carrying him to the ultimate goal, the National championship." Equally important for Tilden was the fact that "Carl has never forgotten his junior tennis days and is never too busy to help one of the youngsters coming to the fore in Philadelphia."[46]

Next up in early September at the West Side Tennis Club was the defense of the Davis Cup against a revamped but strong team from Down Under. James O. Anderson, a giant who dwarfed even Big Bill, now led the Aussies and, more important, had already beaten Tilden a year earlier. Gone were Patterson and O'Hara Wood, but their replacements were young and talented, and they had defeated the best Europe had to offer, including a young but skilled French team. The American squad was a prohibitive favorite until the unthinkable happened the first day of competition: Anderson, the Australian captain, beat Little Bill Johnston in a five-set slugfest. Generally considered "in a class alone with Tilden, and unbeatable by any other player," Little Bill had just won the Wimbledon title. His defeat "came as a shock to tennis followers" around the nation.[47]

Some tennis connoisseurs, stunned by Johnston's surprising loss, predicted "an end of an era had come" and "feared that the invaders might even take the Davis Cup back to Australia."[48] But that was practically an impossibility: the American team was just too strong, especially given Tilden's position as the anchor of the team. In fact, Big Bill would win all three matches that he played: two singles and one doubles. By the end of the weekend Tilden remained unbeaten, and the Davis Cup continued in the possession of the United States.[49]

Once again the action immediately moved south to Philadelphia and the Germantown Cricket Club for the National Singles Championships. The competition was expected to be "one of the most notable in the forty-two years that the tournament." As opposed to the previous year the entry list was cut in half to sixty-four, many from overseas, and America's first ten players. All the smart money, however, was on Tilden and Johnston reaching the final. Would this be the year, many wondered, that Little Bill would finally take down the champ?

There were ferocious struggles and some excellent tennis in the early rounds, as would be expected with a smaller but more elite field of competitors. Startling upsets were the talk of the tournament early on. Frank Hunter, for example, a former navy man during the war and captain of his Cornell tennis team, defeated Vinnie Richards in an exciting five-set battle.

As expected, however, Johnston and Tilden successfully powered their way to the final, the latter losing only one set along the way and discarding the likes of Alonso and Norton as if they were high school players. But Little Bill was now the Wimbledon champ and known for his powerful forehand and big heart. The coming clash, it was pointed out, could prove their most significant encounter and "decide the question of supremacy for all time," as they had evenly decided their twelve matches against each other and the twenty-four sets they had played.[50] Fifteen thousand eager fans packed the temporary wooden stands for what was expected to be another of their monumental grass-court brawls.

Fifty-three minutes later it was over. Tilden had spanked and dispatched his sternest rival in record time. As the *Philadelphia Inquirer* accurately captured the glum scene after the 6–4, 6–1, 6–4 mauling, "There was little applause during the match, and even less when the match came to an end. One doesn't rejoice at a funeral, and this was the funeral of Little Bill Johnston's ambition. No one knows better than he that his racquet is losing his venom while Tilden is rising to more lofty levels every year."

The *New York Times* was even more blunt in its assessment of the battle royal that devolved into a one-sided skirmish. Thousands had filled every available seat, wrote the *Times* reporter, for what turned out to be "the most disappointing finals played in the forty-two year history of the championship. Johnston was defeated before he went on the courts. He knew he was to face one of the greatest players the game has known just when that player was at the crest of form." Only the "very best could cope with such a genius," and Johnston didn't have it.[51]

Try as he might, Little Bill's "best efforts were confounded by the masterly playing of Tilden, who turned back Johnston's finest strokes with daring passing shots made on the run." Tilden's court coverage was nothing short of "marvelous," his stroking exceptional, and his ability to adapt to his opponent's play "irresistible."[52]

Johnston's loyal defenders over the years had attributed Tilden's victories to luck more than superior talent and athletic ability, but the debacle that was plainly evident to anyone watching proved Big Bill was an unmitigated colossus. As one newspaper account chronicled the awesome show of tennis expertise, "Tilden didn't wear down his persistent challenger, and eventually snatch the triumph by virtue of his superior staying qualities. He out-stroked him from first to last, out-steadied him, outgeneraled him, balked him at every point, did everything but out-game him—and did it in a workmanlike way without forcing himself to the limit of his tremendous power."[53]

The following day in a most flattering *New York Times* sports editorial, Bill was called "one of the marvels of the world of sports" and as much "a genius with a racquet as [violinist Fritz] Kreisler is with a bow. There is no stroke he cannot make, no pitch to which he cannot raise his play. He has all the finesse and delicacy of touch of an artist, together with unlimited power and variety, and a surpassing knowledge of the strategy of the court. Today, Tilden stands alone, the master." The admiration-filled piece concluded by saying, "When one remembers that shortly after the close of the 1922 season Tilden suffered the loss of a part of the middle finger of his right hand it becomes difficult to understand how he could have gone up, as he has, instead of down as he predicted. Tilden is hitting the ball harder today than ever before, with every bit as good control, and has lost none of the wizardry in making strokes that require much delicacy of manipulation. He towers above all opponents on the courts."[54]

Incredibly, Tilden celebrated his fourth straight National Singles Championship by returning to the courts at Manheim, as he did the previous year, and taking on "four young players of the Germantown Cricket Club at one time and defeated them five straight sets. The scores were 6–3, 7–5, 8–6, 9–7, and 7–5."[55] Obviously, Tilden's stamina was nothing short of epic and exceeded in size only by his love of the game. He had been playing tournament-level tennis for months, had just expended a tremendous amount of energy over the past few weeks in Davis Cup and national singles action, yet took the court the very next day for an additional five sets against a quartet of players hoping to claim at least one set against the champ. Like those before them, the disheartened foursome came back exhausted and humbled.

For some time after, fawning columns and gushing assessments of Tilden's greatness poured forth from the nation's broadsheets and tabloids like the waterfalls at Niagara. "He played the finest tennis ever seen on a court," "Once, and for all time, whatever doubts might have existed as to the supremacy of Tilden were set at rest," and "It is simple truth to say that his like as a player has never been seen" were just a few plaudits from an *American Lawn Tennis* admirer.[56]

Glowing tributes from overseas were no less impressive. "His backhand is an unbreakable weapon of great power, his more speedy forehand is nearly as reliable," stated A. Wallis Myers, the respected English tennis authority. "I rank him as high as, and perhaps higher, than any other man whoever put a racket to a ball, nor is it certain that he has yet reached his zenith."[57]

No doubt Bill savored the many testaments to his stellar play. He would do some writing as well, but rather than crow about his recent triumphs or his spectacular year, he chose as one of his first pieces a defense of his good friend Little Bill Johnston, whom he had just eviscerated on court. "It was not the old Bill Johnston who went down in three sets to me in the final," wrote Tilden in his "Passing Shots" column. Granted, Little Bill was "a tired, drawn shadow of himself," but it was sheer folly to "think that it is the beginning of the end of Billy Johnston. Never have I heard a more

FIG 1. Captain William T. Tilden Jr. (seated, right) and his 1910 Germantown Academy tennis team. From an early age Tilden had a sense of personal comportment and fashion. Invariably, when not on court he wore a tie, a habit he would maintain throughout his life. Courtesy of the Germantown Academy Archive.

FIG 2. Unlike those of his brother, Herbert Marmaduke, young Bill's years on the University of Pennsylvania tennis team (seated, right) were undistinguished. In 1915 he would drop out of school and soon after witness the deaths of both his father and his brother. Courtesy of the University of Pennsylvania Archives.

FIG 3. Tall, lanky, and athletic, Bill could run like a gazelle and hit shots as if fired from a cannon. But during his college years he was also capable of muddled strategy and an erratic serve-and-volley game. Courtesy of the University of Pennsylvania Archives.

FIG 4. (*opposite top*) While a student at the University of Pennsylvania, Tilden (center, rear) served as the volunteer coach of his former high school's tennis team. His inability to answer players' questions sparked his intense study of the game's history, fundamentals, and tactical nuances. Courtesy of the Germantown Academy Archive.

FIG 5. (*opposite bottom*) Though his collegiate play as a Penn student left most unimpressed, Tilden was actually a national mixed-doubles champion. Young Bill was plucked out of the ranks to partner with Mary K. Browne and win back-to-back titles in 1913 and 1914. Special Collections Research Center, Temple University Libraries, Philadelphia.

FIG 6. (*above*) A perfectionist, Tilden believed his loss to Johnston in the 1919 National Championship was due to a major flaw in his game—a weak back-hand. After spending the winter months developing an attacking backhand in Providence, Rhode Island, he returned to competitive play with one of the most potent weapons in the game of tennis. Photograph by Edwin Levick, Davis Cup Album, 1924, William M. Fisher Lawn Tennis Collection, Courtesy of St. John's University Archive and Special Collections, Queens, New York.

FIG 7. Tilden shocked the sports world in the spring of 1920 when he defeated the brawny Australian Gerald Patterson at Wimbledon. In becoming the first American-born player to win the title as "world champion," the tall Philadelphian with the all-around game and odd mannerisms became an instant celebrity. Photograph by Edwin Levick, Davis Cup Album, 1920, William M. Fisher Lawn Tennis Collection, Courtesy of St. John's University Archive and Special Collections, Queens, New York.

FIG 8. Despite enduring a career-threatening injury and partial amputation of a finger in 1922, Tilden would relearn how to grip the racket and perfect his strokes. Opponents were awestruck by his amazing collection of drives, spins, drop shots, and lobs. Photograph by Edwin Levick, Davis Cup Album, 1926, William M. Fisher Lawn Tennis Collection, Courtesy of St. John's University Archive and Special Collections, Queens, New York.

FIG 9. (*above*) Though he could pound forehands the way Dempsey threw punches and cover ground like Jim Thorpe, Tilden's natural grace and athleticism often had him in flight like a grass-court Nijinsky. Photograph by Edwin Levick, Davis Cup Album, 1920, William M. Fisher Lawn Tennis Collection, Courtesy of St. John's University Archive and Special Collections, Queens, New York.

FIG 10. (*opposite*) William Johnston was unimposing physically, but he was a tenacious court warrior who was blessed with the most feared forehand in the game. His sparkling play and straight-set defeat of Tilden for the U.S. Singles Championship in 1919 confirmed his stature as a fan favorite. Special Collections Research Center, Temple University Libraries, Philadelphia.

FIG 11. (*above*) "Little Bill" Johnston was twice national singles champion and possessed a whiplash forehand, but by 1920 Big Bill Tilden becomes the dominant name in the game. Johnston and Tilden wave to supporters as they sail off for the 1920 Davis Cup match against Australia. Photograph by Edwin Levick, Davis Cup Album, 1920, William M. Fisher Lawn Tennis Collection, Courtesy of St. John's University Archive and Special Collections, Queens, New York.

FIG 12. (*opposite top*) More feared than the New York Yankees' Murderers Row, the U.S. Davis Cup team of Tilden, R. Norris Williams, Vincent Richards, and Bill Johnston during the 1920s established a reign of success that remains unequaled. Photograph by Edwin Levick, Davis Cup Album, 1923, William M. Fisher Lawn Tennis Collection, Courtesy of St. John's University Archive and Special Collections, Queens, New York.

FIG 13. (*opposite bottom*) Though a major celebrity, Tilden volunteered his time to manage the affairs of the Belfry Club at Germantown Academy. Tilden directed as well as starred in a number of the drama club's productions during the 1920s. Alexander "Sandy" Wiener, on Tilden's left, impressed all as both a thespian and an athlete. Courtesy of the Germantown Academy Archive.

FIG 14. (*opposite*) A man of many interests, Tilden was captivated by the dramatic arts and pursued career opportunities as an actor, playwright, and producer throughout the 1920s. Here he is pictured from one of his theatrical roles in October 1926. Permission of *Philadelphia Inquirer*. Copyright 2016. All rights reserved.

FIG 15. (*above*) With an interest in the theatrical arts and a sports hero, Tilden was a natural for Hollywood's burgeoning film industry. Pictured here from a scene in a midtwenties silent film, Tilden often arranged his tennis schedule so that he could take advantage of stage and screen opportunities in various cities across the country. Special Collections Research Center, Temple University Libraries, Philadelphia.

FIG 16. Tilden was a star among stars, and Hollywood royalty gravitated to his side. Pictured here in some freewheeling tennis play alongside Tilden are Charlie Chaplin, Douglas Fairbanks, Mary Pickford, Spanish player Manuel Alonso, and tennis protégé Sandy Wiener. Courtesy of the Richard Hillway Tennis Collection.

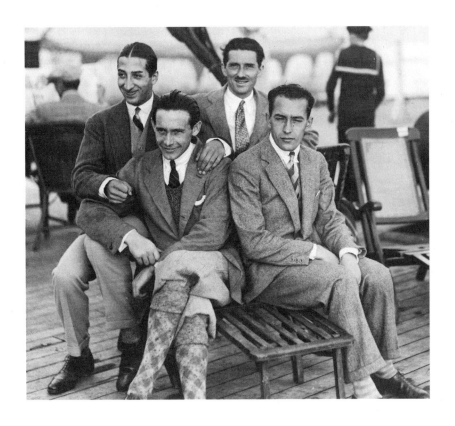

FIG 17. After years of disappointment France marshaled a quartet of exceptional players in the late twenties to challenge America's dominance on the court. Pictured here are the French Musketeers (front) Jean Borotra and Henri Cochet as well as (rear) René Lacoste and Jacques Brugnon. Courtesy of the Richard Hillway Tennis Collection.

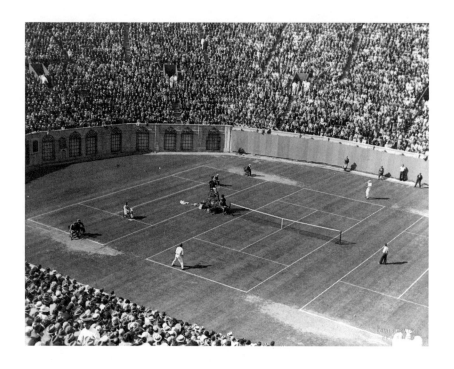

FIG 18. The football-like stadium of the West Side Tennis Club in New York City was the largest tennis facility in America. Thousands routinely turned out to watch "Big Bill" do battle with the game's greats, such as this match against French Musketeer René Lacoste. Photograph by Edwin Levick, Davis Cup Album, 1927, William M. Fisher Lawn Tennis Collection, Courtesy of St. John's University Archive and Special Collections, Queens, New York.

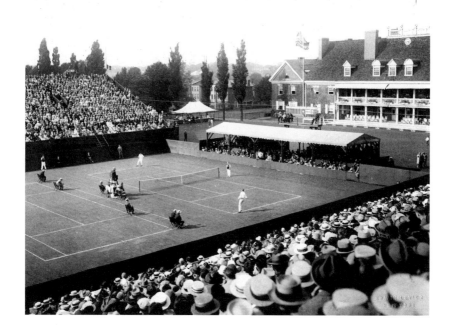

FIG 19. Designed in the late nineteenth century by the nation's premier architectural firm, the Germantown Cricket Club would become one of the world's great cathedrals of tennis and host numerous national and Davis Cup championships. In this 1926 match Tilden is competing against French star René Lacoste. Photograph by Edwin Levick, Davis Cup Album, 1926, William M. Fisher Lawn Tennis Collection, Courtesy of St. John's University Archive and Special Collections, Queens, New York.

FIG 20. (*above*) After more than a decade as the world's most famous amateur tennis player and years of contentious relations with the USLTA, Tilden finally signed a motion-picture contract in December 1930. The act made him a professional. It also triggered the immediate growth of a pro tennis circuit. Pictured alongside Bill at the contract signing is Major Edward Bowes of Metro-Goldwyn-Mayer. Courtesy of the Richard Hillway Tennis Collection.

FIG 21. (*opposite top*) Helen Wills and Tilden watch Davis Cup action at Forest Hills in 1926. Practically unbeatable, Wills and Tilden were America's premier male and female tennis players during the "golden age of sports." Courtesy of the Richard Hillway Tennis Collection.

FIG 22. (*opposite bottom*) Clowning for journalists, two icons of the "golden age of sports" display their trademark weapons in this January 1934 photo. Jack Dempsey's career ended in the late 1920s, but Tilden continued to compete at the highest levels for many years. Courtesy of the Richard Hillway Tennis Collection.

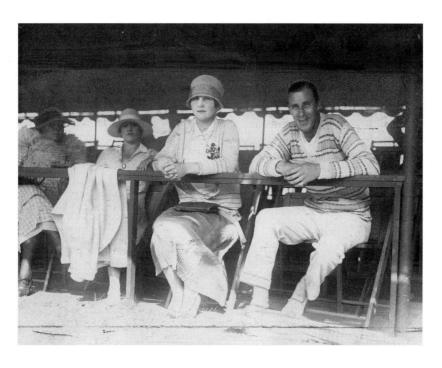

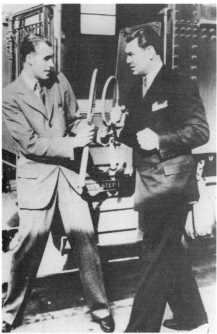

FIG 23. Hollywood stars with an athletic bent stood in line waiting for an opportunity to play a few games against Tilden. One of the film colony's best athletes and most competitive players was Mickey Rooney. Courtesy of the Richard Hillway Tennis Collection.

FIG 24. Tilden and young German star Cilly Aussem were the subject of marital gossip in numerous tabloids and broadsheets in 1930. Though Tilden may have been pleased by the engagement rumors, Aussem was less thrilled and pooh-poohed such talk as silly. Permission of *Philadelphia Inquirer*.

FIG 25. Both young and old in the motion-picture industry gravitated to "Big Bill" for tennis lessons. Pictured here are Skip Homeier and Joan Carroll, young studio actors excited to be getting key tips from the world's most famous tennis player. Courtesy of the Richard Hillway Tennis Collection.

FIG 27. (*above*) Errol Flynn, one of Hollywood's most dashing leading men, was a fine athlete and tennis player. He and Tilden played often and supported each other's charity events. This 1946 fund-raiser also featured John Nogrady and Vince Richards. Special Collections Research Center, Temple University Libraries, Philadelphia.

FIG 28. (*opposite top*) Tilden was arrested in November 1946 and charged with contributing to the delinquency of a minor. Numerous news articles and photos—as with this one showing Bill in handcuffs—illuminated the sports icon's fall from grace. Courtesy of the Associated Press.

FIG 29. (*opposite bottom*) Tilden could have declared his innocence, mounted a vigorous defense, and probably won the case, according to some observers, but he chose a less confrontational path. Here he is pictured in jail consulting with his Hollywood attorney Richard Maddox. Courtesy of the Associated Press/Harold Filan.

FIG 30. A gifted athlete with a curious and creative mind who enjoyed everything from writing books and challenging games of bridge to performing
onstage and listening to Italian opera, Bill Tilden, it can be argued, was as close
to a Renaissance man as the American athletic community ever produced. Courtesy of Allen M. Hornblum.

ridiculous statement. All Billy needs is a rest of six months, a change of thought, a lot of relaxation and he will return the same brilliant star he has always been."[58]

There would be other Tilden-authored articles in the news during the last months of 1923, including several that would have severe bite and underscore the increasingly troubled relationship between the United States Lawn Tennis Association and the organization's most famous player. The dustup originated at the Davis Cup challenge against Australia when Harold Hackett, a member of the Davis Cup committee, took it upon himself to offer some advice to Bill after the third-set rest period. At the time the American team was losing and obviously struggling. Hackett believed Tilden's play was the cause and suggested some tactical changes.

Sensitive to a fault regarding criticism, Bill resented the notion that he, of all people, needed direction on a tennis court. Although the play of the Tilden-Williams duo would improve and they would win the match, it did not end the hostilities. In a series of dueling articles that ran in *American Lawn Tennis* and the *New York Times*, both men took after each other. Hackett was no dub; he was an accomplished player who had won four U.S. Doubles Championships and had helped bring home the Davis Cup from England in 1913. "I am one of the great majority," admitted Hackett, "who consider Tilden not only the greatest singles player of his time, but of all time: still his doubles game is quite another matter for he absolutely fails to understand the great fundamental of the doubles game which is position play." In a line that would receive considerable coverage in the press—and greatly offend Bill—Hackett concluded that Tilden's subpar play showcased "the fact that he chose to park his intelligence outside the stadium during the doubles match" and nearly cost America the Cup.

Insulted that he should be lectured to in such a matter—and publicly no less—Tilden fired back that he was asked to play the right court, a position he did not normally play, and that he and Dick Williams had been given only two days' notice they would be the American doubles team. Moreover, he was going to bring the issue before the next USLTA meeting and strongly considering quitting the Davis Cup team.

In fact, as Arthur Voss points out, there were enough blame and questionable decision making to go around.[59] If Tilden was such an unschooled doubles player, which was untrue, why did they choose him in the first place? Williams could have played with Watson Washburn, his normal doubles partner, and leave Bill his already difficult assignment of playing two singles matches. For Bill's part, he could have been a little less sensitive about being on the receiving end of advice and criticism. Granted, he was the world's best player, but did that make him incapable of error?

The flare-up between player and USLTA official eventually fizzled out— America retained the Davis Cup, and as the three-time winner Big Bill took possession of the American singles trophy—but the relationship between the association and its star player would become increasingly bitter and foster a series of nasty clashes. While one was trying to adapt to a quickly evolving sports scene and a popular culture predicated on strong commercial and professional influences, the other was wedded to an increasingly outdated nineteenth-century ethic that valued amateurism and tradition over all else. Conflict was destined to become a key aspect of their relationship.

8

"Evil Influence"

To present to the foremost player of all the world
the alternative of ceasing to write or to play is so
unexpected and stunning an action that it can be
regarded only as a calamity. To put a period to
Tilden's endeavors in either is almost unthinkable.

—S. WALLIS MERRIHEW

Tilden would begin the 1924 calendar year just as he had the year before: he was ranked America's best tennis player in both singles and doubles. He probably derived even more pleasure, however, from the fact that the USLTA now included categories for juniors and boys in their national rankings—a concept he originated—and that in addition to Vinnie Richards, three of his young pupils had made the list. Carl Fischer, one of his first students, was ranked seventh best in the men's division, Sandy Wiener was number three in the boys division, and Arnold W. Jones was third in the New England section of the national rankings.[1]

Despite overcoming a significant physical impediment in 1923 that threatened to end his athletic career, and a host of worthy foes who hoped to topple him and claim his throne, Tilden not only survived but was believed by many to have become even greater. As satisfying as those triumphs may have been, he was now confronted with another challenge that was every bit as imposing: a sustained bureaucratic broadside designed to sever him from the game he so loved.

The issue that would stalk Tilden throughout the decade had its origin just four days into the new year, when the *New York Times* carried a story detailing a cadre of influential elders inside the USLTA "determined to put an end to the practice of tennis players writing tennis articles for newspapers and magazines for which they receive substantial sums of money." It was their belief the practice had metastasized into a concerted "evil, jeopardizing the future of the players engaged in the practice as well as the good name of the game."[2]

As the *Times* article made clear, if the Amateur Rules Committee's resolution passed muster with the Executive Committee, the USLTA was prepared to severely punish "any player engaged in such practices and receiving substantial compensation" for writing tennis articles. An individual performing such an act, the organization argued, was clearly "not an amateur." Few knowledgeable observers of tennis at the time doubted the traditionalists behind "the big effort" had the numbers to carry out their plan.

The committee trumpeted their belief that the game was under attack. They told reporters there were "certain definite abuses which are beginning to creep into the game of tennis in this country which, and if not stopped promptly, will spoil and ultimately ruin this noblest and most glorious of all games as an amateur sport."[3]

The USLTA stated they were not opposed to players with legitimate professions writing articles about the game, but they "did not approve of any player making what amounts to a living out of writing tennis articles in connection with playing tennis." It was the introduction of significant "money-making or commercialism into the game" that was causing "grave concern and alarm." Anyone who was devoting all his time to tennis—playing it, writing about it, and making a significant wage from it—was not an amateur.

The association admitted that policing the world of tennis was easier in earlier years, when "tennis was a game among the leisure class and the lines of demarcation clear and well-defined." Players then were either of "the leisure class or a toiler." But with the passage of time the game had grown, more people were playing, and it was no longer the preserve of the upper class. And that presented a serious challenge. As E. Digby Baltzell observed, "As the proportion of independently wealthy players declined, amateurism may very well have been doomed."[4] People, the USLTA understood, have to work for a living, but that presented a problem. They did not want them earning a living based on their success as a tennis player.

Obviously, those with the biggest names in the sport, holders of the most titles, and those with the greatest name recognition were the ones of interest to news syndicates. And, of course, the greatest, most recognizable name was that of William T. Tilden 2nd. It was apparent to practically everyone that the USLTA and its star attraction were on a collision course.

Tilden wasted little time: he replied the very next day. He said the resolution was "drastic and the game probably would suffer more through the loss of tennis articles by men who know the game than it would gain by the restriction."[5] Whether he was playing a shrewd defensive gambit or just extremely naive, Tilden went on to argue that the resolution would not personally impact him. "I do not see how it can affect me," said Bill with a straight face, "as I was doing newspaper work three years before I competed in the national championships, and I have written continuously for newspapers and magazines, and have written books." Writing and journalism, he would further argue, were "honorable and recognized vocations," and the use of his name should not be prohibited since he did his own writing and had been doing so for quite some time.

The following day, on January 6, an article on George W. Wightman's probable appointment as the new president of the USLTA at the group's forty-third annual conclave in New York devoted an equal amount of ink on controversial agenda items that were predicted to make the meeting "one of the most eventful ever held."[6] Initiatives to rein in players paid to write articles and players receiving travel expenses to and from tournaments and expenses incurred during tournaments would be the focus of attention.

Prominently situated right next to the Wightman article at the top of the *Times* sports section was another article entitled "U.S. Olympic Athletes May Be Barred from Writing Articles on 1924 Games." Whether sparked by the actions of the USLTA or their own concern of financial improprieties by track-and-field athletes, the American Olympic Committee expressed its intent to prohibit American athletes from writing newspaper articles. Supporters of the ban vigorously argued that athletes needed to train, not waste time writing articles. Moreover, it was argued, most of the athletes "have no fitness for writing, few being trained along such lines, and it is evident that they are employed almost solely for the use of their names."[7]

Clearly, a tipping point had arrived for members of the affluent old guard in both tennis and the Olympic sports. Just days into the new year, 1924 was rapidly becoming one of those seminal years when long-simmering issues crystallized, at least with respect to amateurism versus professionalism in sports. For some hard-liners, action needed to be taken.

Part of their angst had to do with the swiftly moving socioeconomics surrounding athletics in America. Lawn tennis, a leisurely pastime of the well-to-do, was quickly becoming big business. They were on to something, but it was a revolutionary commercial tsunami they could not hold back, though they did not realize it at the time.

The 1920s would eventually become known as the golden age of sports. Iconic names such as Dempsey, Ruth, Grange, Jones, Cobb, Hornsby, Paddock, Gehrig, Hagen, Leonard, and many others sparked images of unprecedented and superhuman athletic accomplishment. Their dramatic triumphs—and the gate receipts they spurred—propelled investment in huge stadiums; the emergence of new careers such as promoters, publicists, and sports agents; as well as increased newspaper and magazine sales.[8] There was no shortage of commercial opportunities for a sports-crazed nation anxious to keep abreast of the exploits of their favorite athletic heroes.

Tilden was one of those iconic figures and arguably at the top of the heap, for his notoriety was international. Tennis was played around the world and quickly increasing in popularity. The game of tennis, however, was controlled by a well-heeled eastern elite that was wedded to ancient notions of amateur play. They disapproved of any form of professionalism in sports and especially shunned the prospect of rapidly advancing commercial opportunities in tennis.

As a birthright member of the well-bred, privileged class, Tilden had long shared many of their values. Though sports entrepreneurs promising big bucks to turn pro would often solicit him, Bill always rebuffed them. "Personally, I have no interest in professional tennis and never have had," Bill would write in an early autobiography. "I play tennis because I enjoy it. I get a great thrill out of hitting the ball. I love the game. It is sport for me, and as long as it remains so, I will play. Professional tennis is a business and I do not care for that kind of business. To me sport and business do not mix."[9]

Bill did not begrudge athletes the caliber of Ruth, Dempsey, Grange, and Hagen capitalizing on their reputations and athletic prowess, but it wasn't for him. He had imbibed the cultural proclivities of his family's social milieu and literally grew up on the grounds of the exclusive Germantown Cricket Club, just a few short yards from the Tilden residence. Bill believed Manheim was a "typical conservative club of the elite" and took itself and its social position quite seriously. In fact, one could say dues-paying members luxuriated in an air of superiority during this "amateur age of innocence," as E. Digby Baltzell referred to it. It is true that Bill was always uncomfortable with the snooty, patronizing attitudes of upper-class Philadelphians, but their belief in amateur play, sportsmanship, and honor became bedrock principles of his. As Baltzell has written, "Tilden was obsessed with honor and sportsmanship." His "flamboyant moralism" was displayed on the court as often as his tamper tantrums. It was not unusual to witness him throw a point, game, or even a set during a match because of what he perceived as an egregious call by a linesman or umpire. A "moral despot," according to Baltzell, Bill knew right from wrong regarding the game of tennis, and, furthermore, he believed he was good for the game.[10]

But that opinion was not universally shared. Tilden's strident attitudes, constant prodding, unprecedented demands, and occasionally outrageous court behavior irritated key members of the USLTA. They could knock him down a peg as well as take a stand against creeping commercialism in the game by adopting an aggressive position on tennis players earning money from writing newspaper and magazine articles. The new player-writer sanction was a dagger pointed at Bill's pocketbook, if not his heart. "When it was necessary to call a spade a spade he did not hesitate," said Edward C. Potter, who has written about Tilden's independent streak. "They attempted to silence Tilden by making a rule aimed, ostensibly, at all player-writers but worded in such a way that it affected scarcely any one but him."[11]

Bill burned through money rather quickly. His father's death in 1915 left him with a tidy sum, but it was not nearly as substantial as rumored. He took periodic jobs in subsequent years as a newspaper reporter, sporting-goods salesman, and insurance agent, but his real profession was tennis player. After winning both American and British titles in 1920, his inheritance nearly gone and only tournament hardware to show for his physical labor, Bill needed the money his tennis articles brought in. Without the income from the syndication of his tennis articles, he would be in very dire straits financially.

There were a few other prominent tennis players, most noteworthy Vinnie Richards, who also published newspaper articles. Richards's articles, however—at least in the early years—were ghostwritten for him. The practice of news reporters ghosting for top jocks was widespread and growing at the time. Vinnie, a great young player but of modest means, appreciated the income. The money allowed him to play tennis full-time. His articles, written by Edward Sullivan (decades later known to the general public as Ed Sullivan, the television impresario), were very much depended on for his economic sustenance.

Though others may have been involved in the practice, most observers saw the USLTA's initiative for what it was, an effort to control, if not punish, the game's greatest player. W. O. M'Geehan, one of the leading sportswriters of the day, saw the USLTA restriction as "a bit far reaching" and mocked the group by imagining what such a rule would have done to other famous part-time writers in history such as Caesar and Xenophon.[12]

M'Geehan was not alone in viewing the association's action as a direct assault on the game's greatest personality. "It is manifest that the resolution is aimed chiefly at Tilden," argued Perry Lewis of the *Philadelphia Inquirer*. "The fact of the matter is William T. Tilden has a mind of his own, a fine sense of proportion and sportsmanship. He would voluntarily sacrifice anything that he felt in his own mind offended the finest ideals of amateur sport, but he will not be dictated to by any man or group of men when he is convinced that such dictation is unnecessary."[13] As Lewis added, "There are evils in amateur athletics sufficient to keep all officials busy, real evils which should be stamped out. It would be well if those in charge would turn their energies toward that end, and cease trying to regulate the private enterprises of athletes who have done more for athletics on the playing field than has ever been done in committee rooms."

Richard Hillway has studied the game and its top players for years and has little doubt Tilden was the true target of the USLTA action, or "the storm center," as the *Philadelphia Public Ledger* phrased it.[14] "It was very personal," says Hillway. "The organization used that rule to put Tilden in his place. They wanted to control him."

"Bill never liked authority figures," says Hillway.

He rebelled against authority. He was very vocal, sure of his opinions, and wrote a lot. No one did as much to foster the growth and popularity of tennis as Tilden, but he wouldn't keep quiet. Moreover, he was always pushing the USLTA to do more, hold more events, do more for young players, and provide American players the money to go abroad and play in foreign tournaments. He was a constant thorn in their side. The Association was not following any international standard when it created the player-writer rule. It appears that only the United States of all the countries tried to keep players from writing at the time.[15]

Very few players were bold enough to speak up at the time about the new rule. One of them was Carl Fischer. "The sport alone will lose by forbidding players who know it to write about it," said Fischer. Not only does Tilden know the game, argued Fischer, one of the champ's former pupils, but "his name over a story . . . assures a large percentage of extra readers who may thus become interested in the game."[16]

Tilden's contributions were not lost on the many who were left scratching their heads at the USLTA's initiative. "Big Bill has done more for tennis," wrote one commentator, "than any man in the game today. He has taken countless hours from his business to teach boys the finer points of the game; he has always been ready and willing to go into schools and recreation centers to spread the gospel of tennis."[17]

Bill's endless proselytizing over the years resulted in numerous examples where his efforts to spread the gospel of tennis had won adherents to the game or kept wavering supporters from leaving. Bill himself, in a "Passing Shots" column, noted a letter he had received from Mr. Rastam Nagarwala of St. Xavier's College, India, who was so frustrated at his own lack of progress that he was about to give up the sport. It was then that he came across one of Tilden's books. Its revelations, claimed Nagarwala, "lifted the veil off my eyes. I vainly looked for a speck of light to raise me up and God sent me help."[18]

Tilden used the letter to underscore the importance of his literary contributions. "Here is a player," said Tilden, "who really feels that my writing helped him. If that is so, I believe I have done the game a real service, one of greater value than any injury, which it may receive because a few people object to a monetary return being paid me for my writing. It gives me courage to go on writing, even though it may cost me my amateur standing, a ridiculously high price to pay to help the game, but still worth it, if by so doing I can develop interest and improve players."

Tilden completed his "Passing Shots" column by writing, "The whole sports world has gone mad on legislation," but everyone should remember that "the whole object of sport is to play it for the game's sake and remember that players are sportsmen at heart who are engaged in their sport for amusement and not with any ulterior motive. Cannot the tennis world," he asked, "lead the way to a finer, freer cooperation and understanding by more play and less legislation?"[19]

The answer, at least from the nation's major tennis association's point of view, was a resounding no. In mid-January the California Lawn Tennis Association endorsed "the proposed change in the rules to bar amateurs from commercializing their tennis ability by writing for newspapers for money."[20] Dr. Sumner Hardy, the state association president, and no friend of Tilden's, wasted little time in getting his large group behind the national association's movement.

A week later the Philadelphia and District Tennis Association went on record. They "voiced their disapproval of the proposed amendment to bar tennis players from writing for the daily press."[21] Standing up for the hometown hero and in opposition to the will of national leadership, more than three dozen Philly-area tennis clubs said they weren't buying it. The fact that a player wrote newspaper articles did not make him a professional.

Another Tilden ally was the nation's best-known tennis magazine and its widely respected publisher. S. Wallis Merrihew, the founder and driving force of *American Lawn Tennis*, found the entire affair mind-boggling. In a pointed editorial entitled "A World Astonished," Merrihew wrote, "Opposition to the new amateur rule grows daily and our apprehension as to the results of the policy adopted has increased enormously."

Admittedly perplexed by the USLTA's action, he wrote, "It defies understanding how anyone can contend that writing about lawn tennis makes a professional of a player?" If Tilden should continue writing articles after the January 1, 1925, deadline set by the association, asked Merrihew, would that make him a professional? "A professional what?" Merrihew pointedly asked. "A professional lawn tennis player? He does not receive one penny for playing lawn tennis, but his playing does bring many thousands of dollars into the coffers of the clubs for which he plays."[22]

In a subsequent *ALT* editorial entitled "It Could Have Been Avoided," Merrihew published an even stronger commentary regarding the USLTA's heavy-handed approach in dealing with tennis players who wrote about the game. "It is inconceivable," wrote Merrihew, "that the governing body of the game in this country which is the champion nation in the Davis Cup competition and admittedly the premier nation in a playing sense, should wantonly jeopardize its intent—the casting out of the amateur ranks of men who have done the most to establish the position referred to." Furthermore, said Merrihew, "We oppose the legislation which has come to be known as the writer-player interpretation because we hold that no principle is involved, no less than because its enforcement would deprive the world of the privilege of watching the foremost player of all time."[23]

Merrihew's recurring broadsides against the game's parent organization could not have endeared him to USLTA officials and policy makers. Neither did the realization that they had sown considerable discord in the ranks of the American tennis establishment, not to mention the many critical articles now appearing in the press. Their one concession, however, was postponing until January 1, 1925, the Damocles sword falling on violators of the amateur rule in an effort to allow current contracts with newspaper syndicates to expire.

Tilden was unimpressed by the gesture and remained wedded to his proclamation that he would sooner quit playing tennis than concede to an elitist group dictating wholly unreasonable and arbitrary rules and regulations. He proved his mettle on that score by announcing on March 12 that he had formally withdrawn his name as a member of the U.S. Olympic team scheduled to participate in the upcoming Paris Olympics.[24] Olympic officials showed no interest in compromise, and Tilden expressed little regret that he would not be going overseas. It should be noted that his last trip abroad, especially to Paris and London in 1921, resulted in an impressive cache of trophies, but the toll on his health was the dominant recollection.

Tilden had recently been granted an audience before the USLTA's Executive Committee to plead his case, but no action was taken. The committee appeared wary of the significant blowback that would arise if they banned Bill from amateur tennis matches. They used the excuse that the new rule would not go into effect until 1925 to avoid making a decision. It was made clear, however, that if "the same conditions exist then as exist today he would likely be guilty of a violation of the amateur rule."[25]

With both parties seemingly intransigent on the subject, cooler heads urged restraint and sought some form of compromise. The *New York Times*, for example, took note that "Tilden has declared that he places his newspaper work above his playing and now that the tennis authorities have given an opinion that can but lead him to believe that he will have to abandon his journalistic work next year, he may decide on immediate action, particularly in view of the fact that he is barred from playing for this country on the Olympic team if he continues to write."

In an attempt to appease all sides, the *Times* threw a bone to each of the warring parties. "Tilden has just cause for resenting the ruling of the Olympic authorities," the paper stated. "He is under contract to write two articles a week for the year and it is unfair to ask him to break the contract." However, the newspaper went on to concede, "The ruling of the Olympic Committee . . . is to be commended. No coach can expect to get the best results from his charges when they are rushing to the telegraph wire to get off stories instead of looking strictly after their training." The *Times* editorial concluded, "It is sincerely to be hoped that his case will receive consideration from the authorities and that some way will be found to make it possible for him to fill his contract and still play for the United States."[26]

Interestingly, in the midst of the heated debate over the player-writer rule, what should appear on bookstands throughout America—Tilden's latest book. Destined to become a classic, *Match Play and Spin of the Ball* was a concise, pithy primer on every aspect of the game. In addition to Merrihew's excellent account of Bill's life, the book delved into such topics as footwork, racket grip, court strategy, intensive practice, and pace versus speed, with each issue given its own chapter, but the importance of spin was the central element of the book. Tilden would argue that spin was more important than speed in controlling an opponent and winning a match.

Tilden was convinced that few players "consciously think about spin in their game, for the great majority of tennis players are not students of the game. It is the love of study of tennis that has led me to the point where I never hit a shot without a conscious application of twist or the deliberate attempt to use none. I believe that only by so doing can the greatest results be obtained."[27]

Though application of spin on a shot was not in and of itself revolutionary, Tilden's use of it was bewildering—especially to opponents—and his written comments on the subject were equally novel. For example, "Let me suggest the ball for a moment as an individual" was the intriguing opening line of his new treatise. "It is the third party in the match. Will this third party be on your side or against you? It is up to you." The grand master went on to assure his readers that with knowledge and practice, "The ball will do as it is told."[28]

Though the book's many interesting stories and recommendations were packaged in a tidy, digestible manner, they were derived from many years of practice, experimentation, and further practice. No one put more time in on-court evaluation of the nuances and possibilities of the game than Tilden. Eagle-eyed readers of the book also took note of something else. The book's many photographs of top players such as Johnston, Richards, Williams, Cochet, Lacoste, Shimidzu, and Alonso demonstrating specific strokes were helpful, but those of the author himself disclosed a remarkable and much-speculated-on curiosity: Big Bill's mangled finger. Written and published after his hospitalization, the photographs of Tilden demonstrating proper racket grip graphically revealed the unsightly damage done by his debilitating battle with blood poisoning and a surgeon's scalpel. The ugly remnant of a finger was clearly visible for those in search of the missing appendage.

Back in the court of public opinion, the war between the game's greatest player and its leading organizing authority went on unabated. In fact, it was increasing in acrimony. The last two weeks of April, for example, were particularly bitter. Newspaper headlines across the country underscored the worsening relations: a problematic relationship had become downright toxic.

In an effort to bolster their position and further damage Tilden's credibility, the USLTA's Amateur Rule Committee made public private documents disclosing Bill's business arrangements with various newspaper syndicates. One document stated that Bill "signed a twelve month contract calling for one 800 word mail letter per week until May 1, two 800 word mail letters per week from May 1 to Oct. 1, and daily wire dispatches covering the 1924 Davis Cup interzone and challenge round matches and the national singles, doubles, and clay court championships. The release price for each article is $2 and the circular states that there will be approximately 100 releases."[29]

The committee went on to surmise that the arrangement would "pay the syndicate $20,000 . . . and if our present champion is half as good a business man as he is a tennis player, his emolument is most likely a very substantial one." Holcombe Ward, a former national champion and no friend of Bill's, released the damaging report. In his press statement he threw in the additional taunt that a true amateur "is one who plays the game solely for the pleasure and physical benefits he derives from it. Can the playing of tennis," Ward asked, "be nothing more than a pastime to a tennis champion whose widely advertised business is tennis writing? Hasn't he turned his tennis pastime into a real business?"

The upshot for the Amateur Rule Committee, and its parent organization, was "the harm that can be worked by a player of prominence violating the amateur rule in setting an example to younger players, declaring that it is a far more serious injury to tennis than is the violation of a rule of the game such as the foot-fault rule." Ward went on to state:

> If these evils which we are attempting to curb really are evils, then the man who holds the position of champion of the United States should be the one to take the leadership in maintaining our amateur standards. . . . [H]e should be more scrupulous than any lesser light in tennis to observe both the letter or spirit of our amateur rule. For if he infringes the letter or spirit of our amateur rule, he can do more damage to our amateur standards than any other player on account of his pre-eminence as a player and as a writer.[30]

For Bill, who had spent a good portion of his life preaching the benefits of tennis at every recreation center, school auditorium, hamlet, and town that could in any way justify his appearance, the accusation that he gave a bad name to tennis and was a "bad example" for American youth, as a *New York Times* headline framed it, was infuriating. No one in the country, possibly the world, had devoted more time encouraging young people to take up tennis and adopt its bedrock principles of sportsmanship, honor, and amateur play. He had no doubt that the USLTA's attack that he was an "evil" influence on the game was personal, blatant, and ludicrous. The association's charges were more than a warning shot across the bow for Tilden; they were a direct assault upon his good name, a total disregard of his past efforts to build the sport, and a brazen effort to finally silence him.

Others shared that view. The *Philadelphia Inquirer*, one of Bill's hometown newspapers, headlined their story "Player-Writer Rule Focused on Tilden." The article claimed, as many newspaper stories across the country would, that the USLTA's effort to punish Tilden had backfired, drawing "widespread criticism" and "condemnation" on themselves, thereby forcing the organization's Amateur Rule Committee to release what they hoped would be perceived as damaging information about Tilden's business affairs. As the article went on to suggest, "If the USLTA sticks by its guns, as it probably will, and Bill Tilden, the greatest player of all time and a man who has done more for the advancement of the game than any single individual, is lost to the sport, after this year, the syndicate manager who constructed this letter and others must shoulder no small part of the blame."[31]

Less than forty-eight hours later Tilden fired back: he announced his resignation from the U.S. Davis Cup and Olympic teams. The unexpected announcement startled the sporting world and "created a sensation in tennis circles." The announcement became the lead item in newspaper sports sections around the nation. In his letter to Julian S. Myrick, chairman of the Davis Cup Committee and former USLTA president, Tilden wrote, "I learn with astonishment that the player-writer in general and I, in particular, am regarded . . . as not only no longer an amateur, but as an evil influence in the game. Since it is inconceivable that the association would desire the presence on the Olympic or Davis Cup squads for 1924 of such an 'evil influence,' I, although I do not for a moment concede either the fairness or correctness of the committee's interpretation of the amateur rule or of my standing there under, tender to you my resignation as a member of both squads." Tilden completed his letter with the slightest of openings for a potential resolution by stating he was resigning "with regret, but self-respect compels me to do so. I wish you and the committee to know that my services are at your disposal when my amateur status is clearly recognized."[32]

Caught off-guard by Bill's surprising action, USLTA leaders were either unavailable for comment, as was Julian Myrick, or, as Holcombe Ward was quoted in the press, "sorry" to learn of Tilden's decision. There can be little doubt that those out to publicly embarrass Tilden were now wondering if they had kneecapped themselves. Instead of Tilden being on the defensive, it was the USLTA that was coming under fire. Even the lengthy *New York Times* article covering the latest developments in the player-writer imbroglio admitted that Tilden's absence from amateur competition

> will rob [Davis Cup] challenge round matches of a great deal of interest. As the world's greatest player he is perhaps the leading drawing card in the game not only because of his prowess but also because of his personality, which has been a source of interest wherever he has played. At Wimbledon, where he won the world's championship in 1920 and 1921, and in Australia where he regained the Davis Cup with Johnston in 1920, the tall, elongated Philadelphia was the centre of interest, enthralling the spectators with the wizardry of his play and entertaining them at the same time.[33]

It was clear to some observers that Tilden had commandeered the high ground in the battle for moral superiority and public approval. The USLTA's oligarchs were on their heels. They never had to deal with a principled but irascible prima donna before. Players previously—no matter their athletic stature or social bearing—had complied with the association's desires and dictates. Tilden, however, was a totally other matter. He would not be dictated to; he could not be controlled.

Like those at the *Times*, other news reporters and editors were taking note of the increasingly venomous relations in the usually demure and ever-so-proper world of amateur tennis. Many newspaper columns trumpeted Bill's righteous stand. In a *Philadelphia Inquirer* story headlined "Tilden Outwitted U.S. Net Solons," Perry Lewis, obviously impressed, wrote, "When William T. Tilden 2nd went in for tennis and literature a great statesman and politician was lost to the nation."[34]

From his perspective as a beat writer who had covered sports for many years, Tilden was a refreshing voice. He had dedicated himself to taking lawn tennis out of exclusive country clubs and bringing it to the nation's playgrounds and neighborhood rec centers. "For many years, Tilden, a progressive devoted to the democracy of the courts and therefore abhor-ring all Star Chamber proceedings," Lewis wrote, "has been in conflict with those who controlled the governing body in this country. Fearlessly, he fought them at every point when he felt that the time had come to fight; he refused to be dictated to, and from beginning to end was a thorn in the sides of his powerful opponents."

Finding it difficult to contain his distaste for the ruling class that ran lawn tennis in America, Lewis wrote that while some were still trying to decide whether the player-writer rule was "an abortion or a blessing," many had made up their mind, and "a storm of criticism" was the result. "The great sporting public of America digested the thing, realized that it was a blow at the champion, their champion, who had made this nation supreme on the courts, and went right after those responsible."

Lewis went on to argue that it was patently obvious that the USLTA had prematurely congratulated themselves on what they considered "a master move" in aggressively going after Tilden. But "their committees overstepped the mark in the business of crushing Tilden." Instead, their heavy-handed approach "proved a huge blunder and the astute Tilden promptly took advantage of it." Making their attack personal, and especially by calling Bill an "evil influence," the USLTA, according to Lewis, had sustained a self-inflicted wound from which they might not ever recover. The champion, Lewis further argued, had responded with "singular clarity." With a "few strokes of his pen he passed the buck to his enemies (for enemies they are and always have been) and placed them on the defensive before the sport lovers of America, who, after all, are the real bosses of tennis. It was a master move."

The majority of the nation's sportswriters were in agreement. Tilden had placed the normally imperious leadership of the USLTA between a rock and a hard place. His "masterly move," as some saw it, not only had "the close corporation which controls the game in this country . . . in an awkward position," but they were now faced with an even worse scenario. If they accepted Tilden's resignation, they would "logically be forced to request the withdrawal of Vincent Richards," another offender of the rule.[35] By cleaning the decks of the nation's first- and fourth-ranked players, would the ship stay afloat in Davis Cup competition against the world's best?

Many believed the USLTA had needlessly placed the nation's tennis dominance in peril, while most tennis fans around the globe were in a state of puzzlement about the entire affair. In England, where the game began, the Tilden-USLTA quarrel over some arcane player-writer controversy "aroused the greatest interest." The British public sided with Tilden; there was a definite "consensus that his amateur status should not be questioned." As one prominent British tennis official remarked, "Writing doesn't make a man a professional, whether he plays or not. It is a good thing for the game to have those who understand it write on the subject. Player-writers have made the game what it is." The British Lawn Tennis Association concurred. According to the group's secretary, "Under our rules players are not regarded as professionals if they write about the game. The public is always ready to hear with interest what first-class exponents have to say, and this is all for the good of the sport."[36]

London newspapers agreed there was serious overreach occurring in the ranks of amateur tennis in America. The *Westminster Gazette* commented, "The purists in this instance have gone much too far. If such a rule were universally applied the public would be cut off from the descriptive and instructive writings of the best exponents of many games, a deprivation which would be seriously resented."[37]

Not all foreign observers were distressed by the squabble. On learning of Big Bill's withdrawal from Davis Cup play, the secretary of the Australian Lawn Tennis Association was heard to cheerfully remark, "Australia's chances to lift the cup were materially enhanced by the development."[38]

Under increasing pressure, Julian S. Myrick, the Davis Cup Committee chairman, was forced to quickly send a letter to Tilden stating, "I was very much surprised to receive your letter" and learn "that you desire to withdraw from the Olympic and Davis Cup squads to relieve the association of embarrassment." Myrick tried to assure him such action was not necessary, nor was it ever the intent of the committee, and he was still "invited to play for your country." Moreover, Myrick requested he join "the committee for dinner" in New York City to discuss the matter further.[39]

Tilden was unimpressed. Reporters who tracked him down at his Hansberry Street home found him resolute in the belief he had been done a great disservice and in no mood to break bread with his offenders. The champ informed newsmen "there was no need to talk." He had no intention of going to Manhattan for a meal and planned to follow through on "a previous engagement to play in exhibition games in the South." In his letter to Myrick Bill wrote he would not have offered his services to the Executive Committee of the USLTA had he been aware of the official wording of the report of the Amateur Rule Committee to the Executive Committee. "Had I had knowledge of the official wording of the report," Tilden wrote, "where-in player-writers are held up as a harmful influence to and an evil in the game, I could not at that time have agreed to play in Davis Cup competition."

Tilden made it clear that "self-respect and a desire to maintain the highest standards of international amateur sport leave me no other course of action but to refuse to play until my amateur status is definitely fixed and clearly recognized by the governing body of tennis. Once my amateur status is established beyond question, it will give me great pleasure to defend the Davis Cup for my country if I am again asked to do so."[40]

Two days later, on April 27, the Davis Cup Committee of the United States Lawn Tennis Association "officially accepted" Tilden's resignation. Committee chairman Myrick, with a straight face, informed the press that this was never the committee's objective. He reminded them that the decision to sanction rule breakers had been postponed: "Enforcement of the player-writer resolution had been held up until January, 1925." When reporters returned to Tilden for his reaction, he had little to say. "This closes the incident so far as I am concerned" was his only comment.

Casual tennis observers but loyal American sports fans were shocked by the rapidly worsening state of affairs. Big Bill was looked upon as the anchor, the "bulwark of this country's tennis hopes." For the average sports fan used to seeing star athletes like Ruth, Dempsey, and Hagen garner increasingly large salaries and stunning financial rewards, the entire episode over some arcane player-writer rule was incomprehensible. Tilden wasn't even a professional; he had not earned any prize money from all his tournament victories. All they truly understood was that the world's best tennis player would no longer be playing for his country.

Vinnie Richards was paying close attention to the ever-darkening skies over American lawn tennis. He was not as big a name as Tilden, nor did he write as much, but he knew he was also in violation of the rule and would probably be next on the hit list. "I can't afford to give up newspaper writing for tennis," he told the press, "so I guess this will be my last year unless the association's attitude is changed. I'm a serious individual nowadays, but my self-respect hardly will permit me to play in the Davis Cup matches. If I am to be declared a professional next January for writing I must be considered one now."[41]

With the amateur lawn tennis scene in disarray, sports entrepreneurs were quick to sniff out an opportunity. As the *New York Times* reported on April 29, "An outgrowth of the sensational controversy aroused over the prospective disbarment from amateur tennis ranks of William T. Tilden . . . and other player-writers, professional competition among a group of stars possibly headed by Tilden, may be developed in 1925."

It did not take a genius to recognize the commercial opportunities presented to the lucky promoter who signed the world's greatest tennis player to a contract. Tilden was tennis during the 1920s. He could be playing a Fifth Avenue traffic light, and people would pay to see him.

One of the quickest to act was Tex Rickard, the famous boxing promoter, who informed the press he already had "a plan to stage professional play next year, when the new player-writer rule of the United States Lawn Tennis Association goes into effect." Rickard expressed his confidence that professional tennis would prove popular and lucrative, "provided it attracted players of the top ranking class."[42] He further pointed to the construction of the new Madison Square Garden sports arena in the theater district as a perfect venue for indoor tennis. Baseball parks would be utilized for outdoor competition during the summer.

When asked by the press of his interest in such a proposal, Tilden was noncommittal on the subject. He had always disdained the prospect of professional tennis and informed reporters that "he still considered himself an amateur." Bill still hoped to play in top singles events such as the National Championship. It did not stop businessmen from proffering lucrative opportunities, such as the owner of the ritzy Briarcliff Lodge, who reached out to Bill to work at his facility. The owner assured Tilden that "the inducements we are prepared to offer are commensurate with your standing as the foremost tennis player in the world."[43] Once again Tilden expressed no interest in the offer, stating, "I am not on the market as a professional. I am strongly opposed to professional tennis, and as I have said before, I will remain an amateur until I am forced out."[44]

Vinnie Richards, however, was more inclined to contemplate such options. He said he would consider becoming a professional if he was barred from amateur play and "expressed the belief that the professional game might hold forth unusual opportunities." Richards added that California was producing a large and rich crop of tennis players and might prove "fertile territory for the development of professional play."[45] After some feeble attempts in recent years to establish a semblance of professional tennis in America, the notion seemed to suddenly have legs. Ironically, it was the USLTA, the archenemy of professional tennis, that was providing the boost.

Critics like the *Philadelphia Inquirer*'s Perry Lewis were not shy about leveling blame for what was being seen as an unmitigated disaster. "Evidently the tennis solons who have blundered into this mess and undermined the imposing structure of tennis built by the master hand of Tilden and others," Lewis angrily lectured, "are seeking a way to get from under the storm of public criticism raised by their action. With professional tennis in the offing, and the court prestige of America tottering, the position of the men who are driving the best players in the world off the American courts, isn't a comfortable one."[46]

Their discomfort would only increase, as the following day Richards submitted his resignation from the U.S. Davis Cup squad. As the *New York Times* informed its readers, "The youthful star . . . followed the example of his former mentor," but with an extra dose of bombast. "The time has arrived," Richards stridently declared, "for all tennis players who object to the obnoxious player-writer to come out in the open and unite in taking definite steps to curb the power of the millionaire clique that apparently is striving to make lawn tennis safe for the idle rich."[47]

With pressure building, internal dissatisfaction increasing, and public criticism on the rise, Lewis Carruthers, president of the West Side Tennis Club, announced that a special meeting of the club would be held "to get an expression of the opinion of the members on the player-writer interpretation of the amateur rule."[48] It was a clear sign that the tennis establishment was feeling the heat and willing to take a second look at their controversial policies safeguarding amateur play. And the West Side Tennis Club was not alone: many of the nation's most famous cricket and tennis clubs were now reassessing their position on the controversial rule.

A good many sports fans, including Tilden, were pleased by the development. "I am delighted," said the champ, "to know that a crystallization of sentiment of the tennis public on the player-writer rule seems imminent. I sincerely hope that some way out of the present difficulty in the association will be effected."[49]

Association leaders were not about to concede anything immediately, however. Richards's resignation letter had to be reviewed, and they asked for a meeting with the young star. Richards was amenable but up front in stating he now earned a living writing articles on a variety of sports, "declared journalism his profession," and expected to continue to do so.

In pleading his case, he would go on to argue, "I took up newspaper work as a profession in good faith, when I could have gone into banking or insurance or any other business. It is my livelihood and I will not give it up." Richards said he did not like the accusation that he was deserting his nation in its time of need. He loved playing the Davis Cup and proclaimed, "I would rather cut off my arm than do that, but the rule is wrong. If I am declared a professional I won't play for myself either."

On that last point the disciple was parting company with his mentor. He called Tilden "inconsistent" in saying that he would still play in the championship tournaments but not in the Olympic and Davis Cup matches. "If the Association declares me a professional," said Richards, "I won't play in any tournament. I won't be seen on a court."[50]

When asked by the press if he would consider playing professional tennis if amateur play was denied him, Richards said he was opposed to the pro game. His one last statement concerned the recent experience of Pat O'Hara Wood, a top Australian player who wrote tennis articles for the *Sidney Referee*. When O'Hara Wood inquired of the Australian Lawn Tennis Association if he could write and continue to play the Davis Cup, the association "gave him permission to write as much as he pleased."[51]

By the end of the first week of May developments were occurring so rapidly, it was not unusual to see three or more articles on the player-writer controversy in the same issue of a newspaper. On May 6, for example, the *Times* published articles on Philadelphia tennis clubs rallying to Tilden's aid and a delegation traveling to New York for a high-level powwow with USLTA chieftains, a large group of disaffected West Side Tennis Club members calling for an end to the controversial player-writer rule, and Chuck Garland, a former Davis Cup player, who had changed his position on the rule from opposed to in favor.[52] It was all quite unusual; a little-known and widely misunderstood tennis stipulation had suddenly become a recurring item in the nation's sports sections.

Rich Hillway believes that in an attempt to contain his increasing outrage, it was Tilden who began writing a series of tennis articles in *Sport Magazine* that were authored by someone calling himself P. Laire Riter. Though feeling much put upon by the powers that be, Bill still had a sense of humor.

Many newspaper sports sections were now printing articles that had more to do with questions of philosophy than athletics and columns entitled "Amateurism vs. Wealth" for readers to mull over. George Wightman often found himself being skewered in the press. "The problem Mr. Wightman presents is this," wrote one perplexed pundit. "Shall we be content to bring American tennis to the level of mediocrity, or to develop the game to its very highest notch? If men such as Tilden, Vincent Richards and others who could not devote the time they do to the game save by virtue of their present activities are debarred, then only those who are endowed with money will be able to give to the game that amount of time and attention that are necessary for the highest development." In short, if Wightman and other elitists got their way, "amateurism might well come to connote nothing save wealth," and that "would not be a good thing at all."[53]

Dissatisfaction and turmoil seemed to predominate throughout the comfortable country-club set. Discord replaced the normal pleasantries of who won what tournament and whose backhand had witnessed the most improvement in recent months; tennis commentary had moved from the athletic to the political. You were either for the player-writer rule or against it.

That Tilden should start such an emotional hullabaloo was a surprise to many. Bill was not political. Unlike his father he had never shown an interest in world affairs or national political developments, and his civic engagement focused on visiting groups and communities interested in learning more about the game he loved so much. Ironically, he had now helped spark one of the bitterest political controversies in American tennis history.

Tennis clubs were rife with pro- and anti-Tilden sentiment. The West Side Tennis Club, a hotbed of anti-Tilden sentiment—at least with regard to the club's leadership—was challenged by a disgruntled pro-Tilden faction demanding a recount. A floor vote of 48 to 4 rejected the player-writer section of the amateur rule, and the "room rocked with the roar of applause," only to discover proxies totaled 181 to 155 in favor of the rule. The democratic exercise had only aggravated the situation.[54]

Another player group led by Sam Hardy, Frank Hunter, and other of Bill's friends dispatched a pointed letter to Wightman, Myrick, and Ward with their own accusations: "to what extent tennis officials benefited in a business way through their connection with the game and how such benefits compared with those alleged to have accrued to Tilden, who was no less a writer than they are business men." The incriminating question was a good one, but was never answered. The letter further stated that the players wanted peace, but not at any price. They pledged to "remain loyal to Tilden—one of the finest characters the game ever knew"—to the bitter end, come what may.[55]

A week later President Wightman of the USLTA, exasperated by the constant bickering, infighting, and embarrassing publicity, called for an immediate and special meeting of the association to finally "end the controversy concerning the player-writer interpretation of the amateur rule."[56] Even that rather modest—and long-overdue—proposal proved problematic. Arguing "it was inappropriate that the player-writer rule be discussed publically while we are sending our own representatives to play in foreign countries, and receiving as guests in our own country the players of other nations, some of whom also write for newspapers," a group of eleven current and former "players of prominence" lobbied Wightman to postpone any high-level conclave on the subject. There were a number of well-known names on the letter, but the most significant was right at the top, Maurice E. McLoughlin, the legendary California Comet.[57]

McLoughlin was no stranger to the sanctimonious dictates of USLTA overseers. In 1913, at the height of McLoughlin's fame, the association hit him with similar charges for his connection to a sporting-goods store. Tilden was only twenty at the time and an undistinguished college player who paid little attention to the accusations. Years later he would write of the incident, "Poor Maury, the most charming and impecunious of persons in those days, was held up as an awful example of dire commercialism, which if not stepped upon by the guardians of the game would quickly ruin the game itself."

As a member of the well-bred Manheim elite and a devout defender of amateur sport, Bill never thought he would one day be hit with the same charge. He owned up to the naive belief that "to be a professional tennis player one must perform tennis for money." Despite his innocence on the subject, "the Association, ever zealous, sometimes over-zealous, in its desire to protect the lily-white amateur game of tennis from the smirching feet of filthy lucre, did not see it this way at all."[58] Now it was Bill's turn to face an onslaught of allegations regarding his supposed professionalism.

On June 5 Wightman announced to the press that his previous call for a "special meeting of the Association" to end the player-writer debacle had been scuttled. Wightman said the controversy "had become so intense and clouded with personalities and is occupying so much time of the players and officials throughout the country that the success of the playing season is seriously threatened."[59]

Commentators across the journalistic world were taking well-deserved shots at the USLTA leadership for what they headlined a circus-like "After-You-Alphonse Act." As one *Philadelphia Bulletin* scribe informed his readers, "It will be most unfortunate if this hair-splitting policy continues on both sides. There is still a way out but it depends on more compromising than has yet been done."[60]

Recognizing the damage being done to his own organization and tennis in general, Wightman devised a new gambit, a "special committee" that would fairly and thoroughly examine the issue, make recommendations to the USLTA's Amateur Rule Committee, and then hopefully gain approval of the Executive Committee. The special committee would consist of two members of the Amateur Rule Committee who favored the player-writer rule and two members in opposition of the rule. Those four would then select three additional members to complete the seven-man membership of the Special Committee.

A week later names were attached to the four members who were assigned to tackle "one of the bitterest controversies ever to rise in the lawn tennis world." The two in opposition to the rule were none other than William T. Tilden 2nd and S. Wallis Merrihew.[61] A formidable duo, but their opponents on the committee were Amateur Rule Committee members with an equal number of votes. The selection and appointment of the final three members would be critical to the final decision. Devereux Milburn, captain of the

U.S. International Polo Team; Grantland Rice, one of the nation's most famous sportswriters; and George Wharton Pepper, a constitutional law scholar and U.S. senator from Pennsylvania, were the final three members.

Most important, the establishment of a special committee allowed all sides to step back, take a deep breath, and call a temporary truce to the war of words and recurring waves of embarrassing publicity. Tilden, Richards, and others affected by the player-writer rule would be allowed to play through 1924 while waiting for the committee's recommendations, which were to be delivered before the end of the year. By this point everyone desired a cessation of the unpleasant commotion and a return to normalcy. "Most sudden was the end which came to the Amateur Rule or player-writer controversy," wrote Merrihew in his *ALT* column, "which has been raging with increasing virulence since the first of the year." Though a partisan and staunch Tilden supporter who had previously trumpeted that "the Amateur Rule interpretation . . . was conceived in sin and born in inequity," Merrihew was delighted "peace and a lasting one" had been achieved.[62]

Bill, of course, used the truce to underscore, if not bless, his status as an amateur. As he would tell everyone within earshot, "This compromise places the player-writer question in the same position it held in 1923 prior to the interpretation, and therefore, my amateur status is clearly and officially recognized by the Executive Committee."[63]

In fact, Bill had never stopped playing, and, even more amazingly, the much-discussed brouhaha never impeded his quality of play. Tilden participated in and dominated a lengthy series of tournaments over the course of the spring and summer that included the South Atlantic Championships, Middle States Clay Court, Orange Lawn Tennis Club Invitation, Rhode Island State (where he played five semifinal and final singles and doubles matches totaling 157 games in one day from ten to six and then spent the evening playing bridge), Great Lakes Championships, New England Championships, Western Championships, National Clay Court, Illinois State, and Southern California Championships.[64] Appearing impervious to both physical and psychological assaults, Big Bill just kept on winning.

By mid-August everyone's attention was focused on the National Tennis Championships scheduled for the West Side Tennis Club's recently constructed stadium at Forest Hills. Though the West Side leadership often castigated Big Bill in the confines of their private clubhouse, his court prowess and popularity propelled them to build a new permanent stadium for the game's growing fan base. The 1924 National Championship was expected to be one of the strongest and most competitive fields ever assembled, as Davis Cup teams from Australia, France, Japan, Mexico, and Canada were entered along with such stars as Babe Norton, Manuel Alonso, Billy Johnston, Frank Hunter, and Vinnie Richards, who had just played the most impressive tennis of his career in winning the Olympic title. Though he had survived his latest bout with the USLTA and was rumored to be quitting tennis to "enter the moving picture profession," Big Bill was still the favorite to win the championship.[65]

As usual for such a large and impressive blend of tennis talent—eighty-two players attempting to survive six or seven rounds of matches—there was a fair share of surprising upsets and scintillating performances, but as was the norm in major events the cream usually rose to the top. By the semifinal matches Bill Johnston, Gerald Patterson, Vinnie Richards, and Bill Tilden were the last four still standing. Most tennis aficionados predicted Johnston would have his hands full with the Australian heavyweight and Tilden a much easier time with young Richards, whom he always defeated in big matches. It proved exactly the opposite. Though the "giant Anzac" had played well in earlier rounds, he was crushed by Little Bill, 6–2, 6–0, 6–0. It was a humiliating thumping by a player half Patterson's size. As Tilden would admiringly write in his syndicated newspaper column, "Johnston was at the very top of his game. Everything he hit went in. There is little to say about the match, for it was all Johnston."[66]

The Tilden-Richards contest, on the other hand, would prove the match of the tournament. Probably due in part to his sterling play in defeating René Lacoste and Henri Cochet, two young, talented players, in succession on French soil for the Olympic title, Richards came into the tournament with confidence. According to Edward C. Potter, "The master was no longer a hero to his valet."[67] Richards was keen on ending his mentor's customary dominance. As the Associated Press would write of the magnificent struggle, "William T. Tilden was forced to five thrilling, gripping sets today before he conquered his youthful former pupil." The score of the long five-set battle under a broiling sun was 4–6, 6–3, 8–6, 4–6, 6–4.

Spectators and news reporters were in awe of the physical effort put forth by both players on a brutally hot day. "Given the fight of his life," according to one newspaper account, Tilden "rose to the greatest heights of his brilliancy to check the young Olympic champion." Normally, the champ could count on his superior array of ground strokes to thwart and bewilder Richards, but Vinnie was hitting deeper now, with more pace, and not just relying on his impressive volley game. Freely admitting he was pushed to the brink and beyond in the tense, exhausting match, Tilden wrote in his newspaper column, "Richards and I staged the match of the tournament. I never have seen Richards play so well, nor have I played better tennis this year. It was anyone's match to the last point."[68]

The fact that Little Bill pulverized his semifinal opponent and Tilden was on the verge of losing to Richards gave heart to Johnston's loyal supporters that this would finally be the year the little Californian regained the national title. "Everyone stated that Little Bill was playing the best tennis of his life," observed one top-ten player and Tilden supporter. "Never did he drive with more severity. Never was his game more effective or his physical condition better."[69] Tilden, they hoped, had been psychologically worn down by the recent amateur-rule controversy and distracted by the prospect of a new career in motion pictures. This would be the year Big Bill would be cut down to size.

As the players took the court under ominous skies, thunderous applause, and a multitude of photographers who trailed after them, those privileged enough to have a ticket to the much-anticipated contest sat on the edge of their seats to await the athletic fireworks. Tilden did his part, holding serve at love. Johnston was unable to return one of the champion's cannonballs or high-bounding placements. Little Bill followed and held his serve, but it would be his high-water mark of the first set. Tilden took every game thereafter, the fourth being "the greatest exhibition of driving in the tournament," as he repeatedly sent bullet-like shots deep into the corners, nicking the lines and leaving Johnston "as helpless as an infant."

Just ten minutes after they had begun the grand vision of a glorious Johnston triumph was torn asunder; Tilden had taken the first set "with a hurricane attack [that] took the heart out of the Californian and ended any doubts which may have been entertained as to his ability to defeat the player who had annihilated Patterson in the semi-finals."[70] That first set—

seemingly over in the bat of an eye—was called "an orgy of speed" by one observer, who attempted to describe the "devastating, irresistible shots" exploding from Tilden's racket. "It did not seem possible that such shots could be made from a human being," wrote the amazed reviewer, who clearly thought he had witnessed something never before seen.[71]

The next two sets would underscore "Tilden's invincibility." The champion would repeatedly display his "marvelous control, uncanny anticipation, flashing speed, and devastating power."[72] Johnston never had a chance.

Incredibly, just fifty-eight minutes after the two net men walked on the court, the match was over. It was as awesome a display of physicality and skill as anyone had ever seen on a tennis court. As the *New York Times* informed its readers, Tilden's performance should have demonstrated to the satisfaction of Johnston as well as everyone else that "there is no player living, probably never has been one, worthy of his steel. As last year, Johnston did not get a set, yielding at 6–1, 9–7, 6–2."

A half hour later when he walked onto the court to collect his big challenge cup during the award ceremony, Bill must have had extraordinary satisfaction in being handed the trophy by George W. Wightman, president of the United States Lawn Tennis Association. As Bill would write a number of years later, the "Little Tennis Snob" had evolved into a "Tennis Bolshevik," and the elite country-club establishment that controlled the game could not do a thing about it.

It was a performance worthy of the gods. From the first serve Tilden came to play and win. Normally, Bill liked to observe, probe, and test his opponent early in a match. But he had seen Johnston destroy Patterson; he could not afford to gradually get into the game. Besides, he knew Little Bill's game as well as anyone. There was no need to survey and analyze; he knew what had to be done, and he did it with lightning speed.

It is an understatement to say newspaper reporters covering the event were impressed. Al Laney, a longtime tennis observer and devoted Johnston supporter, was admittedly starstruck by Bill's performance:

> In practically a lifetime of observing and writing of tennis of the top class, I have never seen such hitting and such astonishing control from both sides as Tilden displayed on this occasion, and I am prepared to believe that no such exhibition had previously been given on any court at any time anywhere in the world.

Johnston, twice United States champion as well as Wimbledon champion surely was one of the finest players the game has known. Little Bill, I think, must be placed on anybody's list of greatest players, and in 1924 he was in full possession of his wonderful powers. Yet Tilden overwhelmed him without coming to the net at all, and I do not believe any player, past or present could have survived against such stuff. That was Tilden at his absolute peak, and I have not seen the like of it.[73]

Tennis officials, generally no friends of Tilden's, were equally awestruck. As one former USLTA president was heard to comment, "Tilden's playing in the first set was the greatest tennis he had ever seen." The *New York Times* reporter was so impressed with Tilden's play that he compared it to "the utter futility of trying to chain lightning. It was a Tilden rampant who went on the court yesterday, deadly in earnest, with the zest for the fray and absolutely merciless."[74]

Bill Johnston was in agreement. His opponent had put forth an incredible performance. "I could not play against that tennis," said Little Bill. "He kept me continually on the defensive and turned my best shots into aces."[75]

In his own column on the match Carl Fischer wanted to end for all time the argument that Tilden's dominance over Johnston was solely based on his "superior stamina." It should now be clear to Little Bill's "most ardent admirers," wrote Fischer, "that Johnston's best is not nearly good enough to conquer the five-time national champion. All hail to Tilden, the greatest player of all time."[76]

Bill certainly had reason to crow. For most of the year USLTA leadership had him in their sights and tortured him with threats of expulsion if he did not comply. In addition to that yearlong bureaucratic sniping, every player the world over had him as the opponent they most wanted to beat. But Bill did not boast, brag, or swagger; in fact, his first article for syndication after his victory was a heartfelt defense of Little Bill Johnston. The match, he argued with only modest success, "was far closer and more bitterly contested" than the score indicated. Still, it was a grand gesture by one competitor for another.[77]

Though it would not become the centerpiece of one of his articles, there was much talk and much written about Bill forsaking the courts for motion pictures. Bill even admitted that was his goal in some postmatch interviews. His intent was to retire right after the Davis Cup match was completed. Most found the prospect of such a dramatic career switch shocking, but Tilden's increasing interest in the stage and the dramatic arts had become well known. Still, "the lure of the game is great," wrote one dubious commentator, "and the thousands who have followed Big Bill's career through its various stages are almost one in the belief that he will never turn from the courts save when compelled to by age."[78]

Just a week later newspapers across the country would once again celebrate Tilden's court heroics, as he led America in another Davis Cup triumph. The United States' 5–0 victory over Australia solidified America's tennis supremacy and was thought by many to be "the most overwhelming performance in the history of the international matches." Staged at the Germantown Cricket Club before an "enthralled" audience of more than ten thousand patrons, the American team was so dominant that the Aussies— who had previously defeated China, Mexico, Japan, and France—were allowed but one set in the entire five-match challenge.

Based on Vinnie Richards's stellar play against Tilden in the national semifinal and Little Bill's struggle with Bill in the final, the twenty-one-year-old New Yorker was rewarded with one of the singles assignments alongside his mentor. Johnston would just play doubles and partner with Tilden, a repairing of the formidable team that had won the Cup five years earlier in New Zealand. Tilden and Richards easily won their singles matches against Patterson and O'Hara Wood. Bill's play was exceptional as usual, his match against O'Hara Wood, for example, a terribly one-sided affair, with the Aussie managing to win just four of the twenty-two games played.

The 1924 tennis season complete, it was the fifth consecutive year Tilden had dominated his sport like no other in the history of the game. Only the great Babe Ruth in baseball and Jack Dempsey in boxing could compare in their majesty, raw talent, and total dominance. They were not just unvanquished champions; they were icons in an era that glorified athletic accomplishment and physical prowess. But unlike Ruth, who was a national figure and relatively unknown beyond American shores, Tilden was an international celebrity and the recipient of effusive praise and laudatory comment throughout the world.

Both at home and abroad, the adoration and tributes were bountiful and recurring. "To William T. Tilden II, master player of the world, all gladly make obeisance," wrote S. Wallis Merrihew in assessing the champ's year in an *American Lawn Tennis* editorial. "Such play has never been known, such transcendent skill was never before us on exhibition. One seeks vainly to decide whether mentality or physics as the superior in his case, and ends by concluding that it is the blending of the two in unmatched coalescence that is responsible for the finished product."[79]

Big Bill, the extravagant rebel, unshakable defender of the Davis Cup, aspiring thespian, prolific author, man of intrigue, and the most spectacular performer his sport had ever known was once again at the very top of the mountain. But just at his gifts were great and his interests varied, his challenges were equally diverse, daunting, and unrelenting. One thing was sure, however: no matter the opponent or obstacle, Bill was not one to back down.

9

"The Greatest Wizard the Game Has Known"

Never in a quarter of a century of first-class tennis have
I seen such amazing hitting and phenomenal control.

—A. WALLIS MYERS

By the end of 1924 and with his tennis legacy firmly established, Bill was spending more time onstage than on court. Early November saw him appear in Edward Salisberry Field's *Wedding Bells* at different Philadelphia venues, including the ballroom of the Germantown Cricket Club. Interestingly, Bill's stage performances occurred just a day or two after he attended a working meeting at the Bankers Club in New York City concerning the cantankerous player-writer rule. As he was a member of the Committee of Seven designed to negotiate a viable settlement to the problematic debate over amateur versus professional athletes, Tilden's head must have been filled with both the playwright's script and his heartfelt views on amateur athletics.

Although the discussions at the Bankers Club were kept secret, Tilden's theatrical reviews were good and the play drawing patrons from as far as New York City. It was certainly not a presentation that foretold the arrival of another John Barrymore or Francis X. Bushman; still, the dramatic bug had bitten Bill, and his forthcoming trip to the West Coast was as much an opportunity to explore the dramatic arts with his Hollywood friends as it was to participate in a series of California tennis tournaments.

As Tilden was the grand monarch of the courts and with nothing left to prove to solidify his place in the hallowed halls of lawn tennis history, even close observers like the editorial staff of *American Lawn Tennis* speculated on the probability of Big Bill exchanging his racket for a motion-picture script.[1] Bill had already accepted a number of theater performance opportunities in locales consistent with his athletic schedule. Bookings for performances in Indianapolis, Cincinnati, and other Midwest cities by theatrical producers like Stuart Walker were being cemented; the moneymen behind expensive productions well understood the attraction and financial impact of a national sports hero on ticket sales. And it was not all that uncommon to find Bill's name in a newspaper's sports and entertainment sections, one article commenting on his forthcoming lawn tennis contest with the other advertising his appearance at a local theatrical playhouse.[2]

Tilden was not delusional. He recognized his limitations onstage, but he must have wondered, would not his belief in intensive practice deliver the same result in his dramatic pursuits as it had for his tennis game? And besides, the support and encouragement he was receiving from his movie-colony friends were exciting. If anyone should know about his potential as an actor, it would be actual actors.

Increasingly drawn to the film world, Tilden was quick to pick up on the possibilities and even penned an article for *ALT* that praised the contribution motion pictures were making in the tennis arena. He specifically cited the improvement one's tennis game would witness by studying new slow-motion films of numerous tennis stars such as Helen Wills, Bill Johnston, Vinnie Richards, and Dick Williams that were taken at Longwood, Germantown Cricket, and the West Side Tennis Club.[3] Proper stroke technique was critical in tennis, and moving footage of the world's best hitting forehands, backhands, and serves would prove invaluable to the tennis neophyte.

While participating in exhibition matches at the Berkeley Tennis Club, Golden Gate Park in San Francisco, and several private and public clubs in the Los Angeles area (Bill loved "the warm, sunny, far-too-comfortable climate of Southern California" and said the gorgeous weather "never failed to hold an irresistible attraction" for him), it was not unusual to spot famous Hollywood stars in the stands who had come out to see the great Tilden display his genius in matches with Bill Johnston, Vinnie Richards, Peck Griffin, and Harvey Snodgrass. Big Bill may have been a novice on the Hollywood back lot, but his appearance on a tennis court brought the likes of Douglas Fairbanks, Pola Negri, Claire Windsor, Ben Alexander, Lionel Belmore, and Peggy Wood as well as directors and tennis enthusiasts King Vidor, Raoul Walsh, and William de Mille.[4] Hollywood royalty was as delighted to receive a tennis tip from the world's greatest player as Bill was in getting suggestions for how to modulate his voice, where to stand onstage, and how to memorize his lines.

It was while he was on the coast that news broke concerning the decision of the USLTA special committee that had been established to address "one of the bitterest controversies ever to rise in the lawn tennis world," the player-writer rule.[5] Newspapers from coast to coast carried accounts of the committee's recommendations, and some papers had two and three articles on the deliberative process, the long-awaited proposals, and the reactions of the players and tournament organizers. As a long article in the *New York Times* announced, the present player-writer rule had been cast out and a new one put in its place that would permit "players to write tennis articles for publication, regardless of the amount of money received for them, so long as they are not daily accounts of tournaments in which they are entered and the players do not use their tennis titles in signing them."[6] Although the new recommendations were scheduled for a vote by the full USLTA membership in February 1925, its passage was a foregone conclusion, as the group's Executive Committee had already given it their unanimous approval.

The new rules under the compromise agreement were designed to leave no doubt as to the limits a player-writer could go. The four key provisions were as follows:

A person will be considered to have forfeited his amateur status by committing any of the following acts:

By permitting or sanctioning the taking of tennis action motion pictures of himself and receiving remuneration in connection therewith.

By permitting or sanctioning his name to be advertised as the author of books or articles on tennis of which he is not actually the author, or by receiving payment of consideration for commercial services which he does not actually render.

By using or sanctioning after February 1925, the use of his titles or statement of his reputation won on the tennis court in connection with books, newspaper, magazine or other written articles, motion pictures of himself, lectures, to radio talks for which he is to receive any payment or compensation.

By writing for pay or for a consideration current newspaper articles covering a tournament or match in which he is entered as a competitor.[7]

Although the rules may appear terribly modest, if not quaint, in their thrust and scope in comparison to today's wide-open, hypercommercialized atmosphere, the struggle by old-guard traditionalists in the 1920s to safeguard amateur sport from the corrupting influence of fame and "filthy lucre" was an all-consuming endeavor. Other sports at the time had quickly answered the siren call of money, popular demand, and commercial opportunity, but lawn tennis was intent on remaining a bastion of athletic purity.[8]

As members of the committee, Tilden and Merrihew argued for more liberal strictures, policies that recognized the new reality of sports in an increasingly commercialized age. Nineteenth-century attitudes and practices, they contended, were no longer sustainable, given the dramatic changes occurring in the sporting world. And ancient bureaucratic dictates established by an undemocratic and entrenched elite only aggravated a rapidly evolving social and economic landscape. "What has always been done before," Merrihew wrote in a stinging editorial earlier in the year, "has been the setting up of a doctrine, extreme in principle and drastic in application, by one party; and the total ignoring of all on the other side. Such action bred strife as inevitably as decomposed matter breeds maggots."[9]

In a concession by defenders of the status quo, the new rule would jettison the prickly and divisive definition of an amateur athlete that caused much of the dissension. The old standard had read: "An amateur tennis player is one who plays tennis solely for the pleasure and physical benefits he derives therefrom, and to whom the playing of tennis is nothing more than a pastime." Anti-Tilden oligarchs repeatedly used the definition to point out that "any player who receives substantial sums of money for writing tennis articles is not playing the game solely for the pleasure and physical benefits derived and that to that person the playing of tennis is more than a pastime; it is a business."[10] Such a person—with Tilden in mind—should be declared a professional and therefore declared ineligible for amateur play.

The new rule stated, "None but amateurs shall be allowed to play in any matches or tournaments played under the auspices of the national association." In addition, a professional tennis player was now defined as someone "who is paid directly, or indirectly, for playing, engaging in, or teaching the game of tennis or any other form of athletic exercise or sport, or who has competed in any game or sport for a stake or purse or for gate money."

Because many tennis cognoscenti already believed the entire rumpus was inspired to cripple—or at least gain control of—the game's reigning monarch, it would appear Tilden came out of the player-writer scrap rather well. He could continue writing tennis articles, there were no restrictions placed on his earnings from such work, player-writers could use their names, and the prohibition against a player-writer identifying himself as the winner of this or that tournament or garnering this or that title may have had import for someone like Carl Fischer, who was not a household name. But for Tilden, it was irrelevant; everyone knew who he was. The only stipulation that might impact him was the one precluding players from writing articles on the day they were actually competing. "The committee deemed it unwise or improper . . . for players to write about tournaments in which they compete." Merrihew and Tilden believed such a provision was "both wrong and a mistake in policy." However, they would ultimately agree to it, though it would seem a restriction that newspaper publishers would find most disagreeable, since timely articles were their stock in trade. Not a deal breaker at the time, the issue would eventually come back to bite Tilden in the rump.

The special committee's recommendations were roundly praised, and there was general agreement that the "vexing problem" had been placed in "well qualified hands." As Ed Pollack, a *Philadelphia Public Ledger* sports columnist, wrote of the agreement, "The special amateur committee which drafted the proposal has rendered diplomatic service to the association. The suggested rule is acceptable to the two factions which were so bitter in their animosity that the whole structure of tennis government was splitting at its foundation."[11]

Even the *New York Times* boasted that there was "no longer a player-writer problem" and was pleased the agreement "promises to restore harmony in the tennis ranks." Players, event organizers, and most important the game's fans, the *Times* crowed, would be delighted to learn all parties "practically guarantee that there will be no repetition of the resignations from the Davis Cup team of last season, jeopardizing the success of the United States in the matches."[12]

Subscribers to the game's bible, *American Lawn Tennis*, were happy to learn where there was once "open and . . . universal strife, there is now peace and a saner, broader outlook on the issues which caused the strife." Merrihew called the recent conflict the "bitterest of all . . . in the history of lawn tennis" and described how it "sundered friends of long standing, hampered the . . . well-ordered conduct of tennis affairs, and destroyed much of the pleasure of playing the game. Had it gone on," Merrihew soberly declared, "ruin was in sight."

The new agreement, according to ALT, provided an amateur code that was "simple, sane, sensible, and plain as the day that follows the night. It compels respect and excites admiration. A new era is before us. The universal game will flourish even more exuberantly than it has in the past."[13]

In retrospect—and by comparison to today's practically indistinguishable amateur-versus-professional standards—the new guidelines that resolved the player-writer tennis controversy of 1924 were rather modest. Their wide acceptance may speak to the intensity of the debate at the time and the great desire to settle the dispute. Almost all wanted an end to politics and a return to tennis without all of the accusations and histrionics. The declarations of peace in our time were welcome, but decidedly premature. The tectonic plates that undergirded sports in the twenties were constantly shifting; even those who firmly held their ground in opposition to encroaching professionalization discovered they were moving in a more commercialized direction.

And for those who hoped the player-writer furor would temper the rambunctious Philadelphian's willful initiatives and rebellious nature, they found themselves sadly mistaken. By any measure Tilden had a well-developed brain, myriad interests that ranged across a wide swath of the athletic and cultural landscape, and supreme confidence in his own judgment. Tennis was his lifelong love and the game's nurturing and expansion his constant passion. No player did more, knew more, or wrote more about who was playing and what was happening in lawn tennis around the world. And naturally, anyone with a different opinion than his on a tennis-related subject was wrong. The bottom line was that the months-long uproar over the player-writer rule did not temper his ardor for constructive suggestions on how to improve the game.

For example, before the ink was even dry on the new USLTA tennis guidelines, Tilden was already active on a number of issue fronts. Despite being a longtime critic of women's tennis play, Bill was quick to see the rapid growth of female players in California and their decided superiority over the gals back east. Part of the reason for their superiority, Tilden reasoned, was that "girls play against men all the time in California," and it showed in the quality of their play. That experience, Bill wrote, allowed them "to learn to judge speed, hit hard, and gain a broader insight into the game." Such an opportunity was not open to women in the East, Tilden explained, because of cultural prejudices that kept women off the same courts as men. "Very few of the leading stars of the East will play against the best boys," argued Tilden, much less hit with girls. "Now is the crucial moment," Tilden preached to all who would listen. "The coming season should be the start of the new campaign to raise the standard of play in the East among the girls."[14]

Tilden was equally dogged on the subject of the USLTA player rankings. He was troubled by the obvious bias toward older established players over the young Turks on the way up. There were too many instances of former stars earning a place in the top ten that should have been awarded a younger player who had entered more tournaments and outperformed the more senior star.

Ironically, it would be at the forty-fourth annual meeting of the USLTA in New York City that was ostensibly designed to endorse the new player-writer rule that a long and vehement argument broke out between Tilden and Julian Myrick over the association's penchant for "juggling" players in the rankings. Tilden was said to have been impressive that night, defiant when challenged, and able to "produce chapter and book to support his objection. It was the younger players like George Lott, John Hennessey, and Alfred Chapin whose cause he pleaded."[15] They were the ones who had played the most tournaments, earned the best records, and deserved the highest ranking, not the big names on the downside of their careers with fewer match wins.

His list of grievances far from exhausted, Bill followed that up by expressing his distaste for the association's last-minute changes in Davis Cup personnel. Bill informed the large and attentive audience that sound doubles play was built on teamwork, and that was impossible when players were thrown together on a court—as he and Bill Johnston had been several months earlier—without the proper preparation and practice time. With Big Bill and Myrick facing off "some forty or fifty feet apart," in front of scores of rapt USLTA members, Tilden "spoke clearly and earnestly with a hint of emotion in his voice . . . while Myrick's voice was low and plainly on the defensive." The champion's arguments were "so cogent, and so clearly in the right, that it added to his popularity with the delegates."[16]

Bill was not done, however. There were additional complaints and suggestions he wanted the association to consider. One concerned his chagrin that the USLTA would not sanction a series of exhibition matches for the benefit of the National Marine and Naval Memorial. Calling it "nothing short of flabbergasting," Bill was outraged that worthy causes, many of a humanitarian nature, were routinely turned down when individuals and organizations came to the USLTA looking for their assistance and blessing. "Evidently some people only know of faith and hope," wrote Tilden in a "Passing Shots" column, "but not charity."[17]

Tilden was a sucker for a whole host of admirable causes and fund-raising events. Groups proffering worthy causes and in need of a big name to attract donors and patrons could always count on him for assistance. The same could not be said for the USLTA, however. Protective to a fault of ensuring players were not taking money for public appearances and a blemish appear on the USLTA escutcheon, they were extremely parsimonious in handing out their endorsement. And in the absence of such an organizational blessing, most established tennis players were scared off. No point in risking one's amateur status for an unsanctioned event, even one for a worthy cause like earthquake relief. Such practices Tilden found unconscionable.

One of the worst examples of such callous bureaucratic thinking occurred a year earlier when Zenzo Shimidzu came to Bill with the heartfelt request that he help raise money for the Japanese people, who had just suffered a devastating earthquake. The September 1923 quake caused tremendous destruction throughout the country, leveled a good portion of Tokyo, and extinguished the lives of nearly 150,000 men, women, and children. Bill quickly signed on to play in a tennis benefit and encouraged fellow players to participate in the fund-raiser. The use of his name alone helped rouse an advance ticket sale of ten thousand dollars, a considerable amount at the time.

Soon after, however, Zenzo called Tilden with bad news. Highly emotional and on the verge of tears, he informed Bill the Jackson Heights charity event had to be called off. The USLTA refused to sanction the event; players were withdrawing, fearful of losing their amateur status. Angered beyond words, Bill told his Japanese friend not to call off anything. The event would go on as scheduled.

"But Bill," replied Shimidzu, "you'll be barred if you play."

Tilden remained adamant. The fund-raising event would go on as scheduled; he would take care of it. Tilden immediately contacted Julian "Mike" Myrick and informed him he would be playing in the Japanese charity event. "You'll be barred if you play," Myrick warned him.

"I dare you to bar me," Tilden erupted. "Try it and I'll spill the whole story to the press. I doubt if the American public will stand for their national champion being barred because he helps the victims of a catastrophe."

Myrick knew Bill meant it and quickly backed down. Not only had Big Bill called Myrick's bluff, but within hours Shimidzu had the USLTA's permission to hold the charity tennis event.[18]

It quickly became apparent to all that the player-writer rule had proven an ill-conceived scheme to force the national tennis champion to tone down his act and fall in line with the rest of the country's obedient contingent of ranked tennis players. The USLTA leadership had egg on their collective faces; the controversy had sown discord in their own ranks and resulted in tons of bad ink for the association and the sport itself. Worse yet, Tilden never missed a beat. He seemed impervious to both reason and a show of strength: he did what he wanted when he wanted to do it. Never before had the organization been confronted with such a defiant and single-minded figure. The USLTA, "composed for the most part of a few near-sighted antiques in Hoover collars," as one critical observer called them, was totally and regularly outmaneuvered by this "unique Ichabod Crane" character with a genius for racket play and a knack for upsetting the bureaucratic apple cart. Tilden had repeatedly proved he had a mind of his own and believed it worked better than any of those in organizational leadership setting the rules of the sport.[19]

Adding to the establishment's general consternation was Bill's restlessness; he was not only an agent provocateur but also one of extraordinary passion, breadth of interest, and stamina. He never seemed to slow down or take time off like most mortals. His days were thirty-six hours long, weeks were ten rather than seven days long, and every minute was geared toward fostering the sport's growth and popularity. Dealing with him, as well as his endless suggestions, requests, and demands, was exhausting. But he was universally celebrated as the world's best player and regarded by most as the greatest to have ever swung a racket. What could Myrick and the USLTA do? When Bill wrote in a column that he "was hoping to be too deeply engrossed in moving pictures to have time to play tennis" in 1925, most tennis fans were stunned and disappointed by the news.[20] A good many USLTA officials, however, secretly welcomed the prospect of Big Bill mothballing his racket and relocating to Hollywood. A smaller Tilden footprint was not all that threatening for organizational types. But the Tilden legend and persona had been the spark, the driving force, that popularized the game, overhauled its sissified image, and gave the sport its aura of aggressive manliness. He was also the raison d'être for the construction of hundreds of tennis courts across the country, including the new Forest Hills stadium. For all his peculiarities and periodic displays of defiance and petulant behavior, Bill was an iconic sports figure. Tennis would survive his departure, but how many years or decades would the sport have to wait to discover another such exceptional talent?

Speculation was rampant and theories varied as to Bill's seriousness about leaving the game, but notices of Bill's departure proved premature. As the days and weeks passed, Tilden's activities seemed as tennis centered as ever. He was participating in indoor winter tournaments, partnering with younger players in doubles matches, and writing both inspiring fiction stories for America's youth and informative nonfiction articles on the game's latest developments for sports fans. By 1925 he had written more than a dozen fiction and nonfiction books, including *It's All in the Game, Lawn Tennis for Young Players, Singles and Doubles, Lawn Tennis for Match Players, The Art of Lawn Tennis, The Common Sense of Lawn Tennis, The Junior Player, The Expert, Better Tennis for the Club Player, The Kid, The Phantom Drive, The Pinch Quitter,* and what was soon to become a sports classic, *Match Play and Spin of the Ball.*[21] At the time one would have been hard-pressed to name another famous athlete who was as prolific with a pen or typewriter. By the time of his death such a task would be impossible.

His many newspaper and magazine articles were as educational and insightful as they had always been. In February 1925, for example, Bill wrote a unique piece that informed readers of the evolving nature of playing surfaces and his shocking prediction that "as greatly as I deplore it, it will not be long . . . before grass courts will be a rarity, and all championships played on clay or some dirt surface." The article went on to describe the style of play most suited for various surfaces—speed on hard courts, which is best suited for an offensive, attacking game, and delicate drop shots for clay courts that require greater touch for the use of chop strokes and soft placements—and America's clear inferiority to Europe in the design and maintenance of clay courts. Bill also predicted "indoor courts are rapidly coming to the fore," and in the "not too distant future every city of importance will have a fine indoor club."[22]

And all of this was happening while Bill was in New York making his first motion-picture film. Entitled *Haunted Hands*, a "crook melodrama," starring Ben Alexander, Marjorie Daw, Walter Long, and Kathleen Martin, the film was being shot at locations in Hell's Kitchen and Long Island. Bill thoroughly enjoyed making the film and associating with the film's actors and crew, and he hoped for more of the same. "I want to make my first screen appearance as a motion-picture actor and not just a tennis player," he told one reporter. "You see this *Haunted Hands* isn't going to be my only picture. At least, hope it isn't, and if I'm not too terrible in it, I want to make several others. I've been eager for several years to go on the screen, and now I'm having my chance."[23]

It was around this time that Bill moved from his Germantown home in Philadelphia to New York City and began residing at the Algonquin Hotel. The hotel was famous for its celebrated roundtable discussion group that included the likes of Franklin Adams, Robert Benchley, Heywood Broun, George S. Kaufman, Dorothy Parker, Harold Ross, Robert E. Sherwood, and Edna Ferber, and Big Bill no doubt enjoyed the occasional camaraderie with some of the literary world's most talented and talked-about writers.

Though his off-court interests were numerous and varied, Bill was still best known for his athletic exploits, which were quickly taking on legendary stature. Universally recognized as the greatest tennis player of all time, Bill was the subject of endless praise and commentary. Even opponents of Bill's not known for their grace or complimentary comments could not help but marvel at Bill's athletic ability and technical skill. "Tilden is the only first-class tennis player in the world," Gerald Patterson, twice a Wimbledon champion, informed the Australian press on his return home after participating in a series of American tournaments. Compared to Tilden, "Richards, Johnston, Anderson, and Lacoste are all second graders." Without Tilden, said Patterson, Australia could give America a "hard tussle" in Davis Cup competition, but with him the United States was "impossible to beat."[24]

Another Aussie with two Wimbledon trophies and an even more impressive tennis résumé, Norman E. Brookes, had much the same to say. With nearly three decades of top-tier tennis behind him, Brookes told members of the press that Tilden was the best he had ever seen.[25]

One European player with a particularly keen eye for the mental side of the game as well as its physical mechanics was "much impressed" with Tilden's play and not hesitant in proclaiming, "I cannot resist saying . . . how much I admire both the strokes and the tactics of the champion." The young Frenchman rapidly working his way up the tennis ladder had been impressed with the great Philadelphian ever since he had first seen him at St. Cloud in 1921. Now on American shores for a series of matches, he paid close attention to the champion's incomparable game. On the grounds of Manheim he sat in the stands and studied Tilden like a trained virologist examining a rare and wondrous microbe under a microscope. It was not unusual for players to watch Bill perform on court—they all marveled at his grace, clean strokes, and endurance—but the young Frenchman was particularly studious in analyzing Bill's overall strategy, his tactical approach in game situations, and his basic thought process as a match progressed. It was this latter aspect—the mental or psychological approach to the game—the Frenchman discovered, that so clearly separated the champion from all others. "In my opinion the greatness of Tilden is more in his conception of the game than in his own game," René Lacoste would write.

> Truly, he is the best player off the ground in the world. He can play a very steady game, topped, flat, or sliced as well as the most forceful attack. The force and twist of his service make it the best singles service ever seen. Despite this superiority of strokes, the decisive factor of his invincibility, and the greatest lesson he gave to the true students of the game, is the manner in which he built up and is now using his game. Tilden built his own game for winning not only on his own efforts

but also by the possibilities given by his opponent. Against a slice serve he uses a topped drive, against a sliced drive he volleys, against a chopped return he serves a slice. Against Richards he speeded up his serve, against Johnston he wants it bounding out of the court, obliging the Californian to extend to the extreme limit of his reach. He showed the objective manner of winning and gave the rules of the battle of minds that is perhaps the most interesting aspect of the art and science of lawn tennis. Tilden is the best tactician ever.[26]

Lacoste, who would go on to establish his own formidable tennis credentials, spent each evening transcribing to his notebooks what he had seen that day on Germantown's lush green fields of combat. Each man's strengths and weaknesses were cataloged and evaluated. "For each of their strokes he sought to find the answering thrust" that would prove the winning parry.[27] Big Bill was of most interest, but he had positive comments about other top American players. He called Little Bill Johnston "probably the most offensive player" he had ever seen on a court. He kept his opponents running from side to side under a hurricane of blistering forehand drives. Olympic champion Vinnie Richards was an "unorthodox" and "natural match player," who was best at using "every mistake of his opponent" against him. But the one he admired most and kept coming back to was Tilden. There were many fine tennis players across the globe, each with his own style and unique attributes, but Big Bill was truly *magnifique*.

As Edward Potter has written about the rise of the French, when Lacoste returned home, "he had a new objective. He no longer needed to study the strokes of Borotra and Cochet. He was analyzing those of the American holders of the Cup. For each of their strokes he sought to find the answering thrust."[28] Though the youngest of what would become known as the Four Musketeers, René Lacoste was the most cerebral, the most analytical, of the quartet. He would become his nation's lawn tennis general with one goal in mind: for France to become the first non-English-speaking nation to win the Davis Cup. To do that they had to defeat Tilden.

Interestingly, Lacoste was not the only one taking notes. Consistent with his finely tuned eye for developments in the game and knack for judging talented newcomers, Bill was one of the first to predict the rise of a new overseas threat to America's tennis hegemony. "The triumph of the two young French stars Jean Borotra and René Lacoste in the singles at Wimbledon," Bill warned in 1925, "should cause the Davis Cup Committee of the United States to sit up and take notice." More so than some others who discounted two Frenchmen facing off in the Wimbledon final as a quirk of fate, Bill was impressed by Dick Williams's loss to Lacoste and Vinnie Richards's defeat at the hands of Borotra. "It seems to me," Bill would plaintively write, "that this is a threat of our supremacy too obvious to be ignored."[29]

In addition to his recent Wimbledon victory, which was memorable for his athleticism and frenetic leaps and jumps to finish off high volleys, Borotra also impressed Bill with his newly earned nickname, "the Bounding Basque." Bill, too, in a moment of self-deprecation, thought he deserved a suitable nickname. Playing off his busy tournament schedule that could have him playing in Boston on Friday, Hartford on Saturday, and New York on Sunday, Bill thought up a couple of appropriate names for himself. "Why not something like the Tumbling Tuna Fish or possibly the Flying Flapjack?" he humorously suggested.[30]

With or without a new moniker, Big Bill was seemingly unbeatable on a tennis court. Whether in the Northeast or the Deep South, or on hard court or clay, large venue or small, Tilden hardly ever lost. Missing part of a finger on his racket hand, in constant battle with USLTA overseers, and performing a variety of dramatic and comedy roles onstage and on-screen, Tilden managed to cast all pretenders aside. Spurred by Tilden's dominance the nation's newspapers and magazines hoped to spark sales by stirring debate as to who was the greatest player in the history of the sport. Was it one of the early players, such as Bill Larned or Malcolm Whitman, or someone more recent, like Brookes, McLoughlin, or Tilden? The answer was always the same. "We believe that the verdict of history will be for Tilden," wrote one of the game's more knowledgeable reviewers. "He is the money player, so to say. The greater the occasion the surer is his likelihood of winning. He is an extraordinary match and stroke player, and no height seems to be too great for him to attain."[31] Doubters to the prevailing wisdom could be counted on the fingers of one hand.

Tilden's universal acclaim did not stop the rest of the field from trying to claim his scalp and immediately earn themselves their own place in the history books. Like Melville's Captain Ahab and his obsessive pursuit of a great white whale, there were scores of tennis players throughout the world who dreamed of doing battle with the lawn tennis leviathan and eventually taking him down in a titanic five-set struggle that would become their contribution to the game's lore. Rarely, if ever, did that dream become realized. Even the sport's greatest players and those with national championships to their credit were routinely dispatched. In one May 1925 match for the championship of Pennsylvania, for example, Bill found himself across the net from a determined and energized R. Norris Williams. No novice with illusions of grandeur, the two-time national titleholder with an intimate knowledge of Bill's game came out on the court at Merion Cricket Club like the "Sultan of Swat," smashing winners to all corners of the court. Tilden, doing his best to return the awesome barrage of high-risk shots, was occasionally made to appear both helpless and hopeless.

It was an overwhelming display of power and precision tennis. No one present could recall Tilden being buried under such an avalanche of expert shot making. Before he was able to catch his breath or figure out what was happening, he had lost the first set in little more than a blink of an eye. Tilden was more than impressed. "The first set was the greatest tennis by Williams (or any other man) I have ever seen," Tilden would write of the match. "Williams ran six games, allowing me but five points and wasting only ten minutes of a beautiful afternoon, yet I was playing my game when I could get my racquet on the ball." Bill would go on to comment on his opponent's "brilliance," "perfect control," and "impeccable ground game," but he was not one to run up the white flag and surrender without a fight.[32] In fact, such an unexpected offensive bombardment only triggered his indomitable will to win. His analytical mind stirred in search of an appropriate defense and viable counterattack. Bill fought back as he was uniquely built to do.

Playing both inspired offense and defense, Bill turned the table on his accomplished adversary to win the second set 6–2. In a stunning turnaround, Williams's robust combination of aggression and precision could not be sustained. The two Philadelphia-area champions traded the next two sets, only to witness Bill win the hard-fought fifth set by a score of 6–4. Tilden remained undefeated and winner of the trophy declaring him the champion of Pennsylvania. The valiant loser garnered a smaller piece of hardware and the headline "Williams Extends Tilden for Title."[33]

For the most part, however, Tilden was rarely pressed. State and regional tourneys competed aggressively for the honor of having Tilden in their draw. His participation guaranteed greater fan and press interest, a profitable gate, and that certain buzz and excitement that only the best in the world can generate. Invariably, Bill walked off with the most impressive piece of silverware and the ever-lasting adoration of the spectators. These smaller tournaments he participated in were more like a leisurely walk in the woods as opposed to a knock-down, drag-out alley fight. In fact, during two consecutive tournaments—the Nassau County Invitational and the Rhode Island State Championships at the Agawam Hunt Club in Providence—Bill managed to win fifty-seven straight games and sixty-three of sixty-four from a collection of decent but severely outgunned players. It was an accomplishment so rare, no one could come up with a comparable example of such sustained excellence. And Bill's opponents, most having played college and club tennis, were appropriately humbled, as only a seemingly endless series of 0–6 scores can fashion.

Ironically, defeating Tilden in the two years that followed his hospitalization and the partial amputation of his finger had proved nearly impossible. He lost no singles match of import, and if he did lose on court, it was most likely a men's doubles or mixed-doubles contest when paired with a youngster like Sandy Wiener and against seasoned players like Little Bill Johnston and Clarence Griffin. Such a record, according to one European tennis authority, solidified "Tilden's greatness" and underscored "his great courage and determination" after overcoming severe physical impairment.[34]

In what should have proved another strong signal to the tennis establishment that the tectonic plates of the earth's tennis landscape were finally shifting, France won the right to take on the United States in the 1925 challenge round of the Davis Cup. Though a neophyte at this level of international competition, France was led by the last two Wimbledon champions—Jean Borotra in 1924 and René Lacoste in 1925—and a supporting cast that was nothing to trifle with. They were making a deliberate, sustained, and well-planned assault on America's preeminence, but many observers refused to give them their due. Although it is true, as Richard Hillway believes, that either Big Bill or Little Bill would have won the 1924 and '25 Wimbledon titles if they had ventured over to the All England Club, it is also true that France was developing something truly special in the realm of lawn tennis.

That should have been apparent to the more perceptive tennis connoisseurs at Germantown Cricket Club, but most were too busy congratulating themselves on America's decisive 5–0 triumph. It was a wipeout in the eyes of most casual observers, but a more discerning examination of individual matches gave hint to a serious threat on the horizon. In what the *New York Times* accurately described as a difficult struggle, Tilden "was extended to the last ounce of his physical strength to overcome Jean Borotra in the opening match, which went to the limit of five sets." With his all-out desperate "rushes to the net where he gave one of the greatest exhibitions of volleying and killing seen in the international matches," the Frenchman was on the verge of grasping victory when he let it slip away, as the physical toll of playing the great Tilden finally left him exhausted and in "helpless condition."[35] The score of the entertaining five-set struggle was 4–6, 6–0, 2–6, 9–7, and 6–4.

In the second match Bill Johnston "played marvelous tennis," his forehand "ripping the turf with his savage drives," leaving Lacoste bewildered and embarrassed. After witnessing two frames of dominating 6–1, 6–1 tennis, the thousands in attendance expected the third set to pass just as uneventfully. But young Lacoste was made of sterner stuff. "Playing beautiful, aggressive tennis that was almost perfect," according to the *Times* account, "the Wimbledon champion thrilled the gallery as he overpowered Johnston's cannonball forehands and stinging volleys." It was a game response from the foreigner and allowed him to claim the hard-fought third set at 8–6. The battle continued into a fourth set, but the little Californian restored order when he won the set at 6–3. Newspaper accounts said Lacoste's "control was a thing to marvel at," his ability to "handle Johnston's powerful ground strokes and service" a thing of beauty. "The cool, expressionless youth across the net," Allison Danzig would write, "was a stone wall that catapulted everything back at him with more force and depth than it came over."[36] America had won both opening-day Davis Cup matches, but not without a fight.

The following day Dick Williams and Vinnie Richards would claim the doubles contest over Lacoste and Borotra in a relatively smooth straight-set victory, 6–4, 6–4, 6–3. Tilden and Johnston would win their final singles matches against the two Frenchmen on the final day of competition, thereby concluding a very impressive and one-sided defense of the Cup. But the effort was far from a walk in the park; that was especially true for Tilden, who once again was forced to play a tough five-setter against the young upstart Lacoste.

Americans celebrated retention of the famous silver bowl emblematic of world tennis supremacy "for the sixth year without a break" and "ninth triumph in the twenty years of play," but the French were not discouraged. In fact, they seemed emboldened and were making audacious predictions. Max Decugis, the French team captain, boasted for all to hear, "The Davis Cup will be ours before 1930." A mighty brash statement after his nation had been throttled and unable to win a match, but the French were on a mission, and they saw enough positive signs in the competition to bolster their hopes. Decugis admitted, "Tilden is still in a class by himself, but he is past thirty. So is Johnston with his great forehand drive. On the other hand," he went on to remind everyone, "Jean Borotra and René Lacoste are nearer twenty than thirty, and still must improve."[37] Few Americans paid any attention to the foreign bluster, but Decugis was on to something.

After dominating the summer tennis circuit as well as being a key member of America's victorious Davis Cup team, Bill was once again the favorite at the National Championships at Forest Hills. The usual complement of perennial challengers such as Bill Johnston, Vinnie Richards, Dick Williams; foreign powers like James O. Anderson, Jean Borotra, Manuel Alonso, Babe Norton, and Takeichi Harada; and young wannabes like George Lott, Wray Brown, and Arnold Jones planned their annual, but always unsuccessful, assent up Mount Tilden.

Interestingly, whether it was designed to stimulate debate, to spur newspaper sales, or for some other reason, the *New York Times* printed several prominent articles on the eve of the national tournament suggesting the Tilden era may be coming to an end. One article was entitled "Tilden Confronts Crisis This Week" and provided a laundry list of first-class challengers with the ability to dethrone Tilden. The other, a *New York Times* sports editorial—probably also written by Allison Danzig—made note of the "tremendous struggles that were waged in Philadelphia" and some less than complimentary comments about Bill's quality of play against the French. "Tilden, the world's recognized greatest player, the mainstay of America for these six years, no longer can be said to stand in a class by himself," the opinion piece argued. "The gulf that has existed between him and the rest of the players of the world has narrowed."[38]

Both articles contained much favorable information about the French stars. In addition to their sterling play, mention was also made of Borotra's athleticism and captivating "personality" and Lacoste's machinelike strokes and steely "temperament." The pieces were so one-sided, a fair-minded person might have wondered, had Danzig and the *Times* grown tired of Big Bill's dominance? Had his tempestuous act finally grown stale? Were they in search of a new lawn tennis hero?

Whatever their motivation, they were left with egg on their faces as the "Bounding Basque" was handed a "crushing defeat" in just the third round by Richard Norris Williams. The score was an embarrassing 6–2, 6–2, 6–2. Playing as aggressively as he had at the Pennsylvania Championship earlier in the summer when he blitzed Tilden 6–0 in the first set, Williams played inside the baseline, took every ball on the rise, and made sure the Frenchman—unlike Big Bill—never got into the match.[39]

In fact, the foreign stars were having a hard time of it. By the end of the third round only two foreigners—Lacoste and Manuel Alonso—were still in the competition. And after the quarterfinals were contested, only American players were left standing, thereby providing further proof that the best tennis was played in the United States. In a battle of talented youngsters, Vinnie Richards put the wood to Lacoste, beating him handily in straight sets, 6–4, 6–3, 6–3. Alonso, despite his "tigerish efforts" and some of the "greatest tennis" he had played since moving to America, was taken out by Johnston and his "murderous forehanders," the four-set battle ending 6–3, 6–8, 6–1, 6–2. Big Bill had relatively little trouble with Wallace Johnson, winning in straight sets, and R. Norris Williams had a similarly easy time defeating Howard Kinsey.[40]

On September 18 the semifinal matches pitted two-time national champions Johnston and Williams against each other and the current five-time champion against his former protégé Richards. Tennis fans salivated over the expected grass-court fireworks, though the majority would have been surprised if any other than Tilden and Johnston met in the final. Now a rite of fall for tennis fans, the Big Bill–Little Bill contest had practically become an annual September event.

And so it was, as Allison Danzig reported in the *Times*, "for the fourth year in succession and for the sixth time in the last seven years, William T. Tilden of Philadelphia and William Johnston of San Francisco . . . met in the final round of the national lawn tennis tournament." Playing with what was described as his old "wizardry" after losing the first set of the semifinal to Richards, Tilden fought back with increasing authority to take the next three sets. By that last set Tilden was so formidable, young "Richards went to pieces"; his game totally collapsed.[41]

Johnston had a much easier time of it; he dispatched Williams in just forty-seven minutes. Though he had played "brilliantly in the extreme" against Jean Borotra and Howard Kinsey earlier in the tournament, Williams delivered "one of the most disappointing matches of the season" in the semifinal, going down in straight sets. As his high-risk game and career record clearly demonstrated, with Williams it was "either the heights or the depths. Magnificent one day, extremely erratic the next."[42]

For the widely anticipated final, "14,000 wild and enthusiastic spectators filled the stadium" in expectation of a battle royal between the world's two best lawn tennis players. Their performance did not disappoint. Little Bill won the first set 6–4 after hitting his nemesis an endless series of "blistering" forehands and no doubt using his embarrassing losses in 1923 and '24 as motivation. "Volleying flawlessly with punching strokes and whipping forehands across the net at low altitude," he managed to keep his opponent on the defensive well into the second set. Johnston forced Tilden to "call upon all his brilliance as a shot-maker to stay on even terms with him." Little Bill played at a high level and did not falter until the eighteenth game of that brutal second set—a set he nearly won three times—but would ultimately lose 11–9 when his "inability to control a couple of key shots in the critical moments cost him" a key game.

Throughout the lengthy set, according to the *New York Times* coverage, "the gallery was in a state of such excitement that it could hardly control itself. Every shot was followed with breathless interest; every winning stroke of Johnston's threw the spectators almost into a state of frenzy."[43] It was lawn tennis at its best, as only the two Bills could play it.

The players would battle on, split the next two sets, and go into a fifth with the championship on the line. Johnston was within a point of taking a 3–1 lead, but he let the opportunity "slip away in the fourth game." Tilden, using every shot in his large arsenal and every court tactic at his command, quickly tied the score at three each and then ran off the final three games. The two-hour-and-ten-minute five-set battle that had spectators on the edge of their seats throughout ended 4–6, 11–9, 6–3, 4–6, 6–3.

Victory over the game's greatest players enabled Tilden to surpass the mark of five consecutive triumphs of William A. Larned, a mark that had stood since 1911. Even the *New York Times* was forced to comment on the champion's record of excellence. Calling Tilden "the greatest player of all time," the *Times* made mention of his various challenges and rumors of his "slipping" in ability, but then cited his tournament play, which they concluded should "end all doubts as to his physical fitness and racquet mastery." Was he not "the greatest wizard the game has known?"[44]

An even more knowledgeable tennis authority would write of Tilden's "undisputed supremacy," refer to him as "the master genius of the game," and proudly proclaim him a "colossus . . . sitting in solitary and unapproachable grandeur on a throne altitudinous and remote."[45]

Bill would finish the year ranked number one in the world for the sixth successive year. As A. Wallis Myers, the respected English sports reporter, succinctly stated of his 1926 list of the world's best tennis players, "Tilden is still Tilden, and therefore still first."[46]

Praise for his recent accomplishments as well as his play over the course of the year would continue to pour in for some time. Many were from prominent individuals, while others were from lesser-known fans of the game. One gentleman from the Los Angeles Tennis Club was appreciative of Bill's "beautiful strokes, placements, services, volleys," and startling ability to hit a ball just where he wanted it to land, but there was another aspect of the champion he had grown to appreciate even more.

As R. E. Callahan would write to the publisher of *American Lawn Tennis*, "In the past twenty years, how many tennis players can you name who have played as Tilden has played?" He was not referring to Tilden's racket wizardry but another facet of the man that he had come to greatly respect.

As Callahan would go on to write, Bill had visited his tennis club "several times and each time we have found him ready and willing to play most any time, anywhere and to be agreeable along any sensible and reasonable line. He goes further than this. It's the high school this afternoon, another one tomorrow morning, San Diego, Riverside, YMCA or some other place that afternoon and the next day. Within two weeks time he has played at a half dozen different places because he loves the game, enjoys playing, and takes an unquestioned keen interest in the juniors and the small boys that are just learning tennis." Callahan would end by remarking how much better it would be "if only the leading tennis players of every club in the country would take the same interest," perform the same public service, and follow the lead of not only a great athlete but also a decent human being.[47]

Big Bill was truly something special. Known for his incomparable racket play, occasional petulance, and demanding mien, he was also a rare, multi-faceted intellect who could write books, immerse himself in anything from Italian opera to the latest Broadway plays, and play some high-level bridge matches on the side. As Tilden approached his thirty-third birthday, 1926 would present some familiar tests as well as a number of new challenges. Whether old or new, Bill was ready for them. He was living his life and doing it just as he desired.

Part 3

A Foreign Challenge

10

"Three against One"

Tilden has everything. His best serve has
no answer. His volleys take your breath away.
He gives you no rest. He has no equal.

—JEAN BOROTRA

The early-January 1926 ruckus was no different from the many others that
spontaneously flared up when the game's top players volunteered for some
worthy cause without the event first gaining the approval of the sport's
high priests. But as everyone already knew, the USLTA was exceedingly
stingy in blessing nonorganizational events. December's *New York American*'s Christmas and Relief Fund tennis exhibition starring a number of the
game's better-known names was such an event. The exhibition's promoters
hoped the participation of such well-known players as Big Bill Tilden, Vinnie
Richards, Molla Mallory, Mary K. Browne, and Frank Hunter would draw
spectators and help raise money for a worthy cause during the holiday
season. As the event's top draw, Bill was busy: he played singles (losing to
Richards 8–6, 6–4), doubles, and mixed doubles, and then he auctioned
off his racket for $117. The other players donated their time and rackets as
well: most sold for between $25 and $45.[1]

Less interested in the surprising upset, the amount raised, or where
the money would be spent, the USLTA had its organizational nose out of
joint because the players had disobeyed a directive and participated in an
"unsanctioned exhibition." The players had done so even after receiving a
letter from the chairman of the Sanction Committee stating it had insufficient time to investigate the event and warned anyone caught playing in it
would be punished. Most of the association's leadership, no doubt, blamed
Tilden for the egregious act. And they were probably right; many, if not
all, of the other players would never have bucked the USLTA and accepted

a charity invitation if they had not had Bill's sturdy umbrella protecting them from the political fallout.

Once the dispute became public and newspapers got wind of it, however, the USLTA had to backtrack and find a diplomatic way to extricate the association from an uncomfortable situation. "Just a tempest in a teapot," Jones W. Mersereau, president of the USLTA, told the press. He assured everyone that it was just a simple "misunderstanding" and too much was being made of it. Mersereau said he "hoped no penalties will be imposed" and "players may be cautioned as to [their participation in] future exhibitions."[2]

Tennis and bureaucratic politics were not the only things on Bill's mind at the time. He was actually preoccupied with another weighty matter, his Broadway debut, where he had a supporting role in *Don Q Jr.* For someone who grew up in a household that encouraged an appreciation of good music and the arts, just the appearance of his name—albeit "Big Bill" Tilden—in the *Times* entertainment section under Broadway shows, alongside that of such well-known plays and performers as *Ben Hur*, Stella Dallas, Hedda Gabler, Otto Klemperer and the New York Symphony, and Arturo Toscanini and the New York Philharmonic must have been gratifying.

Originally entitled *The Kid Himself* and advertised as a "whimsical comedy . . . dealing with the trials and tribulations of a newsboy hero who has a heart of gold," the play left theater critics unimpressed.[3] The production had opened just five days into the new year at the Belasco Theater in the nation's capital to a receptive audience. His "professional stage debut" was well received, and it was said he "tackled his new vocation with as much earnestness as he ever expended on a tennis championship." Bill's opening-night nervousness was obvious, his normal gargantuan appetite much reduced, and he was seen to even decline the offer of a cigarette. The presence of the secretary of war, Dwight Davis, may have also added to Bill's apprehension, but the "play got a dozen curtain calls after the first act, and liberal applause," thereby ensuring its unveiling on Broadway.[4]

Over the years it has been written that Bill's performance was uninspiring, his part overacted and not worth the price of admission. In actuality, his reviews at the time were fairly positive. And there was even optimistic speculation on Bill's potential. The *New York Times* review did call the play "childish" and "painfully naïve," but Bill's performance was viewed far more favorably. The review acknowledged, "There have been several signs in recent years what William T. Tilden, having scaled the heights in tennis, was casting covetous eyes upon the acting profession. Slipping up on it by easy stages, such as the motion pictures and an occasional amateur appearance. Mr. Tilden made the leap last night at the 49th St. Theatre." The reviewer went on to comment about the "many tennis players of only slightly less prowess than Mr. Tilden" who were seated in the audience and "welcomed him with applause and shared the general belief that he has the makings of a pretty good actor." The *Times* reviewer seemed to agree; he wrote that "certainly many worse ones are acting away for dear life in sundry theatres up and down the avenue."[5]

Though Bill would subsequently admit, "It was not a good play by many miles and I was incredibly bad in it," he was impressed with the talent and commitment of his costar, a thirteen-year-old actor named Billy Quinn. Despite what Tilden called "a bad play and bad direction," he was pleased young Billy "scored a great personal triumph."[6] He may have also taken some solace in the final words of the *Times* review, which stated, "There is no reason why Mr. Tilden should not enjoy a successful stage career, although it is unlikely that he ever will mean to the stage what he means to the courts."

Other critics were more complimentary. A *Variety* reviewer said Bill "is not the champion on the stage that he is on the tennis courts [but] with a little more rehearsing, the six time title holder may become more accustomed to the professional stage." Another reviewer summed his performance up this way: "Mr. Tilden is no worse than many young men we have seen in similar parts, and no better. Considering the fact which can't be exactly news to our readers, that he plays tennis and makes acting only his occasional avocation, his talent seems even more praiseworthy."[7]

Interestingly, though Tilden could easily command the enthralled attention of thousands of patrons in a tennis stadium and consume a meal that would stuff a horse before going on court, a Broadway debut was another thing entirely. Bill was extremely nervous and able to drink only a small cocktail consisting of an egg-and-milk mixture before going onstage. His apprehension may have been well founded; the play's modest reviews helped close the show after just two weeks. Entranced by the theatrical experience, however, Bill socked much of his own money in keeping the play going at another Broadway location, the Mayfair Theatre.[8]

In what was probably an unprecedented act and one never to be repeated—at least for a world-class tennis player—Tilden's tennis matches were pushed back an hour or more in order for him to have time to finish his matinee performances and travel uptown to the athletic arena.

On court the United States was struggling to maintain its tennis hegemony in international competition, as France kept nipping at its heels. The French took every opportunity possible to challenge the best and thereby plot the appropriate strategy for the eventual kill. At the mid-February 1926 National Indoor Championship at the Seventh Regiment Armory in New York City, the French put on quite a show. Tilden did not even make it to the semifinals, as Borotra took him out in a quarterfinal match. A week later in the International Indoor Team Tennis Championship, the American team, consisting of Tilden, Richards, and Frank Hunter, won out but just barely. The 3–2 score did not fully illuminate how close the match was from a talent perspective. The fact that Lacoste beat both Tilden and Richards, along with the fine play of Borotra and Brugnon, further confirmed "the grit and improved French play" American tennis officials could now count on from their chief foreign opponent.[9]

Lacoste's performance at both events was so impressive that he was "proclaimed by many as the coming champion of the world." There seemed to be general agreement that both he and Borotra belonged "unquestionably in the world's first ten." Merrihew at *American Lawn Tennis* was impressed by the French team's fine play and thought everyone else should be as well. In an article entitled "The Fate of the Cup," Merrihew wrote that the French team's high quality of play had convinced him they were "within striking distance of victory." Merrihew further encouraged his many devoted tennis readers to take note of another salient fact, the age difference between the French and American players. The players who were the backbone of the great American team—Tilden, Johnston, and Williams—were men in their thirties. "They are due," he soberly predicted, "for their period of decline and fall."[10]

Some had already taken notice that the world's best player was no longer the dominant player who stood regally above all others. Tilden's surprising losses to lesser players was news making. At the Mason-Dixon Tournament at the Greenbrier Country Club in April, Bill lost a hard-fought five-setter to his former disciple Richards, who won 11–9, 6–2, 2–6, 3–6, 6–3. Knowledgeable fans at the White Sulphur Springs, West Virginia, resort, used to seeing Big Bill's incredible comebacks, were expecting another after Tilden won the third and fourth sets and with Richards "appearing . . . to be more worn by the battle," but it did not play out as scripted. Bill was the one making the unforced errors in the final set and going down to defeat.[11]

It was Richards's second victory over his mentor in a month—the earlier one in Jacksonville—and no doubt both were satisfying. Their relationship had been increasingly strained. Richards was now in his early twenties, a top player, and an Olympic champion. He was no longer willing to put up with Bill constantly dictating what he should do on and off the court. Vinnie had long been exasperated over Bill's "habit of dominating the court and not playing sound doubles." Bill's propensity to go after every ball, even though it might be Vinnie's play or his side of the court, was a source of constant friction, as was Bill's habit of making all of the team's big and little decisions. Vinnie was ready to be his own man and would soon end their once close relationship.

Bill was not just losing to Richards, however. Others, some without international reputations, were now beating him. Alfred Chapin, for example, was a fine tennis player, but nobody would expect him to defeat the great Tilden. Yet it happened at the Connecticut Championship. It was a shocking result and, as the newspapers noted, Tilden's "first straight set defeat in outdoor play for six years."[12] Once gain, Tilden was doing double duty as struggling thespian and accomplished athlete, but he never used his nightly appearances in a New Haven play and lectures during the day to a Yale drama class as reasons for his subpar court performances.

In what was more than likely the only time a world-class athlete lectured on the subject of "contemporaneous drama" at Yale University, Bill told the students, "It isn't the producers, nor the actors, nor the scenic effects, nor even the author that makes a play. It is the audience's reaction to the show." Bill went on to argue, "Only Barrie's or Shaw's plays are put on the stage exactly as they are written. Other plays undergo sometimes very radical changes before they reach New York." Bill also tossed the students a compliment, stating that his New Haven theater audiences were some of the most "intellectual" he had appeared before, and this would definitely help polish the play for its forthcoming Broadway premiere.[13]

The losses, however, sparked debate. After playing what was perceived as flawless tennis for the past few years, Tilden finally seemed a member of the human race; he could make errors and lose matches like everyone else. Ironically, it would be the normally critical Allison Danzig in a *New York Times* column who would come to Bill's defense. "There was once a time when it was thought that William Tilden could not be defeated," argued Danzig. "The year is still young and already the champion has been vanquished four times in tournament play." The previous year, Danzig conceded, Tilden also looked vulnerable and had "narrow escapes" against George Lott, Harvey Snodgrass, Howard Kinsey, as well as various Frenchmen. It all "led to questions as to his invincibility." But then, Danzig reminded everyone, "came the national championship," where he once again proved invincible. Danzig, now a firm believer in Bill's extraordinary powers, concluded his piece by writing, "Tilden can go on being defeated almost day after day, but it will change few expectations as to what he will do in the national championship."[14] Years of unequaled excellence had carved the story in stone: Big Bill was the money player.

For anyone else Tilden's four losses out of a ton of matches during the early months of 1926 would have been quite desirable, but for the world's best it was rather pedestrian. Public speculation increased, just as it did for another iconic sports figure of the era, Jack Dempsey. Both men had retained their titles during the twenties, convincingly defeated all challengers, but there were signs, actual physical indications, some believed, that the years and the myriad battles had taken their toll. For Dempsey speculation was rife the champ was not training as hard, was out of shape, and that a solid newcomer, a former marine named Gene Tunney, had a shot of taking the heavyweight title. For Bill there was a triumvirate of French Musketeers seeking his scalp, not to mention a dozen or so others from abroad as well as at home with a similar goal in mind. One of those on the home front who knew him well, Vinnie Richards, thought his mentor was definitely showing some wear and tear, but it was a change in the champ's mental aspect that was most noticeable. He believed Tilden was on the downside of his career. He said the signs were too obvious to ignore.

Richards was quoted in the newspapers as saying the Tilden he faced in recent matches in the South—in which he defeated Bill twice—"was not the Tilden of past years." The champ, according to his former pupil, had "lost something of his daring." Bill, who had been known to all for his "ability to rise to unassailable heights . . . and confound his opponent with the lightning of his strokes," had become more tentative. He was now playing a more "cautious" brand of tennis. In the past, when Tilden was pressed and the play reached a critical stage, he was always able to throw caution to the wind, turn "rampant," in Vinnie's words, and find the tactics and strokes to pull out a victory. The fact that Tilden was no longer doing this, said Richards, was "an omen pointing toward the slipping of the champion."[15]

Allison Danzig, a *New York Times* sports reporter, knew selling Big Bill short was risky business, but as he pointed out to his many readers, Richards knew Bill's style of play better than most and he had the rare privilege of beating him, not once but twice in recent months. So far in 1926 Bill had been defeated four times, twice indoors and twice on clay. Granted, the losses were an oddity that most attributed to Bill spending too much time onstage and too little on court. Richards, however, believed there was more to it than Bill's theatrical performances. As someone who had been playing with and against Tilden for eight years, he no longer believed that the champion was as invincible as he had been. Something was definitely different about his game.

Richards would take his racket and opinions off to Europe for the French and English Championships, while Bill played in a series of domestic matches and applied himself in his various dramatic pursuits. For Richards the trip abroad was far less rewarding than his overseas adventure in 1924. Then he returned as the Olympic champion. This trip was less eventful; in fact, it was embarrassing. Henri Cochet knocked him out of the Wimbledon competition in just the second round. Richard's early exit combined with a third Wimbledon final consisting of two Frenchmen was another clear sign that America's grip on the Davis Cup was in jeopardy. Most tennis fans in America, however, were convinced the threat was overblown. They were spoiled. The two Bills—Tilden and Johnston—

had repeatedly proved themselves unbeatable in Davis Cup play. They would do so again.

Back on American shores Tilden continued to rule the tennis roost with an occasional stumble. He won the middle-states singles and doubles (with Sandy Wiener) titles in June and followed that up with his fifth straight National Clay Court title in Detroit in July. In late July he would lose a New York–area four-set final to Richards but come back in mid-August to win the annual East versus West Tournament and the Southern New York Championship. He would defeat both Bill Johnston and Richards in the process of claiming both titles, but more discerning observers recognized something was amiss with Tilden's game.

A. Wallis Merrihew thought he knew what it was, Bill's backhand. In an *ALT* article he wrote that the champ's "confidence has been shaken." Bill was running around his backhand "in order to hit them on his forehand" side. This amazed Merrihew, who was a serious student of the game. He considered Bill's backhand one of the game's greatest strokes and had little doubt that it had "won him more than one of his six championships." Merrihew wondered aloud if this great stroke "would become a thing of the past." Moreover, it was unlike Bill "to let a thing of this kind happen." Normally, Bill would work assiduously "to get his backhand going again."[16] For Merrihew and others, it was a mystery.

If there was one item that dominated tennis circles across the globe during the summer of 1926, it was one that actually occurred off court: Suzanne Lenglen signed a professional contract. Unbeatable—at least by another woman—Lenglen was becoming progressively disenchanted with her demanding schedule of high-pressure public appearances and much-reported-on matches with little in the end to show for it. Her delicate temperament and gradual disgruntlement were made to order for C. C. Pyle, an enterprising sports promoter who knew how to make a buck from the exploits of top American athletes.

Less than a year earlier Pyle—better known to newspaper readers as "Cash and Carry" Pyle—pulled off a significant coup when he signed University of Illinois star running back Harold "Red" Grange to a professional football contract. The hottest property in college football, a sport that was already much followed and still rising in popularity, Grange left school after his final season of college eligibility to join the professional ranks as a member of the Chicago Bears. Up until this time a turnout of twenty thousand at a professional game was considered pretty good. The appearance of the "Galloping Ghost" (Grange's nickname) now brought out three to four times as many people when the Bears took the gridiron against teams from New York, Washington, and other towns with pro teams. But just as "professional football needed a Red Grange" to spark public interest, "tennis needed a Bill Tilden to develop into a big-time spectator sport."[17] Now that it had arrived as a game patrons would pay to see, it awaited that next crucial step: a professional tour.

A crafty businessman and sports visionary, Pyle knew only amateur stars with the vast following of Tilden and Lenglen could do for tennis what Grange had done for professional football. Tennis, however, proved a tough nut to crack. The amateur ethic was deeply embedded in the roots and fabric of the sport, and getting high-profile players with an upper-class pedigree and elitist sensibilities to go pro was a considerable, if not impossible, challenge. Pyle, if nothing else, however, was relentless.

Viewing the Frenchwoman an easier sell than the irascible patrician from Philadelphia, Pyle pursued her on a regular basis—both here and abroad over a period of months—until she agreed to turn pro. "She demurred at first," Pyle admitted, "but when I made the big financial offer she accepted."[18] Suzanne's selling price to go pro was the object of much speculation. Most observers put it in the neighborhood of $100,000, though others thought it approached $250,000, a staggering amount by the standards of the day.

The internal debate, deciding whether to remain an amateur or go pro, exhausted Suzanne. "The nightmare is over," she informed the press when the decision was made. "I have escaped from bondage and slavery. No one can order me about any longer to play tournaments for the benefit of the club owners. Now I will be able to make some money, have some fun, and see the world."[19]

Criticized by many purists for what was perceived as a heretical act, Suzanne felt obligated to explain her decision and expose what rankled her so about amateur athletics. "In the twelve years I have been champion

I have earned literally millions of francs in entrance fees to be allowed to do so," she wrote in a long article for the *Philadelphia Evening Bulletin* and the North American Newspaper Alliance. "Wimbledon took in about $150,000 at the gate. . . . The Cannes Tournament in which I participated sold 800,000 francs worth of tickets. . . . All the Riviera tournaments in which I have played have averaged more than 10,000 francs in gate receipts. I have worked as hard at my career as any man or woman has worked at a career. And in my whole lifetime I have not earned $5,000—not one cent of that by my specialty, my life study—tennis."[20]

Lenglen plaintively asked her readers, what is a twenty-seven-year-old athlete to do who has been described as having a "genius" for a game but is unable to make any money from it? "Should I smile at the prospect of actual poverty and continue to earn a fortune" for others? "What about the poor man as amateur?" she asked. "How is he to earn his living? Should sports be left to the independently wealthy?" Lenglen argued that amateurism under the current rules "required the player to have an independent income or sentence himself to mediocrity by giving only half his attention to his sport—or be a swindler."

Suzanne Lenglen was not the only one to see the stark inequities in the amateur system, but she now had the fire in the belly as well as the biggest megaphone to express her moral outrage. The current system, she complained, "gives the rich man an advantage on the court. That seems a little strange in a world which has gone through centuries of revolution to establish the principle of equality."

Lenglen revealed her torment, the gradual realization that tennis—a "clean sport," as her father referred to it, and one she would grow to revere as if it were a "religion"—was not as advertised. "As I grew older," she admitted, "little doubts began to creep into my religion—little incongruities, the so-called amateur rules awakened trains of thought in my mind that were strangely agnostic."

For Lenglen—and probably many other athletes at the time—what was occurring was too obvious to ignore. "If we amateurs are to contribute a life's work to learning to play for nothing," she openly pondered, "why isn't there an amateur gallery which can look on for nothing? At last I realized what was happening. The owners of these clubs at which I so often played were mostly shrewd businessmen and they saw to it these tournaments netted them a handsome profit. With few exceptions, the proceeds from these amateur exhibitions went into private pockets."[21]

Lenglen would go on to rail against the many inequities she had witnessed over the years, such as patrons paying admission fees and players paying entrance fees, thereby allowing "club owners getting money going and coming." It was a system, said Lenglen, set up by the wealthy and for the wealthy. But "was such a system fair? Did it advance the sport? Does it make tennis more popular?" The answer was obvious, she argued. Quoting Shakespeare, she barked, "There is something rotten in the state of Denmark."

For some time, Lenglen admitted, she had "been hovering on the brink of doubt and discontent. Then from the west came the deciding impulse that made me renounce my amateurism and protest openly against this unjust state of affairs. I am today a professional; happy in my decision; enthusiastic about my future and sincere in the belief I will preach the gospel of tennis to thousands." As to the professionalism—that bogeyman of tainted sport—Lenglen maintained, "Professionalism cannot hurt the sport, it can only do it good. I know professionals who are perfect sportsmen and I know professionals who are not. There is no valid reason why the professional should not match his skill against the amateur except the amateur might be afraid. As for myself, I can only say that I have always been a clean amateur and that now I am going to be a clean professional."[22]

Lenglen's decision to turn pro jolted the world tennis community. Opinions varied as to the impact. Cynics who were aware of the traditional but covert money grab by the USLTA and the club owners speculated on the outcome as well as the viability of professional tennis. What would it look like? Would there be tournaments or one-night stands in different cities? Would pros and amateurs compete against each other? Many believed such a venture could never get off the ground. Most important, whom would Suzanne play? Pyle must have wondered himself, though one would not know by his public statements. Ever resourceful, he said Suzanne would come to America in mid-September and begin her national tour soon after. He promised "at least seven or eight other famous tennis stars" would join her on a national tour and teased that some of them were on the U.S. Davis

Cup team. This came as a shock to the USLTA and Richard N. Williams, captain of the American squad, which was preparing to defend the Cup. "Personally, I would not consider any proposition to turn professional," declared Williams, who came from money and was quite content with the status quo. But what of other team members? "It's all news to me," said Bill Johnston, who said Pyle had not approached him.

The biggest catch, of course, would have been Tilden, but Big Bill's negative view of professional tennis wasn't a secret. Still, Pyle thought such a venture was worth the effort, as Bill's acrimonious relationship with the game's leadership was equally well known. His efforts proved unrewarding.

Bill would subsequently write that he believed Pyle "gave pro tennis a black eye," but that was before Bill himself became a convert. Bill thought the sports promoter "created a peculiar quality of unreality, of false, circus atmosphere about it that did not appeal to sportsmen." A member of an elite Philadelphia family and an upper-class Germantown club that was immersed in tradition and eschewed professionalism in sport, Bill said he "played tennis because I enjoy it" and the "great thrill" he got out of "hitting the ball. Personally, I have no interest in professional tennis, never had. To me sport and business do not mix."[23] It was a principle he deeply believed at the time, though, like Lenglen, there were nagging doubts and occasional sparks of agnosticism.

As the biggest fish in the sea, however, he was targeted by professional promoters since he became a star attraction. When Tilden returned from Australia in 1920 as the world, American, and Davis Cup champion, Arthur Hammerstein proffered a professional contract. C. B. Cochran, a British promoter, made an even more attractive offer, but Bill remained unpersuaded. "My love of playing tennis for fun proved too great," said Bill, "and I turned down the offer." Pyle made a series of enticing appeals, but Bill rejected those as well. The promoter was shocked an athlete who was no longer rolling in dough could turn down such money.

"Mr. Tilden," said Pyle in exasperation, "I think you are a damn fool."

"I think you're probably right," Tilden replied.[24]

Much like Lenglen, Tilden's views were still evolving. With the game's increasing popularity—due in large part to their stellar play—the sport was increasing in stature, and considerable money was being made, but not by those whom the public was paying to see perform. The financial component, along with the USLTA's dictatorial decision making, made it increasingly difficult for him to defend the exalted institution of amateur sport. By the late 1920s Tilden had moderated his disdain for professional tennis and saw "no cause for the feeling that there is a stigma attached to a professional and that professionalism is a menace to the game. I consider the professional game just as high class and sporting as the amateur, only it is a business and amateur tennis is a sport."

In retrospect, one can detect a slight crack in the window, and like a stealthy second-story man trying to go straight, Tilden was increasingly torn between his bedrock principles and the freedom and money professional tennis represented. Over the course of the next few years, Tilden's view of the amateur-versus-professional debate would continue to evolve. But at the moment Tilden had other tennis concerns. Lenglen was not the only French tennis player making news. In fact, there were four others, all men, who were advancing on Fortress America. Tilden had been one of the first, according to E. C. Potter Jr., to perceive a new menace to American tennis supremacy "rising in France these last few years and this was the first patterning of the raindrops which presaged the storm which was soon to break."[25]

Prior to World War I, France was the leading exponent of lawn tennis on the Continent. Players like Max Decugis, William Laurentz, and André Gobert were generally viewed as respectable and accomplished net men. The postwar years, however, would unveil a new generation of tennis players who not only exceeded their predecessors, but also helped to uplift a war-devastated nation. They would eventually prove peerless in international competition and solidify their place in the hallowed halls of tennis history.

The first to rise was Jacques Brugnon, who as a young man showed promise just prior to the start of the war. In its aftermath he won some tournaments, but it was increasingly clear "his strokes were accurate and well-controlled but they lacked sting." His play was sound, especially in doubles, where his game neatly conformed to whatever style his partner played—Lenglen said, "I know of no man I would rather have for a partner"—but it was doubtful he would surpass men like Laurentz and Gobert in singles play.[26]

It would be in 1921 that two younger players would arrive on the scene and showcase an array of court skills that caused Parisian audiences to sit up and take notice. Jean Borotra was a slim, athletic beret-wearing twenty-two-year-old Basque lad at the time who had come to France's famous École Polytechnique to study engineering. In addition to a fine business mind, he came with a love of sport and an accomplished hand at his native game, pelota. Exchanging his *chistera* for a tennis racket, he won a series of matches more on "verve and impetuosity" than racket skill. Though his ground strokes and tactics were unorthodox, he delighted spectators with his aggressive, acrobatic performances that amazed opponents and won matches. Lenglen was so impressed, she compared Borotra to "a flash, a streak of light, a man bouncing around like a rubber ball and the get you think is impossible shoots back over the net."[27]

For all of his brio and ingratiating personality, he would seem to have met his match against another equally gifted tennis newcomer from the city of Lyons. Shorter and stockier than Borotra and three years younger, Henri Cochet was a city-tough street gamin who was filled with confidence, promise, and a natural feel for the game. Due to his father managing a tennis club, by the age of five Cochet was swinging a racket, learning the rules of the game, and besting players twice his age. By the war's end he was still just a teenager, slightly undersize, "but with the same confidence in himself and the same superiority over" most rivals who had the gumption to step on court with him.[28] Moving up in class he traveled to Paris for better competition and met Borotra in an important contest for both players. It was a tight affair until young Cochet, altering his tactics, began running around his backhand and started walloping volleys from midcourt and smashing forehand winners by deftly hitting balls on the rise. It was an impressive performance that he would replicate in future matches. Though he shunned practice and usually got away with it because of his fine reflexes and athleticism, he never walked on a court feeling inferior. Impressed by his swagger, Lenglen said Cochet "bursts into action like a bomb" and "serves, reaches the net, and kills the return with what seems to be a single effort. On a good day," Lenglen boasted, "nobody in the world can stop him."[29]

With Borotra's and Cochet's potential obvious, France had produced two young players who looked like they were going to take the place of—and possibly exceed in stature—the accomplishments of Gobert, Decugis, and Laurentz. But France was not done; there was one other player in the pipeline who was destined to make his mark on the world tennis scene.

Three years younger than Cochet and six years younger than Borotra, René Lacoste was a large-nosed, olive-skinned son of a wealthy automobile manufacturer who had not seen a tennis court until he spied one in England in 1919. The game immediately intrigued him, and he soon after dedicated himself to mastering the key elements of the sport. His initial efforts were uneventful and he lost most of his matches, but he only grew more determined to play the game at a high level of proficiency. To the displeasure of his father, he focused all his attention and energy on lawn tennis and began taking weekly lessons from the professional Henri Darsonval.

Not as physically robust or athletically gifted as Borotra or Cochet, he brought something else to the table, "a keen and studious mind," plus a remarkable work ethic. As Potter would write of him, Lacoste "approached tennis as he approached a problem in algebra. It was like an equation to which he knew there was an answer. He could find it if he applied himself to its solution in the right way."[30] Lacoste's highly cerebral approach had him examine, and reexamine, his matches as well as those of others. His losses were constantly scrutinized; he investigated not only how a point played out, but also how it could have played out. "Cause and effect" became his mantra. It was a mental form of war games laid out on a grass field of combat. There would be periods when he would practice for months without playing a match, always taking notes, analyzing the reason for unforced errors, and studying the strengths and weaknesses of opponents. By 1922 he was defeating players who had once beaten him; he even bested Roper Barrett, one of England's top players, in a Belgian tournament.

Lenglen was quick to notice young Lacoste's improvement, studious demeanor, and dedication. He "plays methodically and carefully," said Lenglen, and she called him "a stylist of the highest order." He was always "perfecting his game, practicing every stroke . . . until he has mastered it."[31] His workmanlike approach was not unlike Tilden's, his dedication unquestioned. In time his leadership qualities would become equally evident.

There was one other thing about the French newcomers that was as important as their talent, and that was their commitment to excel and bring the revered Davis Cup trophy to French shores. Though they were as different as four men could be in philosophy, playing style, and temperament, they developed a single-minded desire to defeat the United States and make France the world's greatest tennis nation. With the passing of each year, they improved, gained more confidence, and became more assured that their goal was attainable. Borotra rose to prominence first at Wimbledon, "his lithe, athletic figure dashing in for the volley . . . his unconcern for injury as he hurled himself into a lineman's chair in rushing for a wide ball drew applause and laughter."[32] For the first time, a French name appeared on the British championship's roll of honor for men's singles in 1924.

The following year another French name took first prize at Wimbledon. Young Lacoste took out the Bounding Basque, a further sign that the French were stockpiling a stable of exceptional tennis talent. In fact, from 1924 until the end of the decade, a Frenchman held the Wimbledon singles crown, with Borotra, Lacoste, and Cochet each winning the championship title twice. But as Al Laney has observed, "The winning of individual titles, however satisfying personally, was not their principal goal. That was the winning of the cup, and they considered Tilden, who had last been at Wimbledon in 1921, their main enemy and their principal target . . . and if he would not come to them, then they would seek him out at home, challenge him, and try to find out how he could be beaten. They recognized very early that so long as Tilden remained unbeaten, France would remain a secondary tennis nation."[33]

The French would garner other titles on the Continent as well as on American soil. The latter were particularly galling. Borotra would win the U.S. indoor title in early 1926, Lacoste would do the same, and in the French-U.S. team match Lacoste defeated both Tilden and Richards in straight sets. Though most tennis fans spoiled by American dominance of Davis Cup competition refused to see the signs of struggle ahead, for the French the veil of American invincibility was gradually coming down.

Merrihew tried to inform his readers of the approaching storm. "It is more certain than ever," he warned *ALT* readers, "that France will be this year's challenge. With three of the four semi-finalists at Wimbledon, France stands out more than ever as the dominant nation at Wimbledon. It remains to be seen whether she can dominate the Davis Cup contest as well."[34] For the bulk of American tennis fans, however, the formidable lineup of Tilden, Johnston, Williams, and Richards made any serious challenge seem a pipe dream. Past glory overpowered any sense of reality.

Tilden was not mesmerized by the American team's unprecedented success during their stunning run. He had been carefully watching the French net men grow in confidence and capability. He had made a mental note early on in the decade when "an unknown kid in his late teens named Henri Cochet upset the famous Australian star, Pat O'Hara Wood," in an interzone Davis Cup challenge round between France and Australia. The following year another "boy with little reputation at the time," René Lacoste, "threw the fear of God into several top-ranking players." And in 1925 when everyone expected Australia to challenge the United States once again for the Davis Cup, the team from Down Under "was unexpectedly spilled by the young French team of Lacoste and Borotra." For Tilden, "The coming greatness of France became unmistakable."[35] Their early 1926 indoor victories in New York confirmed his fears.

In addition to the Frenchmen's eye-catching performances, Bill was also struck by their "complete contrast" in personalities. Lacoste always appeared "detached, stolid, and phlegmatic." His "shrewd, analytic" study of the game and opponents was so "scientific" in approach, Tilden could well understand why most observers saw him as "ruthless and cold-blooded." Lacoste's nickname, "the Crocodile," seemed most appropriate.[36]

Cochet, according to Tilden, was very different, more like an explosive pocket rocket than a deep thinker. Though he thought the little Frenchman's "technical command was superb," he said when that proved insufficient in a tight contest, Cochet "threw it to the winds and called on that inspirational creativeness which defies analysis." In short, Cochet was a "genius" and complete tennis "revolutionary."

Borotra had an outsize personality and one that drove Tilden crazy. Bill referred to him as the "artist and charlatan" of the group and one of the "greatest showmen and fakers in tennis history." Though Borotra's game left much to be desired from a technical standpoint, "his unbelievable speed of foot, his swift eye, his muscular reflexes so fast that he seemed almost inhuman, allowed him to produce first-class results with a completely second-class technique." More unusual yet, Bill argued, was the Basque's huge but wholly phony personal charm. Borotra could shower an opponent or a stadium audience with recurring waves of warmth and gratitude, but at its heart was a hefty foundation of cunning and "insincerity."

And Brugnon, the last of the four Frenchmen, was the least talented and interesting from a personality and singles perspective, but his doubles play was exceptional. He had the unique ability to augment his partner's strengths and diminish his weaknesses, which was both uncommon and of great value in forming a potent doubles team.[37]

It was the quartet's cohesiveness as a unit, natural talent, and uncompromising dedication to a goal that further set them apart from other national teams. Digby Baltzell was so impressed with their unique collective effort to win and defend the Davis Cup trophy that he would go on to argue that their effort resulted in "surely the finest five years in the history of tennis."[38]

And to achieve that most difficult task, it was necessary to defeat the great Bill Tilden. But how does one surmount such an omnipotent opponent? Many had tried over the years, but in tournaments of great esteem it had proved impossible. There had not been a player alive who had defeated Big Bill outdoors in an important contest after 1919. Great competitors such as Brookes, Patterson, Anderson, Shimidzu, Johnston, Williams, and the French had all fallen in battle. Maybe it was not possible. But wait. Might not a nation accomplish what an individual player could not? Could a team consisting of a diverse collection of talented players sworn to a single objective devise a scheme, a grand strategy, some might say, that would conquer the best lawn tennis player in the world?

As Lacoste, the calculating instigator of the audacious game plan, would one day admit, stories had long swirled of Tilden and his unrivaled ability, but seeing him in person provided the first true sense of the man's greatness. It was a match between Tilden and Manuel Alonso, and young Lacoste sat in the stands and eagerly studied both men. "I admired exceedingly the speed, elegance and ardor of the wonderful Spanish player," Lacoste would eventually write,

> but was amazed by the sight of Tilden's play. It is an extraordinary thing that Tilden, who only became a champion by dint of hard work, shows on the tennis court such facility. Tilden always seems to have a thousand means of putting the ball away from his opponent's reach. He seems to exercise a strange fascination

over his opponent as well as the spectators. Tilden, even when beaten, always leaves an impression on the public mind that he was superior to the victor. All the spectators seem to think he can win when he likes. Seemingly, in two steps Tilden covers the whole of the court; without any effort he executes the most various and extraordinary strokes. He seems capable of returning any shot when he likes, to put the ball out of reach of his opponent when he thinks the moment has come to do so. Sometimes he gives the ball prodigious velocity, sometimes he caresses it, and guides it to a corner of the court whither nobody but himself would have thought of directing it.[39]

If Lacoste was accused of hero worship, of imagining one of the Greek gods descending from the celestial heavens and picking up a racket, or sounding like a love-struck teenager, it is unlikely he would have taken umbrage at the characterization. The young Frenchman was admittedly star-struck. He knew well the difficulty, the endless hours of practice, involved in mastering proper tennis technique. Tilden's grasp of every facet of the game was not only extraordinary; it was inhuman.

Lacoste had immense respect for the game's other top players such as Patterson, Johnston, and Richards. Bill Johnston, for example, was another "great architect of American [Davis Cup] victories." Lacoste recognized the little Californian's popularity, his exquisite "execution," his ability "to impart greater speed to the ball" than Tilden, and his dominance over such fine players as Kumagae, Patterson, Richards, Borotra, and himself, but every time Little Bill stepped on a court with Tilden, he "appeared to be dominated by the athletic superiority and the strong personality if his rival." In Lacoste's close study of the game's best players, "Johnston executed perhaps more perfect strokes than Tilden. He did not give the same impression of a master as Tilden, nor did he seem capable of triumphing over any opponent, in any circumstances, like the wonderful Philadelphian."[40] The American team had other great lawn tennis players, like Dick Williams and Vinnie Richards, with national and Olympic titles to their names, but the chief obstacle was always Tilden. A great mountain climber may have triumphantly scaled Annapurna, Makalu, and Lhotse, but there was always Everest looming in the background. Until the biggest, most dangerous mountain peak had been successfully ascended, one would permanently reside in its shadow.

In order to scale that insufferably difficult lawn tennis peak known as Mount Tilden, Lacoste devised a strategy more suitable for a military campaign than an athletic event. The French team would orchestrate a campaign of attrition; they would simply try to wear Tilden down. According to Rich Hillway, the French adopted a unique team approach with the goal of "tiring Tilden out. In short, their goal was to exhaust him. Run him endlessly; run him from corner to corner. Hit an endless series of lobs and drop shots so that he would never face an easy point. Keep him on the court and make him work for everything. Strive to make each and every match as difficult as possible for him. They sought to put him through a physical and psychological ordeal."[41]

As with all such campaigns of attrition, they do not produce victory overnight. The French were not even sure it would work, but it was worth a try. Nothing else had proved successful. They decided to first employ their new strategy in early September in Philadelphia. The Germantown Cricket Club was once again hosting the challenge round of the Davis Cup. The French had proved themselves the best of the world's twenty-four nations that entered the 1926 competition, with the exception of the vaunted American squad. By now Borotra, Cochet, Lacoste, and Brugnon had been anointed the "Musketeers" by Henry W. Slocum Jr. at a USLTA dinner in their honor. They were intent on achieving greatness on the courts of the greatest tennis nation in the world.

When Bill took the court inside Manheim's huge wooden stadium late on the afternoon of September 9, Bill Johnston had already polished off René Lacoste, 6–0, 6–4, 0–6, 6–0. In stunning fashion Little Bill had decidedly defeated the earnest young Frenchman.

His partner's decisive victory must have spurred Big Bill to go one better, and he defeated Jean Borotra—the reigning Wimbledon champion—in straight sets, 6–2, 6–3, 6–3. With Tilden going at the athletic, beret-wearing Basque with "hammer and tongs" from the very first swing of the racket, the usually jocular Frenchman did not have a chance. "A picture of determination from the outset," Bill had been beseeched by his teammates "to win the match quickly." Apparently eager to comply, Bill unleashed a panoply of weaponry to tame and slay the French and British champion.

"Pretty good for a couple of old men they had dead and buried all year," remarked Tilden after the match. His victory and Little Bill's earlier in the afternoon had given the United States "a firm grip on the Davis Cup for another year." "Many times I have said no man possesses enough stamina to go to the net for five sets," Bill remarked to reporters after the match. "This match proved my point. Any man who can shoot first class tennis can keep Borotra from the net, and he must get to the net to win."[42]

Borotra was practically shell-shocked by the embarrassing tennis lesson, especially in front of fourteen thousand spectators. "Bill Tilden, he's just too good," the Frenchman repeatedly muttered to himself. "Tilden is too good. His service, his volleys, his tactics . . . he doesn't let you breathe. He has no equal."

Lacoste was similarly dejected. He had no expectation of such one-sided defeats. The first day's results were a shock. "Discouraging is the only way to describe it," he told reporters. He even talked of retiring from tennis, though he was just twenty-two years old. If he came back again, he said he would recommend the team come earlier in the summer so that the players became "acclimated" to the weather. Lacoste, it seemed, placed part of the blame for his team's poor showing on the East Coast's oppressive heat and strength-sapping humidity. "There is only one way to become acclimated," said Lacoste, referring to the "sticky weather." "That is to come to America two months before the challenge round." When asked by reporters if the heat had caused their defeat, the stoic Frenchman replied, "We simply were outplayed."

Julian S. Myrick, the powerful USLTA official and referee of the challenge round, was in agreement with both of Lacoste's statements. "The Frenchmen," said Myrick, "have not been here long enough to do themselves justice. My own experience is that a month is needed to become acclimated in a distant land. But, acclimated or otherwise, those terrific service shots of Tilden would be enough to take the wind from anyone's sails."[43]

Pierre Gillou, the French nonplaying team captain, was beside himself with disappointment. He had come to America optimistic regarding the French team's chances and was widely quoted the year before that the French were close to achieving their goal. Gillou's embarrassment would only increase the next day as the doubles duo of Richards and Williams defeated Cochet and Brugnon in straight sets, 6–4, 6–4, 6–3. America had retained the cup and in domineering fashion. As Arthur Voss has written, the French "were bitterly disappointed" and had little to look forward to regarding the following week's trip up to Forest Hills for the National Singles Championship.[44]

But there were still two singles matches to play at Manheim. Even though the Cup had been won by the United States for an unprecedented seventh straight time—a record that still stands—nearly ten thousand spectators turned out for the event's third and final day of competition. It appeared the French were destined for another bitter dose of humility when Little Bill had his way with Borotra in straight sets, 8–6, 6–4, 9–7.

When Tilden and Lacoste took the court, there seemed to be little to play for. That was most evident in Big Bill's lackluster play; he was "making the most lamentable errors on easy shots," and it was all "too obvious that he was not concentrating on the task" at hand. Tennis patrons used to seeing Bill start slow were assured from past experience that when the "elongated Philadelphian" got motivated and "down to business," he would eventually wipe the deck with the Frenchman. Most presumed "the cup already safely defended may have influenced Tilden to shirk at his task for he certainly showed nothing like the keenness and deadly seriousness of purpose that he did against Borotra."[45]

It was a completely different story on the other side of the net. Lacoste "was as earnest in his play as though the cup hung in the balance on this match." His intensity and earnestness, however, got him little in return, as he too made his share of errors as his "control was wretched, and Tilden, in spite of the fact that he was taking matters easily, took the first four games and then the opening set at 6–4." As play continued in the second set, it gradually became obvious the young Frenchman's quality of play started to improve and match his seriousness of purpose. His "machine-like strokes . . . stowed away everything that Tilden sent over and replied with strokes of disconcerting penetration."

More like Tilden in his cerebral approach to the game than any other topflight player, Lacoste had not abandoned the original game plan of running the champion, exhausting him with an endless series of shots to the far edges and corners of the court. As Allison Danzig of the *New York Times* would recount in his coverage of the historic match, by the fourth game of the second set, "Tilden understood that he had his work cut out for him, as his young opponent outguessed him and forced him to abandon pursuit of shots that were too well placed to be returned."

Tilden's play continued to confound spectators. He rarely fired off his cannonball serve, his ground strokes lacked punch, and he repeatedly hit to the same spot on the court instead of trying to move Lacoste around. Moreover, the champion seemed to overrely on a chop stroke, "attempting to lure Lacoste into mistakes with the spin on the ball." To his credit the Frenchman was impervious to such a tactic and seemed "stumped" only when Bill added some heft to his shots and started hitting "flat drives of burning pace."

But the penetrating drives were few and far between; Lacoste won the second set 6–4–mostly through Tilden's many errors—and continued his solid play well into the third. Lacoste won the first three games of the third set. Danzig would write that the champion was being "outguessed, outgeneraled, and out stroked." With no reason to alter his approach, the "young invader" was providing a "marvelous tactical exhibition, driving his opponent to the net with strokes of shortened length and lobbing over his head or passing him down the line, and still Tilden was content to take matters easily allowing shots to go uncontested and making no serious effort to take the offensive."[46]

It was not until Tilden made a comeback and the score was 4–3 in the third set that he began to play his unique style of tennis. Suddenly, his ground strokes had length and pace, his cannonball serves were like bullets, and a deft array of drop shots and tricky slices came off his racket. But the junior member of the French contingent exhibited no signs of his relative inexperience. And he certainly wasn't ready to concede a point, much less the match. He raised his game as well and shocked those in the stands, not to mention his opponent, by returning just about everything hit his way. Despite the riptide of balls with both spin and pace coming his way, Lacoste proved "so impenetrable that the only way the champion could win points was to earn them on clear placements." The rallies, grueling and long, showed off Lacoste's surprising ability to "outsteady" the world's greatest player. The match, which had once been a battle of unforced errors, now became a contest of strategy and highly sophisticated stroking.

Tilden was not reticent about giving the young Frenchman his due. "The monotonous regularity with which that unsmiling, drab, almost dull man returned the best I could hit, seemingly without any effect upon him physically or mentally, piled almost irresistible pressure on my nervous system,"

Tilden would subsequently write. "I used to wish to God he would just once show some form of human reaction. I was often filled with a wild desire to throw my racket at him or hit him over the head."[47]

With the score tied—a set apiece and 6–6 in the third—misfortune struck Tilden in one of the most reliable, if not strongest, parts of his game, his legs. The disastrous event would not only doom any chance of winning the match, but also adversely impact the remainder of his lawn tennis season.

The unlucky "trick of fate," as Allison Danzig would refer to it, came after Tilden had a 40–15 lead in the thirteenth game, and in fact thought he had won the game after Lacoste had hit a ball long, but "the linesman," according to Bill's account, "slept and the ball went for good." Tilden would lose the next point on another delicate Lacoste drop shot. The Frenchman had Tilden on a string, sending well-struck lobs over his opponent's head and then quickly drawing him in on deft drop shots. It was after Tilden had scampered well beyond the baseline to retrieve a lob that Lacoste executed another strategically placed drop shot near the umpire's chair. Tilden charged diagonally across the court toward the net for all he was worth when his left knee buckled just as he weakly struck the ball. As Lacoste hit the ball to the open court for an easy point, Tilden lay in agony on the court.

Tilden had blown out what was described at the time as the "semi-lunar cartilage" of his knee, an already weakened structure that had suffered repeated insults over the years, as well as untold hours of strenuous athletic activity. Regarding what is commonly known today as a meniscus tear or injury, Tilden would say at the time that it was an old injury first suffered as a teenager while playing soccer. Not surprisingly, given Tilden's demanding tennis schedule, the structural damage to his knee never quite healed, and Tilden would be confronted with several significant injuries to the same weakened joint. Carl Fischer witnessed his mentor reinjure the knee in a 1916 match when Tilden "slipped while playing on a very wet court in Wilmington, Delaware."[48] In Tilden's seventh-round match with Zenzo Shimidzu at Wimbledon in 1920, the meniscus would pop once again and leave U.S. tennis officials concerned that Bill, limping badly, would be unable to compete in both the Wimbledon final against Patterson and the subsequent Davis Cup competition. As history would repeatedly prove, Tilden was seemingly impervious to pain and physical injury—and adamantly opposed to defaulting a match—and would go on to defeat the big Australian in both England and New Zealand.

Now Bill would demonstrate the same grit and determination at Manheim as he manually maneuvered the dislocated semilunar cartilage back into place and continued to play. In great pain and limping badly, Tilden struggled back to the baseline, double-faulted, and drove a ball long in the next rally, enabling Lacoste to win the game. Barely able to stand and incapable of setting himself properly to strike the ball, Tilden made five straight unforced errors, thereby assisting the Frenchman in winning the set 8–6.

As Tilden tells the dramatic story of what occurred in the Germantown Cricket Club locker room during the ten-minute rest period between the third and fourth sets, there was much debate as to whether he should default or soldier on, as he was wont to do. "I was told by a doctor to default the contest," Bill wrote years later in his book *My Story*. "But the year's captain, Dick Williams, having seen the cup won in the previous match and Lacoste and I out to play what amounted to an exhibition, had departed for some back court to play tennis himself. No one else had authority to scratch the match, and I was unwilling to do so. So I went out on one leg in the fourth set."[49]

It was a dubious decision at best and one he would pay for dearly. When Bill stepped back on the court for the fourth set, the knee was already swollen and heavily bandaged, and he exhibited a pronounced limp. Making a "stout-hearted" attempt to contest every point with his much younger opponent, Tilden managed to win games on the basis of his serve and "all his cunning and every stroke at his command." Unable to run, Bill did the best he could in retrieving Lacoste's "clever and well placed shots." Never a crowd favorite, Tilden's obvious physical impairment and warrior spirit won him increasing support from a crowd that rarely, if ever, viewed him in the role of a sympathetic underdog. Attempting to stage a rally late in the set utilizing what Danzig called a combination of "utmost daring and cleverness," Tilden received "thunderous" applause that on more than one occasion "brought down the house." When he overcame a two-game deficit and tied the set at five-all, "the Philadelphian aroused the 10,000 spectators to a frenzy of excitement."

Tilden's unexpected and forceful counterattack combined with the crowd's appreciation of his brave effort left the youngest Musketeer "bewildered." He turned toward team captain Gillou with a puzzled expression, signifying his frustration at being unable to quickly end a match against an obviously handicapped opponent. But this was no ordinary opponent; it was Big Bill Tilden, and he was still playing "magnificent tennis." The players traded points and shots, and some exhausting rallies left Tilden decidedly disadvantaged and frustrated. He was having increasing trouble walking, much less scampering for Lacoste's adroit placements. The fourth-set battle went on for some time—twelve games, thirteen, fourteen, far longer than anyone expected—but it was increasingly clear Tilden was playing on fumes and guts. He would eventually be worn down by an excellent player eleven years his junior with two good legs. The final point occurred as Tilden awkwardly chased a ball hit deep to a far corner of the court and feebly launched himself in the air to hit a return, only to see Lacoste take the net and put the ball away. The match ended with Tilden in agony on the grass turf and Lacoste jumping for joy. A Frenchman had finally scaled the mountaintop, 4–6, 6–4, 8–6, 8–6.

According to E. C. Potter, as Tilden limped to the locker room, he could be heard to gloomily mutter, "There it goes."[50] We are left to speculate whether he was referring to his dislodged cartilage, his unblemished Davis Cup singles record, or America's unrivaled dominance as a tennis power.

There was no denying it had been quite a contest—one news organization started their account, "A more sensational match has seldom been played in the twenty-six year history of the Davis Cup than was this epochal struggle"—but most spectators in the stadium must have been slightly perplexed at the reaction of the French team: they were absolutely jubilant. One would have thought they had finally won possession of the Davis Cup, but in fact they had been soundly thrashed 4–1. What the largely American audience could not appreciate was the French team's reverence for Tilden and their long-desired mission to defeat him.

Allison Danzig in his *New York Times* account of the match tried to capture the reason for such celebration by the losing team. "The fruits of victory in the challenge round could hardly have been sweeter to the defenders than was this triumph of Lacoste over the player whose name has brought dread to the hearts of invading teams for seven years. One might have thought from the rejoicing among the French players that at last they had been successful in their long quest for the cup instead of losing the series." In actuality, the excitement was the Four Musketeers' giddy response to the "first taste of blood in a challenge round." And accomplishing it against the great Tilden made it all the sweeter. "I was very lucky," admitted an ecstatic Lacoste in his comments to reporters. "Tilden is the greatest of all tennis players and I am positive that he can defeat any one on the court when he is in his best form. He will come back next year if his knee is in shape and he does not devote too much time to theatricals at the expense of training."[51]

Yes, Tilden had lost, but he had gained something of great value, the public's unreserved admiration. He had been so dominant for so long, many began to view him as a petulant machine. After his valiant but eventual loss under impossible circumstances, those in the stands gave him a greater ovation than if he had been the victor. As one awestruck tennis pundit would go on to describe the scene, "In the hour of defeat William Tilden's star shone more brightly than it had done at any time in the six years that it was the most brilliant luminary in the lawn tennis constellation. As the days, the weeks, and the months pass, the brightness of the former champion's star will increase until its scintillation will almost dazzle the eye. For Bill went down with his colors flying, nailed fast to the mast. Crippled, suffering agonies of body and of mind, he almost flushed victory from certain defeat."[52]

Tilden, at the time, could not fully appreciate what had transpired. Not only had his pristine Davis Cup record in singles—thirteen challenge-round victories over seven years—come to an end, but he had left the battleground physically damaged. According to one witness, the game's greatest player was severely injured. Carl Fischer, who was one of Bill's first students and was now professionally recognized as Dr. Carl Fischer, examined his mentor in the Germantown Cricket Club locker room. "His knee was very swollen, virtually immobile and very painful," recalled Dr. Fischer years later. "I referred him to Dr. Wm. Swartley, Chief Surgeon at Germantown Hospital who had taken care of his right middle finger staph infection four years before. Dr. Swartley said that although orthopedic surgery would be the only cure, the risk was too great. I then referred him to Dr. Mason Beeman in New York, who put an adhesive cast on him and said, 'I don't see how you can play.' The Nationals started at Forest Hills the following week and Tilden was determined to defend his title even if he went on the court with crutches."[53]

Despite the Davis Cup setback, according to Al Laney, "nearly everyone still thought Big Bill invincible." Speculation was rampant in some quarters, however, that Tilden was too injured to play and would be unable to defend his national title. Bill jettisoned those doubts as quickly as they arose. "I'd rather be beaten in the first round," Bill fired back, "than default the title. I'll be in there playing as long as I am able to stand."[54] Drawings and caricatures in newspapers of the world's top players coming to town to compete showed Big Bill with a racket in one hand and a crutch in the other.

What irritated Bill even more than the doubts regarding his forthcoming appearance were the snide comments by some critics that the injury was a hoax, charade, or "alibi" designed to excuse his loss to Lacoste in Philadelphia and gain public sympathy for the defense of his national lawn tennis title. When he took to the court for his first match at Forest Hills, Bill was as intent in thwarting hurtful stories that he was "dramatizing" a relatively minor injury as he was in winning the match. "I have never been more angry about anything in my life than the way some people are saying I'm not hurt but just fooling. The weak knee is due to an old injury," Bill told all who would listen. "It traces back to a kick I received in a soccer game twenty years ago. When the cartilage slipped Saturday, I was unable to cover the court properly any longer. I should never have played that fourth set, but it wasn't my place to default an international match."[55] For those who wanted proof, Bill brought with him "statements from two doctors saying the cartilage in his left knee is out of place and there are some strained tendons and ligaments there."

Bill's first match was against John Van Ryn, an up-and-coming Princeton player who went down to defeat 6–4, 3–6, 7–5, 6–2. The contest did little to improve Bill's expectations or his leg's recovery. It was hard not to notice that Bill stay "rooted on the baseline, returning anything that came near him and letting everything else go uncontested," reported the *Philadelphia Evening Bulletin*. "Honestly, I can't tell how far I will be able to go," he told reporters. "I'll admit I can go better than I did today. I am taking no chances in these early matches. If I am moving toward a ball, I keep on going for it, but if I am moving away from it, I just let it go. I really don't know how my leg would act if I gave it a severe strain. And I have no intention of trying to find out until I have to."[56]

Those who observed that first match at Forest Hills were even more pessimistic about Bill's chances against the likes of Johnston, Richards, Williams, Frank Hunter, and the rapidly improving French Musketeers. The *Times*, for example, saw Tilden's "struggle" with young Van Ryn as a dark omen. "When Tilden loses a set in an opening round of the all-comers there is something necessarily wrong," the newspaper speculated. Tilden's objective of winning a seventh National Championship was considered nothing short of a "herculean test."[57]

His next match was against Neil Sullivan, another former protégé and Manheim club member who even volunteered to default the match if it would help Bill in his goal of amassing a seventh national title. Bill voiced his appreciation of the generous offer, but would never accept such a gift. He told Sullivan to play his best, which is what he did. Like Van Ryn before him, Sullivan managed to take one set off his former coach.

Curiously, Bill's next match would be against another former student, Arnold W. Jones. It had been seven years since Bill had relocated to Providence to rebuild his backhand and teach young Arnold the rudiments of the game. Just a sprightly teenager and tennis novice at the time, Arnold had improved steadily over the years and was now a fine player in his own right. Like Sullivan, Fischer, Richards, and many others Bill had mentored over the years, Jones now stood between him and the championship. As athletic competitors it is doubtful either player gave much thought to their long personal connection once the first serve was offered. In addition to the game's technical aspects, court etiquette, and good sportsmanship, Bill also taught his charges to play hard and play to win. And that is what Jones endeavored to do. He took a long, difficult first set off Tilden 9–7 and was on his way to a second when the champion's frustration erupted. He stopped the match and started ripping off "a yard or so of adhesive tape" and bandages that encased his damaged leg. Now able to move more freely, Tilden went on to win three of the next four sets, 7–5, 4–6, 6–1, 6–2.

Reporters who covered the match were anxious to get Bill's assessment of his effort. "My leg stood up well under the running," Tilden remarked. "My knee is a little swollen, that is all. I will get a new elastic brace and from now on I will go as long as the knee holds up. I hope it will carry me through the final."[58]

Not everyone was so optimistic. Tilden's mobility was greatly compromised, and he was in obvious pain. One need not be a connoisseur of the game to spot it. Some longtime tennis observers were making private predictions: Tilden was in no condition to repeat as champion. A. Wallis Myers, for example, the noted British tennis critic, had Lacoste and Johnston in the final. In the deeper recesses of his mind, Tilden might have agreed.

Interestingly, even Myers, one of the keenest students of the game, would be only half right in his prediction. One of the strange results of the seeding process and the actual contests is that the quarterfinals brought forth "America's Big Four—Tilden, Johnston, Richards, and Williams" against the "French Davis Cup Team of Lacoste, Borotra, Cochet, and Brugnon." In what would be labeled "Black Thursday," three of America's best, Tilden, Johnston, and Williams, would go down to defeat. Only Richards would survive, for Brugnon, a doubles specialist, was the weakest of the French contingent in singles. Borotra had defeated Johnston, Lacoste beat Williams, and Cochet upset Tilden in a long, nerve-racking battle, 6–8, 6–1, 6–3, 1–6, 8–6.

As Danzig described the action, "Fighting from behind all the way during the two hours that the match lasted, the Philadelphian won the hearts of the 12,000 spectators in the stadium as he never won them in victory. He gave himself unsparingly and with reckless disregard for his underpinning in his vain effort to withstand the demoralizing steadiness and craftily placed shots of his opponent." On numerous occasions, according to Danzig, the champion had been outfoxed and outplayed by the much younger man, only for the stunned onlookers to see Tilden "lift his game . . . to unassailable heights" and be "greeted with roars of applause" from an appreciative audience. In the end, however, the younger, healthier competitor proved the better player.

Appearing poleaxed by the enormity of his accomplishment, Cochet did not deny he was slightly dumbfounded by his own success. "When Tilden led 6–5 in the last set, with his own service coming, I said goodbye to my chances," the Frenchman admitted. He reached out to Tilden after the match and said, "Oh, you were unlucky." Tilden would have none of it. He talked of close points, missed opportunities, and having not "quite enough to come through" at the end. "Cochet," he told the press, "deserved his victory."

Stunning in its shock value and of earthquake-like proportions to serious sports aficionados, Tilden's defeat was front-page news around the world. Under the *New York Times* masthead, for example, ran the headline "Tilden Vanquished; His Six-Year Reign in U.S. Tennis End." Allison Danzig began his long first-column page 1 account of the history-making event with "Tilden, the invincible, the player whose magic with a racquet has confounded the greatest players of the world and made America supreme in tennis, at last has relinquished his scepter."[59]

In fact, the magnitude of the event was deemed so great the *Times* printed a special article listing Tilden's career achievements. Reading what was more like an obituary than a column in the sports section, one would have thought Big Bill had succumbed to a dreaded disease as opposed to losing a sporting contest. "By almost unanimous consensus he has been looked upon as the greatest player of all time," the article intoned. "So great a spell had the wizardry of the champion cast upon the tennis world that it had come to be believed that it was impossible to defeat him when he chose to win, and so, in spite of the numerous defeats that he had suffered this year the tennis public still maintained firm faith that he would successfully defend his crown this week."[60]

It was all too much for an American tennis patriot to digest. Tilden knocked off his throne by foreigners and on his home soil; it was unimaginable. Merrihew of *American Lawn Tennis* was, like many close observers of the sport, trying to sort through it all. "There has never been a year like 1926," he would tell his readers. And at the top of the list of stunning turnabouts were the defeats suffered by William T. Tilden, the world's greatest player. "The colossus who in seven years had won twenty-one single rubbers and lost none was found to be vulnerable at last. Thought of the heel of Achilles leaps to mind—except that this time it was a knee instead of a heel."[61]

Tilden's friend Dr. Carl Fischer was less verbose but no less impressed with Bill's courage and ability to endure four matches so soon after a serious knee injury, an injury that would have placed most competitors on the shelf. "What guts" was his emotional two-word assessment.[62]

As the *Philadelphia Evening Bulletin* informed its startled readership, "Never before has a non-English speaking player reached the semi-finals. In fact, never before in the forty-five years of American championship competition had three foreigners, English-speaking or otherwise, gotten that far in the tournament. Now there are three of the latter variety, and one is sure to be in the final."[63]

Shockingly, it would only get worse for American tennis, as Vinnie Richards, despite his exquisite volleying ability and reputation as a "great fighter," was taken out by the equally physically gifted beret-wearing Basque in a long five-set battle. The upshot was hard to digest, two Frenchmen—Lacoste and Borotra—fighting it out for the lawn tennis championship of the United States. The calculating, methodical Crocodile would prove the victor in straight sets, as the bounce in the Basque's step may have been a little less spritely after playing two successive five-set matches.

"At the end of this summer of 1926," Al Laney observed, "Tilden had been beaten twice by Lacoste, indoors and out, by Cochet at Forest Hills, and by Borotra indoors. All these victories had been scored in championship or Davis Cup play and French players now held the national titles on board courts indoors, on hard courts, and on grass outdoors, of France, England, and the United States." They would not sail home with the team title, but they had left their mark on America's top Davis Cup players, each taking a painful loss from one or more of the French Musketeers. As Laney summed up the devastation on this side of the Atlantic, "There was no escaping the feeling that France had put a lien on the Cup for delivery the next September."[64]

American sports fans could no longer delude themselves into believing the Stars and Stripes reigned supreme in the world of tennis. It was the end of an era, and the realization was not all that comforting. Tilden, once thought a demigod in his court supremacy, had been brought down from his lonely mountaintop outpost. The fact that just days later Jack Dempsey, the great heavyweight boxer who also reigned supreme during the twenties, would also be thrown off his throne was another shocking sign that a dramatic change was occurring. The year 1926 had proved quite eventful; many were left to wonder, what was to come?

11

"Decidedly Unlike Tilden"

Real modern tennis started with Tilden in
1920. Since Tilden nothing really new has
been invented. He was undoubtedly the one
who taught us the game of modern tennis.

—HENRI COCHET

In the aftermath of Black Thursday the press as well as the public seemed fixated on the prospect of Tilden turning pro. For many it seemed only a natural progression; he had won every title imaginable as an amateur, albeit without earning a dime of prize money, and more and more athletes in a variety of sports appeared to be taking advantage of the many lucrative offers that were now coming their way.

Bill would have none of it. "Don't think for one minute I am out of amateur tennis," he told reporters after his loss to Cochet at the National Championships. "I intend to carry on and will try to regain my title next year. I took chances with my weak knee, but I have no alibis.

"There has been a lot of talk that I am going to sign a contract with C. C. Pyle to play professional tennis," said Bill with a chuckle, "but that is all ridiculous. I have no such idea in my mind. Neither have I any intentions of commercializing my standing as one of the leading players. I have no laurels to rest upon. I have not hung up my racquet and do not intend to. Maybe I may be fortunate enough to win back the title next year. If I do not, it will not be on account of not trying hard enough."[1]

Bill's declaration to remain an amateur and not commercialize his great stature in the sporting community must have drawn a satisfying smile from USLTA officials, but only to be followed by a quick pang of dyspepsia. He was never an easy person to deal with, and his decision meant the amateur game's bureaucratic leadership would continue to be inundated with requests, proposals, and additional initiatives to spread and improve the game. Bill was relentless in his understanding of what the USLTA should be doing. No doubt some of the tennis oligarchs wished he had taken Pyle's offer. Others certainly were.

Just a few days after the disappointing results at the nationals in Forest Hills, American tennis, and association officials in particular, would receive another unwelcome jolt. Vinnie Richards decided to turn pro. As the natural heir apparent to the aging American stars—Tilden, Johnston, and Williams—Richards was presumed to be the bulwark of a new crew of elite players to help defend the Davis Cup from an ever-improving French squad. His surprise appearance as the guest of honor at a waterfront banquet in New York City for Mlle. Suzanne Lenglen on September 30 and announcement that he was turning pro were as shocking as they were unexpected.

On a stage aboard the ocean liner *Paris*, Richards stood with two additional gems in C. C. Pyle's diamond-studded tiara, Red Grange and Lenglen. Both had abandoned the amateur ranks—one in football and one in tennis— for the big money. Pyle had promised there would be others to follow the French tennis queen on a pro tour, and he wasn't kidding. Just a couple of weeks earlier he had picked off a big name to provide competition for Lenglen. Mary K. Browne's decision to leave the amateur game and turn pro was neither easy nor hasty. She claimed to have given the decision great thought. "Of course, my action will seem like a shock at first," Browne told reporters, "but I feel in the long run, it will be a good thing for the game. It will help to clear the atmosphere for I look upon amateur golf and tennis as expensive luxuries." If nothing else, added the California athlete, "it will take a lot of the hypocrisy out of American lawn tennis." Brown went on to admit that her decision was based on "economics" and "ethics" and her precarious position as a "player-writer." "This step is merely a pioneer move to help clear the game of the taint of commercialism. I have tried to be straight forward and honest, for I think a clear line of distinction between amateurism and professionalism will help the officials and, in the long run, benefit the game."

Browne had been the dominant female player in America ten years earlier and had even won a couple of mixed doubles titles with an unknown college player from Philadelphia named "Junior" Tilden in 1913 and 1914. She had gone on to establish herself in golf as well, nearly winning a national title, but over the years a growing concern had become economic survival. How do amateur athletes support themselves if they are not independently wealthy?

Increasingly disturbed by some of the more nefarious things that were occurring in the amateur arena regarding under-the-table gifts and payments to players, Browne began to "discuss the question with lawn tennis executives and other leading sportsmen." Her decision resulted in newspaper headlines. "I feel professional lawn tennis is bound to come, and if it is handled on a safe and sound basis, it is certain to be a success on the court as it is on the links. There are probably other players like myself who are not independent," she added. "What they will do remains to be seen."[2]

Vinnie Richards now added his name to the list of those athletes who thought if the public was willing to pay to see them perform, maybe the athletes should derive a share of the profits. Though just twenty-three years old, he was no longer a Tilden prodigy. Competing as a player and writing sports articles, he believed he needed to show more responsibility, especially so since as he had just married and had a wife to support. "I had to turn professional in justice to myself and my wife," Richards informed the press. "I have signed a contract for four months and in the contract is a clause giving me the option to sign for two more months if I care to."

Three years earlier during the player-writer controversy, Vinnie had expressed little interest in turning professional, but times had changed. "I only want to say this in regard to my professional tennis career which is before me," said Richards. "I had to turn pro, and now that I am pro I intend to play just as hard as when I was an amateur. I feel very strongly for the professional game and I have no excuses to offer for my action. I cannot see any reason why I shouldn't be getting the money as well as the tennis associations."[3]

Initially recognized as a young "tennis phenomenon . . . under the tutelage of Tilden," he had gone on to have a fine career. Though he had never won an American or British National Singles Championship, he was the 1924 Olympic champion and a topflight player who had won numerous doubles titles. Many believed he had a better year than Tilden prior to accepting Pyle's offer. Now he was a professional and, like Browne, seemed to have few regrets about leaving what would soon come to be known as "shamateurism."

According to Richard Hillway, top players were offered inducements to participate at the more prestigious tournaments. Travel expenses, lodging, and sometimes additional financial payments were offered to ensure a top player's participation. We cannot be sure how many knew the unsavory practice was occurring, but few spoke out about it, much less openly opposed it.

Although it may have seemed counterintuitive at the time, especially to the uninformed, players such as Browne and Richards who had decided to turn professional expressed relief. It was not just that their economic concerns had been resolved. In addition, they no longer had to play a silent, duplicitous game of appearing to uphold high amateur standards while being offered—and accepting—certain monetary inducements or valuable perquisites by tournament officials, many with significant USLTA standing. For those on the inside, the big-name attractions like Lenglen, Richards, and Browne, money was a key component of both amateur and professional operations, but in the former the players—the real attractions patrons paid to see—went unrewarded. The money stayed in the hands of the tennis club owners and the association. This unfair relationship increasingly rankled those whose labor was making other people and organizations rich. "The tennis associations worked the stars for all they were worth, the stars worked the associations for all they could get; it was all one . . . snooty family who made up their own rules," according to Paul Gallico, who covered sports for the *New York Daily News* in the 1920s. "Money was needed more and more as the tennis stars suddenly discovered that there was a racket going on and that if the scales were unbalanced as to sharing the profits, it was against them. The tennis clubs, in addition to publicity and prestige, were hauling in gate receipts."

Though a player or two may balk at the inequity, only the likes of a Tilden or Lenglen "could make, chisel, or hornswoggle" anything of value out of the amateur game's leadership. "The Lawn Tennis Association," argued Gallico, "held power over them that was practically absolute in spite of the fact that these men and women were amateurs and the association was both ostensibly and actually guarding their amateurism jealously." As

Gallico and others have pointed out, "The Tennis Association's solicitude for the amateurism of its players was in part an honest desire to keep the sport reasonably clean and amateur, but in equal part a cool, out-and-out business proposition. Tennis more than any other sport at the time was threatened by professionalism, and the threat hit right to the wallet."[4]

As critics like Gallico and John Tunis would go on to argue, "The Tennis Association had the game and the racket completely to itself on a wonderful basis. It, or rather the member clubs, took all the swag. The players who drew the money got nothing, or at least as little as it was possible to give them."

"Cash and Carry" Pyle, an indefatigable promoter with a shrewd eye for making money from the rapidly exploding sports scene, threw a wrench into that proprietary system with the signing of Lenglen and the subsequent signings of Browne, Richards, and several others for a pro tennis tour. No longer feeling the threat of a Damocles sword hanging above their heads, they were willing to speak out about the indentured servitude–like system called amateur tennis.

Lenglen, in particular, was motivated to address what she saw wrong about the current system. The game's leadership, she wrote, "have intentionally created the amateur rulings to enrich themselves." She took time to describe how the system functioned. Tournament directors needed to attract "six to ten known stars . . . to fill the gallery with spectators (who fill the organizer's pockets with francs). The star would then be invited. His traveling expenses are paid, his hotel bills are arranged for, and sometimes other expenses." Mystified, Lenglen, who benefited by such a system for years, now came to ask, "How is it possible to reconcile this state of affairs with the rules of strict amateurism? I cannot understand that it is yet constantly being done. Why the star should get all his expenses paid for him and the player of lesser rank should pay his own, has also been a mystery to me, for which I can see only one solution—gate receipts."[5]

Lenglen knew the game's so-called purists, the establishment traditionalists, would attack her, but she had marshaled her facts, arguments, and examples of abuse. "It is all very well to talk of playing tennis for the love of the game," said the French star, "but I do not see why the man who honestly makes a little money out of tennis loves it any the less. Art for art's sake who [sic] are forbidden to enjoy the rewards of their art?"

Tilden, like the French star, knew well—and no doubt benefited by—the dirty little secret that pervaded amateur tennis at the highest levels. *Shamateurism* was not a household term, but close observers understood the disingenuous economic landscape that colored the game. Though he had never voiced his concern about it in public—neither did Lenglen, Richards, or the others while they were amateurs—Tilden must have been equally troubled by the deception and hypocrisy. More than anyone else at the time, Tilden repeatedly wrote books about the importance of honesty, honor, and sportsmanship, and he constantly prodded the association for reforms that would open the game to more people, alter its elitist image, and embrace change rather than fight it. In 1926, however, Bill had not yet reached the point where he was prepared to make the leap. As Merrihew of *American Lawn Tennis* said about players crossing the sport's "Rubicon—Once a professional, there was no turning back."[6]

Bill, his friend Merrihew, and the vast majority of tennis aficionados had been brought up in and were still supportive of the tenets of amateurism. As an *ALT* editorial argued in the midst of the high-profile defections, "We are more than ever for amateur play and all that it means. We believe that lawn tennis is an amateur game, that it must inevitably suffer as a game when the amateur spirit is dimmed or snuffed out; that the player who becomes a professional and plays for money loses something that may be termed spiritual, and that at any rate is concrete, cognate, easily recognizable."

And once again the bedrock principle of amateurism was trotted out; for those who "play lawn tennis because they love it, and to whom the thought of profit, either direct or immeasurably remote, has not the weight of a note in the scales by which they measure the really worthwhile things in life."[7] For Big Bill the scales still kept him wedded to the amateur game, despite the defections, the recurring battles with the USLTA, and Pyle's periodic and enticing financial pitches. As Tilden was the biggest fish in the sea, Pyle could not help himself; Big Bill was the one he wanted to hook.

At an Algonquin Hotel sit-down, Pyle made another attempt to have Tilden sign his name to a professional contract, but Bill was not swept off his feet by the offer. Even though the sports promoter repeatedly increased the numbers, Bill resisted what most would consider ever more tantalizing proposals. According to Richard Hillway, "Tilden and other leading players in the United States were willing to consider offers to turn pro, but weren't psychologically prepared to do it." Most were not ready to take the radical step, while others had something else in mind. Tilden, in particular, was set on another "crack at the French. He wanted to defend the Cup and take back the American national titles the French had recently claimed." Sure, Tilden would listen to Pyle's proposals, but the tennis item at the top of his immediate agenda was to go to Europe in 1927 and beat the French.

The rise of the French Musketeers and their impressive accomplishment in capturing the American national title, combined with Bill's losses to Borotra at the indoor championship earlier in the year, Lacoste at Germantown Cricket, and Cochet at Forest Hills, greatly rankled him. Unaccustomed to losing and long thought the king of the mountain in lawn tennis, he found the defeats unsettling. So were the predictions that his reign may be at an end and the negative commentary. E. C. Potter, for example, would argue that the "three Frenchmen were now picking on Tilden."[8] Tilden was a fierce competitor, and the defeats and the loss of the American title revived his competitive juices. With a combination of both personal regret and patriotic outrage, Tilden would write, "Those 1926 Nationals saw the beginning of the end of the United States as the champion nation. . . . For the first time since 1903, our national title left the shores of the United States."[9] Not since 1921 had he actually wanted to go to Europe, but now he did; he wanted to take on the French. As Hillway points out, it was consistent with Bill's long-held attitude that he had been the world's best lawn tennis player, and all those who sought his crown should come to him. Now that he was no longer the American titleholder, it was only right that he go to France.[10]

In a frank statement of his thoughts on the prospect of players turning pro and his intention to return to Europe, Tilden said:

> I see no objection to professional tennis and I blame no player for turning professional. I consider that a matter for the individual to decide for him or herself. Certainly there is no stigma attached to it. Mr. C. C. Pyle made me an offer, which I turned down. It was turned down because I believe that I owe it to amateur tennis to play one more year at least. I have reaped the honor and advantages, which the American title affords for six years. I believe it would be most unsportsmanlike to turn professional the first year that title goes abroad. If I have enjoyed the fruits of the champion's title, I should do what I can to see

it returned to the country next year, whether it is won by some other American or myself.

Tilden's claims of "personal standards of sportsmanship" preventing him from abandoning amateur tennis for the big money are supported by those who have seriously studied Tilden's career. Rich Hillway confirms that "Tilden was very loyal and patriotic" and no doubt troubled by the American title falling to a foreign player. He believed "the best lawn tennis was played in America and the game's best players were American." In short, Bill considered it practically un-American for the American national title to be in the hands of a non-American.

Bill wanted everyone aware that his decision to remain an amateur was not a reflection of his feelings about professional tennis or an aggressive sports promoter. "The amount of money Mr. Pyle offered me did not affect my decision, nor is my decision against the idea of professional tennis. I might sign in 1928, but the year of 1927 presented the peculiar circumstances which I felt demanded my upholding the sporting traditions of amateur sport."[11]

As the *New York Times* would report of Pyle's persistent pursuit of Tilden, Bill informed the promoter, "Even if I were considering turning professional, I would not accept your offer. It would have to be doubled."

"It is doubled," Pyle immediately replied with great expectation.

"No thanks," said Tilden.

And that, according to the *Times*, ended the matter.[12]

Bill's attitudes on the amateur-versus-professional debate were clearly evolving, and some of his notions were a clear departure from the chummy country-club values he had embraced as a child. College football players, for example, were now thought by Bill to be entitled to a wage for their athletic skill as well as their service to the university. "I believe in the old hokum about the amateur sport theory—sport for sport's sake," he was quoted as saying, "but the economic pressure must be considered in this matter as well as other lines of activity. It may seem to be heresy, but I rather wonder why a man shouldn't make money-playing football to pay his way through college. A man can get money if he is a good waiter or a good musician so why shouldn't he make money if he is a good athlete?"[13] Ninety years later an ever-increasing number of Americans are asking the same question.

A man of wide interests, varied talents, and the ability to compartmental-ize, Tilden had more on his plate than just athletic pursuits. Before a trip to Europe to do battle with the French, and less than a month after the devastating Forest Hills debacle, Tilden was performing on Broadway. The play *They All Want Something* was at Wallack's Theater on West Forty-Second Street. The fact that the work debuted so soon after the Forest Hills tournament suggests that Tilden may have been learning his lines at the same time he was nursing his damaged knee and fighting for all he was worth to defeat Henri Cochet.

The play, a comedy by Courtenay Savage, based on *The Dark Chapter*, a novel by E. J. Rath, drew varied reviews. Friends of Bill considered the "farce . . . well staged, well cast and a coherent exposition of the life of today in the country home of the nouveau riche."[14] At the play's conclusion those closest to the stage could see tears in Bill's eyes as he answered curtain call after curtain call.

Bill was cast in the role of a "pseudo-tramp—the son of a wealthy auto-mobile manufacturer who assumes the part to meet and win the girl," and is inveigled in a series of highly improbable, humorous escapades. What the ALT reviewer found "screamingly funny," the *Times* critic thought juvenile. In fact, the *New York Times* critic thought the play left much to be desired. He was apparently unimpressed with both the production and Tilden's performance. The former was seen as "elementary school entertainment" and "at best only moderately entertaining," while Bill's "histrionic gifts" were said to be considerably less formidable than other actors appearing on Broadway. "He strikes a good many poses and manages to play about half of the scenes directly to the audience," wrote the *New York Times* reviewer, though he did so "with none of the vitality that he shows on the tennis courts."[15]

The *Times* review obviously stung, but others were far more compli-mentary. The *New York Journal*, for example, said Bill "moved with all the grace and stage presence of a seasoned actor. Gone was the newness and gawkiness apparent in his first appearance on Broadway. Bill's rule of the tennis court's is over," concluded the review, "but it looked last night as if his rule of Broadway has only begun."[16]

Regardless of the reviews, Bill was on Broadway, patrons were paying to see him perform without a racket in his hand, and newspaper advertisements had him on the same page with the likes of Basil Rathbone, Fanny Brice, Basil Sydney, and a host of other accomplished artists. Though most athletes, especially amateur tennis players, relished the opportunity to get their name into the nation's tabloids and broadsheets, Bill had grown used to the honor of appearing in countless sports-section articles. It was an entirely different accomplishment to be mentioned alongside classical artists and celebrated stage actors. The reviews of his performances did not suggest the rise of a great thespian, but his athletic achievements did not come overnight either. He could only hope that with experience and practice, the result might prove just what the dramaturgy and script doctor ordered. Granted, he was socking a lot of his own money into these productions, but there was more to life than whacking tennis balls. Bill loved the theater; he enjoyed being onstage and took great satisfaction in working with a talented ensemble of actors, scriptwriters, and directors.

With the start of a new year came new challenges. Tilden was forced to come to grips with the fact that for the first time during the sports-crazy decade of the twenties, he was neither the American national titleholder nor the number-one-ranked player in the world. In fact, A. Wallis Myers of the *London Daily Mail* had Bill ranked as the fifth-best player in the world. Frenchmen captured the first three spots and were followed by Bill Johnston and Tilden. In sixth place was Vinnie Richards.

Myers admitted that Bill's "strained knee . . . handicapped" his play during the last key weeks of the tennis season, but also argued that Lacoste might have just "discovered the tactical secret by which he may be confounded."[17] Lenglen, no friend of Bill's, suggested her own world rankings and placed "Tilden in 6th place." It should be no surprise that her French compatriots held the first three spots, followed by Richards, Johnston, and Tilden.[18]

Bill was more troubled by the slight to Richards than his own debatable demotion. That was especially the case when the USLTA filed its own national rankings for 1926 and placed Bill at the top of the list. Richards was struck from the list completely; they wanted to penalize him for turning pro. Bill fought the association's policy of not ranking professional players and voted for his former protégé. He believed Vinnie had earned the number-one ranking as the best American player for 1926. Moreover, Bill would go on to argue, Vinnie had not signed a professional contract until the playing season was over. Despite Bill's gallant gesture, the association was intent on sending a message: professionals were persona non grata.

Though he was performing on Broadway, Bill had not totally divorced himself from tennis. His personal losses to the tricolor's Musketeers combined with the American singles title going abroad annoyed him no end. It was a constant irritation he could not scratch, and the fact that twelve months would have to pass in order to correct the matter only further irritated him. Unable to wait that long to restore order in the world, Tilden made plans just weeks after the Forest Hills tournament to travel to Europe. "If 1927 is to be my Swan Song in tennis," he wrote in *American Lawn Tennis*, "I am going to make it a long one, if not a loud one. I am going to the Riviera in late January for two months." He booked passage on the S.S. *Majestic* and planned to compete in a series of Riviera tournaments and eventually the French championships at St. Cloud and the British championships at Wimbledon. Joining him on the journey would be young Junior Coen of Kansas City. One of Tilden's newest protégés, Coen, according to Bill, was "the most remarkable baseline player for a boy I have ever seen. He has all the mechanical perfection of Lacoste with the promise of a punch like Bill Johnston."[19] High praise indeed, but as Rich Hillway says, "Bill was always in search of the next American star. The next great American player who would take his place in the pantheon of the world's greatest lawn tennis players."

By January, however, Bill was forced to alter his travel plans. Whether it was due to economic concerns, his gimpy knee, or the threat of being overtennised for the big Davis Cup and National Championships later in the year, Bill postponed his departure for Europe until April. He expressed his regret for the delay in his "invasion of France," but the disappointment was even greater on the other side of the Atlantic. News of Tilden's forthcoming appearance at Riviera hotels and tennis clubs spread rapidly and was met with great excitement. Notice of his change in plans produced instantaneous disillusionment at a host of Mediterranean resorts; his appearance would have brought that extra bit of pizzazz that only a world-class celebrity can deliver.

It was during the last few months of 1926 that Bill gave serious thought to having surgery on his damaged knee. He had received a number of medical opinions; many argued for an invasive procedure that "would very likely be successful," but he was also told that "there is a chance that it wouldn't be successful." He could be left with a stiff, immobile leg that was unsuitable for any type of intense physical activity. Though commonplace today, in the midtwenties surgery on joint ligaments, tendons, and cartilage was still in its infancy, and Bill decided an operation was too big a gamble. He chose to give the knee rest rather than a date with a scalpel. By late winter his knee felt strong enough for him to play a series of tournaments in Florida, Georgia, and North Carolina.

Although he downplayed his own interest in returning to Europe in his autobiography, *My Story,* Tilden gives credit for the overseas adventure to "the USLTA [for] desiring first-hand information on the strength of the French team" and their anticipation of "the large financial return from any international matches" Bill and a partner of his choice could scare up.[20] The association envisaged an extended barnstorming tour that would take Bill to Germany, France, Belgium, Holland, England, and Italy.

Initially at a loss as to whom he should select as a partner for such an exhausting travelogue, he was surprised when Frank Hunter volunteered for the job. "I had known Frank a long while but had never considered him one of my close friends," Bill would write in his autobiography, but over a big dinner "consisting of an enormous melon, a half cow with the horns removed that was humorously termed a steak, bolstered up by such minor details as French-fired potatoes, peas, hot rolls, and coffee, and in Hunter's case, a large salad which I scorned, all rounded off with an enormous chocolate soufflé—when Hunter spoke. 'Bill, I think you and I ought to make a great doubles team.'"

Outside of his appetite—which rarely matched Bill's gluttonous consumption level—Hunter's tennis game was characterized as "lopsided" and one-dimensional. He had "one terrific shot," according to Bill, "his crashing forehand drive" that could blow opponents off the court, but little else from a technical standpoint. His lone redeeming feature besides his forehand was his "fighting ability." As Bill would write of his new tennis partner, "His specialty was winning matches after he was apparently hopelessly beaten. The clown never seemed to have a sense enough to know when he was licked."[21]

Built more like a rugged fullback than a lithe tennis player—he was captain of the Cornell hockey team—Hunter was the fifth-ranked American player in 1923 and had some impressive victories to his credit, including teaming up with Vinnie Richards and winning the 1924 Wimbledon and Olympic doubles titles. A year earlier he had lost the Wimbledon singles title to Little Bill Johnston.

Hunter's sturdy physique may have put him in good stead as a doubles partner for Bill, as the animated Philadelphian was a notorious ball hog, pursuing everything hit on his side of the net. He usually got away with such shenanigans due to his stature and the fact that many of his doubles teammates were dutiful protégés. Though his doubles play was often criticized, his records are noteworthy. Tilden won five National Doubles Championships, the first of these with fifteen-year-old Vincent Richards; three National Indoor Championships; four Mixed Doubles Championships; and victories in four out of five Davis Cup challenge-round doubles.

The evening before their mid-May departure, a big send-off bash was held at the Algonquin Hotel. There were many well-wishers and celebrities at the event, including "His Majesty, the Czar, Julian S. Myrick," as Bill would humorously describe his nemesis in an *ALT* column. The next day Bill and Frank Hunter set sail for Bremen, Germany. Among Bill's gear were "three dozen rackets; one dozen strung with gut and two dozen unstrung." Many of them were new Top-Flite models with an open-throat design that Spalding was advertising as the latest technical innovation in the game. The company no doubt saw the tour and Tilden's use of their new product as a tremendous way to market the racket overseas. Whether Bill was paid, promised free rackets in the future, or freely conceded to use the new rackets without compensation is unknown. Awaiting him in London would be another two dozen rackets. Such a vast arsenal was unnecessary, but Bill had a habit of giving tennis equipment away to admirers and sick children in need of a pick-me-up. On the long Atlantic crossing the rackets were stowed away in airtight compartments to protect them from the moist ocean air. Hunter spent most of his time in the ship's gymnasium, while Bill played bridge and hung out in the "dining salon," where he claimed to consume "eight meals a day."[22]

On Tilden and Hunter's arrival at the Berlin train station from Bremen, a large crowd anxious to see one of the world's greatest athletes greeted the players. Bill was easy to recognize. He was not only one of the tallest at the station but the only one with his arms full of rackets. He and Hunter were immediately escorted to the Rot-Weiss (Red and White) Club, Germany's top tennis club, in the beautiful Gruenwald section of Berlin, where upon their arrival and despite the late hour they insisted on inspecting the courts. The next morning hundreds turned out to watch Tilden and Hunter practice on the well-manicured red-clay courts. Their early misfires were puzzling and thought due more to the long boat trip. But Bill inspected the balls and immediately determined the German-made balls he had mistakenly been given "were lighter and less lively than the standard." To ensure a sufficient supply for their upcoming matches, Tilden "wired London for twenty dozen" regulation balls. On their first day Tilden and Hunter played three sets of singles in the morning and another three in the afternoon. The next day they increased their workouts to five sets in the morning and another five in the afternoon. After their workout Bill was asked to officiate a professional match between two top European players.[23] When he ascended the elevated umpire's chair, "spectators packed in the stands rose and gave him a prolonged ovation."[24] Germany had been prohibited from postwar tennis competition, but now they were eligible to compete. Though banished from international play, they had not lost track of the game's stars. Tilden was the brightest star in the galaxy, and they were eager to see him in action.

The Rot-Weiss visit was Bill's first opportunity to observe Germany's top players. As usual, when asked to comment on opposing players, he was quite complimentary. He thought Froitzheim, Landmann, Moldenhauer, Hannemann, and the Kleinschroth brothers "were very sound" and saw them with the potential to "win consistently."[25] The assessment of the Americans by the German net men was equally positive. "Tilden and Hunter are unbeatable by anything Germany has got," said Roman Najuch, the top German professional, who lost four pounds practicing with the American players. "Tilden's cannonball service is something which Froitzheim and Landmann have not encountered before."[26]

It was no surprise when the Americans won their matches handily, Tilden beating Otto Froitzheim 6–2, 6–2, 6–4 and Hunter defeating Heinz Landmann 6–2, 6–1, 9–7. Large crowds, including members of the former kaiser's family and lesser nobility, flocked to the stadium to cheer on their country's representatives, knowing full well their odds of victory were slight. The following day the American duo defeated Landmann and Heinrich Kleinschroth in doubles 6–3, 6–1, 4–6, 6–3.[27] Though the best German talent proved little opposition for the Americans—Froitzheim defeated Hunter on the final day of competition—Tilden came away much impressed with the warm reception, their sincere interest in rejoining the international tennis community, and the large number of young people playing the game in public parks and private clubs. "There is much to tell about sport over here," wrote Bill for his syndicated news column. "Everywhere I see children playing tennis, many of them good enough to make our junior and our boy champions look to their laurels." Bill went on to warn his sports-minded countrymen, "We cannot sit back in satisfaction at our prowess or we will find ourselves outclassed."[28]

In coming days similar results would be registered in Amsterdam and Brussels. Tennis stadiums in both countries had never been so inundated with ticket requests, and hundreds were delighted to obtain standing-room-only passes. The crowds in Germany, Belgium, and Holland may not have had a clue who Red Grange, Rogers Hornsby, Lou Gehrig, and other top American athletic stars were, but they certainly knew the name Tilden. And they were prepared to pay good money to see him. A gifted showman who loved to perform for an appreciative audience—whether it be on court or onstage—Bill enjoyed the gracious receptions he always received and strove to take in as much of each country and its cultural institutions as the schedule allowed. In Brussels, for example, Chevalier de Borman took Bill to the opera one evening to hear *La bohème*. The next night he went back to hear *Madame Butterfly* performed by "a new and glorious little Japanese star," who was honored a great American athlete on tour would take the time to view her performance. In fact, many from the performing arts flocked to the tennis stadium to witness one of the world's great athletic artists practice his craft. John Charles Thomas, the famous American baritone on tour in Europe and currently performing in the Belgian capital, not only came to see Bill play but also took him the next day to view a rehearsal of *Don Juan* in which he was starring.[29] Few American celebrities touring European capitals could have walked so seamlessly between such different artistic and athletic venues.

After a series of relatively easy contests, Bill was now off to what were expected to be much-sterner tests in Paris. First on the calendar would be the Franco-American team competition to be followed by the World Hard Court Championship at St. Cloud. He had a date with the French Musketeers; it was the raison d'être for the trip. The losses over the past year to Borotra, Lacoste, and Cochet still stung; the fact that the winner of the American singles championship resided on French soil only magnified the insult. Commentary from sports pundits such as John Kieran's remark that he was like an aging warrior and his losses to Lacoste and Cochet at Germantown and Forest Hills were "merely the first leaf of Autumn" rankled him.[30] He wanted to correct those impressions.

His purpose was clear, according to acquaintances at the time. Tilden was like a hunter "on safari," wrote Al Laney, looking for "big game." His prey were easily identifiable: Lacoste, the mechanical, cool general with dogged determination; Cochet, the athletic artist who could scale heights few have ever achieved; and Borotra, a player of inspiration, daring, and pure showmanship. They were the objects of Bill's thoughts.

Tilden's arrival in France was a big deal. When Bill and Frank Hunter took to the courts to drill in preparation of their forthcoming matches, one would have thought an actual match was taking place by the size and excitement of the crowds that gathered to observe them. Though France was still in a recovery mode after the Great War, their Musketeers were something to cheer about; their success had become a point of national pride. To achieve France's ultimate goal, however, America had to be defeated in Davis Cup play. And to accomplish that Tilden—or "Big Beel," as they referred to him—had to be tamed. On three separate occasions during the previous year Borotra, Lacoste, and Cochet had accomplished that seemingly impossible task. It was a major breakthrough for each of them and grounds for celebration, but could they repeat their achievement?

The many hundreds who encircled the practice court to watch Tilden gracefully hit forehand and backhand drives, great looping lobs, soft drop shots, and amazing spin shots were entranced by both the balletic elegance and the concerted power that the tall American could summon at will. Even other players, including the Musketeers, who had by now established their own sizable fan base, stood for considerable time to admire the great master's style, strokes, and comportment. One of those who paused nearly twenty minutes to study Tilden was René Lacoste. When asked his thoughts on the tall American, the young Frenchman said with an approving nod, "Tilden appears to be in the best form I ever have seen him. He is the greatest player in the world."[31]

If so, his hold on that title was tenuous. Some, like Laney, would argue he was on the way down. He "had already passed over the divide and begun the long journey down the far slope. Europe thus never did see Tilden in all his majesty, only as he was rising and at the slow decline." Even so, there were still brilliant flashes of incomparable tennis and mind-blowing instances of extraordinary athleticism. Many who witnessed this return visit would declare that "they had seen nothing like it in their lives."[32] And, in fact, they hadn't.

In late May 1927 Big Bill was definitely the man, and it seemed all of France wanted to see him work his magic on the court. Tickets for the team matches were long sold out, and much of Paris seemed to be Tilden-ized. His persona was so great, a "Tilden Cocktail [was] rapidly becoming the most popular drink with rising young tennis players" throughout the area.[33] The cocktail, mineral water without the benefit of a glass or cup, came about after closely watching Bill's every step even when taking a brief respite during an energy-draining workout. French fans noticed Bill taking long swigs of mineral water from a bottle. Instantaneously, a new drink was created and being requested at swanky tennis clubs as well as popular bistros on both sides of the Seine.

Back home the anticipation was building for the Tilden-versus-Musketeers confrontation. Though an American victory in the team competition was much desired, only the most optimistic thought Frank Hunter capable of defeating any of France's Big Three. Tilden, however, was another story. More than a gifted warrior who had repeatedly proved his mettle over the years, he was the champ. Sports fans delighted in the prospect he would right the faltering ship and reestablish America's tennis dominance. Newspaper articles informed readers of Tilden's whereabouts, victories, and associations on a daily basis. Like traveling royalty or a head of state, Bill's every step was big news—even his trip to Le Tramblay, a Parisian racetrack, was covered—and expectation built as the showdown at St. Cloud drew closer.[34]

Newspaper articles desperate for new story lines speculated on Bill's outlook, tactical approach, and the health of his oft-injured knee. Whether they had any basis in reality or were the work of an editor's overactive imagination, much ink was spilled on the ravenous appetite of readers for tales of international conquest. "Tilden Changes Tennis Tactics for First Time in 7 Years" was the headline of one lengthy article that seemed to have inside information regarding Bill's strategy.[35] Apparently, the *Philadelphia Evening Bulletin* had confirmed that just as in the winter of 1919–20 when Bill went off to Providence to master a new stroke in the aftermath of the Bill Johnston debacle, he had now determined in the wake of the recent Lacoste and Cochet defeats to reassess his own game and design a tactical attack that would thwart the French.

Tilden realized "the French, particularly Lacoste and Cochet, were using a block stroke—a stroke with a short back swing and a checked follow through, that returned the ball so accurately it could be played short or deep, to the left or right, with almost complete certainty of falling where they wanted it to. As a result, according to Tilden, their opponents, including himself, when they saw their best drives coming back all the time, started pressing, and thus losing control. That is what beat Tilden and the other members of the American team."

Tilden's counterstrategy, according to the *Bulletin* article, was recognition that "the weak point of the French system is obviously that these defensive, block strokes lack speed. Control was behind the stroke and direction, but the ball lacks pace." Bill's answer to the tactical puzzle: "Why not attack this game from the net? A net attack can be defeated by speed. Their slow, blocked defense so successful against a backcourt game, ought to fail before a fast net game. There is time to get to the net against it. Why not do this?"[36]

Tilden and Lacoste took the court before a packed stadium, every available inch of space being occupied, while the thousands who were locked out grumbled at their misfortune. Attendance seemed mandatory for anyone who claimed to be of import, for foreign diplomats to stars of the entertainment world all journeyed to Club Français at St. Cloud for the much-anticipated clash between the best of America and France.

Tilden, looking "cool and seemingly just as youthful as his opponent, who [was] fully ten years his junior," put on a masterful performance. From the smack of the first ball, Bill was the aggressor. His cannonball serves startled both Lacoste and his many supporters in the stands with their speed and accuracy, while his deep forehand and backhand drives kept the Frenchman on the defensive. Despite their partisan leanings the French fans cheered wildly at Bill's "marvelous returns when it seemed he could not get near the ball." In point of fact the French had heard so much glowing commentary about the American giant over the years that Tilden could have appeared in his pajamas with a flyswatter, and they would have cheered him.

But it was the return of the old Tilden, the one who reigned supreme with both speed and amazing control. And when he closed out the match 6–4, 7–5, dozens of reporters and photographers flooded the court for comment and photos. The crowd gave Tilden rousing applause and cheered his presentation of the winning racket with a little pink bow attached to Mary Garden. The American opera star, whom Bill first met when he was a high school senior, was seated in a box close by the court, and the audience appreciated Bill's gallant gesture.[37]

Two days later Bill continued his masterful display and added another French scalp to his lodge, taking out the flamboyant Jean Borotra 6–0, 6–3. Many observers left with the impression that Tilden "appeared to be simply toying with the Bounding Basque." The normally upbeat Frenchman was duly humble after being taken to the woodshed. "I have no excuses," said a thoroughly defeated Borotra. "I lost to a superior player."[38]

Granted, the French won the team competition by a score of 3–2, Hunter losing both his singles matches against Lacoste and Borotra, but Bill had defeated both Frenchmen, thereby restoring some semblance of order to the world. Attendance at the French American contest broke all records—even exceeding those set by Mlle. Lenglen—but many tennis connoisseurs knew it was only a precursor to the World Hard Court Championship, which was to immediately follow. Would the great Tilden be able to replicate his singles victories against the Three Musketeers? Bill had little doubt he could. "I think I played like my old self again," he informed the press, "and feel sure I will be able to do even better in the five-set matches in the tournament next week."

But Borotra, Cochet, and Lacoste were not about to roll over and allow Tilden to reestablish his dominance, especially on French soil and in front of thousands of patriotic Frenchmen. Although specifically designed for Davis Cup play, their battle plan could also work in singles competition. Wearing the big man down chasing lobs and drop shots and heavily watering the clay courts to blunt the force of his cannonball serves were their form of gang tackling. They believed the collective effort had worked before; it could work again. That along with Bill's age, fragile knee, and the prospect of longer matches could well prove the keys to victory.

Tilden should have been completely mindful of the challenge before him; he had been watching France's improvement for years. "When you played any one of those fellows, you played the whole team," Bill would write in his autobiography. "They were always on hand to support and encourage a teammate, and on the court you could feel the combined psychology of the team pressing in on you from the sidelines as well as from across the net."[39] That oppressive, suffocating atmosphere of being outnumbered and surrounded would be on full display at the finals of the French championships.

Just as many expected, Tilden and Lacoste met in the final. In earlier rounds Bill had defeated Cochet, while René had eliminated Hunter and Borotra. The victory over Cochet was significant and garnered front-page coverage back in the States. It meant Bill had defeated each of the French- men who had beaten him in 1926. The victories were an important psy- chological achievement; the debacle known as Black Thursday needed to be rectified. Now he had to confront the phlegmatic face and methodical play of Lacoste in the final.

As Bill would write of the three-hour-and-forty-five-minute tactical slug- fest that some would come to consider the toughest ever played on the Euro- pean Continent, "Every point was like a chess move as we maneuvered each other around the court. Rally after rally would go twenty or more returns with both of us at our best, hitting hard and accurately. It was a terrific tennis match." It would also prove a very controversial and incident-filled one.

An omen of what was to come occurred when the opening serve was delayed, as "a couple of drunks in the stands" decided to battle it out as part of the match's undercard. In "typical French spirit," according to Tilden's later account, the "thousands of spectators immediately took sides and thunderously cheered on their favorites." Though he could eventually joke about the affair, at the time the unruly crowd and unexpected fisticuffs did little to calm Bill's nerves. In addition to the raucous crowd and inebriated patrons, he was perturbed by the fact that they continued to water the courts after they were already soft from recent rain, and then there was the close proximity of swarming photographers. If any further distraction was needed, it was provided by the rumor that Lucky Lindy would make an appearance at the match in support of his countryman. Just a few days earlier a bold American pilot named Charles Lindbergh would complete a heroic flight across the cold, lonely Atlantic and set off euphoric celebrations in Paris and around the globe. It was considered only natural by many caught up in the stunning achievement that he would appear at St. Cloud to support another American hero.

What was described as "the first really big tennis occasion for France" finally got under way in a most surprising manner: Tilden not only lost his serve, but never won a point in that first game. It was an unexpected turnabout for the possessor of the sport's much-feared cannonball serve. Bill quickly settled down, however, and began playing his normal exquisite game. Through the use of scintillating cross-court and down-the-line backhand shots, Tilden grabbed a 4–2 lead, but Lacoste adjusted his equally potent game. The Frenchman managed to rip off four straight games and win the first set at 6–4. Bill was on notice: anything less than his best would prove unsuccessful.

Coyly testing each other and then launching sudden offensive strikes, they parried through another ten-game set that saw Tilden come out the victor. After an hour's worth of top-tier tennis, they had each taken a set. The temperature and ferocity of play only escalated in the third set, as Tilden managed a series of punishing shots that kept Lacoste on the move, running from sideline to sideline. To the surprise of many it gradually became evident that the older player was in better physical shape. Though he had a slight lead in the third, Lacoste was displaying signs of exhaustion and began to limp. Courtside observers were split; some thought the young

Frenchman was cramping, while others believed he had twisted his knee chasing one of Tilden's shots.

After hitting effective drives that kept his opponent neutralized, Lacoste threw in a series of chop and drop shots to further confuse Tilden. Despite his physical exhaustion under an increasingly broiling sun, Lacoste managed to tie the score at 5–5. The crowd responded with thunderous applause and cheers, but Lacoste had gone to the well once too often. Now expecting a periodic drop shot, Bill was prepared for the stroke and replied similarly, surprising the Frenchman and taking the advantage. He broke Lacoste's serve and won the set at 7–5. Bill now held a 2–1 lead, and the impassive Parisian was noticeably laboring. As he limped off for the normal break between sets, the young Musketeer appeared a beaten man.

It was at this point that a number of students of the sport believe Tilden's sense of sportsmanship cost him the match. Rich Hillway, for example, argues that Lacoste was incapable of returning to the court in the allotted time—ten minutes—and should have been disqualified. The break extended ten, twenty—Hillway notes some reports suggested thirty minutes—beyond what was customary in order that the Frenchman's handlers massage and revive him in order to contest the fourth set. Tilden, ever the chivalrous combatant and someone wedded to a nineteenth-century code of sportsmanship, never objected. If René needed more time, Bill was willing to wait. Such leniency would never occur today.

Bill would write two decades later in *My Story*, "Lacoste was seized with cramps so severe it seemed unlikely he would be able to continue." He learned afterward that Lacoste was "given injections to dull the pain." Bill never mentioned his generous gift of additional recovery time.

To the shock of all, after the players returned to the court, Lacoste appeared a new man. Even though he lost the first two games, he came back to win six of the next seven and take the fourth set at 6–3. The stadium erupted, the applause deafening; their beloved Crocodile was still fighting. The entire stadium was breathless with anticipation as they began the fifth and deciding set.

The midday heat and humidity were now truly oppressive; after each changeover Tilden grabbed a pitcher of water from the umpire's chair and, rather than drinking it, poured it over his head to revive himself. Neither player could sustain a lead. When the Frenchman went ahead at 5–4, Tilden responded with three service aces that brought him back to keep the score even. Again Lacoste would take leads of 7–6 and 8–7, but could not finish off the match. Tilden kept hitting deep shots to the corners and following them up at the net. Finally, the tall American broke the Frenchman's serve to take a 9–8 lead. If he could hold serve, the French championship would be his.

It was at this point that the most controversial aspects of the match occurred. The "critical moment," according to Bill's later account, presented itself when "Alan Muir, an expatriated American living in France, almost created a riot by suddenly calling three successive foot faults on me, one of them on a second service! The fact that he had been sitting on the foot fault line throughout the match without seeing any violation prior to that time was too much even for the hot French partisanship; he was roundly booed by the crowd."[40]

Muir was more than just an impartial expat. He was actually part and parcel of the French tennis establishment and was the nonplaying captain of the French Davis Cup teams of 1922 and 1923. Though Muir would argue he "called the foot faults impartially and squarely" and wanted "no argument with Tilden" on the matter, others question both his veracity and his objectivity. Some, like Hillway, wonder why neither linesman called a single foot fault on Tilden up to this point.[41]

At the time it was not unusual to have partisans and actual players call the lines. As Baltzell entitled his book *Sporting Gentlemen*, the game was rooted in notions of honor, sportsmanship, and gentlemanly behavior. It would be unthinkable for someone to purposefully favor one contestant over another. One cannot deny, however, that such unethical shenanigans must have occurred on occasion. Unfortunately for Tilden, a similarly controversial call occurred just after the questionable foot-fault rulings.

Somehow Tilden managed to jettison his disbelief and ire at Muir's foot-fault calls and buckle down; he could not afford to lose his concentration. "Giving all I had," Bill would recount later, "I overcame this handicap and finally reached match point at 13–12, 40–30 in the fifth set. I felt it was now or never, for I, like Lacoste, was verging on complete exhaustion. Brother, I really wound up on that one, cannon-balling a service that traveled perhaps as fast as any shot hit in the entire match."[42]

The ball whizzed past Lacoste and "seemed a winning ace," according to Al Laney, who was at the match, and to many others, including both Tilden and Lacoste. But the linesman, Henri Cochet, who had come in to replace a linesman overcome by the heat, threw up his hand and "called out, a fault." Most in the stadium were in a momentary state of shock, as they thought the serve was good and the big American had won the match. But they were to play on. Tilden gained another advantage but missed an easy shot. For Laney and other connoisseurs of the game, it was "an ominous sign." Their fears proved correct. Lacoste came back, broke Tilden's serve, and won the match. A double fault by Tilden at match point ended the contest.

The celebration that followed, according to Laney, was something he had not seen before, nor would he again. It was an explosion of national pride and jubilation. "People stood and shouted for minutes and swarmed onto the court," recalled Laney, "to hail the boy champion now grown to a man's stature." He had taken down the great Bill Tilden in a titanic struggle and on French soil, no less.[43]

Though sorely disappointed by the loss, especially when on the precipice of victory, Bill harbored no ill will toward Cochet for the debatable line call. "No more honest sportsman than Cochet has ever graced tennis," Bill would write, "and he would have been just as quick to give the decision to me had he seen it the other way." Not all would be so magnanimous in their assessment. And even Bill was less cordial toward Alan Muir. "Those foot faults were unpleasant incidents, coming strangely, every time at critical stages when either the set or match was at stake," Bill commented. "Never before in my tennis career have I had three foot faults called against me in one match, and I am known as having one legally perfect service."[44] As Tilden would admit several decades later of the controversial match, "I thought I had won. I had let down nervously and mentally; and never again that day could I come back." Bill likened his situation to another iconic figure of the era, Jack Dempsey, and his equally infamous "long count" bout with Gene Tunney. "No athlete who makes a supreme effort and thinks it has brought him victory," Bill would write, "only to find himself still in competition, can pull himself together in time to regain full poise."[45]

There would be much debate over Tilden's loss at the French final, his first at an outdoor national or international championship "when he had admittedly been in good physical condition." His knee had not been an issue, he had the lead in the fifth set, and he needed just a single point to win. Merrihew was convinced Lacoste's victory was tainted. "There were scores, perhaps hundreds," Merrihew wrote, "who followed the ball and who say that it hit the line. A dozen or more, some excellent judges among them, both English and French people, declared that the ball squarely hit the outside of the line. . . . [T]he strongest testimony being offered was that the service was good and that Tilden won the match."[46] But besides the suspicion of favoritism by linesmen, there were other observations. As one American newspaper soberly observed, at the critical point in the match, "the kind of psychological moments Tilden likes to take advantage of, it was Lacoste who did so. It was decidedly unlike Tilden."[47]

The newspaper went on to show that despite winning ten more points than Lacoste during the course of the match, Tilden still lost. Was he cheated out of the victory? Was he overtennised? Was his age finally catching up with him? Speculation abounded. Some blamed the players' diametrically opposed personalities and "contrasting temperaments. Lacoste: imperturbable, phlegmatic, steady under all conditions. Tilden: flustered, annoyed, careless whenever some untoward circumstance arose." The upshot, according to one of Big Bill's hometown newspapers, was that "the cool player will always have the advantage over the nervous one whenever they play before noisy galleries, which can be pretty generally counted on."[48]

Despite the setback Tilden was still favored to win the British championship just a couple weeks off at the relatively new suburban London location. Bill continued to write articles, visit museums, peruse Charring Cross Road bookstores, take in London Philharmonic concerts, and practice with Frank Hunter. Not surprisingly, he also spent time in London's West End theater district, attending various stage plays. No doubt he tried to talk playhouse managers into hosting a run of *They All Want Something*. Still the biggest name in the game, and the first time he had set foot in England since his last Wimbledon triumph in 1921, Bill was a much-discussed celebrity. As in Paris his travels and associations were duly noted in British tabloids and broadsheets.

By the mid-1920s England had few championship-caliber players, but their interest in the sport remained high, and Tilden's return caused a run on tickets. Long lines in hope of procuring tickets before the tournament even started became a daily sight, and by the event's start some were even camping throughout the night in order to be first in line for the next day's general-admission sale of standing-room-only tickets.

As the tournament's second week began, the competitive landscape looked much like what most tennis authorities predicted, Tilden versus the tricolor's Musketeers. Bill easily disarmed Jacques Brugnon, the least threatening of the French quartet. The next morning he was awakened early by knocking at his hotel room door. It was an agent of a major sports promoter wondering what it would take to get Bill to sign a professional contract. "Not for a million dollars, just now," Bill replied. He later told reporters, "I have two extremely hard matches to play before I reach the championships. If I lose either I wouldn't be worth half of what these gentlemen promise me. I play tennis because I like the game. That's how I feel just now. How I will feel six months from now nobody knows."[49]

Back on court Bill had to take on the little but talented Henri Cochet in the semifinals. Cochet had just avoided elimination by overcoming a two-set deficit against Frank Hunter on Monday. Two days later he was scheduled to face the game's greatest name. After watching his friend fall victim to the Frenchman's escape artistry, Bill decided to take no chances; he would aggressively go after Cochet from the start.

"He unleashed a withering attack of unanswerable speed," wrote Al Laney, who covered the match. "Drives from both wings, either flat or carrying top spin, were hitting the lines, out of reach or too swift to return, and the service often brought no reply at all." For Laney and all those with the good fortune of witnessing the extraordinary display, it "was Tilden in all his majesty blowing his opponent off the court with irresistible gusto." The Frenchman was on the verge of blossoming into one of the game's great players, but against Tilden's ferocious attack Cochet appeared a rank beginner. The devastating assault resulted in a quick 6–2 set. The little Frenchman, according to Laney, "had no chance to organize a defense and no time in which to bring his own best weapons into play." Most observers would admit Tilden's array of firepower was overwhelming. "They never had seen anything like it."[50]

The second set saw Cochet try to mount a counteroffensive, but it still was not enough. Tilden took the set at 6–4, and the third appeared to be much like the first set. Like Sherman aggressively marching his Union troops through the Georgia countryside toward Savannah, Tilden appeared unstoppable, a man possessed. As Laney would later recall, "Tilden went steadily on, literally hitting through his man, dominant, domineering, and arrogant." It was a throwback to the player of a couple years earlier, the one who was virtually unbeatable and dominated all by sheer will. After bludgeoning his opponent for a 5–1 lead, Tilden threw the balls in his hand aside dismissively. All expected the next game to conclude the little Frenchman's embarrassing public battering.

It was at this point that the tennis gods intruded, decided to turn the world upside down, and fashioned a match that would become one of the most confounding puzzles in athletic history. Tilden proceeded to do what he had done throughout the match, punish the ball. But now he missed; three successive heavily struck returns of Cochet's serve went long. The score was now 5–2. No matter, Tilden would serve the match out. But Bill continued to overhit, his cannonball serves going past the service line and his ground strokes either long or into the net. He was unable to win a point. The sudden display of ineptitude was stunning. Shocked spectators looked at each other in disbelief. How was it possible that the best exhibition of power tennis they had ever seen had instantaneously deteriorated into a circus of miscues and unforced errors?

As Laney would write, "The earlier stream of winning points became a stream of errors." During one run Cochet won seventeen straight points and began winning game after game until he finally closed out the set at 7–5. The turnaround was astonishing. With no rest periods at Wimbledon between the third and fourth sets, the players continued. Tilden cut down on his errors and began to win points and games again, but the reprieve had given his opponent a chance to catch his breath and mount a counterattack. Cochet chose the sly tactic of letting a frustrated Tilden self-destruct; he hit him soft returns that Bill walloped back in an effort to finally end the match. But more often than not, they were mishits that cost him points and games. Tilden tried to recover his accuracy, but even on those occasions when he did so, Cochet was ready. The Frenchman was now playing top-level tennis. The tide had shifted.

Try as he may in the fourth and fifth sets, Bill was stifled; Cochet maintained the upper hand. The sting and accuracy of Bill's shots had dropped off markedly, allowing his opponent to take the net at every opportunity and close out the point. Even on those occasions when Bill managed through great effort to tie the score, he was not able to sustain his quality of play. Unforced errors and double faults always intervened. As Laney would write of Bill's improbable meltdown, "He was done physically and his face showed it." The unbelievable match eventually ended 2–6, 4–6, 7–5, 6–4, 6–3, and those in the stands having the pleasure to witness such an inexplicable athletic curiosity were either paralyzed by confusion or ecstatic by the unexpected outcome. "Never in the history of British tennis," commented an Associated Press reporter, "has Wimbledon witnessed such a spectacle as greeted Cochet's victory. Staid and venerable gentlemen threw their top hats in the air and the cheers and applause lasted for several minutes. Tilden was so fagged out that he was unable to stand before the scores of photographers who swarmed about him for pictures."[51]

Though the applause and wild cheers would eventually subside, a rational explanation as to what had occurred would remain unanswered. Speculation was rampant. Laney himself would be forever perplexed by what he had witnessed. "I was, if not stunned, completely bewildered," the reporter admitted decades later. "I have discussed this match many times with many persons . . . and I never have arrived at a satisfactory explanation of what happened, of why the greatest player of all could not win just one more game after the most brilliant play of a long career."[52]

Bill, ever the gentleman, credited his opponent with stellar play, but Cochet had little to do with Tilden's sudden lack of ability.[53] In a unguarded moment, Bill was heard to remark, "Age, I think it is." And it may well have been. He was nearing thirty-five years of age, ancient by the standard of championship-level play by the mid-1920s. Granted, there were instances of greatness from top-level players in their midthirties like William A. Larned and Norman E. Brookes over the years, but the game was faster now, it demanded more skill, and there were better athletes who took training more seriously. In fact, finding a player in his thirties who triumphed at the American or British championship required one to travel back to the prewar era. Age—as well as the need to find a profession and earn a living, as Rich Hillway points out—had cleared the decks of many of the game's better players. Despite the inevitable tug of years, however, Big Bill soldiered on. "He still has his style, his generalship, his courage and, in bursts, his speed of foot and stroke," argued one newspaper analysis. "But lacking is his once famed endurance." The column went on to predict that "for years, confident of his own endurance, he has run opponents into defeat," but now "younger players will know, in the future, if they can hold him off, they can win in the end."[54]

In fact, that scenario occurred the very next day. Joining with Molla Mallory in the mixed-doubles competition, his effort was almost an exact copy of what took place in his battle with Cochet. Initially, Tilden showed no signs of physical wear from his lengthy match the previous day, as "he showed plenty of speed . . . [and] his service was as fast as ever," thereby enabling him and Mallory to take the set 6–3. In the second set, however, he "displayed the amazing reversal of form which characterized his play in the closing stages of his match" with Cochet.[55] His errors piled up, his strokes lost their speed, and his play became extremely shaky. He and his partner would eventually lose the next two sets 1–6 and 4–6 to a less than imposing doubles team.

Cochet would go on to win the Wimbledon singles title and provide the French with even more reason to believe 1927 would be the year they would wrest the Davis Cup from America. Both Cochet and Lacoste had recently beaten Tilden, the world's best, as the team once again ventured across the Atlantic "in wonderful spirits. The whole French nation," wrote Laney, "seemed involved in this Sixth Crusade and Les Mousquetaires were heroes going forth to fight for the honor of France and bring home the spoils."

Bill and Frank Hunter, on their return to the States, tried to impress upon the USLTA's leadership the significant challenge that was about to land on American shores. The association, however, had been spoiled by America's success over the years. Tilden and Hunter's report of the French team's "tremendous improvement" and America's tenuous hold on the Cup was quickly dismissed. Psychologically unable to accept such a bleak report, they disregarded it as so much malarkey and fearmongering. At a dinner sponsored by the Davis Cup Committee honoring the two players for their exhausting European tour (which raised ten thousand dollars for USLTA coffers), the fourteen members cordially listened to Tilden and Hunter describe the French team's "remarkable and unmistakable" progress. The members then, both individually and collectively, set aside the prospect of a serious French challenge. They blithely predicted that "the United States would doubtless win four matches to one or even possibly five to nothing."

Tilden and Hunter turned to each other in disbelief and figured America could "kiss the Davis Cup goodbye."[56]

The USLTA's Davis Cup Committee compounded their sublime ignorance by allowing an increasingly out of shape Billy Johnston to remain in California rather than come east and practice with the team. Little Bill had played little competitive tennis during the year as he tried to earn a living, his formidable record against the French leading Davis Cup organizers to believe his dominance would go on forever. In a further display of poor judgment, the committee created unnecessary confusion over which players would be selected to play in the critical doubles match.[57]

Tilden was nearly apoplectic over the association's series of misjudgments. Always one of the more attuned to the game and the personnel playing it, he was adamant that he and Hunter presented the team's best chance for a doubles victory. Though Little Bill was a good friend, Tilden knew Johnston was overweight, "undertennised," and in need of serious court time. For Bill it was painfully obvious the French team was not only championship caliber, but also a juggernaut in the making. America need not aggravate the situation by making indefensible managerial decisions. He would battle with the Davis Cup Committee right up to the start of the doubles match.

Even the game's keener observers like Vinnie Richards—now a pro and also a sports columnist—picked up on these missteps, but still thought the United States would retain the Cup. Yes, Johnston was overweight at 138 pounds and in need of practice, but his record against the French was spotless. Who could realistically challenge him? Richards predicted Big Bill and Little Bill would each win a singles match, and the doubles team would come through, solidifying the third and deciding point.[58]

More objective observers, like Al Laney, were not so quick to predict an eighth straight American victory; they recognized the drive and commitment of the French steamroller and the vulnerability of America's fading stars. The Musketeers had developed themselves into exceptional tennis players and a crack unit built for Davis Cup competition. Granted, Tilden and Johnston were all-time greats, but they were now well into their thirties, with one playing the game infrequently and the other too much.

In addition, according to Laney, was Lacoste's ingenious strategy of slow destruction, a grinding down of the big man's mental and physical capabilities so that either he or Cochet could win that last singles match on the final day of competition. Lacoste, according to Laney, did "not feel at all confident of beating a fresh Tilden on the first day, but on the third day Big Bill's power to conduct a long, tiring match, which Lacoste would try to impose upon him, would be considerably reduced." As the backbone of America's chances, Tilden, he figured, would be forced to play all three days of competition. No one else on either side would be placed under such constant and demanding physical stress. With a day off between singles play (Borotra and Brugnon would be the French doubles team), Lacoste believed he had a good shot of defeating Tilden, especially if his mates had performed their jobs and worn "Grand Bill" down.

More than thirteen thousand excited fans journeyed to the temporary wooden stands on the grounds of the Germantown Cricket Club for the first day of athletic warfare between America and its oldest ally. The French let it quickly be known that the long, warm relationship did not extend to the athletic pitch; they were tired of the annual beat down. Right off René Lacoste crushed Bill Johnston in straight sets, 6–3, 6–2, 6–2. The French youth attacked from the first ball, hitting hard to the corners, thereby keeping Johnston on the run and forced to play defense. It was atypical Lacoste tennis, but it worked brilliantly. For Little Bill's loyal and longtime supporters it was a sad, painful performance to witness. Never had the top French players beaten him and certainly not in the decisive manner Lacoste had fashioned. Bill's normally lethal western forehand had less pace and bite, and his foot speed and reflexes appeared slightly slower. Some, like Al Laney, had to wonder if "this was really the last stand of a great little fighter." The diminutive Californian with the big heart was "only fractions of a second slower . . . but tiny fractions of time are like miles to an athlete."[59] Johnston's convincing loss caused even the staunchest American tennis fan to question America's chances of retaining the Davis Cup.

Fortunately, Big Bill brought some order to the day by defeating Henri Cochet in the second match, but the task was not easy. The young Frenchman won the second set handily and pressed Bill through a fourteen-game fourth set before conceding defeat. The scores were 6–4, 2–6, 6–2, 8–6. After the first day of grass-court combat, each side had earned a point; the American squad was hopeful, the French team buoyant. The first day's contests had developed as Lacoste desired. He was now sure Cochet would beat Johnston on the final day of competition and increasingly optimistic he could defeat Tilden, especially if Bill was forced to extend himself in the doubles match and the weather remained hot, humid, and energy sapping.

Johnston's uninspiring performance caused the U.S. Davis Cup Committee to do as Bill had long argued: replace Little Bill with Frank Hunter in the doubles competition. But Tilden was exasperated by the committee's "shameful exhibition of indecision" and the many weeks of argumentation over which two players would form the doubles duo. He would ultimately place some of the blame for what was to occur on managerial folly and the Davis Cup Committee's abandonment of rational decision making.

The second day's critical doubles match would prove an entertaining one. It would also prove long and exhausting, which was just what Lacoste and the French desired. After all the bickering there was great pressure on Hunter to perform well. He started off tentatively, and the French won the first set, but following Bill's aggressive lead, he gradually started to feel more comfortable and display his own brand of court aggression. As the *New York Times* reported, "The powerfully built New Yorker was lacing the ball with all the might of his strong forehand and working his way to the net for volleys and overhead kills."[60] In addition to full cuts at the ball, Bill often resorted to a more nuanced and stylish game, repeatedly hitting deep lobs and wicked slices to keep Borotra and Brugnon off balance. Hunter fed off Tilden's aggression, "first one taking over the reins and then the other closing in to fill the breach and carry on the offense." Occasionally, their attack was so potent, according to an observer, "one might as well have tried to chain lightning as to stop them."[61]

Borotra and Brugnon were not novices, however. They were topflight players and an excellent doubles team; they knew how to fight. The four combatants would continue to work each other over for most of the afternoon, until Tilden and Hunter asserted themselves and smashed their opponents in a fifth and final set. Exceedingly generous as always, Bill would give his partner credit for "dominating the play" and allowing them to "crash through to a final 6–0 victory" in the fifth set, but the 3–6, 6–3, 6–3, 4–6, 6–0 score was deceptive. Yes, the United States was ahead two points to one, but the French showed no signs of concern. In fact, the French captain, Pierre Gillou, was upbeat. "I think we will win both singles matches tomorrow and lift the cup," he told reporters. He would go on to boast, "Lacoste is playing the greatest singles of his career and I expect him to beat Tilden. Cochet will certainly beat Johnston, if the American is no better than he was Thursday, but he will do it anyway."[62]

There was good reason for such bluster: they had kept "Grand Bill" on court under a blistering sun for several hours. Even a grand prizewinning plow horse can be overworked. "Tilden, on whom everything now depended," according to Al Laney, "had played nine sets in two days in the heat, while both Lacoste and Cochet enjoyed a day's rest," sitting in the shade sipping refreshing iced drinks.[63] One can only imagine their delight as they watched their compatriots extend Tilden through an exhausting five-set battle.

On the final day of the Davis Cup challenge round more than fifteen thousand sports fans squeezed into the temporary wooden stands just yards from Manheim's stately club patio, while thousands without tickets expressed their dismay from afar until they were allowed on the grounds and stood or sat on the edges of the arena. It was the biggest and most important sporting event in the world that day. Most attendees were optimistic: the United States had the lead and Tilden. He would once again prove himself invincible in defense of the Cup.

Shortly after Tilden and his twenty-three-year-old opponent took the court, Bill opened with a barrage of hard-hit shots to all corners of the court. Recognizing he might soon be running on fumes after all the time he had spent on court the past two days, Bill knew his only chance for victory was to play aggressively. Long energy-consuming rallies would be counterproductive. Going for winners and hoping his young opponent had a bad day were the keys to victory. Lacoste, however, threw up a "machine-like defense" while under "the most terrific pressure." That impregnable defense would prove his aggressor's undoing. The Frenchman won the first set 6–3, but succumbed to Tilden's punishing blows in the second, 4–6. By the third set, however, the heat, Lacoste's extraordinary defensive skills, and three days of intense play had taken their toll. "By the middle of the third set," as Allison Danzig of the *New York Times* saw it, "Tilden's racquet, the racquet that had once been the symbol of the most autocratic power that ever held sway on the courts, had become a harmless bit of wood and string in the hands of a physically exhausted giant." Ironically, and possibly with Bill's other love in mind, Danzig would go on to comment, "Nothing that the stage has to offer can equal in drama the scene that was enacted on the hallowed Germantown turf."

The young Frenchman's shrewd plan of transforming a gentleman's game into a brutal battle of attrition had proved successful. Under an onslaught of hard-hit shots, Lacoste "stood adamant against the thirty-four year old veteran's shafts of lightening until the American had shot his bolt and his physical powers disintegrated." For all his virtuosity, creativity, and court genius, according to Danzig, Tilden painfully discovered he lacked the energy and finishing shots to make any headway against a stone wall that "catapulted back his most murderous smashes and he realized the futility of opposition. Lacoste had robbed him of his will to win as well as his stamina."[64]

Progressively wilting under the strain, the onetime court colossus who time and again over the years had the ability to summon the perfect shot, the right strategy, would lose the last two sets 6–3 and 6–2, thereby ending America's best chance of retaining the Cup. Though Little Bill would provide periodic and stunning moments of stellar tennis that resembled his form of earlier years, he, like Tilden, could not sustain the effort. Johnston would go down to defeat; Henri Cochet won 6–4, 4–6, 6–2, 6–4.

There was grand commotion on the grounds of the old cricket club as the Musketeers and their supporters celebrated their unprecedented achievement, but the party paled in comparison to the explosion of emotion and gaiety on the boulevards of Paris. "Victory at Last" was the recurring shout that echoed from Montmartre to Montparnasse. "We have got the Davis Cup after waiting twenty-five years," said M. Canet, president of the French Tennis Federation. "England has had her Dohertys, Australia her Wildings and Pattersons and United States her Tildens, but France has Lacoste and Cochet. We are satisfied." Max Decugis would cautiously add, "I don't want to be mean, but I hope it will take another twenty-five years before the Cup returns to the United States."[65]

Though there would be much talk of Tilden's declining skills and ebbing physicality in the aftermath of the Cup making "its way eastward across the Atlantic," Rich Hillway rightly points out that 1927 was the first year Bill did not have a partner he could count on to gain at least one point in the four singles matches. Just one victory there, as he had always been able to count on with Billy Johnston, would have enabled America to retain the Davis Cup. Without that point Tilden had to shoulder the burden by himself. And just a few months shy of his thirty-fifth birthday, the load was too heavy for one man to carry.

12

"Tilden Has Been a Stormy Petrel"

The Davis Cup played without Tilden would
be like Mona Lisa without the smile.

—L'Auto

When the Musketeers returned to French soil in late September, they carried with them something else of value in addition to the long-sought and much-prized Davis Cup. They possessed the trophy emblematic of winning the American championship. In another tremendous blow to national athletic pride, René Lacoste defeated Big Bill at Forest Hills for the U.S. National Championship.

Though Lacoste won a straight-set victory, the conquest was far from easy, as the 11–9, 6–3, 11–9 score indicates. Described by witnesses as "one of the greatest struggles that ever brought the championship to a conclusion," the two-hour tactical slugfest took on the significance of a "titanic struggle between the player who formerly stood as the invincible monarch of the courts and the youth who has succeeded to his position."[1] Even longtime tennis connoisseurs admitted that nothing in their memory surpassed the "harrowing battle between age and youth in the desperateness of the conflict and its appeal to the emotions or in the magnificent quality of the play."

News reporters covering the contest discovered they were as emotionally caught up in the struggle as the paying customers. Allison Danzig, the *New York Times* sports reporter, was so taken with the encounter that he admitted feeling "privileged to see one of the most ennobling fights a former champion ever made to regain his crown." Like the fourteen thousand spectators who crowded into the concrete horseshoe stadium, Danzig was carried away by the stellar play, combative spirit, and historic import of the event.

Tilden, like Ruth, Dempsey, and only one or two others of the golden age of sports, was the regular recipient of colorful commentary lauding his racket skill and superb physical ability, but it was rare for him to capture the hearts and affection of American sports fans. As Danzig would write of this match:

> Tilden, in the years of his most ruthless sway, was never a more majestic figure, never played more upon the heart-strings of a gallery than he did yesterday as he gave the last ounce of his superb physique to break through a defense that was as enduring as rock, and failed; failed in spite of the fact that he was three times at set point in the first chapter, in spite of the fact that he led at 3–1 in the second set. And once again, in spite of the fact that he held the commanding lead of 5–2 in the third set and was twice within a stroke of taking this chapter.

The tremendous effort was lost on a "youth in the person of an untiring sphinx that was as deadly as fate . . . and assimilated the giant Tilden's most murderous swipes and cannonball serves as though they were mere pat balls. . . . But," as Danzig went on to underscore, "the spirit of Tilden was one thing that never broke. Long before the end of the match, yes, by the end of that agonizing first set which had the gallery cheering Tilden madly and beseeching him to put over the one vital stroke that was lacking, those marvelous legs of the Philadelphian were slowing up." By the end, Danzig would comment in an emotional tone that was not customary for him, "the fires of [Tilden's] forehanders were slumbering," and he had become a "drooping figure, his head slunk forward, so utterly exhausted that not even the pitchers of water that he doused over himself could stimulate his frayed nerves, which must have ached painfully."

Many a scribe who would put pen to paper in an effort to describe "a match the like of which will not be seen again soon" was similarly moved. Descriptions of "utmost daring," the "brilliancy of the shot-making," and extraordinary defense led most to conclude that the contest "had few equals in the history of tennis." And though he would not win a set, Tilden had won the support and respect of everyone in the stadium. As Danzig's eloquent account of the title bout concluded, Tilden's effort was "a spectacle to have won the heart of the most partisan French protagonist, the sight of this giant of the courts, once the mightiest of the mighty, flogging on his tired body in the unequal battle between youth and age."[2]

S. Wallis Merrihew of *American Lawn Tennis* was so taken with the level of play that it reminded him of "a machine against a god of the courts; and just as Jove might have dashed himself vainly against the rocks of Olympus, so Tilden was unable to find a flaw in the armor of his opponent."[3] A proud American, but also the dean of tennis writers, Merrihew gave the Frenchman his due. He called Lacoste "the foremost player in the world" and admitted, "It is doubtful whether anything like Lacoste's play—a mixture of steadiness and brilliance—has ever been seen," but reserved his greatest respect, as the others had, for the losing player. "William Tilden is greater in defeat than he ever was in victory. No greater personal triumph was ever achieved than was his. . . . He did all he could to keep the title home, and he stood on a stricken field a glorious figure to whom the hearts of all went out."[4]

Al Laney, of the *New York Herald Tribune,* refused to take a backseat to the other chroniclers. Equally enthralled by the spectacle, he wrote that "this final of 1927, the last we ever were to see of Lacoste in this country, may have been Tilden's finest hour, for he was magnificent in adversity and defeat as he never had been in triumph." As the great crowd called out his name, urged him on, and cheered his every swat of the ball, he was finally the people's champion.

Though Tilden no doubt enjoyed the heartfelt acclaim and encouragement, the losses were something new for him—and the nation—to digest. Like heavyweight champ Jack Dempsey, who was going through his own reassessment after a series of defeats, only a select few who enjoyed iconic stature fully understood the psychic and physical toll the losses appropriated. Though widely perceived as indestructible, both men were unloved during their reign. And both would experience greater popularity after suffering unexpected defeats.

Although Bill would play on and cast aside the many offers to turn pro, he knew something had changed. He recognized his total dominance on court had come to an end, and as he soberly stated in his autobiography, the loss in 1927 of the American championship and the Davis Cup "marked the end of an era. Billy Johnston, ill, worn, and discouraged, retired from competitive tennis, Williams gave up serious campaigning . . . and most of the older stars only played occasionally."[5] Yes, there were good young players in the pipeline such as John Hennessey, George Lott, Wilmer Allison, John Van Ryn, and Sidney Wood Jr.; it also goes without saying that they lacked the skill set, physical ability, and personal aura of those who preceded them.

Tilden aficionados like Rich Hillway repeatedly underscore Bill's patriotism. And that love of country just may be key to his ardent focus on rebuilding a championship-level Davis Cup squad. He was still set on reclaiming the Cup and American title from France. In early 1928 Bill was lobbying USLTA leadership that a two-pronged approach might be the way to go: form two American teams and enter one in the American zone and the other in the European zone of Davis Cup competition. That way one would surely survive to face the French. Apparently, the novel concept was given little credence.

A more sound suggestion was Bill's argument that if an American team was to be successful, it must go to Europe earlier "to get the necessary competitive play on the ground where the Inter-zone final and the challenge round were to be fought out." Though Tilden's argument was viewed by many as "earnest and persuasive," Julian Myrick and others opposed the notion.[6] Sam Hardy, a former nonplaying team captain, for example, thought it was "all wrong to put tennis first." Taking several months off to practice and play in a variety of tournaments, according to Hardy, interrupted one's educational pursuits as well as his business and professional obligations. Hardy argued that such a program would "make bums out of our tennis players."[7]

Bill, however, was relentless on the subject. "We can't win the Cup without proper preparation and training," he argued. "Those of us who have been through the mill know that it is absolutely impossible for any team reaching France a week before the inter-zone final and two weeks before the challenge round to have any chance whatever to bring back the Cup." He would further argue that with a good six weeks of practice and competition in Europe, "we could come within one match of victory or win" back the Davis Cup.

Though some of the USLTA leadership may have been won over by Bill's optimistic pitch, the powers that be were not persuaded. "I am still Chairman of the Davis Cup Committee, I believe," said Myrick huffily, and then used procedural measures to block immediate passage of any decisions or resolutions.[8] The Tilden-Myrick relationship was prickly at best, but it did not prevent Bill from enveloping himself in USLTA affairs. It is unlikely, in fact, that another top player was so embedded in association operations. In addition to proffering an endless steam of initiatives, Bill was a member of the organization's Junior Ranking Committee, Junior Tennis Development

Committee, Men's National Singles Championship Committee, and Tennis Educational Committee. One can only ponder where he found the time to write his many articles and books and prepare for his stage performances.

Undeterred by Myrick's opposition, Bill not only continued to push for an early departure date, but also doubled down by taking the reins of America's Davis Cup team. Named captain of the team in March, he took leave of his role in a new play by Courtenay Savage entitled *The Buzzard* and directed the country's best players to assemble the following month in Augusta, Georgia. There they would prepare for a qualifying match against Mexico in Mexico City. After a week's practice the team endured a four-day train ride from Atlanta to the Mexican capital, an armored escort due to the presence of bandits along the route, a frightening earthquake, and the debilitating effects of high altitude. But the team acquitted themselves quite well; they did not lose a match.

Taken as a reserve member of the squad was Wilbur F. Coen Jr., a promising sixteen-year-old high school player from Kansas City, whom Tilden had been mentoring for several years. Coen, better known as "Junior," was like another former Tilden protégé on the team, Arnold W. Jones, and the latest of Bill's hopes for the future of American tennis. Because the lad possessed speed and solid ground strokes, Tilden was encouraging him to improve his serve, volleying, and tactical approach to the game. Though young Coen was certainly a talent to be reckoned with, it is unlikely he would have been selected for the Davis Cup squad without Tilden's support.[9]

In quick succession Tilden's squad would defeat Davis Cup teams from China and Japan and then in mid-June sail off for England, where the Wimbledon Championships were due to begin. Frank Hunter, who had the money to follow Bill's suggestion and travel to Europe earlier in order to get properly acclimated, now joined the team. The British championships did not augur well for the U.S. team, however. John Hennessey made more news for his attire (he chose to wear striped white flannel trousers) than his play and lost to Cochet in the quarterfinals, while Bill got one round further, losing to Lacoste in the semifinals, 2–6, 6–2, 2–6, 6–4, 6–3. Lacoste would go on to defeat Cochet for the Wimbledon title. The American Davis Cup team's prospects were further darkened when Tilden and Hunter, the defending Wimbledon doubles champions, were defeated in the semifinals by a good Australian duo in a tough five-set match.[10]

On July 18 Bill published an article announcing that he, Hunter, Hennessey, and Lott would be the quartet that would challenge the Italians and French in the forthcoming Davis Cup matches in Paris. The syndicated article would go on to explain his reasoning for the men he selected, their role as either singles or doubles specialists, and the conditions they would play under regarding weather and court surface.[11] The piece was rather tame by journalistic standards of the day, but such articles by active amateur athletes were under occasional examination by the powers that be, and no athlete's commentary was more closely scrutinized than Tilden's. It would be just such a piece that would set off a firestorm of controversy and spark an international imbroglio.

The very next day, the nineteenth of July, a "bombshell" of an announcement would greet newspaper readers and radio listeners around the world. As one front-page headline put it, "Tilden Dropped Off Cup Team for Breach in Writing." The USLTA's shocking decision to expel the greatest player to have ever swung a racket from America's Davis Cup team was precipitated by his "newspaper syndicate articles on the British Championships at Wimbledon where he had been a participant." The decision was so unexpected, so inconceivable, that even those who made the announcement in Paris, Joseph W. Wear, chairman of the American Davis Cup Committee, and Samuel H. Collum, president of the United States Lawn Tennis Association, were taken aback.

The stunning announcement that "left the people of Paris and France in a state of shock" could not have come at a worse time. Not only did the news arrive on the eve of the U.S.-versus-Italy match, but it was delivered just as tennis officials, dignitaries, and members of the press had gathered for the drawing of the two teams' lineups. "Where is Tilden?" inquired Pierre Gillou, president of the French Davis Cup Committee. "We can't go on with the draw unless the American captain is present."

"Tilden no longer is captain of the American team," replied Wear.

French officials were "staggered," and the "room full of dignitaries and newspapermen gasped." Amid deafening silence, Wear read the following statement: "The Amateur Rules and the Davis Cup Committees of the United States Lawn Tennis Association have preferred charges against William T.

Tilden, 2nd, for having violated the amateur rules by writing newspaper articles for pay or consideration concerning the Wimbledon tournament in which he was a competitor, and whereas it would be improper to retain as a member of the American Davis Cup team any player against whom such charges are pending, the United States Lawn Tennis Association has decided to withdraw Tilden from Davis Cup competition."

With completion of Wear's statement pandemonium broke out, and it took considerable time for Gillou to regain order in the room. Just moments later, as everyone was trying to figure out if a poorly designed hoax was being played on them—and much like one of his Broadway stage entrances—Big Bill himself walked into the room. His dramatic arrival resulted in a spontaneous burst of cheers and applause from French, Italians, and Americans alike. No doubt gratified by the warm reception, Bill immediately raised his hand to silence the crowd. He said he would like to address the highly humiliating controversy that had just exploded in his lap. Though years later he would characterize the brouhaha as a "Gilbertian tragedy," at the time the disconcerting developments had momentous athletic importance and subsequently economic and diplomatic significance as well. With tears running down his face and obviously laboring, Bill said, "I refute all charges. We will win the Davis Cup yet. I hereby apply for a job of training American Davis Cup members for the grueling matches ahead."[12]

There was another round of cheers and applause. Overcome by their support, Bill tried to settle the crowd in order to conclude his remarks. His brief but emotional statement read: "I deny the charge of intent to violate either the letter or the spirit of the amateur rule of the USLTA and state unreservedly that any articles which I wrote during the Wimbledon tournament were to the best of my knowledge straight comment articles and in no way an attempt to contemporaneously report in which I was a competitor. . . . I consider that this is a deliberate misinterpretation of my article and an attempt to embarrass President Collum and Chairman Wear." Moreover, Bill charged there was a cabal out to get him, and they were intent on taking him down. His enemies, he argued, were even willing to embarrass their own by using Collum and Wear to do their bidding. Bill charged:

Two of the three disputed articles were out prior to the sailing of Wear and Collum from the United States. One of the articles was fully discussed in a committee meeting attended by them both but no unfavorable comment was made by anyone present. It seems very strange that the same article was so much worse after Wear and Collum were two days at sea. I deeply regret the embarrassment occasioned Mr. Wear and Mr. Collum as well as to the team, but I am glad to say all these gentlemen feel that there is no intent on my part to evade or violate the rule.[13]

When he had concluded he was once again the recipient of a huge ovation. Many French supporters were yelling, "Vive le Grand Bill!" while Baron Umberto de Morpurgo, Italy's top player, put his arm around Bill's shoulders and whispered, "Poor Bill, this takes all the fun out of it." Hunter, Lott, Hennessey, and the other American players quickly surrounded Tilden, while the rest of those in attendance tried to make some sense out of what they had just heard.

Meanwhile, Chairman Wear, his emotions quickly escalating from mortification to outrage by his role in the embarrassing affair, began drafting his resignation notice. "I hereby tender my resignation as chairman of the Davis Cup Committee to take affect immediately upon arrival in the United States of the American team," the letter began. Wear would go on to write that "holding a meeting in my absence of the committee of which I am chairman to consider the alleged offense of Tilden in writing newspaper articles on July 2 and 6 when the matter could have been considered prior to my sailing on midnight on July 6, and my sincere belief that in this instance Tilden is being unjustly treated are the causes for my resignation." In a further parting shot at the USLTA cabal for orchestrating the unusual athletic coup d'état, Wear wrote, "The action of the committee in demanding the withdrawal of Tilden at the last moment is incomprehensible to competing nations and makes us ridiculous in their eyes."

Embarrassed for his friends—both Collum and Wear were from Philadelphia—Bill believed the entire debacle was a well-planned ambush. He was far from alone in that assessment. Merrihew, one of the closest observers of the game, had long written of the association's distaste for the sport's greatest player. In fact, he had recently written of "Bill's enemies and non-admirers." He believed they were few in number, "but active and virulent." Merrihew went on to argue that the USLTA leadership was totally out of touch with "the feeling of lawn tennis followers all over the world," for it was the view of the "rank and file of our lawn tennis family, that the former American champion occupies a position like unto that of Everest in altitude."[14]

That view was only bolstered by Big Bill's statement and actions following his banishment from Davis Cup competition. In what the newspapers would describe as "swallowing his chagrin at his sudden and unceremonious removal from the team," Tilden stated that the first order of business was still the team's best interest and that he would "devote all his energy to training his younger comrades for the difficult task ahead of them." His gallantry after the unexpected stab in the back from his own leaders "made Tilden a more popular figure in France than even before," according to news accounts at the time. "Always admired because of his surpassing ability as a player," according to one newspaper, "Tilden now has won his way into the hearts of the French people and the sportsmen of the world as a man."

Many American journalists were similarly struck by the French reaction to the public bushwhacking of the game's biggest name. According to the *Philadelphia Evening Bulletin*, "The French believe that no praise can be too great for the dignified, unselfish way he met the blow which removed him from the field of action."[15]

Tilden's stature as an athlete and incomparable racket wielder was long established. Unbeatable for years, he handled defeat in recent months at the hands of French players—sometimes under most difficult and controversial circumstances—in a way that only further highlighted his greatness. Now, in the face of inexplicable stupidity, and "at the eleventh hour, after long months of painstaking efforts to develop a strong American squad to try to wrest the trophy from France," the big man was once again demonstrating class and resolve in the face of concentrated adversity.

News of the perplexing action was immediately met with disbelief. Nations often broke the rules to advance their cause, not to harm their own chances. Universally considered "idiocy," "utter folly," and an "error of historic proportions," the association's actions had some critics already making the prediction that without Tilden, the American team might "not even survive the inter-zone finals with Italy." British newspapers were aghast at the decision, and all the London morning newspapers contained editorial comment that "was adverse to the ruling of the United States Lawn Tennis Association."

F. Gordon Lowe, a former British player once ranked eighth in the world, was quoted as saying Tilden's disbarment was a call-to-arms-like moment. "Tilden wrote many articles, but they were all legitimate comment about players," Lowe argued. "The whole thing is most extraordinary and it will have the effect of thoroughly arousing lawn tennis players to action."[16]

And much like a devastating earthquake, there were immediate seismic aftershocks. As one newspaper summed up the startling series of events, "Tennis sensation followed tennis sensation" when George Lott suddenly announced he would not play in the doubles match against Italy. Then an even more startling jolt was delivered when René Lacoste, the world's top-ranked tennis player, announced he would not be coming to the United States to defend his American title. Both players' announcements were construed as personal protests over Big Bill's unjust treatment by petty tennis tyrants.

Lacoste would admit that he had contemplated remaining on the Continent and not defending his American title for some time, but his public expressions of disillusionment over the Tilden snafu led almost all to believe the real reason behind his decision to remain home was the Tilden beef. Where was the honor, he would remark of France defending its hard-won Davis Cup championship, when the American team lacked its best player and the game's biggest name? "We would rather lose the Davis Cup than retain it when there may be some excuse in the absence of Tilden," Lacoste told the French press.[17] In fact, there were actually rumors circulating that the French star was "seriously considering refusing to play unless Tilden was reinstated."[18]

News of Lacoste not coming to America to defend his crown was met with headlines such as "Tennis Champion's Decision Removes Chief Attraction from the National Tournament," but the negative reaction in the States paled in comparison with what was now occurring in France. A fierce public backlash was under way.[19]

Initially, the French Tennis Federation expressed their dismay at the Tilden conundrum, but was "inclined to keep their hands off the entire matter." Their timid response misjudged the public's indignation. Tennis patrons had a personal stake in the matter; the French were set on seeing the greatest showman in tennis history compete against their *Mousquetaires*. Tilden's matches guaranteed athletic excellence and high drama.

It was to be the greatest show on French soil, but now they suddenly felt robbed, cheated.

To compound the nation's collective chagrin was the economic impact. France, caught up in the groundswell of national pride for its tennis team's unprecedented success, had erected an expensive new tennis stadium, Roland Garros—named after a tennis player and army airplane pilot killed during the war—which was christened in May. It was expected that the highly anticipated defense of the Cup against Tilden and the American team would go a long way in paying for the stadium's hefty construction costs. Ticket sales had been brisk. More than one million francs had been collected, and organizers were jubilant that a gate of two million francs by match time appeared attainable. News of Tilden's disbarment, however, was met with the same reception that the plague would receive: lines evaporated, and ticket sales suddenly stopped. Now the only lines that appeared at ticket windows were customers demanding their money back. Beginning to panic, event organizers feared if the refund pattern continued, the event would be an economic catastrophe. Even "the French tax collector," it was said, "has his grievance, for his percentage in the receipts is going to be much less than had been anticipated."[20]

The French were immensely proud of their Musketeers; Borotra's exciting athleticism, Cochet's natural gifts, and young Lacoste's analytical approach to the game were all attributes to be celebrated. But Tilden was tennis in the 1920s; it was against him that all others were measured. In "packing the punch," an expression coined by John Kieran of the New York Times, to separate and identify the greatest athletes of the era, he wrote, "Bill Tilden packed the punch on the tennis court. Jack Dempsey packed the punch inside the ring . . . and Babe Ruth packed the punch on the diamond."[21] Others, no matter their strengths, achievements, or records, were of lesser rank. The average Frenchman knew little of the "Big Bambino" and baseball, but Dempsey and Tilden were athletic supermen of unparalleled stature.

The reaction by French tennis patrons was not unique; Tilden's mystique was universal. By 1925 Tilden's allure was near godlike, from New Delhi and Tokyo to Melbourne and Pretoria. At least Europeans got a chance to see him, however, and when they did, they did not let the opportunity pass. In London, Paris, and Berlin, for example, it was commonplace for paying customers to watch Tilden practice rather than view a competitive match among highly ranked players. Newspapers regularly printed articles describing the "striking demonstration of Tilden's drawing power with the spectators," as a "general stampede of the crowd" occurred each time an announcement was made on what court Tilden was practicing or playing a match.[22] Invariably, actual players would be part of the excited throng rushing to catch a glimpse of him with racket in hand.

Now fully sensitized to the implications of Tilden's disbarment, the French Tennis Federation sent a cablegram to USLTA leadership in New York. "Without desiring to interfere in your interior regulations," the cable read, "we would be very happy if you could, by way of exception, authorize Tilden to play in Davis Cup, as his absence takes away from game great part of its regularity."[23]

The request received a cool reception in New York. Julian Myrick and Tilden's other implacable foes in the USLTA hierarchy were willing to suffer Davis Cup defeat and international derision in order to bring the Philadelphian down a notch or two. The current crisis supposedly arose when Dr. Sumner Hardy, president of the California Association, read an article in the July 3 edition of the *San Francisco Chronicle* entitled "Tilden Reviews First Week's Play on the Tennis Courts at Wimbledon." He then read articles in the *New York World* that confirmed in his mind that Tilden was once again breaching the association's player-writer rule. Much would be made of the fact that Myrick, Hardy, and other top-level decision makers waited until Collum and Wear were at sea and headed to Europe before addressing the issue that would ultimately sideline the game's best-known player.

Bill and his defenders were adamant that he had done nothing differently than the year before when he had also penned articles about the Wimbledon tournament without incident. But the amateur-versus-professional sports debate was an endless quagmire: prickly, ever present, and a source of continual consternation. And USLTA elders were relentless in pursuing transgressors, particularly Tilden. In fact, the clash between an increasingly potent professional sports culture fueled by greater commercial opportunity and an unforgiving nineteenth-century code of amateurism was hopelessly irresolvable. News of Tilden's disbarment swept across Europe, and athletes preparing for the Olympic Games in Amsterdam brought up the obvious hypocrisy. They could not help but notice "the fact that at least a dozen athletes on American teams, together with coaches and trainers, [were] filing daily dispatches . . . to American news syndicates."[24] The athletes were wondering, if the amateur rules were the same in tennis and Olympic sports, why were some able to write and earn money and others were not?

While the controversy raged, the American and Italian Davis Cup squads squared off in Paris. There was some proven tennis talent on the court, such as de Morpurgo and Hunter, but the crowd's greatest applause was reserved for the tall, lanky fellow in plain street attire. Though no longer eligible to play or captain the team—at least "officially"—Bill remained the center of attention. He continued to encourage his young players and applaud their effort, and he congratulated them with the customary French embrace rather than a handshake after their rather easy 4–1 victory. His unrelenting show of support for the team he had been banished from went over well with the foreign audience, as they repeatedly shouted, "Vive le Grand Bill!"

Tilden, in fact, would be the only American to receive the crowd's favor. The French were miffed that the challenge round they so much looked forward to and was now just a few days off had been sabotaged. And they were not shy about letting one and all know about it. As one journalist would report, "The crowds at the matches roared, cursed, and shouted abuse, some of it obscene, at American officials" for cheating them of seeing "Beeg Beel" against their much-loved *Mousquetaires*.

On his return to the States, Collum would inform all who would listen, "You over here cannot imagine Tilden's popularity in France. The day he entered the stadium as a spectator during the Italian matches, entire stands of spectators arose and cheered so long play had to be stopped. Every time Tilden appeared on the court it was a signal for prolonged and sincere applause."[25]

News of the appeal would become a daily press item, but USLTA officials in New York remained unmoved by the French request and the arguments for Tilden's reinstatement by Collum and Wear. Newspaper headlines such as "Plea for Tilden Gets No Hearing" were prominent on both sides of the Atlantic. In some articles Tilden was quoted as saying, "This is the first time

I have been shot through the body to get at somebody else."[26] Bill never specifically mentioned whom he was referring to, but quite likely it was either Collum or Wear, who were both adamantly opposed to the controversial sanction and understandably angered at the way the entire mess had been orchestrated. Collum, the association's president, felt so blindsided by the action he angrily told reporters, "There is not an ounce of sporting blood in any member of the committee," and the fiasco was making America look "ridiculous" in the eyes of sportsmen around the world.

Vinnie Richards was in agreement. Now a professional player and journalist who had already written of the hypocrisy and dishonesty in the game, Richards argued, "The most ridiculous part of the whole thing is the position of Cochet and Brugnon, who also write for the press." Vinnie thought the Tilden imbroglio may yet do some good. "The whole thing looks like the best thing that could have happened for the game. An entire house cleaning" was needed to restore some dignity and honor to the sport.[27]

S. Wallis Merrihew was equally chagrined and no less outspoken. He called the conflict between the USLTA and Tilden "irreconcilable" and said the association "bristles with hostility towards the man who was for six years champion of the U.S. and who is generally acclaimed the foremost player of all time." A firm supporter of amateur play, but realistic as to its growing challenges, Merrihew thought it a moral outrage for the USLTA to label Bill "a menace to the game," for he, more than anyone, "has done so much to develop and make glorious."

Merrihew would write numerous articles on the suspension and in most lambaste the USLTA for claiming Bill "is not a man of honor; that his word is given lightly and broken whenever he deems it to his advantage to break it." Merrihew assured his readers this was not true and that it was his "good fortune to know Tilden intimately for nearly ten years. I have found that his word is his bond, to be relied upon without even the suspicion of hesitation." Tilden, he believed, was "a man of scrupulous honesty, with the very highest conception of honor, and the last person in the world" who would harm the game of tennis.[28]

As sports pundits contributed their thoughts on the international furor, event organizers and Roland Garros officials were in an increasing state of panic. What was once expected to be a wildly successful athletic cele-bration in Paris was looking more like a national period of mourning, not to mention a financial disaster. "The French are frankly desolate at the turn of affairs," wrote a columnist of the impending catastrophe. At one of the largest advance-sales ticket offices in the city, an agent was asked, "Is business looking up?" With a glum expression on his face, the ticket agent replied there were ten people in line. "Eight of them want their money back and only two of them want to buy," the agent said sadly.

French tennis authorities were now pressing Collum and Wear for some sort of positive resolution to the debacle. The two American officials were sympathetic but hamstrung. They themselves had been hoodwinked, and their many telephone calls to Myrick, Hardy, and other high-ranking USLTA members were long, bitter, and unproductive. According to Hillway, they were also expensive and totaled more than seventeen hundred dollars.

French newspapers carried the association's cable to Collum that read, "All members endorse your message charges against Tilden should stand and agree he should not be reinstated."[29] It was clear: as far as those at the USLTA in New York were concerned, the issue was closed. Newspapers throughout the world were asking, "What, if anything, will be done, and when?" while others resigned to the worst were reporting, "There was virtually no chance that the order dropping Tilden from the team would be rescinded."

It is at this point that the embarrassing affair took on a life of its own. Over the years exaggerated tales have been attached to the 1928 Davis Cup brouhaha as barnacles fasten to the hull of an ocean liner. One of the most repeated may have been the serious diplomatic controversy that it sparked. Many accounts have the Quai d'Orsay, the French Foreign Office, being enlisted to intercede and make it known to the American ambassador to France that an international incident of some magnitude had arisen, and the French people demanded an immediate resolution to the issue. As the story goes, the American ambassador made a plea to the State Depart-ment in Washington, and they in turn pressured the USLTA to lift Tilden's suspension. There may be some truth in the account, but reflections from those who witnessed the affair tend to argue a less sensational course.

In fact, actual events reported at the time were less dramatic, but still of equal import. It is true that Collum, Wear, and the French Tennis Federation felt besieged: being on the front line of the controversy necessitated immediate action. Under pressure to do something, the two American officials discovered an ally sitting right in the stands at Roland Garros. Myron T. Herrick was not only an American sports fan residing in Paris but also America's ambassador to France. He had attended the U.S.-versus-Italy interzone matches and was keenly aware of the USLTA-Tilden controversy. As his government's top official in France, he fully understood its impact on French sports and finances and, more important, U.S.-French relations. And as an American living overseas, he was aware more than most of the impact the unpopular USLTA decision was having on the nation's image. French publications as well as street conversation were increasingly bitter about America's attempt to spoil France's first defense of the Davis Cup. As one American journalist would write of the growing anti-American mood, "All the old epithets about Uncle Shylock were pulled out again," as the French were feeling cheated out of their rightful glory.[30]

It was during the U.S.-versus-Italy Davis Cup contest that Herrick told Joe Wear, chairman of the Davis Cup Committee, "It seems to me that all the particulars about Tilden were as completely known at home many days before the decision to suspend him was communicated here as they are now." The ambassador did not want to comment on the merit of the player-writer issue, but did express his dismay that Tilden's suspension occurred at the eleventh hour, just when the French had such high expectations for the Davis Cup challenge match. The entire nation was preparing for a grand celebration. Quickly recognizing a potential angle of pursuit, Wear replied, "Well Mr. Ambassador, won't you write me a letter on the subject?"

Ambassador Herrick did as requested, and Chairman Wear immediately cabled the letter to USLTA offices in New York. Increasingly sensitized to the universal disapproval of their Tilden decision—they had now united French and American tennis fans, as well as sports fans around the world, against them—the association may have been looking for a face-saving way out of their most recent skirmish with Tilden.

According to reports, the association asked Herrick if he would make "a more definite demand for Tilden's reinstatement." Apparently, the ambassador was reluctant to take such a bold initiative without presidential approval, but he was willing to draft another letter that underscored the impact of Tilden's suspension on France. He also threw in a negative comment or two on the manner and timing of the entire regrettable episode.[31] Once the letter was received, Collum and Wear felt emboldened enough to void the association's sanction, thereby allowing Bill to play in the challenge match, but informing him that the charge of breaching the player-writer rule would be reimposed once Davis Cup play was over and he returned to America.

As soon as news of Tilden's reinstatement was announced, there was resounding excitement throughout Paris. Tennis fans, once again, rushed to purchase tickets, and those who had canceled their purchases now worked feverishly to reacquire tickets. Within hours French tennis officials were confident the event would be a sellout, and the Musketeers were reenergized and practicing with increased vigor and commitment. And for the moment at least, Ambassador Herrick had solidified his place in French history, if not the hearts of sports fans throughout the country. "In his first venture into the diplomacy of the world of sport," according to one newspaper account, "Herrick endeared himself still more to the French people."[32]

Bill, who was said to have "maintained a diplomatic reserve" throughout the entire "riotous rumpus," as one newspaper columnist referred to it, and repeatedly cautioned anxious parties to act not as juveniles but as adults, was cautious about any show of delight. He waited for confirmation from the USLTA in New York before expressing his feelings. With each passing day during his suspension, rumors flooded the tennis world regarding Bill's future. Some had him turning professional; others had him leaving tennis entirely for the stage. When asked for comment, he respectfully declined.

When he was assured the suspension had been lifted and finally felt comfortable talking to the press, Bill admitted, "It felt queer to have that tennis guillotine hovering above my head." And as far as the speculation went, he replied, "No, I am not thinking of turning professional, but if we should fail to win back the Davis Cup this time, I feel someone else should try it next year. I am glad to be given the chance to play my last Davis Cup matches with the United States." Bill went on to say, "If I don't come through the next two battles with flying colors, I am through. I never will play international tennis again. Therefore, all France must do to win the cause for amateurs is to get Lacoste and Cochet to trim me."[33]

Though the elation was palpable over Bill's reinstatement, there were some who believed Tilden was in no shape for a contest as high pressure as a Davis Cup challenge match. Merrihew, one of Bill's staunchest defenders, thought the suspension, the subsequent political turmoil, and the heated atmosphere it sparked could not help but drain Bill both physically and mentally. With Tilden having little time on the practice court over the past week, fending off reporters' questions, and the constant worry, Merrihew thought it best Bill express his appreciation for everyone's support but gracefully allow another team member to play in his place.

Considering all that had transpired, however, such a move was out of the question. He had to play; the Musketeers deserved it, and all of France demanded it. Married to the highest ideals of sportsmanship, the team leader, and dedicated to reclaiming the Davis Cup for his country, Bill took the court against René Lacoste with every intention of winning for himself and his country.

The match that all of France and the world beyond anticipated began with Tilden receiving "the greatest ovation ever accorded a tennis player in France as he entered the court at the start of the match and the thousands told him with handclaps how glad they were that he had been allowed to play."[34] Some were so taken by the outpouring of respect and affection, they believed Napoleon himself could not have garnered such a reception. And Tilden wasn't even French.

It was a joyous, heartrending greeting from a foreign audience that probably no other athlete in the world could have received. "Tilden seemed at first surprised by this reception," wrote Al Laney, who witnessed it, "but then his manner indicated that it was, after all, his due." Laney had the impression that Bill was "as pleased as surprised" and was able to "confirm later that he was immensely stimulated, even inspired," by the thunderous greeting.[35] But impressed as Lacoste must have been by his countrymen's show of appreciation for the tall foreigner, the "boy stylist of Europe with the nervous system of an oyster" was resolute and not one to be awed or intimidated. He had gotten the better of Bill in their most recent encounters and expected to have his way again.

The long layoff and protracted politicking during his suspension, as Merrihew feared, did little to help Bill's game. He had a hard time getting started, had little command of his strokes, and struggled mightily to penetrate his young opponent's defense and varied arsenal of court weapons. Before the sold-out crowd had even settled in, Lacoste had taken the first set

6–1. "That wasn't what the crowd had expected," the *New York Times* would report, "and there were discussions as to Tilden's age and failing powers." True, the French groundskeepers had heavily watered the courts to subdue the bounce of the American's hard-struck balls, the air was muggy and the temperature climbing, and a persistent wind made hitting the ball difficult. In addition, the normal Musketeer strategy of wearing Big Bill down over three days was still operative, but few expected the young Parisian to steamroller the former champion from the opening serve. Things looked bleak, but Tilden had not been declared a "master," "genius," and "colossus" over the years for nothing. Realizing he could not blast his opponent off the court with powerful drives to the baseline, Tilden now resorted to a deft array of slices and drop shots—in truth, an endless variety of exaggerated spin shots—to confuse his opponent and pull himself back into the match.

Laney would go on to describe the next "two sets of tennis as interesting as any I have seen." During that critical time Tilden never took a full swipe at the ball; he undercut it and topped it so that the spin and wind appeared to make the ball do eyebrow-raising tricks. Not only was Lacoste forced to repeatedly run from sideline to sideline and baseline to net and back again, but once he got to the ball he was almost mesmerized—like a snake charmer's trance—in order to judge which way the ball was going to bounce and what sort of stroke he would need to reply.

French tennis fans had never witnessed their young hero take so long to swing at the ball or hit so many balls into the net. Everything was so heavily cut by Tilden, including his serves, that Lacoste seemed either perplexed or paralyzed most of the time. And if Lacoste did not strike the ball soundly, which was often, Bill put the ball away for a winner. "That he could wring so much spin from that stubborn surface in the high wind was astonishing," Laney would comment, "and gradually we began to realize that if Lacoste did not soon find the answer Tilden was going to win the match."[36]

Try as he may—and Lacoste was the world's number-one-ranked player at the time—he could not solve the mystery of returning Big Bill's bizarrely spinning shots. Over the next hour the "phlegmatic plugger of France" managed to win four games in each of the second and third sets, but he still lost both. At the break Tilden had orchestrated a shocking turnaround and now held a two-set-to-one lead.

Incredibly, when the players returned for the fourth set, Tilden departed from the tactics that had gained him the lead and began as he had the match, by pounding the ball. This proved a godsend for Lacoste, and not until the set was nearly lost did Tilden revert to his extraordinary collection of spins, chops, and slices. But it was too late, the Frenchman took the set decisively at 6–2, and the packed crowd wondered if Big Bill could withstand another set like the last. Broiling heat and the long exchanges that sometimes lasted fifteen and twenty strokes of the ball left many to ponder if it all was "too much for the older man."

As expected the final set showcased some extraordinary play by both players. Tilden took a lead and Lacoste initiated a vigorous counterattack, but the exhausted veteran could still perform and outfox athletes many years his junior. In exchange after exchange the two men parried, hitting deep drives, soft drop shots, and exquisite chops and slices, but Tilden invariably had the legs, mind, and strokes to weather the storm. Several long rallies left spectators as breathless as the players. Despite the Frenchman's valiant last-gasp efforts, Bill employed whatever energy and tactical skill he had left to win that last set 6–3 and thereby set off another explosion of cheers, applause, and admiration.

All agreed it had been an incredible match, possibly the best they had ever witnessed. Relieved, Tilden told the press that "it was the best tennis match I ever played in my life." Lacoste was gracious in defeat. "Tilden was unbeatable today," admitted the Frenchman, "by me—at any rate." He told his countrymen, "Keeping the Davis Cup will be harder than our admirers appeared to think, but we players were never under any illusion as to the task ahead of us. I played the best game I know."[37]

Back in the clubhouse, forlorn and physically drained, Lacoste appeared baffled, if not slightly shell-shocked, as he sat on a bench in front of his locker answering reporters' questions. Al Laney, who would call the match "the finest of Tilden's career," was in the locker room to hear young Lacoste exclaim sadly, "Two years ago I knew already how to beat him. Now I do not know any more. Now on my own court he beats me. Is he not the greatest player of all?" The talented youngster shook his head in dismay; the defeat stung. He had no answer to the riddle; how does one defeat the inscrutable master? "I never knew how the ball would come off the court," said Lacoste, "he concealed it so. I had to wait to see how much it was spinning.

Sometimes it didn't spin at all. I thought the wind would bother him too much, but he played the wind better than I."

Tilden would subsequently call the victory "the climax of my whole tennis career, the match of which I am most proud. I played very bad mechanical tennis," Bill admitted, "but never have I tried so hard, wanted so desperately to win, and been so certain I could not; never have I used what few brains the Lord gave me to such good advantage as I did that day." When Lacoste hit a shot out-of-bounds, ending the match, and he heard the French cheer, Bill called it "the greatest moment of my life."[38]

If Lacoste voiced amazement at the racket control he had just witnessed, he was not alone. But as great as his victory was, Bill still lacked the partner who could claim another point for the American team in the best-of-five competition. In the following singles match Cochet defeated Hennessey, and the second day's doubles match saw Tilden and Frank Hunter lose a tough five-set battle. Extending Tilden and forcing him to play ten grueling sets over two days and then having him face possibly the most gifted Musketeer on the final day of play were just what the tricolor's warriors had hoped for. Bill would lose to Cochet in straight sets, but as all agreed the contest was highly competitive and "packed with tennis drama." The first set alone went on for sixteen games before Cochet managed to win it. In the second set, "Tilden had a lead of five games to two and was at set point no less than seven times, but could not put across the needed punch." As the newspapers would soberly recount, "Just when every one breathlessly was watching to see Tilden as Tilden has for so long shown himself, he wilted and failed."[39]

The *New York Times* led off their account with, "On the central court at the Roland Garros Stadium at Auteuil, that Napoleon of tennis, Big Bill Tilden, met his Waterloo."[40] "I played as good tennis as I did against Lacoste on Friday," said Bill after the contest. "That's the best I can do. It appears I can't defeat both of these French players the same year. In 1927 Lacoste defeated me in Davis Cup play but I won from Cochet. This year it is the other way around."

No matter as far as proud French patriots were concerned: they had retained the Davis Cup and gotten to see some extraordinary tennis. And as

René Lacoste would frankly write, more than a few Frenchmen left Roland Garros believing that even though "Beeg Beel" had lost the majority of his matches, he was still the one paying customers wanted to see. Then as well as years later, he was the one they would most remember.

It was not, however, just the paying customers who would remember the Tilden-Lacoste match. Polished tennis players who witnessed it were equally transfixed. George Lott, for example, would regularly point to that contest as one of the greatest, if not the greatest, he had ever seen. He called it "an exhibition of tennis that has never been equaled. Tilden used every shot in the game—topspin forehand, flat forehand, slices, chops, lobs, drop shots."[41] Lott was not surprised to hear that in postmatch interviews Lacoste complained that he could not do anything. The Frenchman had completely lost his timing. No one who had ever played the game, Lott and others believed, could have withstood such a wicked mix and bizarre barrage of shots.

Despite Bill's heroic effort to bring back the Cup, he still had enemies in high places. Not long after the match and before Bill departed France for America, he received notification his suspension had been reimposed. A "trial" by the USLTA's Executive Committee had been scheduled for August 24. "No matter how much we may admire Big Bill's courage and nerve," puffed Sumner Hardy, one of Bill's main adversaries, "I believe he does the game much more harm than good."[42]

Bill was outraged at such statements. "I am willing to stack my services to American tennis up against that of any individual official on the committee which barred me and let the public choose which has been and is of more value to the game," Bill shot back. "I am far more amateur in spirit than some of the men who have run tennis for years with an eye to the gate and have exploited me for its advancement."[43]

Bill certainly had his defenders. One of the staunchest was Merrihew of *American Lawn Tennis*, and he was not reluctant in skewering Bill's detractors or emphasizing how out of step they were. "My conclusion is that if the people of the U.S. could be polled on the Tilden matter there would be scarcely more than a corporal's guard on the anti-Tilden side," Merrihew argued. "As to the remainder of the lawn tennis world, the vote would be unanimous."[44]

Frank Hunter, another of Bill's close friends, initiated a letter-writing campaign to players and clubs, calling on them to support Bill and prod the USLTA to postpone any hearing on Tilden until after the tennis season. He repeatedly referred to Bill as "the supreme player of all time" and informed all that if sports fans thought Tilden was a heroic figure on American soil, "in Europe it was almost beyond realization." In all his presentations he would make mention that kings and members of the royal houses of Europe such as King George of England and King Albert of Belgium attended a tennis match only when Bill Tilden was on court.[45] For no other players did European royalty make an appearance. For such an iconic figure, argued Hunter, to be banished from the game was madness.

Hunter's efforts, like those of others, proved unsuccessful, as the "trial," not a hearing, was held as scheduled in New York City. Found guilty, Bill was severed from amateur play indefinitely. Bill did not participate in his defense; he was onstage in Boston at the time "doing a vaudeville monologue before an audience that included Cochet, Borotra, and Brugnon." For the Frenchmen, who were in America to compete in a series of tournaments, seeing Bill onstage or on court was always worth the price of admission.[46]

The absence of both Lacoste and Tilden put a damper on the U.S. National Tournament at Forest Hills, but the leadership of the USLTA evidently thought it a small price to pay. They had already displayed their propensity for principle—or retaliation, as some considered it—over public interest. Henri Cochet became the odds-on favorite for the American title and eventually won it in a "bitterly contested" struggle with Frank Hunter. In what was portrayed as "one of the greatest and most exciting championship matches in tennis history," according to one scribe, Cochet won the prestigious American title in five "magnificently" competitive sets.

The sportswriter who authored the complimentary account of the final—as well as daily updates throughout the two-week tournament for newspapers across the country—was none other than "William T. Tilden 2d."[47] Whether he intended to stick a finger in the eye of the USLTA or it was just a natural predilection to practice his economic profession as a journalist, Bill was contracted by a news syndicate to cover the national tournament. Though more prudent advisers may have cautioned Bill to keep a low profile and avoid ruffling the organizational feathers of the association any more than he already had, Bill had no intention of hiding. His opponents may have kept him from playing in the event, but they could not keep him from attending and writing about it.

His unwillingness to play the guilty transgressor and plead for forgiveness—as well as his musings on the tournament, which were the reason he was sanctioned in the first place—was rewarded by the USLTA deferring his "application for reinstatement as an amateur." In a possible game of one-upsmanship, the unanimous decision was delivered during the national tournament.[48] The next meeting of the committee was not scheduled until December, and even then Bill's reinstatement was considered a long shot, thereby ensuring Bill would be shelved from tournament action until the spring of 1929 at the earliest. Capable of incredible obstinacy on matters of principle, Bill refused to display the chastened spirit or express the contrition the USLTA demanded of him regarding the player-writer rule.

The time off from tournament play did not go to waste. A man of many talents and interests, Bill now had more time for his other pursuits, including his penchant for putting pen to paper, especially in the areas of tennis commentary and fiction. Most noteworthy during 1929 and 1930 would be the publication of two books: *Me: The Handicap* and *Glory's Net*. The former was an interesting and well-written autobiographical account of Bill's early years in Germantown and his initial attraction to the game of tennis as well as his current challenges and what life might present in posttournament play. Dedicated to his parents and signed "Junior," the book was released in January '29 and provided a frank and sometimes self-deprecating portrait of his rise as a world-renowned celebrity and his professional struggles.

With his current suspension in mind, the book's opening paragraph began with the poignant admission, "I guess I have always been the Bolshevik of Tennis. Certainly I have differed with the stand pat conservatism of officialdom ever since I was old enough to think for myself. If that constitutes Bolshevism, I am the Bolshevik of Tennis. Personally I called it Liberalism, Progressiveness."[49] Bill would go on to admit he was probably "born to be a little tennis snob" in the "usual comfortable well-to-do society of Philadelphia at the end of the nineteenth century" and was "practically born into the Germantown Cricket Club." But with all that going for him, "somehow and someway, the Little Snob turned out the Tennis Bolshevik."

After addressing a multitude of subjects ranging from his greatest triumphs and worst defeats to the importance of sportsmanship and the many friends he had made over the years, he seemed to recognize by the book's end that "the story of The Handicap [was] nearly over." Now "barred from tournaments," he insisted he would remain an "amateur" and had "no thought or intention of turning professional." Moreover, he had "no intention of giving up playing tennis. I shall play it as long as my two wobbling legs will function and my aged and enfeebled arms will swing a racquet, as long as my age-dimmed eyes can see a ball."[50]

Glory's Net, published the following year, was another one of his dubious forays into the world of fiction. His stories were usually designed for young adults and emphasized such values as gentlemanly behavior, bravery, clean living, and athletic accomplishment. Bill's fiction was rooted in the formulaic Frank Merriwell stories on which his generation of upscale youth had been weaned. In *Glory's Net* tennis was the backdrop for a troubled romantic relationship between a gifted young player from a small midwestern town and his love for his hometown sweetheart. The book's hero, David Cooper, is a handsome, athletic prodigy who attains early success and wins the National Championship on his first attempt, but the trappings of success and the big-city lifestyle he comes to embrace usher in a series of significant challenges that impact his game, his marriage, and his core beliefs.

The scenes, dialogue, and overarching message of the novel are straight out of the Merriwell playbook that celebrated courage, manliness, and the upper-class moral rectitude that colored his formative years a quarter century earlier. The story lines and often melodramatic exchanges between protagonists were never intended to imitate the Hemingways, Fitzgeralds, or Sinclair Lewises of the literary world, but that did not stop reviewers from taking potshots at Tilden for what they perceived as his literary failings. Bill probably would have been one of the first to admit the flaws of his fictional oeuvre, but even if only one boy was positively influenced by his stories of young men overcoming obstacles in their lives, the negative criticism would have been well worth it.

As in earlier confrontations with Tilden, a point was reached where USLTA decision makers felt they had taken enough heat and punished their petulant star enough. At their February 1929 annual meeting, the association revoked his suspension, and his request for reinstatement was granted. As Merrihew would comment on the critical vote, "There was pulling of wires, subterranean rumblings, and the playing of politics by men well versed in the intricacies of that game," but the apprehension and fears of another setback "proved to be ill-founded."[51] In fact, just two months later, and in what most would consider a highly ironic move, Tilden was engaged by the association to write "a complete forecast and analysis of Davis Cup play" for 1929. News of the article was advertised in association publications and proudly scheduled to appear in the USLTA's own magazine.[52]

Bill's first foray back on court underscored the impact of the long layoff: he would lose both his singles and his doubles finals at the Heights Casino Tournament. For months Bill had invested more time in his stagecraft than his physical conditioning and court play. Though he had agreed to travel overseas with Frank Hunter to partake of the many spring and summer European national tournaments, the biggest being in France and England, Bill was not in good form. He had been spending the majority of his time performing onstage at theaters in Passaic, Hackensack, and other North Jersey towns and cities.

Though still the center of attention both here and abroad, and capable of drawing vast crowds for his matches, he was losing more frequently and occasionally to those he would have never considered a true threat. On one long day in Philadelphia prior to sailing on the *Aquitania* for Europe, Bill lost to both John Hennessey and John Van Ryn. Not surprisingly, Bill was said to be "visibly fatigued" after the disappointing contests. Such results sparked critics to suggest Tilden's spot on America's Davis Cup team should go to one of the younger players who represented the team's future. His old partner Vinnie Richards was one of those calling for change. As a journalist wrote of the growing criticism of Tilden remaining the centerpiece of the country's Davis Cup team, "He was the greatest of all stars when the French first started coming over here six or seven years ago. They naturally studied him in painstaking detail, so today they know all about him and what he will do in every given situation."[53]

In the French championships Bill lost to Lacoste, the eventual champion, in the semifinals, and at Wimbledon Bill would lose to another Frenchman. This time it would be Cochet in the semifinals who would go on to claim the British title. The 6–4, 6–1, 7–5 straight-set loss was "the most one-sided Cochet ever scored on Tilden," and the ten games won were a low mark for Tilden in any championship match in more than a decade.

Cochet and Lacoste were unusually successful against Tilden. The little man from Lyon, however, would actually capture a winning record against Big Bill during the twenties—a unique feat that other players could only dream of—but he took a totally different tactical approach than his more analytical partner. "To beat Tilden, one had to play a game that suffered no weaknesses," Cochet would argue in an article written for *American Lawn Tennis*. "Lacoste thought the best method was to tire him by returning the ball indefinitely and wait for an opportunity to win the point. This was very difficult, requiring knowledge of every shot as Tilden always tried to discover the weakness in his opponent's play. I personally tried another method, a very fast return of every shot, expecting that Tilden would make mistakes, not having enough time to prepare his returns. This, of course, meant that I had to send back very quickly any ball from any place on the court."[54] Cochet would go on to write that the strategies he and Lacoste employed proved successful, but there was no guarantee it would always work. They both knew they were competing against a legendary opponent.

Despite further evidence that Big Bill was no longer the titan of the courts, he received a huge ovation as he collected his rackets and sweater and walked off the court after his match with Cochet. He may no longer have been the game's best, but spectators at Wimbledon that day were mindful that Tilden was like no other. He had devoted his life to the game, loved it more, and had given it more than anyone else in memory.

Soon after, Bill would suffer another stinging defeat to Cochet in the Davis Cup challenge round. This time he would only win six games in a decisive 6–3, 6–1, 6–2 thumping. Though he would come back on the final day of competition to beat Borotra in four sets, it did not dissuade tennis pundits from predicting an abrupt end to one of the greatest careers in the game's history. Even Bill had to admit that "age has won its battle and after nearly a decade of serious tennis," he was being forced to consider "laying aside" his rackets. "The year 1929 sees the end of my international tennis. I have had a grand time," he informed the press, "but I must hereafter write and speak of my triumphs and failures in world tennis in the past tense."[55]

Sportswriters submitting tennis obituaries for Tilden to their editors would be proven a bit premature, however. Back in the States Bill would win tournaments in Rye and Newport, and with the Musketeers choosing not to come to America, Bill was again made one of the favorites to win the national title at Forest Hills. There was a gang of young homegrown toughs coming after him, just as the French had done. After Bill proceeded to knock off the best young talent America had to offer, including the likes of Frank Shields, John Van Ryn, and John Doeg, even Vinnie Richards was forced to admit that Tilden "still has the old fighting heart that he has had since the first day he held a racket in his hand." Emerging triumphant after one hard tussle—in two matches Bill was forced to overcome a two-set-to-one deficit—Bill happily boasted, "They had the grave ready and even the headstone, but they can't bury the old man yet."[56]

In the final Bill was able to once again overcome a two-set-to-one deficit, this time against his old friend Frank Hunter, and win his seventh American championship. Only a few months short of his thirty-seventh birthday, and with untold tennis mileage on his thin legs, Bill displayed incredible "staying power" and the unique ability to raise his game to inhuman heights in order to grasp another big victory.

Rather than extend the celebration with a series of public appearances and media interviews, Bill was off to Europe on the S.S. *Berengaria* the very next week to pursue another of his passions, the dramatic arts. He was to star in the London debut of the play *They All Want Something*.[57] Retitled *I'm Wise* for British audiences, the play's sold-out premier at Golder's Green Hippodrome Theatre was well received, and Tilden was called back for eight curtain calls by an appreciative audience.[58]

Just weeks later the USLTA did its own performance review. The association named Tilden the nation's top-ranked player for the tenth straight year. The milestone—as well as the predictions that he was on his way out—may have influenced Bill to write a particularly thought-provoking piece on the arc of his career for *American Lawn Tennis*. Entitled "My Tenth

Anniversary" and beginning in his normal self-deprecating style, the article ·
reflected on a career where he "had passed from the rising star to become
the fading veteran" and now, at a ripe old age, was "considered a marvel
of antiquity, regarded somewhat like the ruins of Pompeii, or the Great
Wall of China."

Teasing critics for proclaiming him a "hollow shell" and "a mere shadow
of my former self," whose "venerable bones creek" and whose "age dimmed
eye" is no longer clear, Bill fired back. He considered their analysis rubbish.
"It is not age or physical decay that has hit me" or any sports champion
under forty years of age. It was something else, but something equally
devastating to a top athlete's ability to perform. "A man of thirty-six is not
seriously slowing up physically," Bill argued, "but a champion in any sport
who has stood at or near the top for a decade, a target for all to shoot at,
must inevitably feel and fall before the mental pressure of his position."

Prior to gaining success, Bill soberly reflected, he was a "player of crude
game, incomplete experience, uncertain physical reserve," but he possessed
"an overwhelming will to win." It was that "will to win" that overcame all
other deficits and "swept [him] to victory. In those days, I could not tolerate
the thought of defeat. Victory was a crying necessity."

Such unappeasable drive, according to Bill, was an "attribute of extreme
youth, this victory urge. The will to win, ambition, call it what you will,
would drive me on above handicaps and even above better players. It is the
will to win that makes champions like Bobby Jones, Ty Cobb, Babe Ruth,
Jack Dempsey and Henri Cochet. It is its loss that causes their downfall."

Tilden's revealing treatise would further inform his many fans that he was
twice on the verge of retiring from competitive tennis due to the waning
of his will to win, but on both occasions unexpected events interceded and
renewed his desire to continue on. The first incident occurred shortly after
Bill won his third National Championship in 1922. "The will to win in me was
burning still," Bill admitted, "but with a lesser brilliance and a lesser heat."

Then came the loss of his finger, an unprecedented event for a top tennis
player. Everyone believed—Bill included—it was the end of his career. But
as Bill now wrote, "It was a challenge that could not go unanswered, a defeat
I could not suffer without at least a fight. Within me rose once more a wild
urge of will to win." That inner drive motivated Bill to not only recapture his
prior form, but also "make a definite step forward. This new urge carried

me two years, but gradually once more the feeling that there was nothing new in tennis, no new experience, began to sap my will to win."

It would be "the rise of the French stars . . . and their magnificent game" that would propel Bill back into the thick of the fray. The Musketeers' varied and stylish play was a direct "challenge" to Bill's "tennis intelligence," and it was that new challenge that kept him involved at a high level in the sport.[59]

The question of what succumbs first in a top athlete has raged for generations. Is it an athlete's legs, or is it his reflexes? Is it one's vision that goes first, or is it the loss of stamina? Tilden, who had endured health problems, physical injury, and years of competitive play at the highest level, believed it was the slow, inexorable decline of that inner fire, that inner drive. The waning of the will to win, Bill argued, was key to the decline of many a great athlete.

Though much overlooked through the years, Tilden's article resonated at the time, especially with some of sports' more cerebral commentators. J. Parmly Paret, for example, a top player at the turn of the century and later a serious tennis writer, compared Tilden's "My Tenth Anniversary" article to an "epic poem" that broke new ground on the subject of athletic longevity among the world's best sportsmen. The piece clearly showcased Bill as more than just "the high water mark of all time for lawn tennis history."[60] Tilden looked beyond the obvious; he was a thoughtful commentator. For Paret and many others, Bill's keen insight into what motivates upper-echelon athletes was both revealing and provocative. The belief that individual psychology was as important a factor in an athlete's success and longevity as were his physical gifts was in its infancy at the time.

Bill was no doubt pleased with the favorable feedback, but he was preoccupied with another matter at the moment. The last month of 1929 saw his "debut as a cabaret entertainer" at London's Trocadero Restaurant.[61] The two-week engagement was further confirmation that the once shy boy from Germantown not only relished being the center of attention but could also draw a crowd, regardless of the stage or court he chose to perform on.

The year 1930 would be a critical one for Bill, and he would start it on one of the European Continent's most beautiful settings, the French Riviera. The Côte d'Azur, the enchanting Mediterranean coastline from Boulogne on the west to Menton on the Italian border, was a sought-after retreat for the affluent and well-to-do tennis enthusiasts during the cold winter months. Resort hotels in picturesque seaside towns like Cannes, Nice, Biarritz, Deauville, and Le Touquet sponsored tournaments, and top European players were frequent guests. During his heyday earlier in the decade Bill seems to have eschewed foreign travel and preferred having challengers come to him, but since 1927 he had been crossing the Atlantic and was now the recipient of an offer he had difficulty refusing. George Pierce Butler, scion of an American tobacco fortune and a devoted tennis patron, had built a swanky tennis club overlooking the bay of Monte Carlo and sponsored a doubles tournament that top players found both attractive and rewarding. As the game's biggest name Bill might have been a particularly enticing "reward" (Bill called his time there "the most delightful trip in my tennis life"), though under-the-table financial inducements were a well-kept secret.

With the exception of one inexplicable loss, Bill routinely captured tournament after tournament, defeating the likes of Britain's Bunny Austin, Italy's Baron de Morpurgo, and France's Jacques Brugnon. He even took an impromptu 6–4, 6–4 match from the Czech Karel Koželuh. Advertised as the world's professional champion, Koželuh had defeated Vinnie Richards a year earlier to earn the title. The Czech was a sound defender, canny shot maker, and fine athlete, but Bill could do everything better. However, the match presented a risk for Tilden. Just playing a professional before paying customers could have placed Bill in hot water with American and international tennis authorities, but in their inscrutable manner this was one transgression they chose to ignore.

Bill not only proved the "dominating personality" of the season, but was often referred to in grandiose terms such as a contemporary "Caesar," "Monarch," and "the Colossus of the World's Greatest Winter Playground."[62] Bill easily swept an overwhelming majority of his matches—he would eventually "win 13 singles cups, 13 doubles cups, and 9 mixed doubles trophies"—and contributed both guidance and some rising star power to his doubles partners "Junior" Coen and Cilly Aussem, a young German girl with championship-caliber potential.

After conquering the Riviera, Bill moved on to the championships of Holland, Germany, Italy, and Austria, where he again dominated and enthralled large audiences who flocked to see the famous American athlete, author, and stage performer. He did not disappoint: in the Austrian tournament, for example, he would win the singles, doubles, and mixed-doubles titles.

As expected France's World Hard Court Championship proved a greater challenge. He reached the final against the tough little Frenchman Henri Cochet and started out well, winning the first set 6–3. But Cochet fought back to make up a deficit in the second set and go on to win three sets in a row, 8–6, 6–3, and 6–1. Though Bill and Coen would get knocked out in a quarterfinals doubles match, he would win the mixed-doubles title with Cilly Aussem as his partner.

Bill then crossed the English Channel to take on the world's best lawn tennis players at Wimbledon. Along with two French Wimbledon winners, Cochet and Borotra (Lacoste was no longer playing at this time due to his business interests and the initial indications of tuberculosis), Bill was deemed one of the favorites to win the tournament. As expected Bill easily swatted away his early-round opponents. His semifinal match, however, was against another crowd-pleasing showman, Jean Borotra. Both men were two-time Wimbledon champions, and both had outsized egos that demanded center stage. As much a showman as athlete, Borotra knew how to unnerve opponents with his running commentary and court theatrics. His humorous tricks and pranks pleased the crowd, but opponents were usually thrown off stride. Tilden was particularly appalled by the naked gamesmanship and developed a strong distaste for the talented Basque thespian.

Many close observers of the game knew of the players' mutual dislike—if not outright animus—and looked forward to the game's two greatest theatrical prima donnas squaring off. Al Laney, covering the tournament for the *New York World Herald*, was one of them. Tilden, according to Laney, was so intent on not being distracted by Borotra's antics that "Tilden refused to go near him. At each change of courts Bill would wait to see which way Borotra went and then would cross over at the opposite end of the net so as to be out of reach of the Basque's needle."[63]

Bill's "intense dislike of Borotra and his tactics" was matched only by his confidence, of which he was willing to share with the *World Herald* reporter prior to the match. "He's got the best overhead game in the world, hasn't he?" asked Bill. "Well watch me. I will do nothing but lob and I will beat him."

From the opening serve Bill threw up nothing but lobs, but the French-man was on his game and fired back a series of missiles. The result was disastrous for Tilden: he did not win a game. The 6–0 first-set thumping made Tilden's game plan look amateurish, if not ridiculous. In the second set, however, Bill shifted his tactics and began mixing his well-placed lobs with rapid-fire passing shots and biting serves to take the set at 6–4. Borotra fought back to take the third set 6–4 and gain a two-set-to-one lead, but the effort was taking its toll physically. Forced to run hither and yon, his legs started to tire and his overheads were less assured. Inexplicably, he decided to gather himself for a final push in a final fifth set, as he lost the fourth 6–0. Intermittently showing off for the "crowd's amusement"—and with excessive gesturing "with a towel" on one occasion—Borotra repeatedly "disturbed Tilden who engaged in conversation with an official" about his opponent's constant clowning. His complaints accomplished little. Seething, Bill struck back the only way he knew how: with a series of lightning-bolt serves. One cannonball ace even "toppled a linesman off his stool."[64]

In the final set Borotra started afire, as he had in the first set, and quickly took the lead. At every opportunity the Basque attacked the net, looking to close out points or force his opponent to rush his shots and commit errors. Though the crowd was awed by Borotra's resurgence, the old campaigner across from him was too savvy to be swayed by an opponent's last-ditch effort to salvage a match. Bill had Borotra just where he wanted him, on the verge of exhaustion, both mentally and physically. Bill unleashed a fusillade of magnificently disguised shots. Some were bullet-like passing shots and deep overhead lobs, while others were delicate drop shots and balls that spun wildly. Occasions now arose where the Frenchman was either so surprised or out of place, he did not even bother to chase after a ball. The outcome was so obvious at one point that during a crossover, "Tilden stopped by the umpire's chair and said something to Borotra." It was a clear sign to Laney that Tilden had taken control and "didn't fear what his old enemy might say now." Tilden's 0–6, 6–4, 4–6, 6–0, 7–5 triumph would be widely hailed as "one of his most remarkable achievements."[65]

The all-American Wimbledon final stunned many. In the shock of the tournament, young Wilmer Allison of Texas upset Henri Cochet in straight sets, 6–3, 9–7, 6–4, in the other semifinal. Arguably the world's best tennis player, Cochet, as Rich Hillway points out, was capable of playing up or down, depending on his competition and motivation at the time. As the longtime king of the mountain, Tilden always received the Frenchman's best. Allison, however, was another story. The youngster was a fine player on the rise, but his rather short résumé did not inspire Cochet to put forth a herculean effort. The sin of commission—underestimating his opponent— would come back to haunt him.

Laney and a packed stadium that included the British king and queen watched "Allison put up a gallant battle, storming the net at every oppor- tunity, but Tilden's finesse, great variety of strokes and experience were too much" for the Texan.[66] Though spirited and twelve years younger than the aged campaigner across the net from him, by the end of the 6–3, 9–7, 6–4 match, it would be Allison who seemed the more physically spent. Big Bill was once again the Wimbledon champ.

The victory garnered front-page headlines around the world, and Bill was often lauded as "the game's finest stroke maker," the "most heart- breakingly regular and accurate" player to have ever swung a racket, and the consummate combination of "power plus precision." Others were struck by the history of it all, the long interval between Big Bill claiming owner- ship of the British and American titles at the same time, a feat that was first accomplished in 1920. Commentators like Merrihew were impressed that "a man midway between 37 and 38 years old [could] reappear at Wim- bledon . . . and win the title that he had relinquished nine years earlier," an achievement he called "unparalleled in the annals of the game."[67] And it did not pass notice that most of the intervening champions during that span had long since retired. Awed by the rare if not unprecedented accom- plishment, Merrihew referred to Bill as nothing short of an unadulterated "wonder. Whether viewed as a player, writer, or a man." And whatever remained of his career as a tournament player, his place in history was already solidified, for "his monument has been erected for all to see, and none are likely to overlook."[68]

It should be noted that Bill's Wimbledon victory took place at just about the same time as the publication of his latest book, *Shooting Stars of 1930*, a biographical and stylistic survey of the game's current stars and those who were expected to make a name for themselves during the coming decade. His list of publications was quickly approaching two dozen in number, and they were just his books.

Upbeat and optimistic due to the dual triumphs on his return to the States, Tilden was looking forward to the defense of his national title at Forest Hills in September. "But fate stepped in," according to Bill, and he would take a bad fall while playing in an August tournament in Rye, New York. He not only "split a tendon in his right leg but he suffered a dislocation of his sacroiliac joint" that impeded his movement and placed him in severe and constant pain.[69]

Loath to pamper himself, take time off for injuries, or accept the recommendations of medical experts, Bill played on. He felt obligated to his good friend and partner Frank Hunter to play in the National Doubles Tournament in Boston the following week and then travel back to New York for the defense of his national title. In really no shape to compete, especially against top players, he "managed to stagger through to the round of eight," where he met the young and talented John Van Ryn. Though he would defeat the former Princeton player and fellow Davis Cupper, the contest proved long and difficult. Tilden was exhausted, lame, and in severe pain after the contest. Almost completely incapacitated by the time he stepped on court in the semifinal to face Johnny Doeg, the twenty-one-year-old Californian with a big serve and strong net game, Bill suffered what he admitted was a "decisive defeat."

It was at that point that his medical adviser, Dr. Beeman, put his foot down and "forbade him to play any tournament tennis for a month," which included the Pacific Southwest Tournament, for which he was about to depart. The Forest Hills event would be the last serious tennis Bill, hobbled and in constant pain, would play in 1930.

But it would not be the last time Bill's name would be in the news that year. In fact, on the last day of the year, Bill once again dominated news in the sports world. As the *New York Times* headline succinctly captured the attention-grabbing story: "Tilden Joins Movies; Quits as Amateur."[70]

Part 4

From Professional Success to Villain

13

"A Burning Affection for the Game"

As a professional Tilden racked up an even
more amazing record than as an amateur . . . and
between 1931 and 1935 he compiled 340 victories to 147
losses, against such competition as Kozeluh, [Hans]
Nusslein, Richards, Hunter, Cochet, and Vines.

—PAUL GALLICO

Long rumored and much speculated on over the years, Big Bill Tilden's decision to jettison the amateur ranks for the money finally occurred as the year 1931 appeared on the calendar. Interestingly, it would be just days after another of the golden age's Big Four, Bobby Jones, gave up his amateur status to go pro. Both athletes, it seems, had decided to make motion pictures about their respective sports—Jones making instructional golf films for Warner Brothers and Tilden making instructional tennis films for Metro-Goldwyn-Mayer (MGM).

Bill's letter of resignation—something of a belated Christmas present to the USLTA—must have been received as a mixed blessing. His short and direct letter to Holcombe Ward read:

Dear Mr. Ward,

I wish to inform you that I have signed a motion picture contract with the Metro-Goldwyn-Mayer Film Corporation, the terms of which will violate the amateur rule of the U.S.L.T.A. Therefore I am announcing my retirement from Amateur tennis to take effect immediately.

Wishing the game of amateur tennis and the United States Lawn Tennis Association all success in the future and thanking you for many courtesies to me,

Sincerely,
William T. Tilden 2d.[1]

Bill knew his signature on a contract automatically made him a professional in the opinion of the USLTA, an outfit that watched him like a hawk eyes a cunning fox. Section 5 of article 3 of the association's bylaws stated that any player would forfeit his amateur status by "permitting or sanctioning the taking of tennis action motion pictures of himself and receiving remuneration in connection therewith." Section 5 of the same article was equally strict: any player "paid directly or indirectly for playing, engaging in, or teaching the game of tennis" was a professional.

The announcement from one of the sporting world's greatest names caused quite a commotion, and newspaper reporters flocked to his residence at the Algonquin Hotel in Midtown Manhattan, but he had already departed for parts unknown. Some believed he had left directly for Hollywood, while others had him heading back to his home in Philadelphia. The shocking act from "the most dramatic figure the game has produced . . . and whose exploits on the court and multiple controversies with the scions of the National Association had made his name a by-word wherever the game is played" led to much speculation and commentary. The *New York Times*, for example, devoted three columns to the story, with an additional sidebar section listing Tilden's "twenty-nine United States national tennis championships, comprising singles, doubles, and mixed doubles" over the years. Editors obviously decided that a list of Bill's international titles would have been excessive and required an additional column. In fact, *Times* fact-checkers had difficulty calculating them all, and a few national titles that Bill had earned before he became a household name were omitted.

Allison Danzig's lengthy *Times* account of Bill's unexpected decision to turn pro was like many others underscoring the impact of Bill's loss from the international tennis scene. He predicted there would be "dismay by thousands of tennis followers the world over," for Bill had been "so much a part and parcel of tennis, his name has been so synonymous for the game for the past decade."

As he wrote of Big Bill's "gifted racquet" and "flamboyant personality," he lamented the prospect that the greatest tennis player may have departed big-time tournament tennis forever. For his many fans around the globe, wrote Danzig, "it is almost inconceivable to them that he has played his last Davis Cup match, made his final bid for the national crown that he won the record number of times, and waged his last controversy with the lawmakers over the amateur rule and international play policy."[2]

Recounting Bill's career, from beginning to end, Danzig wrote, "The tall Philadelphian's amateur career has been a continuous series of dramatic episodes that have kept him in the international limelight above every other player even when his powers had begun to wane and his irresistible sway had been successfully challenged by Henri Cochet and Rene Lacoste of France." Addressing Bill's many disputes with the game's intransigent USLTA authorities—the *Philadelphia Evening Bulletin* called him a veritable "storm center"—Danzig wrote that most disagreements "centered around the famous player-writer provision of the amateur rule and while Tilden generally came off second best there were times when the association compromised and either changed its rule as in 1924, when a committee of seven redrafted the code, or waved provisions, as last Summer when Tilden was allowed to write advance articles on the Davis Cup Challenge round while a member of the team."

No better example of Tilden's influence, power, and aura, wrote Danzig, was there than the 1928 Davis Cup imbroglio, a conflict "so great as almost to bring about an international stringency and lead to the intervention of the late Ambassador Myron T. Herrick."

Even without mentioning Tilden's many books, articles, and public presentations regarding tennis, the *Times* article assured tennis fans that very few athletes, if any, had so personally and dramatically impacted their sport as Tilden had done. And his contributions and majesty did not go unrecognized by his legions of followers, as was proved in 1929 when "classic Wimbledon paid tribute to the victory of the aging, doddering veteran who had come back almost a decade after his last triumph to reclaim the most treasured individual prize the game offers" with repeated rounds of thunderous applause.[3]

According to Bill's autobiographical account, he may have been as surprised by the sudden turnabout in his plans as his many fans. Jettisoning the amateur game was not a step he had seriously contemplated as he spent the fall resting his aching back and injured leg in the aftermath of his painful Forest Hills performance in early September. In fact, as Bill would subsequently write in *My Story* two decades later, he had "every intention of defending at Wimbledon the following year" and "taking another crack at the United States Championship." But fate—or, more likely, an opportunity too good to pass up—was to intervene. One day early in October, as Bill would recount, he received a telephone call from Bert Cortelyou, whom he knew as a theater producer. Cortelyou, however, was not calling about a forthcoming stage performance. He wasted no time; he had a question for Bill. "Are you interested in turning professional?"

The proposition was not new. Similar overtures had been made over the years. As far back as 1920 Bill had been implored to turn pro. Arthur Hammerstein, son of the operatic impresario, had offered twenty-five thousand dollars if Bill would sign a pro contract. A few years later "Cash and Carry" Pyle, the sports entrepreneur who organized the Suzanne Lenglen tour, came forth with a lucrative offer, but Bill was still wedded to the amateur game and looked at the professional tennis tour with a skeptical eye.

But when Cortelyou proffered the notion of turning pro in October 1930, it was neither a novelty nor as unappealing as it had once been. "I had reached the point," Bill admitted later, "where I wanted to play tennis and not have to worry about what action the officials of the USLTA might be taking behind my back." The freedom to both write and play without the ever-constant association sword dangling over his head was very attractive, but Bill was still not sold. "Frankly," Bill would later write, "I was still uncertain; I could not take the leap."

"How about movies?" Cortelyou then replied. "Have you ever considered making educational pictures?"

Without realizing it, the promoter had hit upon a subject that Tilden was increasingly tantalized by, the prospect of making talking pictures. "Here was something I had always wanted to do," Tilden later admitted. "The question about movies really intrigued me. I had made three silent pictures but now the talkies presented an opportunity irresistibly beckoning."

Bill told Cortelyou, "If you can get me a contract to make pictures, I'll sign it. It'll professionalize me, but if it's good enough I don't care."[4]

Cortelyou persisted. "Will you play professional tennis too?"

Bill's reply underscored his desire for a motion-picture contract. "Sure," he replied, "you get me the picture contract and I'll play tennis."

It quickly became clear that neither was Cortelyou representing a particular film company nor had he a deal in hand, but he did have Hollywood contacts. More important, he knew he had a highly marketable commodity in tow and proceeded to usher Bill to several picture studios in New York. Whether MGM saw the sport of tennis as a new market to be mined or just wanted to stay competitive with Warner Brothers, it signed Bill to a contract. As Bill would one day write, his signature on the contract "wrote *finis* to my amateur career, but opened a new and far more interesting chapter in my tennis life."[5]

From day one Bill said he never regretted his decision. "The very moment I signed that contract," he would write, "I threw my energy into the new career." He had hoped the instructional tennis films would lead to Hollywood movies, but the dream was slow to be realized. When the press finally caught up with him, he was told of the public's chagrin at the news and asked if his decision was final. "I've had my fling at it," Bill replied. "Of course, I'll still play tennis, whether it's for the movies or not. I love the game too much to quit altogether."[6]

In actuality, there may have been another very important reason Bill turned pro, one he never mentioned publicly. He needed the money. Though his books and newspaper and magazine articles brought in a regular salary, Bill was a big spender. Very often what came in went out just as quickly. Generous to a fault, he usually picked up the check when out dining with friends, stayed at the best hotels, maintained an expensive and stylish wardrobe, and was known to have sunk an exorbitant amount of money in various theatrical projects. And though his freewheeling spending habits may have been ill-advised, what really put him in a financial hole was the one that ultimately sank a lot of people at the end of the wild-and-woolly Jazz Age, the Great Depression. Unlike millions of other Americans who lost money and were left destitute, Bill was still in relatively good shape, but whatever nest egg he had nurtured was gone.

According to a United Press report, Bill could withstand the loss of one hundred thousand dollars in a dramatic product gone bad, but after 1929 such dubious financial misadventures were greatly curtailed. Like many others, Bill took a hit in the stock-market crash. It was reported that Bill lost at least seventy-five thousand dollars in one stock alone. His good friend Frank Hunter was said to have lost more than ten times that on the same stock. As United Press came to believe, "This misfortune caused Tilden to turn professional."[7]

Regardless of the actual reason or reasons for finally giving up his amateur status, Tilden's legions of fans were disconsolate. They were less interested in instructional films than seeing him on court doing battle with the world's best, and the prospect of his absence after a decade of dominance was disillusioning. Just a few months after watching him win Wimbledon as well as a slew of other European titles, devoted tennis patrons found it inconceivable Big Bill would give up competitive play for Hollywood. Many just refused to believe it. "The man who bestrode the lawn tennis world like a colossus for more than a decade simply could not cease to wage joyous combat while sound of body and mind," lamented S. Wallis Merrihew in an *ALT* editorial. "The war horse sniffing the fray from afar and unable to enter it can be likened to Tilden in such case."[8]

Not to be outdone, Edward Stillman commented in an *ALT* piece entitled "Tilden the Artist" that Bill's contributions and retirement from the amateur ranks were "epoch-making." He considered Bill's significance "unique" in sport, with "nothing in the game comparable to it." Repeatedly referring to Bill as a "genius . . . who loved his art," he compared his matches to pure artistry, and "like a true master" with acclaimed works to his name, he had a "school" of disciples who learned the game from him and hoped to follow in his footsteps.[9]

Rather quickly, however, the worst-case scenario—Bill giving up competitive tennis altogether—was put to rest. Though he may have aspired to a full-time gig in Hollywood making talkies—he would eventually make a few unremarkable movies—the dream of a film career would go unfulfilled. The result was his availability for the pro tour. It was not long before Bill assembled a traveling squad of players. His close friend Frank Hunter joined the troop, along with lesser-known amateurs Emmett Pare of Chicago and Bobby Sellers of San Francisco. Karel Koželuh, one of the world's top professional players, would provide the main competition for Tilden's series of one-night stands at auditoriums and stadiums across the country. A Czech with solid tennis credentials, Koželuh had been battling Vinnie Richards during the late 1920s for pro supremacy.[10]

Though professional tennis had started with great bombast when Suzanne Lenglen signed a pro contract in 1926, her departure after that initial tour caused a significant drop-off in public interest. Attendance figures plummeted, and newspaper articles on pro matches were few and brief. Others, like Vinnie Richards and Koželuh, soldiered on, but the events were often sparsely attended, and Richards began to lose his appetite for the extensive traveling and underappreciated matches. Professional tennis needed another superstar to inject some interest and excitement in the game; only then would it be on a firm financial footing. There was only one person who had the star power to accomplish that.

In a business-savvy but still controversial move, Bill signed Jack Curley as a promotional and booking agent. Curley had relations with every stadium operator in the country, but he came with some baggage. As Curley was a former promoter of the "odious" wrestling game, or what Bill referred to as the "grunt and groan circuit," Bill had to keep a watchful eye that Curley played it straight and left all management and playing arrangements to others.

Curley was soon inundated with numerous offers from both domestic and foreign sources. Tilden's availability sparked a host of intriguing business opportunities and attractive monetary offers. Athletic promoters in Australia, for example, were willing to put up fifty thousand dollars if Bill would come Down Under for a two-month stay and participate in a tennis program that included "six matches against three approved players."[11] Aussie champ J. O. Anderson, now a professional himself, was "greatly pleased" by the prospect of Tilden coming to Australia and said that Bill's visit "would help us immensely, particularly our younger men, who will have a chance of seeing a master in Tilden."[12]

Almost immediately, full-page advertisements announcing the Tilden-versus-Koželuh match appeared along with forthcoming matches in Baltimore, Boston, Cincinnati, Chicago, Detroit, and other cities. Sponsored by Tilden Tennis Tours, Inc., the ads also listed the undercard for events as well as many of Bill's books, including *Glory's Net, Match Play and Spin of the Ball, Phantom Drive, Pinch Quitter,* and *Shooting Stars.*[13]

Tilden's pro debut took place on a frigid mid-February night in 1931 at Madison Square Garden against Karel Koželuh. The players took the court to a thunderous ovation after a prelim bout between Hunter and Pare. Before the first ball was struck, however, Bill took the microphone and announced the names of the many celebrities in attendance, including the much-loved "Little Bill" Johnston and respected sportswriter Grantland Rice. "Applause," newspapers would report, "rang down from all sides of the building."[14]

Tilden, whom the *Times* proceeded to label "the invincible monarch of amateur tennis," had his way with the "foremost European professional." As Allison Danzig described the encounter, "From beginning to end there was never any question of Tilden's superiority." Tilden's cannonball serves drew roars of approval from the nearly fourteen thousand in attendance, and "his drastic forehand drives and his far greater variety of attack put Kozeluh squarely on the defensive" and often several feet beyond the baseline throughout the contest.[15] As the 6–4, 6–2, 6–4 sixty-five-minute match attested, there was a new kid on the professional tennis block, albeit a thirty-eight-year-old one who was getting a little long in the tooth. But as the large and "highly enthusiastic crowd that turned out for the . . . debut of the recognized greatest player of his time" confirmed, Tilden's maiden voyage as a professional tennis player and sports entrepreneur appeared most promising. It was estimated that ticket sales had totaled more than thirty-six thousand dollars for the event. Not a bad night's work during the height of the Great Depression, and there would be more to come.

The very next evening and a few hours south, more than three thousand spectators turned out in Baltimore to see a repeat performance. Tilden's straight-set victory over Koželuh put to shame some of the publicity bluster that pitted "the man of flamboyant attack against the man of the Gibraltaresque defense, or brilliance and daring of shot-making against machine-like faultlessness in the methodical returning of the ball."[16]

As the troupe put on performance after performance and traveled from city to city, Tilden's dominance was reaffirmed on a nightly basis. "Match after match I consistently won," Bill would later write, "and I sensed, perhaps mistakenly, that someone might try to suggest that I toss a few matches to Kozeluh." Deciding "to beat them to the draw," especially Curley, who was in a "state of squirming anxiety" over the string of one-sided decisions, Tilden laid down the law. "Just in case anyone might get any false ideas, let me tell you right now that if I can I'm going to beat Kozeluh in every match on this tour." And years later Bill would proudly proclaim, "Every match ever played on any tour with which I have been connected has been decided on merit alone."[17]

Koželuh's embarrassing string of defeats finally ended after Bill had run off eleven straight victories. His accomplishment would be ever so brief, however, as the players continued to barnstorm across the country, with Bill quickly reclaiming his superiority. The Czech caught a brief reprieve when Bill required a month off to travel to Hollywood and make his instructional films. On Bill's return in early April Koželuh was no better prepared to deal with Tilden's vast array of court artillery.

By mid-May Tilden led Koželuh 27–6, and by the tour's completion he had accumulated an impressive 63–13 advantage. But now that Bill was a professional, there were other numbers that were equally if not more important; specifically, how much money had the tour earned? He would be pleased with those numbers as well. According to Bill's account, "The tour grossed close to two hundred thousand dollars and broke tennis attendance records from one end of America to the other."[18]

In fact, the Tilden troupe's cross-country travelogue was so successful that it brought Vinnie Richards out of retirement. Believing that he had been snubbed, for he considered himself and not Koželuh the rightful 1930 world professional champion, he proceeded to challenge his onetime friend and mentor for pro supremacy.[19] "I'll play Tilden anywhere he says with one match to decide the title or play him two out of three matches on clay, turf, or indoor court for the championship," blustered Richards. He was even willing to put a side bet of twenty-five hundred dollars on his chances against Tilden.

The 1924 Olympic champion got his wish and more. They agreed on a series of ten matches, with the first at Madison Square Garden. A crowd nearly as large as the one that turned out for the Tilden-Koželuh match greeted the players, but besides the lucrative payday Vinnie had little to show for his braggadocio and effort. He lost the Garden match 5–7, 6–0,

6–1, 6–3 as well as the nine others that followed. Though he was ten years younger than his former mentor, Vinnie was losing his once sleek, athletic physique. Big Bill, on the other hand, remained trim and "in the pink of physical condition." Moreover, he still had that deep reservoir of stamina and extraordinary shot-making ability, as the last three sets of their Garden match plainly demonstrated. He was still the master.

Bill's domination of players many years his junior left observers scratching their heads. Was it truly possible, they asked themselves, that now that he was approaching forty years of age, he might be better than he was a decade or two earlier? Granted, Tilden was not playing Borotra, Cochet, or young American amateurs like Allison and Doeg on a daily basis, but Koželuh and Hunter weren't exactly inexperienced dubs.

In fact, there would be many close observers who actually believed Bill was playing the best tennis of his life. Babe Norton, for example, wrote a piece for *American Lawn Tennis* in mid-1931 that argued, "No player in the world has ever played with such sustained pace as Tilden is using today." Norton, who played Bill many times during the twenties, said Bill always "hit hard" as an amateur, but it was his "accuracy and change of pace that enabled him to beat the world." Now, Norton contended, Bill's "tennis is almost certainly better. He is playing an almost entirely different game. Instead of the long rallies he is now hitting with such tremendous power, depth and confidence that it makes it impossible for his opponents to do anything but play defensive tennis."[20]

Bill was not consumed with accumulating victories and paydays, however. He continued to be generous with both his time and his money, especially when it concerned worthwhile organizations in need. When the Actors Fund of America, for example, came up with a deficit of fifty-five thousand dollars, Tilden volunteered his troupe for a tennis fund-raiser. With Koželuh, Hunter, Pare, and Sellers in tow, Bill showed up at the Westchester Country Club in Rye, New York, for a series of exhibition matches. The club was the site where Bill had taken a bad fall and sustained a severe injury the previous September that nullified his chances of winning an eighth American title, something he wanted badly. As Allison Danzig wrote of the event, Bill was "always ready to serve the cause of charity during his amateur days," and it should be no surprise that he "was particularly sympathetic to the appeal of the Actor's Fund, for aside from his playing and writing activities, his time has been given to the theater, and he won his spurs as a thespian on the New York stage several years ago."[21] In appreciation of his generosity, the theatrical society held a dinner in his honor at the country club.

It should be mentioned that it was quite common for Bill to give lectures and presentations at local schools in the various cities and towns in which his tour appeared. At one school in Montreal, more than four hundred children sat rapt on the edge of their seats, listening to Bill talk of his great American and European tennis battles. In addition to a lively recounting of his career highlights, his talks always emphasized the long-term benefits of tennis over other sports, the importance of mastering the key strokes of the game at an early age, and embracing good sportsmanship in whatever athletic activity one chose to pursue. In addition to his competitive play and lectures, there were assorted other duties he needed to perform. His personal schedule, in fact, was nothing short of daunting, as it was not unusual for him and his cast members to hop in a car after a late-night match and drive for hours to the next city, and while others like Koželuh and Hunter got some sleep, Bill would be checking out the stadium where they were to play, fielding interviews with journalists, and doing what he could to promote the evening's event. The grueling regimen would go on for weeks and months at a time. Just contemplating the physical and mental demands of such an intense schedule is exhausting.

Though much would be made at the time and later concerning Tilden's dominance in these matches, the pro tour served another important purpose. Most Americans knew tennis from newspaper copy. They had never seen an actual match and probably would never step on the grounds of a ritzy country club where the game originated and was usually played. They almost certainly would never have the opportunity or comfort level to visit such august playgrounds of the rich and famous as Longwood, Newport, Forest Hills, and Merion Cricket. Bill's tennis caravan, however, brought the sport to them. Granted, some of the aura and aesthetics would be lost in the game's relocation to an array of venues such as high school gymnasiums, National Guard armories, and cramped civic centers across the country, but it was still Big Bill. He and his colleagues' appearance was often a sports fan's first exposure to topflight tennis. Tilden's pro caravan made stops in towns such as Poughkeepsie, Waterbury, Crawford Notch, Scranton, Fort Wayne, and Grand Rapids as well as the big cities. The excitement generated in small-town America by the opportunity to see one of the nation's greatest athletes in competition cannot be overemphasized.

In addition to all his other burdens and obligations as both player and event organizer were his various writing assignments. Some were for pay with established newspaper syndicates, while others were of his choosing. One contract, for example, with the North American Newspaper Alliance had him providing one column a week to newspapers such as the *New York Times* on a variety of tennis subjects, ranging from updates on tennis tournaments around the world and who was looking most likely to earn a spot on America's Davis Cup team to his predictions regarding upcoming matches and the names of youngsters whom he deemed stars of the future.[22] And it was not all that unusual to have Bill authoring an article and being the subject of another on the same page of the newspaper's sports section.

All in all, it was a pretty good life. As tennis historian Rich Hillway argues, "For the first time, Tilden had the freedom and independence to do what he wanted without someone or some association looking over his shoulder. He loved playing tennis and was now being paid to do so. And he could write and not be penalized for it. Bill made his choices," argues Hillway, "and never regretted them."[23]

Being paid for what he enjoyed most was a novelty. He had always played the game of tennis for the sheer enjoyment, the athletic and mental challenge it presented. Yes, there were ornate silver cups and brilliant trophies that went to the victor, and the celebrity status that came with tournament titles had its appeal, but for a longtime defender of ama-teurism making money from one's athletic prowess proved surprisingly agreeable. And though the nation was in the grip of a serious depression, athletes of Tilden's stature could still do quite well. In addition to his pro tour and syndicated columns, Arthur Voss believes, Bill was earning con-siderable money from endorsements. Products such as Spalding rackets, Dunlop tennis balls, Armour tennis gut, and other sport and consumer items proved a financially rewarding side business. "Bill cleared some-thing over $100,000 during the Depression year," a sum that rivaled what Babe Ruth was earning. After "six years of professional play," according to Voss, "Bill's earnings totaled at least a half-million dollars."[24] But as many of his friends and associates knew, he was capable of spending it as quickly as it came in.

Though he was loath to manage his personal finances, one area he was keener to monitor was the marketability of his pro tour. He needn't have his father's business acumen to realize the need to refresh or restock his stable of Tilden Tours players. One could not go back to the same town and city on an annual basis with the same players. An injection of new blood was necessary to maintain public interest. As major an athletic figure as he was, he knew he could not unilaterally carry the day forever, especially when those across the net from him seemed to be putting up little resistance. As Voss quite rightly points out, "There had to be some fresh faces on the other side of the net."

In 1932 Tilden brought in two German pros, Hans Nusslein and Roman Najuch. He also added Albert Burke, an Irishman who played most of his tennis on the French Riviera circuit, and Bruce Barnes, a fine young player from Texas whose quick jump from college play to the pros—which other young players were to follow—underscored Tilden's impact on solidifying the future of professional tennis. None of the four was a household name, however, and combined with the sour economy, the tour suffered financially. "In spite of the money lost," argued Tilden, "the tour consolidated the position of pro tennis as a major sport."

Throughout 1933 Tilden sought out the game's biggest names: France's Henri Cochet and the young American Ellsworth Vines were the players he wanted. After considerable effort and much persuasion, the French star signed a pro contract in September and agreed to a series of matches against Tilden soon after. The very next month the sports world was stunned to learn that "Ellsworth Vines has played his last Davis Cup match. . . . [P]rofessional tennis has wooed another prized recruit from the amateur ranks."[25] Just twenty-two years old and a former American and British champion, Vines was considered by many the game's finest player, but his play had recently suffered due to assorted pressures, expectations, and rumors.

Talk of his turning pro became so widespread during the year that the USLTA initiated an investigation as to whether Vines had violated the amateur code. "All this talk about my turning professional," said Vines, "is only so much talk. I have not turned professional." But he did admit, "It isn't pleasant to play tennis in an atmosphere of suspicion, with people charging you almost every day of being a professional."[26] Just a month later, however, Vines was once again making headlines, but it was not for any on-court triumphs. After months of indecision, he had finally decided to leave the amateur ranks and join Tilden's "professional movement." "I have become a professional tennis player," wrote Vines in an article for the *New York Times* explaining his decision, "because it is the only thing for me to do. When a fellow reaches a certain point in his life where he begins to think about the future, where he begins to feel responsibilities, he has to start figuring an answer to the important question: Where do I go from here?"[27]

Vines owned up to his "tremendous debt to amateur tennis," but went on to explain, "Being an amateur tennis champion isn't entirely a bed of roses. From the very moment I began to win big tournaments people were after me with one proposition or another. I've been offered every proposition in the world, from doing a hoofing act on the stage to teaching tennis by mail and most of these propositions have been coming to me during the last year. People wouldn't let me alone. Is it any wonder that I couldn't play tennis?"

The young, beleaguered champion admitted that it was "a relief to have finally arrived at the decision to become a professional" and said he expected "to play the best tennis of [his] life now that some of the strain and worry was over."[28]

As part of his effort to publicize the tour and sell tickets, Tilden, who had just defeated Vinnie Richards for the title of national indoor professional champion, threw a dinner for newsmen at the Algonquin Hotel. Bill talked about his goals, what he hoped to accomplish, and how professional tennis would add rather than detract from the sport. He then introduced Vines to the attendees.[29] "Boy, this is great," said a jubilant Vines in reference to his newly signed employment agreement. "I feel swell; better than I have in years."[30]

With his future settled and his economic problems resolved, Vines's biggest concern was how to play Tilden. "My problem with that big guy will be to get him as far as the fifth set," said Vines. "Maybe I can win if I can get that far. He'll try to clean me up as quickly as he can, but he's going to have to be pretty smart about it."

As he listened to the two players field questions in the relaxed postmeal atmosphere of scotch and cigar smoke in a private dining room at the hotel, it dawned on Robert F. Kelley, a *Times* sports reporter, how much the "Old Maestro" loved the game. "Tilden sat for hours talking tennis, eagerly and with plainly evident relish," Kelley would write in a column that was originally designed to feature Vines. But it was Tilden, a player who seemingly had been around forever, who captured his interest and became the centerpiece of his article. "As [Tilden] chatted it quickly became apparent once more why this man, probably the greatest of all tennis players in history, still remains among the best at the decrepit age of 41. There is in him almost a burning affection for the game, which had increased, rather than diminished, with the passing of time. Hundreds perhaps thousands of matches have left him still hungry for more."

Kelley was not the only reporter who became entranced listening to the sport's greatest player and its finest student answer questions. His encyclopedic knowledge of tennis history, his views on the strengths and weaknesses of various players, and his call for open tournaments where both amateurs and professionals could compete provided for both an informative and a highly entertaining evening.

Like true sports fans, reporters were especially interested in Bill's opinion of how the stars of yesteryear would match up with current stars and whom Bill would rank as the greatest he had ever seen or played. His answers, no doubt, surprised some, though a number may have agreed that Henri Cochet was at the top of his list "on the basis of genius for the game and wealth of stroke production," and the German Gottfried von Cramm the best of the current crop based on "shear stroke equipment and brilliance of execution."[31]

Several days later Tilden and Vines were together again, but it would not be for a fancy meal at a Midtown hotel. In what would be described as "the greatest professional tennis attraction ever staged in New York," they were now combatants eyeing each other across a taut net cord. Although Vines was nearly two decades younger than the old man who took the court with him before a packed Madison Square Garden crowd in January 1934, it would be the younger man who was taken to the woodshed. The sixteen thousand in attendance that evening—the largest crowd ever to watch a tennis match in America—repeatedly rose to applaud Tilden's stellar play and extraordinary shot making. He may have been forty-one, but the spindly-legged, ancient court warrior could still play the game. He defeated Vines by a score of 8–6, 6–3, 6–2. Total receipts for the evening brought in more than thirty thousand dollars. Tilden and Vines each earned more than seven thousand dollars. Not bad for a few hours' work.

The large turnout that night and the following nine matches in other cities basically cemented the foundation for professional tennis in America. Fifty-eight hundred spectators turned out two nights later in Philadelphia, three thousand the next night in Washington, and well over twelve thousand patrons in Boston two nights later. And so it went, from night to night and from city to city. If the physical demands, extensive travel, and organizing aspects of the tour wore on Tilden, he seemed not to show it. Although many predicted Big Bill could not hold up on such a demanding and lengthy national tour, he proved them wrong. After a week on tour Tilden and Vines had split their six matches. By the initial tour's completion Vines had won eleven matches against Tilden's nine.[32]

A new tour, America versus France, with Tilden and Vines pitted against Henri Cochet and Martin Plaa, was then organized and equally well received. Cochet may have had the upper hand in their amateur bouts, but as professionals Tilden clearly dominated. He would take eight of their first ten contests. They both, however, profited financially. "The combined tours," according to Bill, "grossed well in excess of a quarter of a million dollars."

Those impressive numbers confirmed something important: sports fans not only accepted professional tennis but embraced it. "With the signing of Cochet and Vines," observed the *New York Times*, Tilden had masterfully given a "decided impetus" to the game's professionalization. In addition, Tilden had also contributed "considerable pressure" for "an open championship" between the amateur and professional ranks, an issue of long and bitter debate.[33]

Often an orphan in the grand scheme of things, professional tennis had been thought a lesser, somewhat tainted offshoot of its parent—tradition-bound amateur lawn tennis. Suzanne Lenglen along with Vinnie Richards and Mary K. Browne had thrown a momentary spotlight on play for pay in 1926, but much more was required for such a revolutionary, if not unsavory, concept to take hold and flourish. That was especially the case with the well-bred, self-appointed guardians of the game opposing the notion of professionalism so vigorously. Big Bill, however, supplied the necessary star power. Only an iconic figure like Tilden had the athletic gravitas, dogged determination, and entrepreneurial skill to orchestrate such a campaign.

By the end of the year Bill was looking abroad and announced that players from America, England, France, Germany, Ireland, Czechoslovakia, and Belgium would "inaugurate international play along Davis Cup Lines."[34] It was his dream to start a World Team Tennis League that would play scores of matches throughout the summer months in major cities throughout the world.

And though he was still barnstorming around the country with his band of professionals and continuing to seek talented college players for future tours, he could still be talked into performing some of his court heroics for worthy charities, especially if it was a cause close to his heart, such as the Actors Fund of America. After crushing Vinnie Richards in straight sets at one Manhattan fund-raiser, Bill helped event organizers auction off various items, including the racket with which he had just walloped his former protégé. Actor Clifton Webb, who outbid other entertainment stars in attendance such as comedian Harold Lloyd and singer John McCormack, paid sixty-five dollars for the racket.[35]

Tilden became something of a soft touch for organizations in need. His charity work became legendary, and his name and presence were often associated with fund-raising efforts for myriad nonprofits. At one major fund-raiser for the American Federation of Actors, Bill swatted autographed tennis balls to attendees, while Mayor Fiorello La Guardia directed the police and fire bands and Babe Ruth reminisced about his career. Interestingly, while the Babe reaffirmed, "As a ballplayer I'm finished," only the more perceptive in the audience probably recognized that Big Bill—two years older than Ruth—was still competing against the world's best.[36]

Though Tilden's pro tour "set new attendance records" at venues from coast to coast and inspired young champions like George Lott and Lester Stoefen—Wimbledon and American doubles titlists—to join the professional caravan, Bill's racket was not a magic wand.[37] Some of his entrepreneurial initiatives proved underwhelming and others "a flat failure." One example was his effort to incorporate women players in the tour.[38] Suzanne Lenglen had electrified crowds in the midtwenties. Tilden hoped to replicate that rare moment in time when men celebrated female athleticism. Tennis patrons, however, were unmoved by the prospect of watching Ethel Burkhardt Arnold and Jane Sharp. Even the presence of Bill and Bruce Barnes on court with the ladies did not help. "I cannot understand why," Tilden would write years later, "because both girls, especially Ethel, were grand players and charming to look at. Yet for some reason," Bill conceded, "the public stayed away in droves."[39]

But when Bill toured with top male players, enthusiastic crowds could be expected on a nightly basis. And Bill expected his players to perform at a high level, even though they may have gotten out of a car or off a train just an hour or two before setting foot on court. The physical demands of a cross-county barnstorming tour were great, even more so for Tilden, who was older, usually doing the driving, the event organizing, and all the publicity. His stamina amazed everyone. On one tour, for example, after Tilden defeated George Lott in straight sets and then played doubles at Madison Square Garden, the troupe was off to Philadelphia for a performance the following night. Less than twenty-four hours later and after playing 109 games in seven sets of singles and doubles, Tilden was back on court in Philadelphia before sixty-three hundred patrons at Convention Hall. There he would play another 100 games in eight sets from 9:30 p.m. to 12:50 a.m. After the last autograph was signed and a quick bite to eat, he was back in the car, driving the crew to the nation's capital and Catholic University, where they were scheduled to play later that night. Where and when he got the time to write his newspaper articles and read his detective novels remain a mystery. Years later when players reflected on the pro tour, their recollections of Big Bill's work ethic were unanimous; Tilden, they all agreed, was an indefatigable workhorse.

Ellsworth Vines, who was in his prime and half Bill's age, was constantly amazed by Tilden's deep reservoir of vim and vigor. "His stamina would kill a horse," he told Grantland Rice, the famous sportswriter. Vine's recounted for Rice the time he and Bill played an exhausting match in Buffalo, with one set alone going 17–15. Vines not only lost but was also physically drained after the match. "I was whipped," Vines recounted. "I stumbled to our hotel . . . flopped down on the bed and just lay there. For twenty minutes I couldn't move. In bursts Bill, looking like he just stepped out of the barber's chair," recalled Vines. "He's had his shower . . . is all decked out in that long polo coat with a bushel of racquets under his arm. He's pulling out for Cincinnati—right then at one a.m.–with an eight-hour drive staring him in the face. His only admonition was, 'Be there . . . on time, boy! We should do well in Cincinnati' . . . and he was gone."[40] Vines could only shake his head in astonishment.

The men's professional tour, however, was so bullish that alarms were constantly ringing in those once formidable bastions of amateurism. "There is much talk of the growth of professionalism and what its ultimate effect will be on the game as a whole," stated an *ALT* editorial. And one subscriber commented, "It does seem as if professionalism takes an ever firmer hold on the leading players . . . and the time is drawing near when the first ten will be no longer an even match for a like number of pros." The threat of professionalism was both intense and universal. "A considerable portion of the lawn tennis world appears to be attacked by the jitters," lamented S. Wallis Merrihew in an *ALT* editorial. "The spread of the professional movement . . . is the cause of widespread discussion and comment. One hears little else."[41]

Tilden's impact on the professional movement was not peculiar to America; it was just as profound in other parts of the world. As one European tennis observer commented, "Win or lose, Bill's magnetism is after all the great magnet which draws the crowds. They love his court manner, his frequent remarks, which few understand, and above all his crabbing at a bad decision." The writer went on to note, "Many eyes were more concerned with Bill's reactions and extrovertive [*sic*] comments than with anything which was going on the court."[42]

That unique personality and aura, as well as Tilden's court mastery, gave credibility to whatever he was associated with, and that was currently his campaign to transform professional tennis into a widely accepted sport. Talented young players, even those in Europe, recognized for the first time that their avocation—smacking fuzzy white balls with a racket—could become their profession. Their delight at the prospect of making money from what they loved doing, however, was giving a nervous condition to traditionalists. The comfortable old guard who had always feared commercialism and professionalism as if it were the plague remained intransigent on the subject.

Not all were in a panic overseas. Less alarmed observers—especially the players—saw the sport's expansion and evolution as a positive step. "In truth, tennis is going through a crisis," argued British player H. W. "Bunny" Austin. "But a crisis of growth." The sport's "immense increase"— both natural and at Tilden's urging—had the game being played "in the four corners of the earth." Tennis, according to Austin, "has ceased being a pastime of the unoccupied as it was thirty years ago."[43]

On the other end of the globe the Asian tennis establishment was considerably less threatened by the game's professionalization. And if it can be believed, Big Bill was even more revered on the far side of the Pacific. Japan, in particular, was a hotbed of Tildenmania. Bill had earned near godlike stature among sports-conscious Japanese not only for his impact on tennis, but also for his critical role in the 1923 Japanese earthquake incident. His stalwart stand against "Little Czar" Julian Myrick and the USLTA not only won the affection of Zenzo Shimidzu, who asked Bill to participate in the emergency fund-raiser, but also endeared him to an entire nation.

Bill's much-anticipated visit in October 1936 was greeted with tremendous joy and pride. He was met with huge crowds wherever he traveled. Some of the first to welcome him on the dock at Yokohama were Kumagae, Shimidzu, Harada, and other top Japanese players, past and present. Bill and Ellsworth Vines, who joined him on the Asian tour, were given a ticker-tape parade that rivaled what Lindbergh had received in Paris and New York after his solo flight across the Atlantic. The parade route along the Ginza was mobbed with adoring fans under colorful clouds of falling confetti. One would have thought Big Bill was a native-born national hero.

Like the French a decade earlier with Roland Garros, the Japanese had recently constructed a new tennis stadium in Tokyo of which they were most proud, but "that Big Bill should ever be seen on a local court was too much to hope for."[44] Record numbers turned out for the matches, among them members of Japanese royal families, including Prince Yasuhiko Asaka,

Prince Takahiko Asaka, and Princess Kiyoko Asaka. Like a head of state, Bill deserved respect, but for his personal accomplishments and principled stands he was showered with complete and warm adoration.

And with all the athletic, entrepreneurial, journalistic, and travel demands placed on him, Bill still found the time to indulge his Hollywood pursuits. In late 1935, for example, he signed a contract with Carl Laemmle, head of Universal Studios, "to play a featured role in a motion picture to be entitled, 'The Amateur Racquet.'" In a nod to Tilden's headline-grabbing capabilities, the announcement was placed just above a bold advertisement for Bette Davis's appearance in *Special Agent* in the *New York Times*.[45]

Given that there was probably no one in the world who had played more tennis than Bill during the first third of the twentieth century, it was no surprise that he had arm surgery in 1936. His thin but potent right arm—an appendage that struck fear in the hearts of the world's top players for a decade and a half—had surely endured its share of physical abuse. The demanding pro tour only exacerbated the situation. Travel schedules were unforgiving: one of his 1935 tours covered eighty cities in one hundred days, a gruesome schedule that gave a player's arms and legs little time to recover. After going under the surgeon's knife, Bill's arm was much improved. For the first time in two years, he told the press, he actually felt like playing tennis. "I am playing a good deal better than I did last year," Bill told reporters. "I couldn't hit a balloon then, but since I had my arm fixed up my game has improved noticeably."[46] He was now looking forward to a new American tour and one in Europe to follow.

As he prepared for his seventh year as a touring pro, Bill was upbeat and said he had no regrets regarding his decision to become a professional. "I wish I had turned pro long before I did," Bill told newsmen as he introduced members of his latest traveling squad. As usual there would be a new member for the 1937 tour, but a lesser-known one. Hyotaro Satoh was a thirty-year-old Tokyo journalist who had dreams of duplicating Bill's ability to both play tennis and write books and newspaper copy. "We've always taken only four players before. The extra one's in case I drop dead along the way," Bill joked. Also in the traveling party were a manager, a ball boy, a thousand pounds of canvas court, a few net posts, and dozens of detective novels. Over the years Bill had become addicted to police procedurals and detective yarns. "I read literally hundreds of them every tour," Bill explained. "They're usually scattered all over the room." When he had time to read them remained a mystery.

As for his thoughts on the prospects of open tennis, Bill was hopeful. "They'll have to do something," said Bill assuredly. "Von Cramm, Budge, and Borotra are the only amateurs in the world today with any real color." As far as playing ability, Bill thought von Cramm was "the world's best amateur," and Budge was "not far behind."[47]

On January 6, 1937, the latest big-name amateur to turn pro took the court at Madison Square Garden against Ellsworth Vines. Fred Perry, an Englishman with extraordinary speed and maneuverability, was a three-time winner at both Wimbledon and Forest Hills and the undisputed king of tennis during the midthirties. A capacity crowd of eighteen thousand—the largest turnout so far for a professional match—greeted Perry's long-rumored transition to the pro game. Interestingly, though Perry and Vines were in their prime and possessed no shortage of ability or fan appeal, it was Tilden, now forty-four years old, who received the biggest applause of the night when he walked on court to play doubles as part of the night's undercard. "The tremendous ovation received by Tilden when he came out for doubles," a *Times* article stated, "testified to the continuing popularity of the remarkable veteran, and the tennis he put forth brought the house down."[48] The crowd's overwhelming show of appreciation for the aging court warrior spurred promoters to quickly schedule a Perry-Tilden match the following month at the Garden.

More than sixteen thousand excited spectators turned out for a match that might have been billed as a generational battle between the best present-day racket warrior against an aging relic of yesteryear. Perry would win that match, but the old campaigner would take two of the following five played in other cities. Although the years and matches that ran into the thousands were finally catching up with him, Tilden could take solace—albeit with a hefty dose of irony—that he had almost single-handedly established professional tennis as a popular, thriving commercial entity. "By that time," he would write with some degree of pride in his autobiography, "the goal of every amateur was to reach a point where he could turn professional and reap the golden harvest."[49]

Later that year Tilden watched with great interest as the United States took on Germany in the semifinal round of the Davis Cup. The winner would earn the right to play in the challenge round against the defending nation, Great Britain. Because Fred Perry had turned pro, it was generally believed that the winner of the U.S.-Germany match would go on to claim the Davis Cup. On this occasion, however, Bill would not be cloaked in the red, white, and blue of Old Glory, for he was a key adviser and occasional coach to the German team. Though Bill's position with the German Davis Cup squad was never officially stated, publicized, or even rumored at the time, there is little doubt he had become close to several of the players, especially Gottfried von Cramm.

From his first trip to the country in the twenties, Bill was impressed with the reception he was given by the German people and their love of tennis. Though he thought their style of play was "rather old-fashioned owing to the long period following the war when Germany was barred from competition with the other nations," he thought that Otto Froitzheim and Hans Moldenhauer were fine players and expected even better ones to emerge as Germany was gradually welcomed back into the family of nations.[50] That expectation was firmly realized with the arrival of von Cramm. Though Perry and Budge dominated amateur tennis in the mid- and late thirties, the regal blond-haired, green-eyed German baron, according to Tilden, was second to none when it came to "beauty of stroke and for grace and appearance on the court." In addition to the German's forehand drive, backhand, serve, and overhead all being of exceptional quality, his physical fitness and ability to pressure opponents well into fifth-set matches were equally noteworthy. Moreover, von Cramm was a charming and cultured man who fluently spoke three languages and developed many and varied interests. Tilden would eventually "place von Cramm among the world's all-time greatest, an equal of the Immortals of Tennis.[51]

For all his personal attributes and his many impressive court triumphs, including two French titles and a three-time Wimbledon finalist, Germany's top player was in an increasingly precarious position. In addition to being a homosexual in a society that was becoming rapidly and pathologically intolerant, von Cramm was not a Nazi and, according to Bill, had a "deep hatred of all that Hitler's gang of cutthroats stood for." Tilden had played in Germany every year from 1927 to 1938 and "watched the insidious evil of Nazism change a friendly people into a mob of suspicious, war-drunk animals." As Hitler's power and brutality increased, Tilden witnessed his friend's growing apprehension. When Bill voiced his concern and quizzed von Cramm on his plans, the German replied, "You don't understand, Bill. I'm playing for my life." It was von Cramm's belief that as long as he won and remained the nation's number-one player, Hitler would not touch him. But he had to win.

There was more to Tilden's support of the German team than just his friendship with von Cramm, however. Though his much-ballyhooed sense of patriotism as Hillway and others cite is generally correct, Bill was highly offended by the USLTA's rejection of his repeated offers to coach or work out with the American team. As far back as June 1933 Bill had offered his services to the American Davis Cup squad. He volunteered to coach or train the team in its match against France, but his proposal was met with a diplomatic "Thanks, but no thanks."

Tilden was a living legend and prolific tennis author, universally recognized as the greatest player to have played the game, and any nation would have jumped at the chance to have him coach or provide guidance and tactical tips to its players. The Davis Cup Committee's rejection must have stung. Taken aback, Tilden admitted he was "surprised" at the decision and told reporters that "the offer was made in good faith and the belief that my long experience against the French on their home grounds might be helpful to an American team that is so anxious to win back the cup."[52] Obviously, some of the old guard at the USLTA still had it in for Bill.

Two years later that head-scratching scenario would reprise itself, as Bill, along with Ellsworth Vines this time, volunteered to work out with the American Davis Cup team before their match with Germany. As the *New York Times* would describe the embarrassing episode at a London hotel, "Big Bill Tilden and Ellsworth Vines sat around their hotel lobby today, as expectant as ambulance drivers awaiting a call to action, but the summons never came. America's two foremost professionals had been assured indirectly that their services were desired to help whip the United States Davis

Cup team in trim for the interzone matches with Germany at Wimbledon this week-end." As Joseph Wear, the team captain, lamely explained to the press, "I decided there would be nothing gained by such practice. Vines and Tilden have entirely different styles from our opponents. Playing against them might only unsettle our players."

Reporters found the statement odd, and tennis fans around the world must have been stupefied by the mind-boggling slight. Vines at the time was still thought by many to be the world's best player, and Tilden was known for his unique ability to play any style at any time. Even accomplished players would have learned much from the two champions. After this obvious slap across the face, Bill maintained his composure and told the press, "I'm sorry we can't help, because I believe the more work they get the better chance our boys will have against Germany. They have a tough match on their hands."[53] For the man who carried American Davis Cup hopes on his back for a decade and attained an incomparable 25–5 singles record in Davis Cup play—as well as his seven National Championships and three Wimbledon titles—it was quite a blow. To add insult to injury, the American Davis Cup team had periodically retained the services of Hans Nusslein, a German pro, to serve as coach.

The actual Davis Cup contest between the United States and Germany was a highly competitive one and not decided until the last few games of the fifth set of the final match between Don Budge and von Cramm on July 20, 1937. Though the German had a two-set lead and appeared on his way to a great victory, Budge managed to come back and play some stellar tennis. From 1–4 down, he would win that final set 8–6 and leave many thinking they had seen one of the greatest, if not the greatest, tennis matches of all time.[54]

As the nation gradually eased out of the Great Depression in the late thirties, Tilden's personal finances remained complicated. Though the years and the seemingly endless string of tennis matches had begun to take their toll, Bill kept busy. He was still campaigning on the pro tour, writing articles, and endorsing products. Money was coming in, but his lifestyle was robust and his ability to spend money equally hardy. He seemed unable to maintain a realistic budget. Periodically unpaid bills would come back to haunt him—and in a public manner, no less—as one did with his favorite Manhattan hotel. In November 1938 Bill was slapped with a judgment by a New York City court for unpaid rent. He owed the Algonquin Hotel "$2,329 on a claim of unpaid rent." The famous Midtown hostelry on West Forty-Fourth Street was Tilden's favorite when in the New York area. As someone who admitted to a "strong compulsion to write" and "toward personalities of the literary world," the Algonquin provided an intellectual cocoon for New York–area sleepovers.[55] But even when playing on the West Coast or in Europe or Asia, he would remain on the books as an official guest at the hotel. According to Algonquin management, Bill "maintained a suite at the hotel for more than fifteen years at the current rate of $120 a month."[56] The practice was unrealistic and unmaintainable. Official papers would be served on him while he was at the Hotel Savoy, his favorite hotel in London.

While in Europe—and possibly on the run from his American creditors—Bill was said "to have swapped matinee idol ambitions for playwriting ones" and to be working vigorously "to peddle a couple of plays" to London theater producers. Written in collaboration with Stephen Vernon, a London playwright, *Knave's Trick* and *Net Profits* met with little excitement by West End stage impresarios, but the fact that a world-famous athlete was even proffering such literary and dramatic fare was newsworthy. Newspaper commentators at the time were reluctant to predict "what effect his latest literary efforts will have on the future seeding of Shakespeare, Ibsen, and Shaw," but they took note that Big Bill was not only adept with a racket, but also "a handy man with a dangling participle since way back."[57]

Vinnie Richards, just back from Europe, had planned a pro tour on the Continent with Bill before a Copenhagen taxicab door accidentally slammed shut, taking off part of Vinnie's finger. He informed the press Bill was doing quite well in London, but might never return. "I hate to say this," Vinnie admitted, "but I'm afraid Big Bill never is coming home. . . . I'm afraid he's going to stay. What's wrong? Oh, I guess Bill has some financial troubles over here. It's too bad we can't get him back. To almost everybody Tilden means tennis and tennis means Tilden."

Vinnie insisted, however, that Bill's friends need not worry for his safety. He was doing quite well. "Bill always lived in Babylonian splendor," said Richards. "He does even now. He has a very large and very swanky apartment in the ritzy Mayfair section of London, a flock of servants and the smartest-looking chauffeur in town."[58]

Bill would eventually return from Europe in early 1940 and almost immediately decide to resettle on the West Coast. The Southern California clime was far more agreeable for any serious tennis player, and Los Angeles was home to the Hollywood film colony, another of Bill's passions. Moreover, he felt it long overdue he quit Philadelphia. The city's stuffy, elitist atmosphere that he had grown up in had always annoyed him. Bill was far more inclusive, democratic, and welcoming in his social tastes, and the snobbish exclusivity of Philadelphia high society and area cricket clubs caused him much discomfort. Southern California, however, was far less concerned with stature and family lineage. It was also a hotbed of rapidly improving tennis talent and year-round outdoor play.

Southern California was an incubator of top court talent; it was definitely where the action was. Informal high-quality matches could arise at a moment's notice. Art Anderson, just a neophyte at the time, remembered Perry Jones asking Bill if he would like to test a rapidly emerging Jack Kramer in the twenty-two-year-old's preparation for the nationals at Forest Hills. Bill agreed, and a match was scheduled for the courts at the Château Élysée Hotel. Word spread rapidly of the May–December scrap, and more than two hundred spectators quickly jostled for seats. Confident he could outfox the young net rusher, Tilden made numerous wagers he would come out on top. In fact, Kramer would get quite a lesson that day. He lost 6–4, 6–3 to a man who was nearly three decades older than he was. Art was duly impressed with his teacher's total mastery of the game. Tilden repeatedly thwarted Kramer's serve-and-volley tactics, and Art was left wondering how good his coach must have been in his prime, twenty years earlier.

In addition to the area's reputation for high-quality tennis play, there was also the financial appeal. As he began to cut back on his pro-tour activities, he needed another source of income. Teaching tennis was the answer, and there were numerous Hollywood film stars who were willing to pay for lessons from a Wimbledon and Davis Cup champion, especially one who shared their theatrical interests. For the average American movie-theater patron, the appearance of Errol Flynn, Katharine Hepburn, Mickey Rooney, or Greta Garbo would surely cause one's heart to flutter. But the excitement of being in close proximity to an international celebrity is also the way film stars reacted to Tilden. A lesson or friendly match with him was something to boast about.

It became increasingly common to find Tilden on the private courts of Charlie Chaplin, Clifton Webb, or Joseph Cotten giving tennis lessons when not on tour. As word circulated from one movie star to another that they could get a lesson from Tilden or play a friendly game with him, his schedule quickly filled. "I had the pleasure of working five days a week with three of Hollywood's most celebrated glamour girls," Tilden crowed in his autobiography. He was referring to Tallulah Bankhead, Katharine Hepburn, and Greta Garbo. "Not in my wildest dreams had I ever anticipated facing such a battery of stars, nor had I ever expected that they could be such fun."

Bill, however, may have feigned his starstruck reaction; he wasn't exactly a Midwest farm boy blinded by the glow of the celebrity class. He had grown up with presidents visiting his Germantown home, and major celebrities of the entertainment world were common at the Tilden family's summer retreat at the Onteora Club in the Catskill Mountains. Moreover, through-out the early 1920s he had garnered audiences, if not relationships, with King George V and Queen Mary of Great Britain and played tennis with the Duke of York (later King George VI) and King Gustav of Sweden, whom he often referred to as "probably the number one tennis fan of the world."[59] For European royalty, Tilden was the celebrity.

As to his Hollywood friends, he had met Tallulah Bankhead in England years earlier, and she was to become one of his most loyal supporters. Kate Hepburn was a new acquaintance he had met through actor Clifton Webb. Her athletic talent immediately caught his eye, and he soon came to believe "she could also have attained fame" on the court as she did on the screen. She loved the game, played often, and possessed a forehand that many female champions would have envied. Garbo, according to Bill, was more "awkward and unorthodox" on court, but enjoyed the sport and the frivolity of being with a few close friends and not having to be followed by hoards of fans and newspaper cameramen. Tilden found her fearful of large crowds and suffering from "a kind of inferiority complex," but quite pleasant to spend time with when around friends she trusted.[60]

During the early 1940s Bill spent numerous mornings either giving les-sons or playing friendly doubles matches with famous Hollywood stars. A mixed-doubles quartet of Tilden, Kate Hepburn, Greta Garbo, and Charlie

Chaplin was not unusual. "This match played for our own amusement," Tilden mused of the collective star power assembled on the court, "could have drawn a hundred thousand dollar gate."

There were many other film stars who did their best to angle some playing time with the great court monarch. Joseph Cotten often practiced with Bill and let him use his court for private teaching sessions. Child stars Mickey Rooney and Jackie Cooper often hit with Bill, Rooney being particularly competitive on court. Another athletically gifted Hollywood star who became good friends with Bill was Errol Flynn. Not surprisingly, the athletic Flynn, who was known for his onscreen swordplay, was one of the Hollywood film colony's better tennis players. Regardless of the stars' unorthodox racket technique, limited court coverage, or tactical shortcomings, Bill enjoyed playing with the likes of Clark Gable, Carole Lombard, Robert Montgomery, Paulette Goddard, Judy Garland, Robert Taylor, Barbara Stanwyck, Gary Cooper, Humphrey Bogart, Lauren Bacall, and a host of other top entertainers after his move to the West Coast.

But Bill did not restrict himself to teaching Hollywood's rarefied elite. He had many tennis clients who were not famous, adults who just loved the game and simply desired to improve their footwork, ground strokes, or serve, as well as children whose parents wanted them to take up the sport. Eleven-year-old Art Anderson was one of them. His mother, Marrion, had learned from another mother at her son's elementary school that the woman's daughter was taking lessons at the Château Élysée Hotel. A noted professional was teaching. Marrion was interested. When she learned the pro was Bill Tilden, she was sold.

Bill was the teaching pro at the Ambassador and Château Élysée Hotels in the early years of the war. The conflict in Europe had abruptly ended any form of pro tour on the Continent and severely limited both pro and amateur play in America. Teaching the game Stateside, therefore, became an increasingly larger part of Bill's activities and income. For a package of ten one-hour lessons, according to Rich Hillway, Bill charged one hundred dollars.[61] The hotels also supplied Tilden free room and board for his services. Bill's students were both hotel guests and Los Angeles–area residents like young Art Anderson.

The boy had never played tennis before, but he was a good athlete and picked up the game quickly. Under Bill's tutelage Art progressed rapidly and won ten tournaments, including the thirteen-and-under tennis championship of Southern California. As Hillway points out, Bill had ceaselessly worked over the years to discover and then develop a young champion who would carry on in his footsteps. He sought a lad who would value the game as he did and play it the way Bill thought it should be played. Granted, it was an unlikely scenario and monumental challenge, but Bill thought it possible and spent many a year teaching the nuances of the game to young boys around the country. Carl Fischer, Vinnie Richards, Arnold Jones, Sandy Wiener, and Junior Coen were just a few of the tennis prodigies he developed, with the hope, if not expectation, that one of them would become the next great American champion. All of them became excellent players— Fischer winning an intercollegiate championship, Richards an Olympic gold medal, Wiener several doubles championships—but Bill wanted more. A national, Wimbledon, and Davis Cup singles champion was his goal.

Over the months and years Bill would become increasingly close to Art and Marrion Anderson, who was divorced and living with her elderly mother. Eventually, they became something like a family, and he moved in with them when Art went into the army. But during those early years and throughout the war, Bill was not exclusively focused on teaching. Coordinating and participating in charity events related to the war effort would become central themes of Bill's activities throughout the conflict. Well before America even entered the war, Bill was helping to raise money for worthwhile causes related to the growing international conflict. In March 1940, for example, Bill pulled together a stellar cast consisting of Budge, Perry, Vines, and Richards to perform on court for the Finnish Relief Fund. The five thousand spectators who turned out for the event at the Seventy-First Regiment Armory in New York City raised more than eight thousand dollars for the beleaguered Finns.[62]

Such fund-raising initiatives would only increase in number and frequency with America's entry into the widening conflict that was to become World War II. Uniquely experienced with over-the-road travel and nightly performances, Bill would now periodically continue the practice but no longer was it geared for the players' financial benefit. Now he was traveling and staging exhibitions for the benefit of the Red Cross, selling war bonds, and uplifting the spirits of wounded soldiers. "I saw at first hand how valuable the game's contribution could be," Bill would write of his performances at army, navy, and marine bases and military hospitals around the country. Bill encouraged both pros and amateurs to join him in these therapeutic and entertainment sojourns, though he would once again be stymied by the USLTA's "official displeasure" with amateurs participating in unsanctioned events. As he would proudly write of the players response, "To their everlasting credit, I found most amateurs more than willing to play despite the risk."

Committed to putting on quality performances for recovering soldiers and those contributing to War Bond and Red Cross fund-raisers, Tilden "dared" the USLTA to "declare two of the amateur players who competed with him as professionals." As he prepared his troupe for performances at Merion Cricket Club that would raise more than three million dollars to benefit Valley Forge General Hospital and the Naval Hospital of Philadelphia, he was spoiling for a fight with an insufferable tennis bureaucracy that seemed constitutionally opposed to rationality and charitable events. "We are battling for the right now to put on amateur-pro matches," Bill told the press, "and there is no excuse for not allowing such matches to aid the war."[63]

Not all of his troupe's efforts paid off so handsomely. At many events such as the Red Cross fund-raiser held at the West Side Tennis Club in June 1945, Bill pulled together top players like Vinnie Richards, Frank Shields, Alice Marble, Manuel Alonso, Welby Van Horn, and Gardnar Mulloy, only to be disappointed at the modest turnout. The Red Cross much appreciated the sixty-five hundred dollars raised, but Bill thought there was so much more potential if only the USLTA would have relaxed their prohibition against pro-amateur play. The association's position, however, was adamant. "The professionals haven't proved they are able to control their own players," argued Holcombe Ward, USLTA president, "and it is possible abuses might creep in, which would be detrimental to the amateur game."[64]

"The utter stupidity of the existing amateur rule of the USLTA as regards professionals and amateurs meeting for the war effort" was Bill's reply to such incomprehensible arguments. It was bad enough in Bill's mind that pros and amateurs were arbitrarily kept apart in times of peace, but when the nation and the free world were fighting for their survival, one would

have thought "the stupid rule" would have been scrubbed in order to benefit worthwhile causes.[65] It should be noted that Bill, at the ripe old age of
fifty-two, walloped Dick Skeen 6–0, 6–0 at the event, a man half his age.[66]

Regardless of the constant bureaucratic frustrations, Tilden soldiered on,
organizing Red Cross drives and programs for military hospitals from coast
to coast. Such fund-raising and entertainment missions could last days or
weeks at a time, such as one travelogue that took him to the Amphibious
Training Base and Naval Hospital at Norfolk and then on to Camp Lee for
a U.S. Army exposition, back to Quantico for a Marine presentation, and
finally to Curtis Bay for a Coast Guard station show. On that one excursion
alone Bill estimated he "played thirteen matches in fifteen days at twelve
different installations to better than 20,000 men." As he would write of
trekking to military base after hospital after military base, "the only losses
were fifteen pounds from Vinnie Richards and my health."[67]

According to Bill's calculations, he performed for "well over 100,000
men" at two hundred bases during the war. He insisted players always try
to put forth a solid effort, but the primary goal was more often than not to
produce a few lighthearted moments. A good "laugh whenever possible"
gradually took precedence over quality of play. Many of the visits were at
military hospitals, where the wounded had little to smile about and laughter was rare. It was at these generally gloomy surgical and rehabilitative
installations that Tilden performed some of his most humorous skits.

One of the most famous was Bill and Walter Wesbrook, a close tennis
buddy, dressing up as a pair of old ladies from the Gay Nineties and taking the court with antiquated rackets in hand. Attired in long Victorian
dresses, bonnets covering their "Mary Pickford sausage curls," bright-red
lipstick, and peculiar mannerisms, "Miss Sophia Smearone" and "Miss
Wilhelmina Shovelshot" always put the audience in stitches. And like Bob
Hope's subsequent road shows at military bases, Bill always had several
pretty female tennis players along as part of the visiting troupe "to make
the scenery beautiful as well as play good tennis." Gussie Moran and Gloria
Butler, attractive young women and solid players, were the eye candy for
the recovering soldiers. Adorned in short, form-fitting athletic wear, Gussie
and Gloria always received whistles of approval when they walked on court.
Their humorous routine opposing the hilarious "Miss Sophia" and "Miss
Wilhelmina" was always a high point of the hospital visits.[68]

"Gloria and I wrapped up the exhibitions at whatever service base or hospital we visited," wrote Gussie Moran in a letter to Rich Hillway, regarding her many travels with Tilden to California military hospitals during the war. "Facing [the Victorian-attired Tilden and Wesbrook] across the net was always the program's finale, and the servicemen did indeed enjoy the comedy. Gloria and I were dressed in our regular tennis togs; usually colored shots with lace tops. Bill and Walter, however, were something else. They brought down the house every time."[69]

Each and every hospital performance caused Bill and his traveling companions to reflect on their good fortune and increase their admiration for the patriotic contributions of the maimed and wounded. That so many had personally sacrificed so much to protect the nation and fight tyranny was awe-inspiring. After one hospital visit, Bill was moved to write, "Some seven hundred patients were clustered around the lines, with fully half the crowd in wheel chairs or on crutches or in casts, casualties from the Pacific. Right beside the baseline sat a youngster in a wheel chair. He couldn't have been over nineteen. Both his legs gone, and shot all to hell, he was making a game fight under the wonderful care and treatment of our medical corps."

As Bill went on to describe the sobering scene, he was running hither and yon and generally being given a tough time by a much younger player. "Complaining bitterly of the way an old man was being treated, a patter audiences always enjoyed and exchanging wisecracks thick and fast with all the gang. This legless boy contributed a couple of cracks of his own, grinned a few times, even chuckled now and then. It wasn't long after that the kid was heard to say, 'Gosh, this is the first time I've laughed in six months!'" Tremendously moved by the encounter and the boy's comment, Bill would plaintively write, "I'd play a thousand matches for one remark like that."

Despite the lengthy travel, financial expense, and organizing difficulties associated with recurring hospital exhibitions across the country, Tilden let it be known, "I wouldn't have missed playing these service matches for anything. Those boys, most of whom knew little of tennis and cared less, turned out to be the greatest galleries in the world."[70]

Gardnar Mulloy, a top-ten player at the time who would go on to be a successful coach at the University of Miami, was often part of the Tilden hospital caravan. "I remember we'd drive to a military base or naval station and several thousand soldiers and patients would be outside waiting for us. You really wanted to put on a good show for them," recalled Mulloy. "I played him many times. I was twenty years younger than Tilden, but he could still give you a game. He played to win. We traveled all over and played before big crowds. He was up in years, but everyone wanted to see Tilden. Even the top Navy brass came out to meet him." One of Mulloy's strongest recollections is of Tilden's generosity with his collection of personal trophies. He not only auctioned them off to raise money for war bonds, but also "gave them up for scrap. They needed metal," said Mulloy, "silver, lead, everything, and Bill gave many of his trophies to the government. He turned some of his trophies over to the military to melt down to use in the war effort. I never saw anybody else do that," said Mulloy. "He was quite a guy."[71]

And though he was getting along in years—he was now entering his midfifties—Bill was still pushing himself and participating in professional tennis events. More than just a big name from the "golden age of sports," Bill could still play, as many young pros painfully discovered. In fact, Bill and Vinnie Richards won the national professional doubles championship in 1945, a feat they had first accomplished as amateurs in 1918, twenty-seven years earlier.

By the autumn of 1945 the war was over, and Bill, like the nation, was looking forward to a return to normalcy. Rebuilding the professional tennis circuit and reestablishing its fan base, working toward the acceptance of open tennis tournaments in America and throughout the world, teaching his many students—both Hollywood celebrities and average clients—and just possibly a slightly less frenetic schedule were all part of his wish list.

Very quickly, however, 1946 would augur something that not only was very different but would present a series of personal challenges as imposing as anything Big Bill ever had to face. More than overcoming just a difficult match, a spat with USLTA authorities, or an unfavorable Broadway review, Tilden would now be confronted with a devastating charge that would leave him fighting for both his freedom and his reputation.

14

"Contributing to the Delinquency of a Minor"

The success of the comeback I hope to make
will depend on the public and the newspapers.
I know I made a mistake and I've paid for it. I
hope you fellows will treat me kindly.

—WILLIAM T. TILDEN 2ND

With Germany's surrender in April 1945 and the war in Europe finally at
end, Tilden was like millions of war-weary citizens on the home front
delighted the brutal conflict across the Atlantic was finally over. Everyone
was looking forward to a return of normalcy. But though news of Hitler's
death and the Allied victory had sparked joyous celebrations, America
was still at war in the Pacific. Lives continued to be lost, and wounded
soldiers were returning home for repairs. Less than a month later Bill
announced another of his many tours of military bases and hospitals.
This one would hit thirty-five service centers, stretching up and down
the East Coast from Jacksonville, Florida, to Ferndale, New York, and run
through the summer until its completion in mid-September.[1] Bill and the
other members of his troupe hoped it would be the last one they would
have to undertake.

Still hot under the collar concerning the USLTA's intransigence on pro-
amateur play—especially regarding charity events—Bill blasted the organization at various stops on his summer tour. Newspapers were increasingly
taking Bill's side in the never-ending skirmish. "War Fund exhibitions,"
commented one newspaper columnist, seemed a reasonable venue for
professional-versus-amateur play and often cited "the ancient mariner of
the tennis seas" for his unrelenting persistence on the issue. As one article
went on to argue, "Personally, we think he has a point this time as, the
world being on fire as it is, it seems rather silly to insist that amateurs and
professionals must not rub shoulders, even for charity."[2]

In addition to the fall of the Third Reich, there was other news from Europe. Bill's cousin Selena Greenwood Hey, whom he called "Twin" and lived with for nearly three decades in the Germantown section of Philadelphia before he relocated to California and she to Scarborough, England, had died and declared Bill the "principal beneficiary [of her] $23,000 estate."[3] The inheritance would come in handy. His many and lengthy military base tours brought in little money, and his normal tennis-related sources of income were much reduced during the war. His spending capacity, however, remained as vigorous as ever. Other than Bill, for example, rarely did a member of Tilden's traveling troupe pick up the tab for a meal or trip. If a sponsor of an event such as Spalding or Gimbel's did not pay the freight, Bill took the responsibility for such necessities and was apparently happy to do so.

The year 1946 would begin with a bang. In truth, it was the sound of an automobile going off the road and crashing into a ditch on a deserted strip of desert near Wenden, Arizona. Traveling back to Palm Springs with a friend, Jack Jossi, from a tennis exhibition in Phoenix in late March, Bill was alarmed to discover the steering wheel of his Buick coming off the steering column. Though he was known for driving fast—occasionally reaching speeds in excess of one hundred miles per hour—on this particular excursion he was well within the legal limits when the steering column broke apart. Able to maintain his composure as they headed toward a concrete culvert, a fifteen-foot drop, and "certain death" in Bill's mind, he struggled to keep the car on the road, but it eventually swerved off the roadway and into a desert gully. The vehicle rolled over, finally resting on the roof, with Tilden and Jossi "spilled all over the car." Though they were pretty well shaken up and taken back to a Palm Springs hospital, neither had broken any bones or sustained serious injury. Bill "strained his shoulder, wrenched his neck and back, and [had] an assortment of cuts and bruises," which kept him off the court and away from serious competition for a couple of months. Only after an additional four months would he be pain free.[4] One could argue the highway wreck was an ominous omen of what would befall Tilden later that year.

On a more positive note the first year after the war would prove a significant one for professional tennis in America. As Bill would declare a short while later, "The entire pro-amateur scene changed in 1946 with the formation of the Professional Players Association. With one stroke this group greatly improved the professional's position by organizing a tournament rivaling the amateur one."[5]

Tilden's jump to the professional ranks fifteen years earlier had laid a solid foundation for the establishment of the professional game, but only the sport's biggest names, such as Vines, Perry, Budge, and Cochet, made any real money. "Young netmen coming up," as Bill would write, "would more or less openly hope they could acquire enough reputation to turn pro and tour with the pro champion." What the pro players lacked was a long tournament season like the amateur game. Without one, players lacking celebrity credentials had little chance of making serious money unless they were part of a tour group with headliners like Budge and Tilden.

One of the first steps in rectifying that situation was the formation of the Professional Players Association, headed by Budge as president and Tilden as tournament manager. A second step followed shortly after in May 1946, when the pro association signed a five-year agreement with the West Side Tennis Club to hold the association's annual national tournament at the Forest Hills stadium. "The West Side Club," said a club official, "is setting out to put pro tennis on the map."[6]

The third impactful development was the formation of an official tennis season that included "thirty-four tournaments in which the money would be divided on performance, not reputation." That last point, as Bill would point out, was like a lighthouse beacon to a distressed vessel at sea. "Now," Bill would claim, "the lure of big money to any man good enough to win found many of the leading amateurs gazing speculatively in the direction of pro competition."[7] Young players increasingly recognized that if they were good enough, they could make quite a handsome living playing their favorite sport.

Records would soon show a prize-money payout of seventy-five thousand dollars for 1946. Bill expected the 1947–48 season to exceed one hundred thousand dollars and that sum doubled by the end of the decade. Not a bad start for a neophyte sports organization and one that had serious organizational opposition. "The world has changed in everything else," wrote an ecstatic Tilden. "Why not in amateur sports?" It was a far cry from the days when top players like Tilden, Bill Johnston, and Dick Williams were paid in ornate silver plates, elaborate trophies, and other forms of decorative hardware. After years of stunted growth—if not outright stagnation—professional tennis was beginning to tender the commercial opportunities in baseball, boxing, and golf.

When the 1946 Professional Championship tournament began at Forest Hills just a few days after the July 4 holiday, it should have been no surprise to anyone that Big Bill was not only entered but also one of the headliners. Described in news articles as "one of the real miracle men of sport at the age of 53," it was also repeatedly mentioned that Bill was still playing competitive tennis a quarter century after he had first won the national amateur crown at the same location.[8]

Bill did not let his many fans down. In his first match against a much younger opponent, Bill was forced to chase down an assortment of deep drives and drop shots, giving many pause; they feared the old man would be run into the ground. "The former world champion resolved these doubts," wrote Allison Danzig of the *Times*, "by making the chalk fly with his service and pounding his forehand into the corners to open the court for his volley."[9] Tilden, displaying extraordinary shot making and limitless reserve, won the match 7–5, 6–2, 6–8, 6–4. Incredulous spectators could only shake their heads in wonderment.

Two days later Danzig would be even more complimentary in describing Tilden's play against Wayne Sabin, an accomplished player in his prime and one of the contestants thought capable of giving the likes of Budge, Perry, and Riggs some serious competition for the pro title. As Danzig recounted the day's highlights, "William Tilden gave one of the classic performances of his unparalleled career yesterday. . . . For two sets against Wayne Sabin, Tilden turned back the clock and hit backhands such as had not sprung from his racquet in years. The 53-year old master exploded his cannonball service, responded under pressure with blazing forehands and used up energy with the prodigality of a colt in covering the court."[10]

Danzig continued to praise the old court warrior: "No one dreamed that Tilden could bring back to life the shots he had made when he first won the amateur crown in 1920. Was it a dream, or was he really stroking his backhand as in the days when it was as wrathful as Don Budge's today, instead of taking the defensive undercut pokes at the ball characteristic of his play in recent years?" In order to assure his readers he was not imagining things, Danzig informed them, "It was not the invincible Tilden of 1920 to 1926, but it was a Tilden nevertheless, every inch the miracle man he had been labeled, and the spectators thrilled to the show and cheered and shrieked in enjoyment."

Regrettably, after winning the first two hard-fought sets, Bill's fabulous half-century-old legs began to show their age, and Sabin's youth became the decisive factor. The younger player would go on to win, 4–6, 7–9, 6–1, 6–1, 6–0. As the match went on, lamented Danzig, "Tilden no longer had the legs or power to make the winners of the first two sets . . . but those first two sets had been his glory and a lasting memory for those privileged to see them."[11] As most serious connoisseurs of the sport—and certainly everyone in the stadium now had to concede—over a set or two Big Bill could still outplay anyone in the world.

Over the next several months Tilden continued to encourage the purchase of war bonds, raise money for the Red Cross, and entertain wounded soldiers recovering at military hospitals around the country. In between tours Bill gave tennis lessons to a cross-section of Los Angeles residents, ranging from widely known Hollywood luminaries to average citizens interested in the sport. There were also more serious students of the game—many of them established or soon-to-be-established players like Alice Marble, Noel Brown, Gloria Butler, and Gussie Moran—coming to Tilden for advice and further refinement on their strokes. Young Art Anderson was one of the latter. Though he would initially start as a complete novice with group lessons, Art soon began taking private lessons with Bill. His tennis progression was plainly evident, as was his relationship with Bill. Forever searching for his heir, a young player who was a strategic thinker, excelled at all the strokes, and mastered the nuances of tactical play, Bill increasingly thought Art Anderson just might be the next great American star.

Art and his mother were delighted by Bill's interest, his investment of time, and certainly the much-reduced instructional fees he charged them. The trio spent considerable time together, eating out at restaurants, taking many meals at the Anderson home, and traveling to Art's tournaments together. Though he could be a tough taskmaster and demanded Art take the game and his lessons seriously, Bill could also be a gentle father figure for a boy whose parents had divorced while he was still quite young. If Art had any grievance, it was Bill's penchant for picking up and taking off on another pro tour or fund-raising trip for the Red Cross or USO. Art lamented how much better he would have been if his tennis education had not been interrupted so often due to his famous mentor's barnstorming around the country.

From the very first time he stepped on court with Big Bill, Art was amazed at Tilden's "pinpoint accuracy." Tilden could "hit the ball to anywhere from anywhere. He could hit any shot any time anywhere" he wanted, Anderson told Rich Hillway in a series of interviews before he died. Anderson attributed this to not only Tilden's athleticism, but also his "double-jointed wrist that allowed him to do things that other players couldn't."

After many of their practice sessions, they would often go out to eat. "Bill loved food," said Anderson. He ate big meals and loved expensive steaks—always medium rare—and sent them back to the kitchen if they were too well done. "He liked his steak red in the middle," said Anderson, "and that was the way he ordered it." Eaton's Restaurant on Ventura, the Brown Derby, and Armstrong and Schroeder in Beverly Hills were just a few of restaurants Art became accustomed to when training with Tilden. "After a full day of teaching and playing anywhere between five and ten sets of singles," recalled Anderson, "Bill loved to go out to dinner at a fine restaurant. He enjoyed a good meal. He would always be well dressed, usually in a tie and jacket. Tall, distinguished, very recognizable," said Anderson. "Everyone noticed him."

During the war years Art gradually grew accustomed to his mentor's frenetic lifestyle, intense training sessions when Bill was home, and then a more relaxed pace during his periodic absences. There would be one interruption, however, an extended one at the end of 1946 and through most of 1947 that was much different from the others. This one, unfortunately, would come with the force of a tsunami and the drama of a good crime novel. His absence and the reason behind it would prove not only a sobering shock to Art and Marrion Anderson, but also a devastating blow to Bill, one from which he would never quite recover.

In late November, just two days before Thanksgiving, Bill would take a car ride that was fraught with as much danger as the one earlier in the year that resulted in a frightening roadside crash and a trip to a hospital emergency ward. When Bill's big Packard Clipper was pulled over on Sunset Boulevard by Beverly Hills police officers, a fourteen-year-old boy was found behind the wheel of the auto, with Bill in the passenger seat, his one arm suggestively around the boy's shoulders and the other on the boy's lap. When they asked the boy to get out of the car, they noticed four of the buttons on his fly were undone. Arrested and charged with "contributing to the delinquency of a minor," Bill retained the services of attorney Richard Maddox, who immediately appealed for and was granted the defendant's liberty after paying a bond of five hundred dollars.

There is much speculation on Tilden's choice of lawyers and legal strategy—a number arguing another attorney and a more aggressive defense would have resulted in a different outcome—but after two continuances juvenile-court judge A. A. Scott had no intention of treating the celebrity athlete with kid gloves.

On January 17, 1947, appearing hardly the international champion that he was universally acknowledged to be, and less than a month before his fifty-fourth birthday, Bill "shuffled up to the bench . . . shoulders slumped . . . tears in his eyes," where Scott let him have it. "You have been the hero of youngsters all over the world," chided Scott. "Many adults have admired you for your sportsmanship. It is a great shock that you are involved in an offense like this."

Looking haggard, his eyes vacant, Bill mumbled that it had all been a "terrible lesson—one which I will never forget." Asked about his life, Bill said he had never run afoul of the law and earned about seventy-five hundred dollars a year teaching tennis—not a bad sum by 1945 standards and during the last year of the war. He made some remark that his trouble started "when I was very young and stupid many years ago."[12] Bill would go on to admit his "regret" for the entire episode.

Judge Scott, a no-nonsense jurist who was known for his antipathy to Hollywood excess and what he considered egregiously bad behavior by members of the movie colony, was unmoved. "It has been a great shock to sports fans to read about your troubles," the judge replied. "I am going to make this an object lesson." Scott then "imposed a sentence of one year, but suspended it and put Tilden on probation for five years, the first nine months in jail." He further stipulated that on release, Tilden should obtain psychiatric treatment and not associate with juveniles except in the presence of responsible adults.[13] "Let this serve as an object lesson to parents," the judge concluded. "Too much of this is going on."

Sitting "glumly" throughout the embarrassing ordeal, Tilden had "conceded his guilt and hoped for clemency." But the judge stunned him with the sentence. Scott even turned down his lawyer's request for a stay of execution in order that the defendant could get his affairs in order. His head down, his world crashing around him, the greatest tennis player in the history of the game was taken away by sheriff's deputies. "There won't be any tennis courts," a deputy was heard to remark concerning where Bill was likely to do his time. The county sheriff had already determined his famous—now infamous—prisoner would be "sent to a road farm where he will labor 40 hours a week."[14]

With the publication of newspaper articles and photos—many showing court officers escorting the prisoner and Bill in consultation with his attorney—the once revered Tilden brand suffered an ignominious fall. Long considered one of the iconic figures of sport, Bill was now a common criminal, guilty of one of the most reviled crimes. For many Tilden would become a tragic, shunned figure. Even members of the renowned Germantown Cricket Club, a lawn tennis cathedral celebrated for some of Bill's greatest athletic triumphs, decided to remove photographs and trophies belonging to him from the institution's walls and display cases. Dunlop severed their relationship with Tilden. No longer would they manufacture a "Tilden"-model racket for the market or supply their famous client with free tennis gear. Few American athletic heroes had ever witnessed such a public and precipitous banishment.

Curiously, many newspaper sports sections and tennis magazines gave little or no coverage of the case. That may have been due to Tilden's no longer being a headliner or more likely the controversial nature of the charges. Long the custom of respectable newspapers and magazines to bury or hide stories involving sex crimes from their readership, it would still be some time before such stories would be given the ink they are today.

Even *American Lawn Tennis* attempted to bury the story. Normally, Big Bill was mentioned in every issue. It might be his appearance on a pro tour, a hospital charity performance, or one of his pithy articles. Now months went by without a mention. One exception was an article entitled "The King of Tennis" in the magazine's June 1947 issue by Alice Marble. A four-time American titleholder and Wimbledon champ, Alice was now a regular columnist for the magazine. Her article lamented the tragic circumstances that had befallen the game's greatest player and one of her childhood heroes.

In the article Marble recounted her nervousness when first meeting Bill on an evening train ride from San Francisco to Los Angeles. Just eighteen at the time, she wanted to thank him for his kind comments about her play. He had watched her in a tournament, and the next morning she and her family were flabbergasted to see a glowing article in the newspaper headlined "Tilden Raves at First Glimpse of Alice Marble."[15]

Marble hesitantly approached Tilden, who she said was "attacking the biggest steak I had ever seen." To her pleasant surprise Bill asked her to join him, and they talked all the way to Los Angeles. "He was kindness itself, making me feel completely at ease," wrote Marble. "It was a lovely experience and one which began a friendship which I have valued for fifteen years."

She went on to describe her travels with Bill years later as part of his pro tour with Don Budge and Mary Hardwick. "Four people in close quarters covering sixty-five cities can get on each other's nerves, but Bill was always the model of decorum, extremely considerate, and made sure that Mary and I had comfortable dressing rooms in the various auditoriums, arenas, and gymnasiums." Alice described how Tilden made sure to watch Mary and her every night, encouraged them when they thought they played poorly, told them stories to entertain them, and read to them from plays he was writing while on the tour.

"Bill at forty-eight, could not beat Don often," wrote Alice, "but he rarely gave a bad performance and he always tried his best to win." Regardless of what occurred on court, the next day's headline announced "Budge, Marble Win; Tilden Steals the Show." For Marble, "He was the king and always will be to those who love this game of tennis. Bill, the temperamental, strange man whom nobody really knows; the genius of the courts, the man who has done much to inspire young and old." In closing Marble gave a heartfelt wish that the public "not pass judgment on him. I, for one, want to thank him for his generosity to tennis and to wish him every success in this, his most difficult battle."[16]

Not everyone was as gracious or as brave as Alice Marble. Many of those who still supported Tilden did not want their names associated with him. The public shunning was not universal, but it was there all the same. In addition to the humiliation, Bill had to contend with imprisonment. Located about forty miles north of Los Angeles near Saugus and Castaic Lake, the prison-road camp, or honor farm, as it was sometimes called, was actually a far better place to serve a prison sentence than either the Los Angeles County Jail or one of California's fearsome state penitentiaries, like Folsom or San Quentin. Consisting of nineteen barracks holding approximately five hundred men, the operation was more like an army camp than a penal institution. There were no walls, violent prison gangs, or claustrophobic cell blocks. However, everyone was expected to work, usually in the hog or dairy ranch, the kitchen, or out in the field farming.[17] Though work assignments could be physically exhausting, for someone like Tilden, a professional athlete used to pushing himself through ten sets of singles a day, the honor farm was more like a vacation, at least from a physical perspective.

On arrival Bill was assigned to the "scouring gang" in the kitchen and shortly after as one of the table setters and waiters in the main mess hall. He was then promoted to the "commissary store room," where he filled orders for camp cooks and the kitchen crew. All in all it was quite tame and fairly manageable.

Inmates were allowed visits on Sundays. Marrion Anderson was a regular visitor, and sometimes she brought Art. She had had a serious discussion with Bill about the charges early on and apparently believed him. He said he was not a threat to Art or anyone else.[18] Marrion felt there was little reason to doubt him. Over the past few years Art had spent considerable time with Bill—both on and off the court—and there wasn't a whiff of something untoward occurring. Marrion, according to Rich Hillway's many interviews with Art, trusted Bill. They were friends, and she was going to support him.

In addition to performing his supply-room duties, it is likely Bill began to pen *My Story*, his autobiography, which would be published the following year. His last serious account of his life and tennis career, the work was probably also designed to provide an explanation of the unfortunate behavior that would result in his being severed from polite society.

Though Bill's subsequent public comments and statements in *My Story* regarding his incarceration at the honor farm were unusually complimentary of the camp's operations and treatment of prisoners, he was far from happy there. In actuality, he wanted out badly. Through his attorney, Richard Maddox, Bill appealed at least twice "for modification of the sentence." It was their hope that Bill would be released to "the care of a physician and placed in a rest home." On both occasions Judge Scott turned the petitioner down. Unsympathetic, Scott bluntly fired back after the second appeal, "This man can't be free. If the doctors can't cure him, he should be put in a state hospital and kept there for the rest of his life."[19]

Just six weeks later, however, Bill got his wish. On September 1, 1947, after seven and a half months' incarceration, he was set free. Tilden had been let out early for good behavior and was relatively upbeat and optimistic about the future as friends and reporters were there to greet him. "I served my time at the County Farm," said Bill. "I have nothing but praise for the way the institution is operated. I worked hard, got plenty of fresh air and had wholesome and adequate food." As to his future plans, Bill rightly conceded that "remains with the American public."[20]

Some months later *My Story* would hit bookstores. The 311-page tome that included photographs of some of his greatest victories and toughest opponents such as Little Bill Johnston (to whom he dedicated the book), Dick Williams, Frank Hunter, René Lacoste, Henri Cochet, and Baron von Cramm; top female players Helen Wills, Helen Jacobs, and Alice Marble; various Hollywood stars like Mickey Rooney and Judy Garland; and several of his younger students. Although the book was a well-written and certainly interesting personal account from one of the twentieth century's greatest athletes, more curious crime sleuths were searching for some sort of mea culpa or explanation regarding Tilden's fall from grace. They did not find it until page 307. It was in those last few pages that Bill addressed the mysterious "nervous strain" that led to his arrest and incarceration. A hint of what was to come, however, appeared twenty-five pages earlier, when Bill addressed the subject of "romance."

Recognizing the need to firm up his masculinity and heterosexual image after his embarrassing criminal conviction, he recounted his many love interests, though the term itself required some qualification. "Frankly," Bill forthrightly admitted, "I doubt that I have ever been seriously in love. Some people choose to believe otherwise, but the trouble lay not in any deficiency of mine."[21] There was certainly some truth in his claim that tennis was a "jealous mistress," but slightly less when explaining that the game "rarely let me rest long enough . . . to really investigate a lady . . . so romance often boiled, but never got a chance to jell."

Seemingly intent on proving himself a regular red-blooded American with a normal sexual appetite, Bill offered a list of women who fell into the categories of "first girls in my life," "adolescent crushes," and "strong attractions." There were even a few whom he considered serious marriage material. The effort to prove his interest in the opposite sex began when he was ten at summer camp, and then during his teenage years, which were interrupted by his mother's debilitating illness and the sudden deaths of his father and brother in 1915. The repeated blows, according to Bill, took the "wildness" out of him, and he was no longer in the "mood for wild oats or anything else."

With the passage of years there were many occasions when Bill claimed attraction "to this girl or that" and even "considered marrying" a couple of times. Peggy Wood in 1918 and movie actress Marjorie Daw, whom he appeared with in the silent film *Haunting Hands* in the midtwenties, were the women mentioned as early love interests. Other women he associated himself with as a romantic partner were film star Pola Negri as well as a bevy of well-known female tennis players, including Mary K. Browne, Cilly Aussem, and Wimbledon champ Helen Jacobs.[22] Though much of the general public may have bought this account, those closer to Bill and the game knew the flimsy foundation on which these stories were built.

At the end of the book when he finally addressed the scandalous incident that resulted in his arrest and conviction, he had his work cut out for him. Bill wrote that the junior high school student he allowed behind the wheel of his car was a "lad" he had met on court, "had known casually for some time," and "wanted to help. He and I worked together several times and became good friends." Somehow, Bill goes on to explain, they "drifted into a foolishly schoolboy-ish relationship," which Bill admits he "should have prevented." He attributed his bizarre behavior to a rare occurrence: "My nervous strain was such that at the time I seemed to lack will; I seemed dissociated, and beyond control of my own actions."

As he went on to describe the sorry episode, after attending a movie together, Bill allowed the boy to drive his car. His poor judgment continued when they began "fooling around [and] indulging in horseplay." Spotted and stopped by police, Bill "gave a complete statement . . . hoping to save the youngster" any embarrassment or notoriety. It was Bill's desire to take "full responsibility" for the entire episode.

Over the course of seven additional paragraphs, Bill embarked on a strangely evasive—some would say sanitized—explanation of something he saw as rather common: "athletics throw[ing] the same sex together constantly and intimately, with strong, close friendships growing up often based at least in part on admiration for physical perfection, an attraction may arise almost like that of love." Bill believed that throughout "history there has been a record of occasional relationships somewhat away from the normal."[23] As with his other comments, he was not specific, and readers are forced to speculate as to what he meant.

"Rumor today has it that amateur tennis is rife with this situation," he went on, but Tilden claimed he had "never seen any evidence . . . that the rumor has any justification" and considered the allegation "the basest kind of libel on the game." If such behavior did occur, Bill argued, "it was neither more nor less than in any other walk of life." Moreover, "the list of celebrated people in this age and previous ones who have deviated from the norm makes it obvious that this is not a sign of degeneracy in the usual sense." For Bill such behavior was indicative of "an illness . . . a psychological illness," one that could be "cured by reconditioning or re-education." Was he addressing homosexuality, hebephilia, ephebophilia, or something else?[24]

It was not long after, unfortunately, when a wave of new stories appeared in daily newspapers across the country. "Big Bill Tilden Is Accused Again," "Bill Tilden Arraigned on New Morals Charge," and "Bill Tilden Seized on

Morals Charge" are a sampling of headlines that greeted newspaper readers around the country in late-January 1949.

Tilden was arrested at his Westwood Village apartment, based on "the complaint of an Inglewood High School student who said that the tennis champion made improper advances last Friday morning, after he allegedly had picked up the youth in his automobile in Westwood."[25] According to Santa Monica juvenile officers, the student had provided a description of the individual and the license number of the car.

The juvenile, whom some newspapers identified as sixteen-year-old Michael Schachel of Inglewood, had a provocative story to tell.[26] He claimed "he was picked up by a man he identified as Tilden at the intersection of Wilshire and Westwood Boulevards. He rode west with the man, who he said made a series of improper advances to him."

When police went to pick Tilden up at his apartment, he reportedly "seemed surprised but accompanied them without argument." At the Santa Monica jail, Tilden told reporters, "I feel pretty sure I can account for myself between 8 and 8:30 a.m. Friday. I'm sure it must be a case of mistaken identity." Bill went on to explain that "at that time he must either have been eating breakfast at a café on Hollywood Blvd. near Vine St. or giving tennis lessons to some of his pupils." When someone suggested he might be the victim of a frame-up, Bill replied, "Nobody would frame me, although there are many who don't like me."[27]

Compounding this second Tilden run-in with the law was the presence of a juvenile when the police arrived with a warrant for Bill's arrest.[28] His five-year probationary period order specified another responsible adult always be present when he was in the company of juveniles. This stipulation was not always observed.

The frame-up issue was not something that Los Angeles residents cavalierly dismissed. Organized-crime figures and members of the Hollywood film colony, just to name two, often cried foul, arguing they had been set up. A number of Tilden supporters—particularly Marrion and Art Anderson—were convinced such a scenario had ensnared Bill. Their assurance of such a sinister plot was being orchestrated when pressure was placed on seventeen-year-old Art to divulge his abuse at the hands of the internationally famous tennis player. Art was threatened that if he did not admit to Tilden's harming him, he would be sent to reform school. In fact, there had never been any abuse. Moreover, Art and his mother had grown so close to Tilden that the boy looked on Bill as something of a father figure.

Art Anderson's account of the troubling incident was related to Richard Hillway in a series of interviews over many years.[29] According to Art, he suspected the LA police witnessed his getting in Bill's car "without a chaperon" while "taking Art to school." Police subsequently "questioned Art and told him that he couldn't see his parent until he confessed that Tilden had done something to him in the car. They told him they were sure Tilden molested him and wanted him to tell them how." Art repeatedly told the police that Tilden "was like his dad and never touched him."

When Marrion Anderson discovered what was happening, she "immediately called the lawyer who had defended Errol Flynn." Harold Lee "Jerry" Geisler was an Iowa boy by birth but moved to California after high school and had done quite well for himself. He became a successful attorney and had defended a number of prominent clients over the years, including Clarence Darrow, a former LA district attorney, and a number of Hollywood stars. His defense of Errol Flynn from some potentially career-threatening allegations was a particularly nasty and heavily publicized affair. It was said that "by 1942 his reputation in Hollywood and Beverly Hills was such that 'Get me Geisler' was slang for big trouble."[30] It was Geisler that Marrion urged Tilden to hire when he was first arrested in 1946, but Bill did not take her advice.

Marrion, however, made sure Geisler represented Art when he was taken before a judge and questioned about his relationship with Tilden. Geisler told Art and his mother he would do all the talking and informed the judge, "I won't allow the court to take this straight A student who is going to be a top tennis player and has no offenses, and against whom there is no evidence, and slander him." Geisler was not shy. He aggressively argued, "The police department was looking for well-known Hollywood figures to make examples of," and it would be a crime if an innocent lad were unnecessarily injected into such a controversy. The judge apparently agreed and dismissed the case.

The episode—specifically the pressure exerted on Art to admit to something that never happened—confirmed to a number of Tilden supporters that Bill was a target and should have hired Geisler from the first. Art, who had grown used to playing tennis with many famous Hollywood stars, remembered Errol Flynn telling Tilden, "Goddamn it, Bill, get Geisler to defend you." Art had obviously been present at certain conversations when Geisler maintained that "there was no case against" Bill. "There were no witnesses," and the "parents of the boy [making the accusation] wanted no publicity. He thought they'd drop it" rather than appear in a courtroom. Geisler, according to Art, would have urged Bill in the first case to "plead not guilty and demand a jury trial where the boy would have to testify." Tilden, however, chose not to accept such a tactically sound but brutal legal strategy.

The questionable governmental shenanigans could in part explain Tilden's surprisingly light sentence, considering the court found him guilty of both a probation violation and a new charge. "When I gave you probation, you gave me your word as a sportsman that you would abide by all its rules," trumpeted Judge Scott in the courtroom. "You have failed as a sportsman and I have no sympathy for you."[31]

When Tilden was asked if he had anything to say, he replied, "No sir, I concur with everything Mr. Maddox has said." The judge then handed Bill another one-year sentence at the county work farm. "Society is doing you a favor by sending you to jail because someone might be tempted to shoot you," blustered Scott. It was February 10, 1949, Tilden's fifty-sixth birthday.

Now a seasoned con and familiar with the prison routine at Castaic, Bill tried to keep his spirits up as best he could. Art and Marrion Anderson would prove his most devoted supporters. Marrion visited him just about every other Sunday and Art on occasion. They wrote often, and Bill was most keen on Art's progress on the tennis court. He regularly gave him tactical advice, encouraged him in his forthcoming matches, and promised to make up for his many absences when released. Bill's many letters to Art—most of them written in pencil and two pages in length—usually began "Dear Pal" or "Dear Bratto" and ended after offering advice regarding an upcoming match with the comment, "I'm counting on you, but I'm very proud of you. Always, Bill." Sometimes he signed off, "Your Old Man." One missive, responding to Art's news of a loss but to a top-ranked player, closed with Bill's uplifting comment in capital letters, "GREAT STUFF, KID!" Not every teenager was receiving almost daily letters from a world-famous athlete. It is safe to assume that very few knew what type of establishment was at the address on the envelope. They all read: "W. T. Tilden, Barrack 19, Box 999, Route 3, Saugus, Cal."[32]

Art and his mother were not the only ones who kept in touch with Bill while he was incarcerated. A number of athletes, actors, and others maintained lines of communication with him. One of the most dutiful and concerned was Gloria P. Butler, daughter of the tobacco magnet and one of Tilden's troupe of players who performed for rehabilitating soldiers at military hospitals a few years earlier. She was not yet an adult herself when she was sent to America during the war, and Bill was her friendly guardian in addition to her tennis coach. She even took a room across the hall from him at the Ambassador Hotel in Los Angeles and was viewed as one of his rare female protégées.

Bill's second arrest and imprisonment troubled her greatly, and she wrote Bill as well as members of the Anderson family (Art, his mother, and his grandmother Mrs. Ada Philipps) regarding his well-being. As she wrote Art's grandmother, from Park Avenue in New York City, after learning of Bill's second conviction, "I am terribly sorry for Bill as I think he deserves a better break than he is getting in Los Angeles."

Butler was of the opinion that Bill "obviously must have some very powerful enemies out there . . . and cannot possibly eke out a decent existence nor give himself enough to do on a few tennis lessons and I'm afraid public appearances for him are over." It was Butler's opinion that Bill should leave the United States, and on her return to Europe she "intended to explore every possible avenue open towards getting an opening for Bill" in any reasonable line of work, including employment "in a sporting goods store."[33]

Though Butler's proposal was made with the best of intentions, there is little to suggest Bill would have ever seriously considered leaving America to work in a European sporting-goods store. Though many a tennis player over the years—especially a number of top Australian players—formed contractual relations with sporting-goods firms in order to earn a living, Bill's life was predicated on being outside, in the fresh air, playing tennis. And as Rich Hillway points out, although Tilden was born into the upper crust and could spend money like an "Indian prince," his life wasn't predicated on earning money.

In fact, prior to his imprisonment, Bill's life had become rather simple and pedestrian. He played tennis during the day, and in the evenings he read paperback mysteries, listened to classical music, and played games of bridge with friends. The days of carefree spending and lengthy stays at the Algonquin were over. And Marrion Anderson, a professional bookkeeper, assisted further by helping Bill manage his finances. She put him on a schedule and budget that greatly tempered his once profligate spending. In short, Bill had no doubt he could sustain himself once he got out of jail.

On December 18, 1949, a week before Christmas, Tilden was released from the Castaic Honor Farm after serving ten and a half months. "Well, here's Big Bill Tilden again," said a sarcastic jailer as the prisoner reentered the free world. "Yeah," said the former tennis champion. "Here's Tilden again." Newspaper accounts said he then "walked out of the jail and into the rain."[34]

Epilogue

Dear Bill:

> I just want you to know as far as your real
> admirers and pals are concerned, you're
> just one set down with plenty of games to
> play. Your old rooters are pulling for you.

ERROL FLYNN

As one would expect, Tilden's personal friendships and economic opportunities were much in decline after his release from a second imprisonment on morals charges. No longer viewed by all as a shining exemplar of the golden age of sports, Bill was often shunned and considered persona non grata by individuals and organizations that once aggressively competed for his favor.

Few people in public life over the past century attained such heights only to experience a sudden and shameful fall. From a revered guest of European and Asian royalty, a frequent visitor to the White House, and an admired figure to the most celebrated names in the arts and entertainment world, Tilden held an honorable place in the pantheon of accomplished Americans. Now it was gone. It is doubtful that any other athlete during the first half of the twentieth century—including the Manassa Mauler, the Galloping Ghost, or the Sultan of Swat—was ever so venerated by such an illustrious collection of world famous personages, only to see much of it vanish.

After his second stint at Castaic Honor Farm, there were no more invitations to the White House, visits to European castles or houses of parliament, or publicity-driven excursions to Hollywood movie sets. Even many tennis clubs encouraged him to keep his distance. Ironically, the man who was most obsessed with honor—both in his books and on the court—was the one who had become the moral outcast. Whether embarrassed for him or outraged by his actions, more than a few gave him a cold shoulder and turned away when in his company. It was made painfully clear some people no longer wanted to associate with him. Some of his famous Hollywood students and benefactors who had paid handsomely for lessons and the privilege of claiming a Wimbledon champion as their instructor now severed their relations with him.

Perry Jones, the autocrat of Southern Californian tennis and the czar-like head of the Los Angeles Tennis Club, told Tilden he was no longer welcome at the club. He would now be relegated to courts on public playgrounds and those few private courts that belonged to friends like David O. Selznick, Joseph Cotten, and Charlie Chaplin who weren't afraid to be associated with him. His much-circumscribed social situation impacted his earning potential and may well have forced him to move to ever-smaller and more affordable living accommodations.

Though he was occasionally shunned and ostracized, Tilden's Mount Olympus–sized accomplishments on the court over the years were too numerous and monumental to overlook. His dominance and importance in the game's history were prominently confirmed when in February 1950, just a few months after his release from the honor farm, "the ultrasophisticate of the world's tennis courts" was selected as the "greatest netman" of the first half of the twentieth century. The widely publicized Associated Press poll of the nation's top sportswriters and radio newsmen selected Tilden on 310 of 391 ballots.[1] The runners-up, Jack Kramer and Donald Budge, were far back, drawing 32 and 31 votes, respectively. In fact, Tilden dominated his athletic specialty like no other athlete, according to the experts; even the great Babe Ruth had some competition for the greatest baseball player, as he defeated Ty Cobb by a relatively narrow two-to-one margin. Tilden, on the other hand, demolished the opposition, winning by ten to one.[2]

"Genuinely gratified that he had been named the greatest tennis player of the past 50 years," Tilden told the press he was "truly grateful for the honor." Being that it was Big Bill, however, it was not surprising that he had some concerns about the voting. Not that he disagreed with his overwhelming margin of victory—that was well deserved—but his unease rested with the runner-up category. Where were the names Henri Cochet, René Lacoste, Little Bill Johnston, Fred Perry, Ellsworth Vines, and Vinnie

Richards? In Bill's mind they were every bit as good as, if not better than, Kramer and Budge.

The Associated Press poll was certainly a much-appreciated respite from the new reality that Big Bill was forced to confront. As one well-known sports pundit attempted to describe the former champion's constrained environment, the convictions had "turned Big Bill into a non-person, [where] younger fans and players today, and even members of the tennis press who never saw him in action, have no real recognition of Tilden the player."[3] Though there is a kernel of truth to Frank Deford's account of the dark shadow that eclipsed Tilden's once brilliant aura in the eyes of casual sports fans, it is Deford's own off-putting depiction of Tilden, especially his last years, that has contributed so greatly to the public's hazy recollection of the man and his remarkable accomplishments. But his life was not nearly as bleak and barren of friendships and enjoyment as certain chroniclers would have people believe. Serious connoisseurs of the game, as well as the nation's leading tennis historian, offer another narrative, one they believe to be historically sound, evidence based, and free of Deford's melodramatic psychobabble.

Frank Deford's 1975 book, *Big Bill Tilden*, was well written by one of the nation's most recognizable sportswriters, entertaining (how could a book about Tilden not be?), and filled with interesting personal vignettes. But it was also laced with historical inaccuracies and much amateur armchair psychoanalysis. In what was originally designed as a magazine piece, Tilden, in Deford's eyes, was a tremendously gifted athlete but severely flawed human being. And it is the latter that he hammers away at. Tilden is repeatedly called "nearly friendless," "pitifully alone," "ashamed of himself," "malodorous," "a penniless ex-con" who was forced to sell his trophies, and "a figure of pity" whose "sad, shameful last years . . . hastened the tennis establishment to reject him."

Tilden's "homosexuality"—its origin, nature, and impact—also receives considerable attention. Deford ascribes Tilden's problematic sexual orientation to everything from fictitious rumors of a childhood accident that left him a "sexual amputee" to growing up in a dysfunctional family guaranteed "to produce a homosexual male: the neglectful father who was devoted to another brother; the overprotective mother, warning her baby about the dirt and disease of sex."

After considerable time pondering the subject of psychosexual pathology, Deford basically throws up his hands and states, "For as much as Tilden was a homosexual, it was because he chose to be one, not because he had to."

Though the temptation to tackle and rebut each of Deford's many controversial allegations and conclusions is great, that was never the intent of this biography. However, one cannot help but address a few of the most outlandish allegations concerning Tilden's later years, such as his banishment from public performances, his propensity for effeminate behavior, his inability to keep himself clean and free from foul-smelling body odor, and his need to pawn his vast collection of tournament hardware.

In fact, Bill remained quite popular with the general public. Just a little more than a year after Bill was released from the honor farm, he was back on the pro tour with Pancho Gonzales, Frank Parker, George Rogers, and Frank Kovacs. To his great relief he was always well received. Newspaper photographs often captured him playing or giving lectures to scores of young people in various cities across the country. At one tennis venue in Salt Lake City, members of a women's tennis team seemed enthralled that one of the game's greatest names was available to give them instruction. Accounts of these sessions repeatedly mention "eager" students hoping to gain valuable tips on how to improve their game, and there were as many as "150 boys and girls . . . on hand to hear the famous maestro of the court" explain the key elements of winning tennis.[4]

And the corporate sector was far from monolithic in regarding Tilden as a pariah. Bancroft, for example, quickly replaced Dunlop as a supplier of tennis gear. Sam Doaks, a Bancroft representative in the Los Angeles area, made sure Bill was well stocked with custom-made rackets and anything else he required in the way of athletic gear. In fact, Bill had such a surplus he sent four rackets to Art in Japan in 1952 while Art was serving in the military.[5]

Regrettably, few remain who knew Tilden—and even fewer who were across the net from him—but legitimate attempts were made to reach out to those who do present a contrary narrative to Deford's unflattering characterization of the man. In fact, no one recalled anything resembling peculiar behavior or unattractive personal characteristics. Gardnar Mulloy, who went on a half-dozen hospital visits with Bill during the war, never witnessed any odd behavior. Tilden always carried himself in a dignified manner and managed events very professionally. "He wasn't treated properly," said Mulloy of Bill's arrest and incarceration. "Today it [his being gay] wouldn't matter. It would be no big deal."[6]

Dick Savitt, who would go on to win the Wimbledon singles title in 1951, spent time with Tilden on several occasions, including an exhibition match in Memphis for the U.S. Navy in 1945, and observed "no gay affectations." What was made particularly clear, however, was that "he was still pretty good. He could still play high-quality tennis."[7]

Vic Seixas, one of America's top players in the early 1950s and a Wimbledon singles champion, has only positive memories of Tilden. Just before Seixas was drafted into the military during World War II, Tilden was on one of his pro tours and invited Vic and another young female player to join him for dinner at the Bellevue-Stratford Hotel in downtown Philadelphia. Tilden, according to Seixas, was the model of decorum throughout the entire evening. "Bill was dressed immaculately and was certainly not malodorous," said Seixas. "Nor was there any hint of effeminate behavior."[8]

Even those who spent considerably more time with Tilden shared the same opinion. One person who was with Tilden on a daily basis during the last months of his life was Angela Buxton. Just seventeen at the time—Tilden had no probationary constraints regarding his association with minors after his second conviction—the young British player hoped to improve her game by temporarily relocating to America in late 1952 and training with California's best. She took a five-month lease for an apartment overlooking the Los Angeles Tennis Club and was playing there daily when she learned her application for membership at the prestigious club would never be accepted. Buxton was Jewish, and Jews along with a number of other religious and racial groups were denied membership. She had experienced similar discrimination in England, but it did not curtail her interest in the game. Searching for another high-quality tennis site, she discovered the courts at LaCienga, a public playground, where everyone was accepted. When she inquired about tennis instructors, many names were suggested, but one name stood out—Bill Tilden.

Though Buxton was cautioned that Bill was a homosexual and had recent run-ins with the law, she was not as quick as some to distance herself from someone considered a social outcast. Besides, said Buxton, "most people spoke highly of him." Admittedly naive about much of the sexual talk surrounding Tilden, she was more attuned to something else that was repeatedly said about him: he was a three-time Wimbledon champion. "When I informed my father I was being coached by Bill Tilden," recalls Buxton, "he was thrilled."

"Bill had the keys to Charlie Chaplin's court, and we played every day," said Buxton. "Sometimes he would bring Art [Anderson] along, and we'd hit against each other or against Bill." After their workouts, according to Angela, they would often go out to eat together or visit some of his Hollywood friends and tennis acquaintances. "On other occasions," said Buxton, "there would be Hollywood film stars playing and taking instruction from Bill." Buxton still enjoys recalling those unforgettable moments when film stars would come to watch Bill practice with her. "There were many Hollywood stars living in the area, and they all loved tennis," recalled Buxton, who would go on to be a Wimbledon singles finalist and win several major titles with Althea Gibson as her doubles partner. "When I told my father that Katharine Hepburn and Walter Pidgeon had acted as ball boys for us," says Buxton, "he got quite a kick out of it."[9] Buxton would train under Tilden from January through April without observing any of the unhygienic personal traits that Deford repeatedly cited.

No one, however, spent more time with Tilden during his last months than Art Anderson. Over the course of their eleven years together, their relationship evolved into something beyond teacher-student. Bill had become more like a father to Art. He not only taught him tennis but also mentored him, spent a great deal of time in the Anderson home, and wrote in his will that Art should receive whatever revenue was derived from his last tennis book. In addition, Bill's personal collection of tournament trophies—a financial haul of considerable value—was turned over to Art in 1950. Tilden and the Andersons had become family. When Art was drafted into the service in 1951, Bill moved into the Anderson household and into Art's room. The idea was Marrion Anderson's, as she was always looking to maximize Bill's savings and limit his expenditures.

For Marrion, who acted as his accountant during his last years, it seemed especially unwise for Bill to pay rent for his own place when he was away from home so often. For several months at a time Bill would often be on one of his pro tours. It was while Art was stationed at Fort Ord, and later in Japan, that Bill moved in with Marrion and her mother. While living with the Andersons, Bill not only contributed financially to the upkeep of the apartment, but also helped care for Marrion's mother, who was dying of cancer. It was Bill who often carried Mrs. Ada Philipps from one room to another when she was unable to do so on her own. And when Art returned from the service in early 1953, Bill once again got his own apartment near the Andersons. A frequent dinner guest, he was always immaculately dressed—invariably attired in a jacket and tie, as was his custom going back to Germantown Academy—and never displayed any of the flamboyant homosexual affectations that Deford ascribes to him in his book.[10]

On Friday, June 5, 1953, Bill began his day as he did most mornings: a large breakfast followed by a couple of tennis lessons and then a more rigorous workout with Art Anderson. They would play anywhere from three to five sets of strenuous singles. Though Art was twenty-two and a former college player and Bill sixty, the old man was still capable of pushing his younger opponent. When they parted that afternoon, they agreed they would see each other later that night at the Anderson home. Bill was leaving the next morning for Cleveland and the U.S. Pro Championships, and Art and his mother wanted to see Bill before he left for the Midwest. It was their goal to send him off with a good home-cooked meal.

Tilden was very punctual, and when he failed to show up for dinner at five, Art attempted to phone him. There was no answer. He then called Mrs. John Bray, the landlady, and was told Bill's car was still in the parking lot. Suspicious, Art drove over to Bill's Hollywood apartment at 2025 North Argyle Avenue and asked Mrs. Bray to open the door with her passkey.

On the court that day Bill had complained of feeling tired and struggling with a bad cold. He had stopped on the way home for some cold medication at a local pharmacy. Despite feeling under the weather, he had been quite active of late. In addition to teaching a series of clients, he had attended the professional tennis matches at the Balboa Bay Club last Sunday and watched the matches between Jack Kramer and Frank Sedgman at Pasadena and La Jolla. Though he was having difficulty kicking his cold symptoms, Bill continued his physically vigorous schedule of teaching clients, hitting with Art for a couple hours, and looking forward to the pro championships in Cleveland, where he would be both a participant and a production assistant. He even planned on stopping in Wichita to give a tennis exhibition for tennis fans in Kansas.[11]

When Art and the Mrs. Bray entered the apartment, they discovered Tilden lying fully clothed on his bed; he was dead. A mystery novel was by his side, and his bags were already packed for his cross-country journey the next morning. Emergency units were called, and firemen worked feverishly for a half hour, but Tilden could not be revived. He was just sixty years old, the same age as his father when he died.

Knowing Bill's schedule and habits as well as he did, Art assumed Tilden arrived back at his apartment after their workout, showered, put on a tie and jacket as was customary when he went out for dinner, and laid down on his bed to read a new mystery novel until it was time to leave for the Anderson apartment. Art could only assume a heart attack had taken one of the greatest champions in American history. A short while later an autopsy was performed that confirmed Art's suspicion.

Over the weekend front-page stories appeared in newspapers around the world announcing Tilden's death. The articles were long and fact filled, and they often delved into Big Bill's assorted interests outside the athletic arena. Few athletes had written books—more than thirty fiction and nonfiction in Bill's case—or appeared onstage and on-screen. As for an accounting of his tennis records, they deserved a newspaper column in themselves: the first American-born player to win a Wimbledon singles title; an American titleholder seven times; the winner of thirty-one national crowns as an amateur indoors and outdoors in singles, doubles, and mixed doubles; the nation's number-one-ranked player for ten straight years; the backbone of America's undefeated Davis Cup squad from 1920 to 1926; and on it went.[12] Also mentioned were Bill's quarrelsome relationship with the USLTA, the amputation of his finger, the 1928 French brouhaha that nearly became an international incident, and his critical role in establishing professional tennis as a popular and profit-making venture. One would be hard-pressed to think of another athlete who had such a profound impact on a sport.

In following days the nation's best sports columnists waxed eloquent about the "great court colossus" who had "dynamite in his racquet" and "belonged to sports' Golden Age, the glorious decade of the Twenties when the athletic gods patrolled this mortal sphere." Tilden was described as "a tennis player without a weakness on the court. He could blast away with the same overpowering force from forehand or backhand. His cannonball serve was untouchable. His drop shots were deft and delicate. He could play the net or the base line with equal facility and roamed with space-eating strides from sideline to sideline. Not only had he all the physical equipment to beat any opponent but he also was smarter than anyone else."[13]

Not surprisingly, those sports scribes who went back to Tilden's heyday such as Al Laney and Allison Danzig were the most effusive in their praise and tributes. Laney considered Tilden a "unique personality," in addition to his "unmatched achievements as a tennis player." He hailed Bill's technique as "without a peer," his control a gift from the heavens that included an "incomparable forehand," a cannonball serve that was struck "as hard as any ball ever hit," and an assortment of "spins and slices" that opponents found "bewildering." In conclusion, Laney believed that Big Bill was not only the equal of Bobby Jones, Jack Dempsey, Red Grange, and Babe Ruth, but quite possibly "our greatest athlete in any sport."[14]

Danzig of the *Times* would call him "the autocrat of the courts" and unlike any other player who ever played the game. "An absolute monarch in a period when American tennis was at its most resplendent and great players were developed in many lands," Tilden was not only "supreme," but the "most complete player of all time, and also one of the most colorful and controversial figures the world of sports has known."[15]

For Paul Gallico it was Tilden's sheer "artistry" that separated him from other top athletes. It was Tilden's ability to overcome "every one of his handicaps, his little tantrums and gestures of pique, sulks, pets, glares and, believe it or not, shouts of 'Oh, sugar!' when he missed one. They simply did not matter in the light of the heights to which he was able to rise when he wished, or needed to, and in rising he would sweep us all along with him."[16]

But now it was over for both the man and an era. "And so it ends," wrote Red Smith, "the tale of the gifted, flamboyant, combative, melodramatic, gracious, swaggering, unfortunate man, whose name must always be a symbol of the most colorful period American sports have known."[17]

Just a month later Tilden's will was admitted for probate, and news quickly circulated that "the assets of his estate amount to practically nothing."[18] The articles were similar to those at the time of Bill's death, which emphasized the former tennis champ died with only a few dollars in his pocket and living in a tiny apartment. It was true, Tilden's economic circumstances were much different from when he came into the world, but the reports of financial destitution were clearly overblown. As Art Anderson told Rich Hillway, Bill's finances were in constant flux, "but he was never broke" and "never complained about money problems." Granted, there were low periods, as when he died, but the next month or next week, he could find himself flush with cash again. As Art pointed out, Bill was always giving tennis lessons and going out on tour. Both brought in a respectable middle-class wage. And as Rich Hillway points out, for all his lavish spending and high living over the years, Tilden enjoyed the simple pleasures of life: playing tennis, reading books, listening to music, and playing bridge with friends. These went a long way to keeping him happy.

Tilden's articles and books were another source of income. Bill's 1950 publication, *How to Play Better Tennis* (which was dedicated to Art, and all royalty payments were to go to Art upon Bill's death), not only came with a nice $5,000 advance but also continued to earn annual royalty payments through 1983. And as to the ever-fluctuating highs and lows of Bill's finances, just a few months before his death Bill was so comfortable financially that he purchased two brand-new Ford Fairlane automobiles. Bill put down $2,250 in cash for the one car and gave it to Art as a gift; the other one Bill kept for himself and was purchased on a monthly payment plan.[19]

Moreover, there was Bill's large treasure chest of trophies. A collection in size and quality fit for a national museum, Bill originally had them stored at his Germantown home. He then put them in storage when he moved to the West Coast. They would later be moved to the Anderson apartment and given to Art as a gift. Marrion and Art were both angered by stories at the time of Bill's death that he had pawned three of his trophies when he was in need of cash. They knew the stories were untrue. But Bill was guilty of giving trophies away to so-called friends, especially movie people, only later to discover his friends had sold them for profit. In 1950 Tilden gave all of his trophies to Art, who was eighteen at the time. They would remain in Art's possession, just as Bill's will dictated. Not until four decades later did he decide to sell a number of them at a well-attended national auction in July 1992. The Renshaw Cup, a stunning trophy representative of the Wimbledon men's singles champion of 1920, sold for $71,500. The Perpetual Trophy, Bill's prize for winning the United States Clay Court Championship from 1920 through 1922, went for $48,400, and the 1923 U.S. Clay Court trophy was auctioned off for $27,500.[20] In all more than $250,000 was earned, and that was just a portion of what Tilden left Art in trophy hardware.

On June 10, 1953, while newsreel cameras clicked just as they had a quarter century earlier when Big Bill was in his amateur playing ascendancy at Wimbledon and Forest Hills, a standing-room-only crowd of two hundred "friends and admirers" gathered at Pierce Brothers Hollywood Chapel for the final rites of William Tatem Tilden 2d. The Reverend Charles Howard Perry of St. Stephen's Episcopal Church delivered the eulogy that began with the words, "I remembered him as an ideal . . . a great figure in the sports world."[21] In attendance were an assemblage of well-known tennis players and Hollywood celebrities. Players from the game's amateur era included John Hennessey, Harvey Snodgrass, Alfred Chapin, and John Doeg. Ellsworth Vines, Pancho Segura, Noel Brown, Gussie Moran, and several others represented a more recent vintage of top tennis talent who came to say good-bye to the tennis legend. A number from the Hollywood artistic community were present to pay their respects, ranging from established stars like Joseph Cotten to aspiring young actresses like Nancy Davis (who would go on to become First Lady of the United States as the wife of President Ronald Reagan).[22] As usual Tilden looked immaculate in a jacket, slacks, and a new sweater purchased for the occasion by his good friend Joseph Cotten.

The body was then cremated and the ashes shipped across the country to his sister-in-law, Mrs. Hazel MacIntosh, and a nephew, William Tilden 3rd, for burial in the Tilden family plot at Ivy Hill Cemetery in northwestern Philadelphia.[23] His ashes were buried under a simple flat stone that read "William T. Tilden 2nd 1893–1953." Joining his brother, Herbert, and his father thirty-eight years after their deaths in 1915, "Junior" Tilden was interned at the foot of his beloved mother and within a few feet of the three older siblings he never knew. The granite stone, no more than two feet by one foot in size, remains the only identifiable marker or monument honoring one of America's greatest and most interesting athletes.

Notes

1. "A GAME OF SOCIETY"

1. Stephen Wallis Merrihew, "Intimate Talk with My Readers," *American Lawn Tennis* (August 20, 1928): 355.
2. Laney, *Covering the Court*, 72–73.
3. Hart, *Lawn Tennis Masters Unveiled*, 20.
4. "Tilden Barred from Davis Cup Play," *American Lawn Tennis* (July 5, 1928): 251.
5. Hart, *Lawn Tennis Masters Unveiled*, 12.
6. Interview with Ken Benner. One of the nation's leading dealers of tennis memorabilia, Benner has collected and sold Tilden photos, clothing, and racquets for decades. Named for the great nineteenth-century player and Wimbledon champion in 1893 and '94, Dr. Joshua Pim, the racquet became a popular item for the growing number of tennis adherents at the turn of the century.
7. Tilden, *My Story*, 16.
8. Tilden, *Me: The Handicap*, 8.
9. Voss, *Tilden and Tennis*, 1.
10. Tilden, *Me: The Handicap*, 19.
11. Tilden, *My Story*, 17.
12. Tilden, *Me: The Handicap*, 8.
13. Tilden, *Me: The Handicap*, 20.
14. *Prominent and Progressive Pennsylvanians of the Nineteenth Century*, 3:435.
15. Tilden File, Special Collections Research Center, Temple University Library, Philadelphia.
16. Tilden birth certificate obtained from the City of Philadelphia Archives.
17. Alotta, *Mermaids, Monasteries, Cherokees, and Custer*.
18. Keyser et al., *History of Old Germantown*.
19. It would appear that war with Germany caused a popular backlash in America. Many individuals, institutions, and customs came under scrutiny and criticism. From the end of the war on, the term *Manheim* is used much

less frequently, and the athletic club is almost always now referred to as the Germantown Cricket Club.

20. *One Hundred Years of the Germantown Cricket Club*, GCC-produced historical account.

21. *Germantown (PA) Telegraph*, January 17, 1902, 7.

22. Additional acreage would be purchased in coming years, which added the lot at the corner of Manheim and Morris Streets, and the Clement property adjoining it, thus securing all the land from the line of Laurens Street on the west, to Morris Street on the east, and from Manheim Street on the south to Hansberry Street on the north.

23. *One Hundred Years of the Germantown Cricket Club*.

24. *History of Germantown C.C.* (1910).

25. Baltzell, *Sporting Gentlemen*, 24.

26. The club's building committee reported, "The character of the work speaks for itself and the committee does not see how it could as a whole have been better done. . . . [T]he club has got more of a building and a better one for the money than we could have been at all likely to get from any other contractor." *One Hundred Years of the Germantown Cricket Club*, 5.

27. Baltzell, *Sporting Gentlemen*, 40.

28. Tilden, *My Story*, 29.

29. Annual report of the Germantown Cricket Club, 1900, 10.

30. During the yellow-fever epidemic of 1793, many Philadelphians fled the city for safer environs. George Washington and much of his cabinet relocated to the higher altitude of Germantown. During his time there his cabinet often met at the school. Sometime later he enrolled his adopted son, George Washington Parke Custis, as a student.

31. Tilden, *My Story*, 18.

32. Tilden, *Me: The Handicap*, 20.

33. Interview with Dr. Mark Rabuck, member of the Germantown Academy History Department and school archivist who provided numerous documents and photographs of Herbert and William Tilden while students at the school.

34. Burt and Davies, "Iron Age," 471.

35. Burt and Davies, "Iron Age," 482.

36. *Prominent and Progressive Pennsylvanians*, 436.

37. *Prominent and Progressive Pennsylvanians*, 436.

38. *Journal of Commerce* (1911).

39. "Wm. T. Tilden, Union League President, Dies," *Philadelphia Evening Bulletin*, July 30, 1915.

40. Several documents held by the Germantown Historical Society disclose names of prominent members of the Germantown Cricket Club during the 1890s. Many of the club's most famous and active members from this time now have their silhouettes on display near the ceiling of the club's grand ballroom. William T. Tilden is among them.

41. Tilden, *My Story*, 18–29.

42. Tilden, *Singles and Doubles*, 95.

43. Baltzell, *Sporting Gentlemen*, 18.

44. Tilden, *Me: The Handicap*, 7.

2. "A USELESS KID"

1. Tilden, *Me: The Handicap*, 21.

2. Tilden, *Me: The Handicap*, 24.

3. Herbert M. Tilden was a member of the Germantown Academy football, cricket, baseball, and bowling teams. Ironically, he did not play on the school's tennis team, a sport he would become most closely associated with after college and one in which he developed some bit of regional recognition.

4. Tilden, *Me: The Handicap*, 24.

5. Tilden, *Me: The Handicap*, 26.

6. *Ye Primer* (Germantown Academy, 1910).

7. Academic record of William T. Tilden Jr. at the University of Pennsylvania.

8. Tilden, *Me: The Handicap*, 26.

9. Tilden, *My Story*, 15.

10. "The Toll of Death," *American Lawn Tennis* (March 20, 1941): 12.

11. "Lay Corner-Stone at Union League," *Philadelphia Evening Bulletin*, October 9, 1909.

12. Testimonial dinner to William T. Tilden, the Union League of Philadelphia, January 25, 1915. Tilden's cautious comment about expressions of love between men might provide an indication of the growing discomfort between the oldest and youngest Tildens. By this time there can be little doubt that Junior Tilden knew he was gay. It could not have been an easy situation for either man.

13. Tilden File, Special Collections Research Center, Temple University Libraries, Philadelphia.

14. Tilden File, Special Collections Research Center, Temple University Libraries, Philadelphia.

15. "W. T. Tilden, Ex-President of the Union League, Dies," *Philadelphia Inquirer*, July 30, 1915.

16. "WM. T. Tilden Buried," newspaper article from Tilden File at Temple University Library, Special Collections, Philadelphia.
17. Such observations were a clear indication that by 1915, young Bill had become the dominant tennis player in the family. In earlier years Herbert was the star player, and there was little to no mention of his younger brother. By the time of his father's death, however, the tables had turned.
18. *Campbell's* 79 (July 1915).
19. "Dewhurst Regains Pennsylvania Title," *American Lawn Tennis* 2, no. 4 (1908): 121.
20. "Pennsylvania State Championships," *American Lawn Tennis* (July 1, 1910): 118.
21. "R. N. Williams Is Pennsylvania Champion," *American Lawn Tennis* (June 15, 1912): 78.
22. "Miss Brown Wins Three Championships," *American Lawn Tennis* (July 1, 1913): 121.
23. *American Lawn Tennis* 7, no. 2 (1913): 42.
24. Tilden, *Me: The Handicap*, 34.
25. Interview with Richard Hillway.
26. Tilden, *My Story*, 20.
27. *American Lawn Tennis* (July 1, 1913): 120.
28. Voss, *Tilden and Tennis*, 4.
29. "Team Matches at Philadelphia," *American Lawn Tennis* 9, no. 2 (1915).
30. Tilden, *My Story*, 20, 21.
31. "Pennsylvania Title," *American Lawn Tennis* (May 15, 1915).
32. "Death of Herbert M. Tilden," *American Lawn Tennis* (January 15, 1916): 519.
33. Letters of administration obtained from Orphan's Court, City Hall, Philadelphia.
34. There appears to be no evidence that Tilden ever bothered to officially change his name with either city or state agencies. Apparently, such name changes were rare at the time, especially so for the type of modest change as in this case, from Jr. to 2nd.
35. Tilden, *My Story*, 18.
36. Regrettably, there are few, if any, ways to check on this century-old event. There is only one slim academic document in William T. Tilden Jr.'s name, and that is frustratingly difficult to decipher. It is clear, however, despite comments to the contrary, Tilden never graduated from the University of Pennsylvania. The real issue is whether he withdrew early in 1915, as his Wharton record indicates, or late in the year after the passing of his older brother.
37. Because of his subsequent fame, Tilden would become known as the "Pierce Boy of 1915" in some school publications. Although unusual that a Penn

(Wharton) student would take business courses at a less renowned two-year institution, it has been known to happen. Tilden's association with the school may have also been based on another of his father's many business connections. According to Bart H. Evarts, Pierce's reference librarian, William T. Tilden presented the dedication speech of the Thomas May Pierce Elementary School in 1910.

38. Tilden, *My Story*, 19.
39. Tilden, *My Story*, 32.
40. Hillway, "Tilden according to His First Protégé," 12.
41. Tilden, *Me: The Handicap*, 27; interview with Hillway.
42. Hillway, "Tilden according to His First Protégé," 13.
43. Hillway, "Tilden according to His First Protégé," 14.
44. Baltzell, *Sporting Gentlemen*, 172.

3. "ALWAYS KEEP MENTALLY ALERT"

1. "Indoor Meeting for Philadelphia," *American Lawn Tennis* (March 15, 1916): 586.
2. *American Lawn Tennis* (July 15, 1916): 206.
3. Tilden, *Me: The Handicap*, 35.
4. Hillway, "Tilden according to His First Protégé," 12.
5. *American Lawn Tennis* (March 15, 1917): 598.
6. *American Lawn Tennis* (May 15, 1918): 37.
7. *American Lawn Tennis* (April 15, 1918): 9.
8. Collins, *Tennis Encyclopedia*, 116.
9. Richard Hillway provided a list of the deceased players as well as *American Lawn Tennis* (May 15, 1918): 9. Hillway did one of the better retrospectives on Robert B. Powell that can be found in the *Tennis Collector* (Spring 2012): 16.
10. Tilden, *Art of Lawn Tennis*, 4.
11. Tilden, *My Story*, 21. Tilden would argue in his book that "almost all tennis players have first degree flat feet," from the "pounding the feet take in sneakers" on hard surfaces.
12. Tilden, *Me: The Handicap*, 41.
13. Tilden, *My Story*, 22.
14. Tilden, *Me: The Handicap*, 42.
15. Voss, *Tilden and Tennis*, 6.
16. Voss, *Tilden and Tennis*, 43.
17. Annual Report of the Germantown Cricket Club, 1918, 14.

18. *American Lawn Tennis* (May 15, 1918): 35. Prewar prices for tennis clothing were, approximately, sneakers, $1.50; trousers, $3.50; socks, $0.50; three shirts, $3.00.

19. *American Lawn Tennis* (April 15, 1918): 4.

20. *American Lawn Tennis* (May 15, 1918): 37.

21. *American Lawn Tennis* (June 15, 1918): 71.

22. *American Lawn Tennis* (June 15, 1918): 74.

23. *American Lawn Tennis* (July 1, 1918): 115.

24. *American Lawn Tennis* (July 15, 1918): 127.

25. Tilden, *My Story*, 23.

26. *American Lawn Tennis* (September 1, 1918): 25.

27. Collins, *Tennis Encyclopedia*, 484.

28. *American Lawn Tennis* (September 15, 1918): 246.

29. *American Lawn Tennis* (January 15, 1919): 353.

30. *American Lawn Tennis* (January 15, 1919): 354.

31. Tilden, *My Story*, 25.

32. *American Lawn Tennis* (January 15, 1919): 359.

33. William T. Tilden, "Variety Is Essential for Tennis," *American Lawn Tennis* (March 15, 1919): 408.

34. Tilden, "Variety Is Essential for Tennis," 408.

35. Tilden, "Variety Is Essential for Tennis," 408.

36. Interview with Hillway.

37. "Opinions of Tilden's Article Differ," *American Lawn Tennis* (May 15, 1919): 50.

38. "Fischer Wins in Junior Tennis," *Philadelphia Evening Public Ledger*, February 16, 1919; "Wants Junior Ranking," *Philadelphia Evening Public Ledger*, February 7, 1919.

39. "No Admission Fee to Tennis Tourney," *Philadelphia Evening Public Ledger*, February 11, 1919.

40. "Philadelphia Has a Roof Meeting," *American Lawn Tennis* (February 15, 1919): 391; "Stars Battle on a Roof Court," *American Lawn Tennis* (March 15, 1919): 410.

41. Voss, *Tilden and Tennis*, 7.

42. "Vincent Richards Is Suspended," *American Lawn Tennis* (May 15, 1919): 43.

43. Voss, *Tilden and Tennis*, 7.

44. There were a small but growing number of players like Tilden—who was in magazine advertisements for a tennis racket manufacturer and might have worked at Mitchell & Ness Sporting Goods Company—who were participating in the perks derived from their athletic fame. The commercial possi-

bilities would only increase during the 1920s, a prospect that only further frustrated leaders of the USLTA.

45. Tilden, *My Story*, 30.
46. Collins, *Tennis Encyclopedia*, 102.
47. Tilden, *My Story*, 29.
48. Tilden, *Me: The Handicap*, 37.
49. Robert T. Paul, "Tilden Victim of Gotham Yarn," *Philadelphia Evening Public Ledger*, March 24, 1919, 18.
50. Voss, *Tilden and Tennis*, 9.
51. Tilden, *My Story*, 34.
52. Voss, *Tilden and Tennis*, 10.
53. Laney, *Covering the Court*, 41.
55. Voss, *Tilden and Tennis*, 12; Laney, *Covering the Court*, 73.
55. "Championships Outstanding Matches," *American Lawn Tennis* (August 30, 1919): 350.
56. "Championships Outstanding Matches," 352.
57. Laney, *Covering the Court*, 43.
58. *American Lawn Tennis* (August 30, 1919): 323.
59. Voss, *Tilden and Tennis*, 12.

4. "A YEAR OF LIVING TRIUMPHANTLY"

1. Tilden, *Match Play*.
2. According to Arthur Voss, Tilden actually sold an Equitable Life Assurance Policy to the great Irish tenor John McCormack. Voss, *Tilden and Tennis*, 13.
3. Tilden, *Match Play*, 115–19.
4. Tilden, *Match Play*, 114.
5. Stump, "Big Bill Tilden," 61.
6. Voss, *Tilden and Tennis*, 13.
7. Baltzell, *Sporting Gentlemen*, 175.
8. "Brookes Praises American Players," *New York Times*, January 1, 1920.
9. "Harte Defeats Tilden," *New York Times*, February 22, 1920.
10. "Tilden Is Twice Victor in Tennis," *New York Times*, February 16, 1920.
11. Many have speculated on the reasons for America's less than impressive showing during the first four decades of Wimbledon competition. Rich Hillway believes there are three main reasons for the poor record: First, the best American players didn't always make the long and expensive journey overseas. Second, there were different conditions—the courts, balls, and climate

were all different. Finally, English players were noted for their all-around ability, whereas Americans tended to be net rushers, a style that didn't fare well in international competition.

12. *American Lawn Tennis* (June 15, 1920): 127.
13. Tilden, *My Story*, 262.
14. *American Lawn Tennis* (July 1, 1920): 163.
15. Potter, *Kings of the Court*, 137.
16. Tilden, *My Story*, 54.
17. *Philadelphia Public Ledger*, July 3, 1920, 14.
18. *Philadelphia Public Ledger*, July 3, 1920, 14.
19. "Tilden's Injury Causes Anxiety," *American Lawn Tennis* (July 1, 1920): 205.
20. Voss, *Tilden and Tennis*, 20.
21. Olliff, *The Romance of Wimbledon*, 50.
22. "American Wins English Championship," *American Lawn Tennis* (July 1, 1920): 163.
23. Stump, "Big Bill Tilden," 62.
24. "Some Extracts from English Papers," *American Lawn Tennis* (August 1, 1920): 271.
25. "Editorial Department," *American Lawn Tennis* (July 1, 1920): 174.
26. "Tilden Is World Tennis Champion," *Philadelphia Public Ledger*, July 4, 1920, 1.
27. "Editorial Department," *American Lawn Tennis* (August 1, 1920): 271.
28. William H. Rocap, "Tennis Solons Are Skating on Thin Ice," *Philadelphia Public Ledger*, July 5, 1920.
29. Rocap, "Tennis Solons Are Skating on Thin Ice."
30. F. J. Bancroft Co. advertisement, *American Lawn Tennis* (July 15, 1920): 238–39.
31. Tilden, *Art of Lawn Tennis*, vii.
32. Tilden, *Art of Lawn Tennis*, 69.
33. Tilden, *Art of Lawn Tennis*, 143.
34. Voss, *Tilden and Tennis*, 22.
35. "Garland's Defeat at Tennis by Washburn Surprising," *Philadelphia Public Ledger*, August 11, 1920.
36. "Will Tilden Upset Tennis Tradition?," *Philadelphia Public Ledger*, August 28, 1920.
37. "Comment on Current Events in Sports-Tennis," *New York Times*, July 8, 1920.
38. Laney, *Covering the Court*, 42.
39. Voss, *Tilden and Tennis*, 26.
40. "Brilliant Court Play Seen at Forest Hills," *Philadelphia Public Ledger*, August 31, 1920.

41. "Williams Eliminated in Big Tennis Match," *Philadelphia Public Ledger*, September 3, 1920.

42. "10,000 See Plane Kill Two in Crash at Tennis Tourney," *New York Times*, September 7, 1920, 1.

43. "10,000 See Plane Kill Two."

44. "10,000 See Plane Kill Two."

45. "10,000 See Plane Kill Two."

46. Tilden, *My Story*, 36.

47. Voss, *Tilden and Tennis*, 27.

48. Tilden, *My Story*, 38.

49. Tilden would write of that moment in *Me: The Handicap*: "When the end of the match came, after nearly three hours of the most nerve-wracking effort in either of our lives, Johnston collapsed on a chair and became physically ill, while I actually staggered into the club-house too tired to even attempt to get out of my clothes. Such a match is not fun. It is torture. It is a terrible thing to play, a disaster to lose and no great joy to win, yet of such matches are champions born" (151).

50. "William T. Tilden, 2nd Is Champion," *American Lawn Tennis* (September 1, 1920): 363.

51. "Tilden Beats Johnston for Tennis Crown," *Philadelphia Public Ledger*, September 7, 1920.

52. Tilden, *Match Play*, 119.

53. "Tilden Beats Johnston for Tennis Crown."

54. Finance Committee Report of the Germantown Cricket Club, March 5, 1920.

55. "Tilden Beats Johnston in Brilliant Battle," *Philadelphia Public Ledger*, September 12, 1920.

56. "Tilden Beats Johnston in Brilliant Battle."

57. "W. J. Clothier, Then and Now," *American Lawn Tennis* (October 15, 1920): 482.

58. "W. J. Clothier, Then and Now," 476–77.

59. Minutes of the Tennis Committee of the Germantown Cricket Club, October 4, 1920.

60. "Internationalists at San Francisco," *American Lawn Tennis* (November 15, 1920): 500.

61. "Our Davis Cup Men Stop at Honolulu," *American Lawn Tennis* (December 15, 1920): 541.

62. According to Collins, *Bud Collins Tennis Encyclopedia*, Shreve, Crump, and Low, a Boston jewelry firm, commissioned the trophy. It was designed by Rowland Rhodes and crafted by William Morton and Warren Peckman at the William B. Durgin Company in Concord, New Hampshire. The silver

bowl's creation cost one thousand dollars. It is estimated that it would cost at least a couple thousand dollars today.

63. Tilden, *My Story*, 52.
64. "Tennis Lovers Hail Return of Davis Cup," *New York Times*, January 1, 1921; Major R. M. Kidston, "U.S. Rightful Owner of the Davis Cup," *Philadelphia Inquirer*, January 2, 1921.
65. "United States Wins the Davis Cup," *American Lawn Tennis* (January 15, 1921): 571.
66. "Editorial: The Win of the Davis Cup," *American Lawn Tennis* (January 15, 1921): 576.
67. "United States Wins the Davis Cup," 571.

5. "YOU HIT TOO HARD"

1. "Tilden Heads Tennis Rankings," *New York Times*, January 2, 1921.
2. "Bill Tilden Heads 1920 Ranking List," *New York Times*, January 2, 1921.
3. "World's Best Players," *American Lawn Tennis* (February 15, 1921): 634. The other Americans to make the top-ten list were Johnston at number three, Williams at number five, and Murray at number nine.
4. William T. Tilden, "Open Tennis Championship for Boys Urged by Tilden," *Philadelphia Evening Bulletin*, January 1, 1921.
5. Tilden, "Open Tennis Championship for Boys."
6. "U.S. Tennis Players Arriving after Victorious Trip to Australia," *Philadelphia Inquirer*, February 21, 1921.
7. "Tilden Says Cup Is Here to Stay," *Philadelphia Inquirer*, January 17, 1921; "Tilden and Johnston in San Francisco," *American Lawn Tennis* (February 15, 1921): 607.
8. "Bill Tilden Home, Received by Mayor," *Philadelphia Inquirer*, February 22, 1921.
9. "Bill Tilden Home, Received by Mayor."
10. "Bill Tilden Home, Received by Mayor."
11. "Bill Tilden Home, Received by Mayor."
12. Notes of the Germantown Cricket Club Tennis Committee Meeting, March 25, 1921, 288.
13. Notes of the Germantown Cricket Club Tennis Committee Meeting, May 16, 1921, 113.
14. "Bill Tilden Home, Received by Mayor."
15. "Bill Tilden Home, Received by Mayor."
16. Alex H. Frey, "Champion Tilden's Book," *American Lawn Tennis* (April 15, 1921): 34.

17. "Editorial," *American Lawn Tennis* (March 15, 1921): 660.

18. Tilden, *My Story*, 65.

19. Tilden, *My Story*, 65.

20. Voss, *Tilden and Tennis*, 36.

21. Tilden, *My Story*, 66.

22. Tilden, *My Story*, 66.

23. Voss, *Tilden and Tennis*, 36, 37.

24. Tilden, *My Story*, 66.

25. Interview with Hillway.

26. Laney, *Covering the Court*, 36.

27. Tilden, *My Story*, 67.

28. Tilden, *My Story*, 67.

29. "Hard Court Title Taken by Tilden," *New York Times*, June 5, 1921.

30. "Hard Court Title Taken by Tilden."

31. In fact, Tilden still had a doubles match to play with his sixteen-year-old partner, Arnold W. Jones. In a long five-set match against the French team of André Gobert and William Laurentz, who was also ill, the Americans lost just as Laurentz collapsed on the court and could not be revived until hours later. Tilden avoided a similar fate, but was in bad shape.

32. "Tilden Enters Hospital for Rest; Condition Not Serious," *New York Times*, June 6, 1921.

33. William T. Tilden, "New Tennis Star Is Rising in Manuel Alonso of Spain," *Philadelphia Evening Bulletin*, July 2, 1921.

34. Herbert L. Bourke, "Tilden Rallies, Retains Net Title in 5-Set Battle," *Philadelphia Inquirer*, August 2, 1921.

35. "Story of 1921 English Championships," *American Lawn Tennis* (July 15, 1921): 204.

36. "Challenge Round against Babe Norton," *American Lawn Tennis* (July 15, 1921): 206.

37. Olliff, *The Romance of Wimbledon*, 54.

38. Olliff, *The Romance of Wimbledon*, 54.

39. Olliff, *The Romance of Wimbledon*, 54.

40. Tilden, *My Story*, 69.

41. Bourke, "Tilden Rallies."

42. Tilden, *My Story*, 69.

43. "Tilden Retains His Tennis Title," *New York Times*, July 3, 1921.

44. Tilden, *My Story*, 70.

45. Bourke, "Tilden Rallies."

46. "Tennis," *New York Times*, July 4, 1921; Perry Lewis, "Hard Task Ahead for U.S. Athletes," *Philadelphia Inquirer*, July 6, 1921.

47. S. Wallis Merrihew, "Editorial," *American Lawn Tennis* (July 15, 1921): 240.

48. Potter, *Kings of the Court*, 142.

49. Tinling, *Tinling*, 68.

50. "Tilden Apologizes for His Poor Showing," *Philadelphia Inquirer*, July 7, 1921.

51. William T. Tilden 2nd, "Pick Williams and Washburn to Beat Japan in Doubles," *Philadelphia Evening Bulletin*, July 29, 1921.

52. William T. Tilden 2nd, "Pick Williams and Washburn to Beat Japan in Doubles," *Philadelphia Evening Bulletin*, August 29, 1921; "Tilden and Richards Win Doubles Title," *Philadelphia Inquirer*, August 28, 1921.

53. Tilden, *Art of Lawn Tennis*, 163.

54. William T. Tilden 2nd, "Washburn Earned Place on U.S. Davis Cup Team," *Philadelphia Evening Bulletin*, August 28, 1921.

55. Perry Lewis, "American Net Stars Defeat Jap Opponents in Opening Matches for Davis Cup," *Philadelphia Inquirer*, September 3, 1921.

56. Lewis, "American Net Stars."

57. Lewis, "American Net Stars."

58. Tilden, *My Story*, 61.

59. Tilden, *My Story*, 61.

60. Laney, *Covering the Court*, 60.

61. Laney, *Covering the Court*, 61.

62. William H. Rocap, "Opposes Blind Draw in National Tennis," *Philadelphia Public Ledger*, September 11, 1921.

63. Rocap, "Opposes Blind Draw in National Tennis."

64. Public and player outcry would be so great by this situation that the USLTA would be forced to adopt a seeding system the following year.

65. Perry Lewis, "Cannonball Service Draws Heavily upon Reserve Powers of Man Who Uses It," *Philadelphia Inquirer*, September 9, 1921.

66. "Kelleher Jolted Johnston," *Philadelphia Inquirer*, September 12, 1921.

67. William T. Tilden 2nd, "Johnston Could Not Hold Swift Pace, Says Tilden," *Philadelphia Evening Bulletin*, September 15, 1921.

68. "Tilden Is Champion for a Second Time," *American Lawn Tennis* (September 15, 1921): 399.

69. "Johnston Conquered by Tilden's Brilliant Play," *Philadelphia Public Ledger*, September 15, 1921.

70. Tilden, "Johnston Could Not Hold Swift Pace."

71. Perry Lewis, "Tilden Wins from Johnston; Norris Williams Beaten," *Philadelphia Inquirer*, September 15, 1921.

72. Editorial, *American Lawn Tennis* (September 15, 1921): 414.

6. "NO ORDINARY MAN"

1. "International Ranking by A. W. Myers," *American Lawn Tennis* (November 15, 1921): 467.

2. Cullen Cain, "Tilden's Radiant Type Best Seen in Matches," *Philadelphia Public Ledger*, September 21, 1921.

3. Cain, "Tilden's Radiant Type."

4. *American Lawn Tennis* (November 15, 1921): 467.

5. Laney, *Covering the Court*, 59.

6. Laney, *Covering the Court*, 70.

7. Laney, *Covering the Court*, 71.

8. "Tilden Victor at Squash Racquets," *Philadelphia Inquirer*, January 12, 1922.

9. *Philadelphia Inquirer*, January 14, 1922.

10. It is unlikely that Tilden actually coached the Penn team for any length of time. He probably provided some periodic advice and counsel to players, but most of the real day-in, day-out coaching was done by Wallace Johnson, who was the Penn tennis coach for many decades.

11. *Ye Primer* (Germantown Academy Annual Yearbook), 1922.

12. *Ye Primer* (Germantown Academy Annual Yearbook), 1922.

13. Wiener, "What I Learned from the Champion," 359.

14. Wiener, "What I Learned from the Champion," 359.

15. Wiener, "What I Learned from the Champion," 359.

16. Tilden, *My Story*, 49.

17. Olliff, *The Romance of Wimbledon*, 56.

18. Olliff, *The Romance of Wimbledon*, 57.

19. Tilden, *It's All in the Game*, vii.

20. Tilden, *It's All in the Game*, 14.

21. Tilden, *It's All in the Game*, 15.

22. Review of *It's All in the Game*, *American Lawn Tennis* (March 15, 1922): 665.

23. Voss, *Tilden and Tennis*, 47.

24. Voss, *Tilden and Tennis*, 48.

25. "Tilden to Play Only in American Matches," *Philadelphia Inquirer*, February 22, 1922.

26. "USLTA Will Not Send Tilden," *American Lawn Tennis* (April 15, 1922): 39.

27. Voss, *Tilden and Tennis*, 48.

28. *Philadelphia Inquirer*, February 22, 1922.

29. "Tilden Wins Eastern Pennsylvania Title," *American Lawn Tennis* (July 1, 1922): 166.

30. Perry Lewis, "U.S. Retains Davis Cup When Johnston Defeats Patterson," *Philadelphia Inquirer*, September 9, 1922.

31. Perry Lewis, "Net King Captures Title after Losing Two Sets to Rival," *Philadelphia Inquirer*, September 17, 1922.

32. Tilden, *My Story*, 40.

33. Tilden, *My Story*, 41.

34. Baltzell, *Sporting Gentlemen*, 182.

35. "The Battle of the Tennis Titans," *American Lawn Tennis* (September 15, 1922): 420.

36. "Tilden Retains the Championship," *American Lawn Tennis* (September 16, 1922): 399.

37. Lewis, "Net King Captures Title."

38. Lewis, "Net King Captures Title."

39. Lewis, "Net King Captures Title."

40. Perry Lewis, "Manheim Musings," *Philadelphia Inquirer*, September 18, 1922.

41. "Tilden Takes Them, Four at a Time," *Philadelphia Inquirer*, September 18, 1922.

7. "THE BOSS OF ALL TENNIS PLAYERS"

1. "Tilden and Mathey Win Princeton Exhibition," *Philadelphia Public Ledger*, October 12, 1922.

2. Tilden, *Me: The Handicap*, 96.

3. Most newspaper accounts cite a cut and blood being drawn such as "Tilden Is Expected to Suffer No Harm," *Philadelphia Inquirer*, October 27, 1922, while Tilden's own account years later mentions no abrasion (*Me: The Handicap*, 97).

4. "Champion Tilden May Lose His Finger," *American Lawn Tennis* (October 15, 1922): 443.

5. A newspaper article from October 28, 1923, entitled "Lance Tilden's Infected Finger," cites Dr. H. B. Andrus as the physician who informed Tilden his finger was "seriously infected" and that he should see a surgeon. The photocopy does not provide the name of the newspaper.

6. Tilden, *Me: The Handicap*, 97.

7. "Champion Tilden May Lose His Finger."

8. "Tilden Is Expected to Suffer No Harm."

9. "Champion Tilden May Lose His Finger."

10. "Lance Tilden's Infected Finger."

11. "Champion Tilden May Lose His Finger."

12. "Tilden Will Lose Joint of Finger," *Philadelphia Inquirer*, November 6, 1922.

13. "Another Bit of Tilden's Finger Off," *American Lawn Tennis* (December 15, 1922): 530.

14. *Philadelphia Inquirer*, November 6, 1922.

15. "Big Bill Forecasts Loss of Net Title but Will Carry On," *Philadelphia Inquirer*, November 14, 1922.

16. Voss, *Tilden and Tennis*, 58.

17. "Big Bill Forecasts Loss of Net Title."

18. "Big Bill Forecasts Loss of Net Title."

19. Tilden, *Me: The Handicap*, 99.

20. "Tilden Encouraged at First Workout," *Philadelphia Inquirer*, December 30, 1922.

21. "Tilden Encouraged at First Workout."

22. "Tilden Encouraged at First Workout."

23. Tilden, *Match Play*, 121.

24. "Chicago Holds a Mid-winter Indoor Meeting," *American Lawn Tennis* (January 15, 1923).

25. "Tilden Shows Form by Downing Hunter," *Philadelphia Inquirer*, January 6, 1923.

26. "Tilden Shows Form in Tennis Match," *New York Times*, January 6, 1923.

27. "Tilden Again Heads U.S. Tennis Rankings," *Philadelphia Inquirer*, January 8, 1923.

28. "Big Bill to Play—Not on Tennis Court," *Philadelphia Inquirer*, January 12, 1923.

29. Belfry Club handbill for the performance of *Dulcy*, Bellevue-Stratford Hotel, January 12, 1923.

30. Interview with Hillway.

31. Perry Lewis, "Champion Tilden an Uphill Fighter, Is Hard to Count Out," *Philadelphia Inquirer*, January 30, 1923.

32. Robert Edgren, "Tilden's Injury May Make Him Better than Ever, Says Edgren," *Philadelphia Evening Bulletin*, April 26, 1923.

33. Lewis, "Champion Tilden an Uphill Fighter."

34. "Dean Mathey Beats Champion Tilden," *American Lawn Tennis* (February 15, 1923): 622.

35. "Tilden Wins Buffalo Indoor Meeting," *American Lawn Tennis* (April 15, 1923): 17.

36. "Champion Plays in Central Park," *American Lawn Tennis* (May 15, 1923): 53.

37. "Champion Plays in Central Park," 57.

38. Partial news article of the Germantown Academy event from an unknown Philadelphia newspaper.
39. "Champion Plays in Central Park," 57.
40. "Champion Plays in Central Park," 59.
41. "Champion Plays in Central Park," 74.
42. "Tilden Gets Back at Manuel Alonso," *Philadelphia Inquirer*, July 16, 1923.
43. "Three Books for Tennis Lovers," *American Lawn Tennis* (July 1, 1923): 180.
44. Tilden's "Passing Shots" columns during the summer of 1923 appeared in *American Lawn Tennis* on July 1 and August 15, 1923.
45. "W. T. Tilden in Press Agent Thriller," 1923.
46. William T. Tilden 2nd, "Tilden's Passing Shots," *American Lawn Tennis* (September 1, 1923): 395.
47. "Tennis," *New York Times*, September 3, 1923.
48. "Davis Cup Singles to End Play Today," *New York Times*, September 3, 1923.
49. Though a serious challenger and top-ten player, James O. Anderson, the Australian captain, was so exhausted from playing two singles and a doubles match in Davis Cup competition that he withdrew from the forthcoming National Singles Tournament in Philadelphia.
50. "Champion Crushes Johnston in Three Straight Sets," *Philadelphia Inquirer*, September 16, 1923.
51. "Tilden Again Wins U.S. Tennis Crown," *New York Times*, September 16, 1923.
52. "Tilden Again Wins U.S. Tennis Crown."
53. "Champion Crushes Johnston in Three Straight Sets."
54. "Tennis," *New York Times*, September 17, 1923.
55. "Champion Tilden Defeats Four Men in Straight Sets," *Philadelphia Inquirer*, September 17, 1923.
56. "Tilden Wins His Fourth Championship," *American Lawn Tennis* (September 15, 1923): 427.
57. "Extracts from 'America Re-visited,'" *American Lawn Tennis* (October 15, 1923): 484.
58. William T. Tilden 2nd, "Tilden's Passing Shots," *American Lawn Tennis* (September 15, 1923): 445.
59. Voss, *Tilden and Tennis*, 61.

8. "EVIL INFLUENCE"

1. "United States Ranking for 1923," *American Lawn Tennis* (January 15, 1924): 626.
2. "Player-Writers Hit by Tennis Officials," *New York Times*, January 4, 1924.
3. "Player-Writers Hit by Tennis Officials."

4. Baltzell, *Sporting Gentlemen*, 112.
5. "Tilden Opposes Rule on Writing," *New York Times*, January 5, 1924.
6. "Wightman to Head U. S. Tennis Body," *New York Times*, January 6, 1924.
7. "U.S. Olympic Committee Athletes May Be Barred from Writing Articles on 1924 Games," *New York Times*, January 6, 1924.
8. Stadium expansion during this period, for example, witnessed fantastic growth. In 1920 the University of Washington built a 46,000-seat stadium, in 1921 Stanford built an 86,000-seat stadium, in 1922 Ohio State built an 85,000-seat stadium, and in 1923 the University of Nebraska built a 74,000-seat stadium. But football was not the only sport to witness phenomenal fan interest. In New York City alone 1923 saw the New York Yankees open a 67,000-seat stadium and the West Side Tennis Club construct a 14,000-seat for major tennis events.
9. Tilden, *Me: The Handicap*, 141.
10. Baltzell, *Sporting Gentlemen*, 210.
11. Potter, *Kings of the Court*, 148.
12. W. O. M'Geehan, "Big Boys Writing Dates Back Ages," *Philadelphia Inquirer*, January 6, 1924.
13. Perry Lewis, "Tennis Solons May Push Bill Too Far," *Philadelphia Inquirer*, January 7, 1924.
14. "New Tennis Rule Will Lift Ban on Player-Writers," *Philadelphia Public Ledger*, December 14, 1924.
15. Interview with Hillway.
16. "Tennis Will Suffer Most, Says Fischer," *Philadelphia Inquirer*, January 4, 1924.
17. Lewis, "Tennis Solons May Push Bill Too Far."
18. William T. Tilden 2nd, "Tilden's Passing Shots," *American Lawn Tennis* (February 15, 1924): 673.
19. Tilden 2nd, "Tilden's Passing Shots."
20. "Coast Tennis Body Endorses Rule against Player-Writers," *New York Times*, January 16, 1924.
21. "Philadelphia Tennis Body Opposes Player-Writer Rule," *New York Times*, January 23, 1924.
22. "Editorial: A World Astonished," *American Lawn Tennis* (March 15, 1924): 740.
23. "Editorial: It Could Have Been Avoided," *American Lawn Tennis* (April 15, 1924): 22.
24. "Tilden Bars Self from Olympic Team," *Philadelphia Inquirer*, March 12, 1924.
25. "Net Solons Declare Tilden Risks Status," *Philadelphia Inquirer*, March 15, 1924.
26. "Tennis," *New York Times*, March 17, 1924.
27. Tilden, *Match Play*, 25.

28. Tilden, *Match Play*, 1.
29. "Tilden Arraigned as a Bad Example," *New York Times*, April 20, 1924.
30. "Tilden Arraigned as a Bad Example."
31. Perry Lewis, "Player-Writer Rule Focused on Tilden," *Philadelphia Inquirer*, April 20, 1924.
32. "Tilden Quits Place on U.S. Tennis Teams," *New York Times*, April 22, 1924.
33. "Tilden Quits Place on U.S. Tennis Teams."
34. Perry Lewis, "Tilden Outwitted U.S. Solons," *Philadelphia Inquirer*, April 23, 1924.
35. Lewis, "Tilden Outwitted U.S. Solons."
36. "British Net World Sides with Tilden," *Philadelphia Inquirer*, April 24, 1924.
37. "Tilden Refuses to Meet Officials," *New York Times*, April 24, 1924.
38. "Tilden Refuses to Meet Officials."
39. "Tilden Quits Place on U.S. Tennis Team."
40. "Tilden Refuses to Meet Officials."
41. "Tilden Is Officially Off Davis Cup Team," *Philadelphia Inquirer*, April 27, 1924.
42. "Pro Tennis Events," *New York Times*, April 29, 1924.
43. "Briarcliff Lodge Asks Tilden to Go There If He Turns Pro," *New York Times*, April 30, 1924.
44. "Tilden Opposes Pro Tennis; Amateur until Forced Out," *New York Times*, May 1, 1924.
45. Perry Lewis, "Enforcement of Player-Writer Rule May Spark Pro Tennis," *Philadelphia Inquirer*, April 29, 1924.
46. Lewis, "Enforcement of Player-Writer Rule."
47. "Tennis Solons Put on Defensive as Richards Also Quits," *Philadelphia Inquirer*, April 30, 1924.
48. "Club Will Discuss Player-Writer Rule," *New York Times*, April 29, 1924.
49. "Tilden Is Highly Elated," *New York Times*, April 30, 1924.
50. "Tennis Body to Act on Richards Case," *New York Times*, May 1, 1924.
51. "Tennis Body to Act on Richards Case."
52. "Tilden Supported by Philadelphians," "Opposition Formed to Tennis Ruling," and "Garland Opposes Tilden," *New York Times*, May 6, 1924.
53. Lawrence Perry, "Perry Sees Flaw in Tennis Letter," *Philadelphia Bulletin*, June 6, 1924.
54. "Special Meeting of West Side Tennis Club," *American Lawn Tennis* (May 15, 1924): 69.
55. Voss, *Tilden and Tennis*, 66.
56. "USLTA Meeting Asked by Wightman," *New York Times*, May 30, 1924.

57. "Tennis Stars Want Meeting Deferred," *New York Times*, June 1, 1924.

58. Tilden, *Me: The Handicap*, 36.

59. "Tennis Body Decides Not to Call Meeting," *New York Times*, June 5, 1924.

60. *Philadelphia Bulletin*, June 13, 1924.

61. "USLTA Names Four on Rules Committee," *New York Times*, June 13, 1924.

62. S. Wallis Merrihew, "Player-Writer Controversy Ends with Suddenness," *American Lawn Tennis* (June 15, 1924): 123.

63. "Compromise Made Announces Tilden," *New York Times*, June 6, 1924.

64. Voss, *Tilden and Tennis*, 68.

65. "Tilden May Quit Tennis," *New York Times*, August 28, 1924.

66. William T. Tilden 2d, "Match for Title Should Be Close Fight, Says Tilden," *Philadelphia Public Ledger*, September 2, 1924.

67. Potter, *Kings of the Court*, 146.

68. Tilden, "Match for Title Should Be Close Fight."

69. Carl Fischer, "Tilden's Defeat of Johnston Due to Champion's Superiority," *Philadelphia Public Ledger*, September 7, 1924.

70. "Tennis for 5th Year Is Tennis Champion," *New York Times*, September 3, 1924.

71. "Forty-Third Singles Championship of the United States," *American Lawn Tennis* (September 15, 1924): 483.

72. "Tilden Takes 5th Title in Row," *Philadelphia Public Ledger*, September 3, 1924.

73. Laney, *Covering the Court*, 72.

74. "Tilden Takes 5th Title in Row."

75. Fischer, "Tilden's Defeat of Johnston."

76. Fischer, "Tilden's Defeat of Johnston."

77. William T. Tilden 2d, "Tilden Tells How He Retained Title Beating Johnston," *Philadelphia Public Ledger*, September 3, 1924.

78. "Tilden to Retire after Defending Davis Cup," *Philadelphia Public Ledger*, September 3, 1924.

79. S. Wallis Merrihew, "On the Roof of the World," *American Lawn Tennis* (September 15, 1924): 508.

9. "THE GREATEST WIZARD"

1. "All the World's a Stage," *American Lawn Tennis* (October 15, 1924): 580.

2. "Tilden to Become Actor," *New York Times*, September 9, 1924.

3. "The Movie Camera Writes," *American Lawn Tennis* (November 15, 1924): 597.

4. William T. Tilden 2d, "California—Here I Come," *American Lawn Tennis* (December 15, 1924): 635.

5. "Tennis Committee Will Report Today," *New York Times*, December 13, 1924.

6. "Tennis Committee Reports on Writers," *New York Times*, December 14, 1924.

7. "Executives Adopt New Rule Which Allows Stars to Write on Tennis," *Philadelphia Inquirer*, December 14, 1924.

8. It should be noted that the "player-writer" controversy was not solely a lawn tennis phenomenon. The Pacific Coast Intercollegiate Conference adopted a rule making ineligible for competition any football player who wrote an article concerning football for publication in any journal except his college paper. Hence, a football player could write about baseball or track providing he did not participate in them. Equally, the track or baseball man could write about football, but must not touch on his own sport. "Pacific Coast Conference Adopts Player-Writer Rule," *New York Times*, December 14, 1924.

9. S. Wallis Merrihew, "Editorial," *American Lawn Tennis* (June 15, 1924): 138.

10. "Tennis Committee Makes Its Report," *New York Times*, December 12, 1924.

11. Ed Pollack, "Suggested Changes in By-Laws Should End Tennis Dispute," *Philadelphia Public Ledger*, December 14, 1924.

12. "Tennis," *New York Times*, December 15, 1924.

13. "A Solution That Solves," *American Lawn Tennis* (December 15, 1924): 642.

14. William T. Tilden 2d, "Tilden's Passing Shots," *American Lawn Tennis* (December 15, 1924): 650.

15. "44th Annual Meeting of the USLTA," *American Lawn Tennis* (February 15, 1925): 773.

16. "44th Annual Meeting of the USLTA."

17. Tilden, "Tilden's Passing Shots," *American Lawn Tennis* (December 15, 1924): 650.

18. Stump, "Big Bill Tilden," 64.

19. Gallico, *Farewell to Sport*, 161.

20. William T. Tilden 2d, "Here and There," *American Lawn Tennis* (December 15, 1924): 651.

21. Tilden book publication list compiled by Richard Hillway.

22. William T. Tilden 2d, "The Game and the Court," *American Lawn Tennis* (February 15, 1925): 750.

23. Conlon, "Big Bill Tilden," 48.

24. "Tilden the Only First Rater in World, Patterson States," *New York Times*, October 29, 1924.

25. "Tilden Leads All, Brookes Declares," *New York Times*, October 9, 1924.

26. René Lacoste, "Players I Met," *American Lawn Tennis* (November 15, 1924): 592.

27. Potter, *Kings of the Court*, 161.

28. Potter, *Kings of the Court*, 161.

29. William T. Tilden 2d, "Tilden's Passing Shots," *American Lawn Tennis* (August 1, 1924): 330.

30. William T. Tilden 2d, "Tilden's Passing Shots," *American Lawn Tennis* (June 15, 1925): 134.

31. "Editorial," *American Lawn Tennis* (August 1, 1925): 307.

32. Tilden, "Tilden's Passing Shots," *American Lawn Tennis* (June 15, 1925): 134.

33. "Williams Extends Tilden for Title," *Philadelphia Inquirer*, May 23, 1925.

34. Olliff, *The Romance of Wimbledon*, 60.

35. Allison Danzig, "Borotra Extends Tilden to 5 Sets," *New York Times*, September 11, 1925.

36. Danzig, "Borotra Extends Tilden to 5 Sets."

37. "How the United States Held the Cup," *American Lawn Tennis* (September 15, 1925): 450.

38. Allison Danzig, "Tilden Confronts Crisis This Week," *New York Times*, September 14, 1925; "Tennis," *New York Times*, September 14, 1925.

39. "Williams Crushes Borotra on Court," *New York Times*, September 17, 1925.

40. Allison Danzig, "4 Americans Left in National Tennis," *New York Times*, September 18, 1925.

41. Allison Danzig, "Tilden Gains Final; Johnston Also Wins," *New York Times*, September 19, 1925.

42. Danzig, "Tilden Gains Final."

43. Allison Danzig, "Tilden Wins Title Sixth Year in Row," *New York Times*, September 20, 1925.

44. "Tennis," *New York Times*, September 21, 1925.

45. "Editorial: The End of the Drama," *American Lawn Tennis* (September 15, 1925): 458.

46. "Two First Ten Lists," *American Lawn Tennis* (December 15, 1925): 488.

47. "About Tilden," *American Lawn Tennis* (October 15, 1925): 503.

10. "THREE AGAINST ONE"

1. "Richards Beats Tilden," *American Lawn Tennis* (January 15, 1926): 628.

2. "Mersereau Quiets Tennis Stars' Fear," *New York Times*, December 21, 1925.

3. Voss, *Tilden and Tennis*, 134.

4. "Tilden Becomes Regular Actor," *Philadelphia Evening Bulletin*, January 5, 1926.

5. "Tilden, Tennis Star, Acts in *Don Q. Jr.*," *New York Times*, January 28, 1926.

6. Tilden, *Me: The Handicap*, 100.

7. Review of *The Kid Himself*, *Variety*, January 6, 1926; review of *The Kid Himself*, *Wilmington (DE) News*, January 12, 1926.

8. Voss, *Tilden and Tennis*, 135.

9. "United States Wins," *American Lawn Tennis* (March 15, 1926): 718.

10. "The Fate of the Davis Cup," *American Lawn Tennis* (March 15, 1926): 726.

11. "Richards Defeats Tilden in Final," *New York Times*, April 25, 1926.

12. "Tilden versus Borotra," *American Lawn Tennis* (March 15, 1926): 734.

13. "Tilden Speaks at Yale," *New York Times*, June 4, 1926.

14. Allison Danzig, "Tennis," *New York Times*, April 15, 1926.

15. Allison Danzig, "Decline of Tilden's Tennis Star Foreseen by Vincent Richards," *New York Times*, May 21, 1926.

16. "The Champion's Backhand Shots," *American Lawn Tennis* (August 15, 1926): 351.

17. Voss, *Tilden and Tennis*, 104.

18. Ross E. Kauffman, "Says Davis Cup Ace Will Play Lenglen," *Philadelphia Evening Bulletin*, August 27, 1926.

19. Voss, *Tilden and Tennis*, 105.

20. Suzanne Lenglen, "Lenglen Tells Why She Became Professional Lawn Tennis Player," *Philadelphia Evening Bulletin*, August 28, 1926.

21. Lenglen, "Lenglen Tells Why."

22. Lenglen, "Lenglen Tells Why."

23. Tilden, *Me: The Handicap*, 141.

24. Tilden, *Me: The Handicap*, 142.

25. Potter, *Kings of the Court*, 149.

26. Suzanne Lenglen, "Lenglen Likens Borotra to Tilden, Lacoste to Johnston in Cup Tennis," *Philadelphia Evening Bulletin*, September 9, 1926.

27. Lenglen, "Lenglen Likens Borotra to Tilden."

28. Potter, *Kings of the Court*, 154.

29. Lenglen, "Lenglen Likens Borotra to Tilden."

30. Potter, *Kings of the Court*, 156.

31. Lenglen, "Lenglen Likens Borotra to Tilden."

32. Potter, *Kings of the Court*, 162.

33. Laney, *Covering the Court*, 80.

34. "Lessons from Wimbledon," *American Lawn Tennis* (July 15, 1926): 255.

35. Tilden, *My Story*, 80.

36. According to Arthur Voss, *Tilden and Tennis*, Lacoste got his nickname in 1923 when a sportswriter covering the French Davis Cup team in Boston used the image of a crocodile in describing how difficult it was to defeat Lacoste. Moreover, Voss argued that a crocodile-skin bag Lacoste had seen in a shop window had enchanted Lacoste. His coach, it is said,

promised him the bag if he won his next match. Lacoste lost, but he was so taken by the newspaper article comparing him to the fearsome amphibian that he had a likeness of the animal embroidered on his athletic garb. Not long after, Chemise Lacoste became a worldwide fashion statement.

37. Tilden, *My Story*, 81.

38. Baltzell, *Sporting Gentlemen*, 187.

39. Lacoste, *Lacoste on Tennis*, 217.

40. Lacoste, *Lacoste on Tennis*, 221.

41. Interview with Hillway.

42. Side Line, "Pretty Good for Two Old Men Says Tilden of Davis Cup Wins," *Philadelphia Evening Bulletin*, September 10, 1926.

43. Side Line, "Pretty Good for Two Old Men."

44. Voss, *Tilden and Tennis*, 129.

45. Allison Danzig, "Tilden Is Beaten by Rene Lacoste," *New York Times*, September 12, 1926.

46. Danzig, "Tilden Is Beaten by Rene Lacoste."

47. Tilden, *My Story*, 82.

48. Hillway, "Tilden according to His First Protégé."

49. Tilden, *My Story*, 84.

50. Potter, *Kings of the Court*, 166.

51. Danzig, "Tilden Is Beaten by Rene Lacoste"; "Lacoste on Tilden," *American Lawn Tennis* (October 15, 1926): 509.

52. "In the Hour of Defeat," *American Lawn Tennis* (September 15, 1926): 473.

53. Hillway, "Tilden according to His First Protégé."

54. Laney, *Covering the Court*, 130; "Tilden Still Limps as Tourney Opens," *Philadelphia Evening Bulletin*, September 13, 1926.

55. "Bill Tilden Coasts to Opening Victory," *Philadelphia Evening Bulletin*, September 14, 1926.

56. "Bill Tilden Coasts to Opening Victory."

57. Allison Danzig, "Tilden Pressed as Title Play Opens," *New York Times*, September 14, 1926.

58. Side Line, "Tilden Ready to Shoot the Works," *Philadelphia Evening Bulletin*, September 16, 1926.

59. Allison Danzig, "Tilden Vanquished; His Six-Year Reign in U.S. Tennis Ends," *New York Times*, September 17, 1926.

60. "Tilden Long Rated as Greatest Player," *New York Times*, September 17, 1926.

61. "Editorial," *American Lawn Tennis* (October 15, 1926): 525.

62. Hillway, "Tilden according to His First Protégé."
63. Side Line, "Defeat of Tilden and Johnston Arouses Foreign Tennis Hopes," *Philadelphia Evening Bulletin*, September 17, 1926.
64. Laney, *Covering the Court*, 133.

11. "DECIDEDLY UNLIKE TILDEN"

1. "Tilden Will Try Again," *Philadelphia Evening Bulletin*, September 18, 1926.
2. "Mary K. Browne Turns Tennis Pro," *Philadelphia Evening Bulletin*, September 6, 1926.
3. "Richards a Pro; Pay Not Revealed," *New York Times*, October 1, 1926.
4. Gallico, *Farewell to Sport*, 148.
5. Suzanne Lenglen, "Amateur Tennis Stars Often Paid for Drawing Crowds, Says Lenglen," *Philadelphia Evening Bulletin*, September 4, 1926.
6. "Editorial," *American Lawn Tennis* (October 15, 1926).
7. "Editorial," *American Lawn Tennis* (January 1, 1927).
8. Potter, *Kings of the Court*, 166.
9. Tilden, *My Story*, 84.
10. Interview with Hillway.
11. William T. Tilden 2d, "Tilden's Passing Shots," *American Lawn Tennis* (December 15, 1926): 612.
12. "Tilden Declines Offer," *New York Times*, October 26, 1926.
13. "Tilden Says College Football Should Recompense Players," *New York Times*, May 18, 1927.
14. "Tilden on Stage," *American Lawn Tennis* (October 15, 1926): 526.
15. "Tilden Pseudo Tramp in a New Comedy," *New York Times*, December 13, 1926.
16. "Big Bill Tilden Wins Broadway Audience," *New York Journal*, October 13, 1926.
17. "A World's First Ten Ranking," *American Lawn Tennis* (October 15, 1926): 527.
18. "Mlle. Lenglen Ranks Tilden in 6th Place," *New York Times*, October 22, 1926.
19. "Tilden to Play on the Riviera," *American Lawn Tennis* (December 15, 1926): 607.
20. Tilden, *My Story*, 71.
21. Tilden, *My Story*, 72.
22. "U.S. Team Off to Europe for French and English Championships," *American Lawn Tennis* (May 20, 1926): 69; Tilden, "Tilden's Passing Shots," *American Lawn Tennis* (May 20, 1926): 92.
23. "Tilden Inspects Courts at Night," *New York Times*, May 1, 1927.
24. "Tilden Officiates at Berlin Match," *New York Times*, May 2, 1927.
25. "Tilden Sees German Net Stars as Dangerous Tourney Rivals," *New York Times*, May 4, 1927.

26. "Tilden and Hunter Drill 4 Hours," *New York Times*, May 6, 1926.

27. "Tilden and Hunter Win German Series," *Philadelphia Evening Bulletin*, May 7, 1927.

28. "Tilden Impressed by German Tennis," *Philadelphia Evening Bulletin*, May 17, 1927. In another Tilden column two days later dealing with the prospect of Germany sending a team to America in coming years, Bill addressed the quality and character of their play as well as the efforts of William Paul Arnelt of New York in fostering Germany's tennis profile and his annual financial support that may have offset the cost of Tilden and Hunter traveling to and playing in Berlin.

29. William T. Tilden 2d, "Tilden's Passing Shots," *American Lawn Tennis* (June 20, 1927): 150.

30. John Kieran, "Sports of the Times," *New York Times*, June 7, 1927.

31. "Lacoste Sees Tilden in Drill; Calls Him Best in the World," *New York Times*, May 20, 1927.

32. Laney, *Covering the Court*, 137.

33. "Tilden Cocktail, All Water, Popular on French Courts," *New York Times*, May 20, 1927.

34. "Tilden Loses at Track," *Philadelphia Evening Bulletin*, May 19, 1927.

35. Side Line, "Tilden Changes Tennis Tactics for First Time in 7 Years," *Philadelphia Evening Bulletin*, May 19, 1927.

36. Side Line, "Tilden Changes Tennis Tactics."

37. "Tilden Conquers Lacoste, 6–4, 7–5," *New York Times*, May 21, 1927.

38. "Big Bill Tilden Conquers Borotra," *Philadelphia Evening Bulletin*, May 23, 1927.

39. Tilden, *My Story*, 82.

40. Tilden, *My Story*, 86.

41. "Lacoste Defeats Tilden in 5 Sets," *Philadelphia Evening Bulletin*, June 6, 1927.

42. Tilden, *My Story*, 86.

43. At the end of the physically draining match, the players shook hands, and Lacoste immediately collapsed. Tilden managed to walk off with the assistance of friends. Both players were spent, and Lacoste, according to Tilden, would never be the same that year. Lacoste's loss to Borotra at Wimbledon, Bill argued, was directly attributable to his inability to recover from his earlier match with Tilden.

44. *Philadelphia Evening Bulletin*, June 6, 1927.

45. Tilden, *My Story*, 86.

46. "Side Lights on St. Cloud," *American Lawn Tennis* (July 5, 1927): 204.

47. Side Line, "Tilden Earned Ten More Points than Lacoste, but Lost Match," *Philadelphia Evening Bulletin*, June 7, 1927.

48. Side Line, "Tilden Earned Ten More Points."

49. "Tilden Says $1,000,000 Would Not Cause Him to Become a Tennis Pro Just Now," *New York Times*, June 29, 1927.

50. Laney, *Covering the Court*, 148.

51. "Tilden Defeated by Cochet's Rally in British Tennis," *Philadelphia Evening Bulletin*, June 30, 1927.

52. Laney, *Covering the Court*, 151.

53. Cochet's 1927 Wimbledon run would be one of the high points of his career. He not only overcame two-set-to-love deficits against Hunter and Tilden, but also did the same in the final against Borotra, a former Wimbledon champion. France would now have three Wimbledon champions gearing up for their pursuit of the Davis Cup.

54. "Age Conquered Tilden? Tennis History Answers Yes," *Philadelphia Evening Bulletin*, July 2, 1927.

55. "Tilden Defeated in Mixed Doubles," *Philadelphia Evening Bulletin*, July 1, 1927.

56. Tilden, *My Story*, 75.

57. As far as Bill was concerned, the best doubles team was self-evident. Richards was now a pro and no longer on the team. Johnston was out of shape, and Williams was getting on in years. Moreover, Bill and Hunter had won a series of major doubles titles on both sides of the Atlantic. "I am convinced," Bill would subsequently write in *My Story*, "we might have saved [the Davis Cup] and held it another year or two except for the mismanagement and senseless bickering that destroyed the morals and upset the nerves of the American team."

58. Vincent Richards, "Richards Picks U.S. in Cup Tennis," *Philadelphia Evening Bulletin*, September 3, 1927.

59. Laney, *Covering the Court*, 158.

60. Allison Danzig, "Tilden Gains Final, Johnston Is Beaten," *New York Times*, September 9, 1927.

61. Allison Danzig, "Tilden and Hunter Put U.S. in Front," *New York Times*, September 9, 1927.

62. "French Captain Undismayed, Sees Davis Cup Victory Ahead," *New York Times*, September 9, 1927.

63. Laney, *Covering the Court*, 160.

64. Allison Danzig, "France Wins Davis Cup as Lacoste Conquers Tilden," *New York Times*, September 11, 1927.

65. "Paris Jubilant over Cup Victory," *New York Times*, September 11, 1927.

12. "TILDEN HAS BEEN A STORMY PETREL"

1. Allison Danzig, "Lacoste Defeats Tilden in 3 Sets to Keep U.S. Title," *New York Times*, September 18, 1927.

2. Danzig, "Lacoste Defeats Tilden."

3. S. Wallis Merrihew, "2nd U.S. Title for Lacoste," *American Lawn Tennis* (September 20, 1927): 440.

4. S. Wallis Merrihew, "Editorial," *American Lawn Tennis* (September 20, 1927): 460.

5. Tilden, *My Story*, 79.

6. "47th Annual Meeting of USLTA Held at Chicago," *American Lawn Tennis* (September 20, 1928): 680.

7. "United States Not to Divide Its Davis Cup Squad," *American Lawn Tennis* (March 20, 1928): 727.

8. "United States Not to Divide Its Davis Cup Squad."

9. Allison Danzig, "Coen, Only 16, Gains U.S. Davis Cup Post," *New York Times*, May 20, 1928.

10. Voss, *Tilden and Tennis*, 157.

11. William T. Tilden 2d, "Hennessey-Lott to Play Doubles," *Philadelphia Evening Bulletin*, July 18, 1928.

12. "Tilden Stricken from Davis Cup Team," *Philadelphia Inquirer*, August 9, 1928.

13. "Tilden Has Been a Stormy Petrel," *Philadelphia Evening Bulletin*, July 19, 1928; "Tilden Controversy," *American Lawn Tennis* (July 20, 1928): 252.

14. S. Wallis Merrihew, "Intimate Talks with My Readers," *American Lawn Tennis* (December 20, 1927): 614.

15. "Tilden Intimates Plot behind Ban," *Philadelphia Evening Bulletin*, July 20, 1928.

16. "Tilden Stricken from Davis Cup Team."

17. "Lacoste Refuses to Compete Here," *New York Times*, July 25, 1928.

18. "Tilden and Lacoste to Open Play Today," *New York Times*, July 27, 1928.

19. "Lacoste Refuses to Compete Here."

20. "U.S. Studies Plea to Lift Tilden Ban," *New York Times*, July 21, 1928.

21. John Kieran, "Sports of the Times," *New York Times*, July 23, 1928.

22. "British Stampede to See Tilden," *New York Times*, June 20, 1928.

23. "U.S. Studies Plea to Lift Tilden Ban."

24. "Tilden Ban Stirs Ire against U.S. Olympic Athlete-Writers," *New York Times*, July 22, 1928.

25. "Tilden, Home, Says He Won't Turn Pro," *New York Times*, August 8, 1928.

26. "Plea for Tilden Gets No Hearing," *Philadelphia Bulletin*, September 20, 1928.

27. Vincent Richards, "Tennis in Need of Good Cleaning," *Philadelphia Bulletin*, July 20, 1928.

28. S. Wallis Merrihew, "Intimate Talks with My Readers," *American Lawn Tennis* (September 5, 1928): 442.

29. "Lott and Hennessey, Probable US Team," *New York Times*, July 25, 1928.

30. Laney, *Covering the Court*, 178.

31. "Cochet Defeats Tilden 3 Straight, France Keeps Cup," *Philadelphia Evening Bulletin*, July 30, 1928.

32. "Tilden and Lacoste to Open Play Today."

33. "Tilden and Lacoste to Open Play Today."

34. P. J. Philip, "Tilden Comes Back and Beats Lacoste," *New York Times*, July 28, 1928.

35. Laney, *Covering the Court*, 179.

36. Laney, *Covering the Court*, 131.

37. Philip, "Tilden Comes Back."

38. Tilden, *Me: The Handicap*, 162.

39. P. J. Philip, "French Win Twice to Keep Davis Cup," *New York Times*, July 31, 1928.

40. Philip, "French Win Twice."

41. S. Hart, *Once a Champion*, 183.

42. "Chairman Ward and Dr. Hardy's Charges," *American Lawn Tennis* (October 20, 1928): 540.

43. Voss, *Tilden and Tennis*, 164.

44. S. Wallis Merrihew, "Intimate Talks with My Readers," *American Lawn Tennis* (September 20, 1928): 548.

45. "The Dinner after the Meeting," *American Lawn Tennis* (February 20, 1928): 717.

46. Voss, *Tilden and Tennis*, 162.

47. William T. Tilden 2d, "Cochet's Net Play Won Tennis Title," *Philadelphia Evening Bulletin*, September 18, 1928.

48. "Tennis Committee Turns Down Tilden," *Philadelphia Evening Bulletin*, September 15, 1928.

49. Tilden, *Me: The Handicap*, 1.

50. Tilden, *Me: The Handicap*, 162.

51. S. Wallis Merrihew, "Editorial: Peace with Progress," *American Lawn Tennis* (February 20, 1929): 730.

52. "Tilden Writer for Tennis Body Which Banned Him as Reporter," *New York Times*, April 30, 1929.

53. "Van Ryn, Hennessey Beat Tilden in Final Play before He Sails," *New York Times*, July 7, 1929; Davis J. Walsh, "Wants to Scrap Tilden and Hunter," *Philadelphia Evening Bulletin*, June 5, 1929.

54. Henri Cochet, "Tennis Trends," *American Lawn Tennis* (July 1929): 69.

55. "Tilden Announces That He Will Retire from International Tennis after 1929," *New York Times*, May 25, 1929.

56. Vincent Richards, "Tilden's Fight Won over Van Ryn," *Philadelphia Evening Bulletin*, September 13, 1929.

57. "Tilden to Act in England," *American Lawn Tennis* (September 5, 1929): 436.

58. *American Lawn Tennis* (October 20, 1929): 556.

59. William T. Tilden 2d, "My Tenth Anniversary," *American Lawn Tennis* (December 20, 1929): 584.

60. J. Parmly Paret, "The Will to Win Lawn Tennis Victories," *American Lawn Tennis* (January 20, 1930): 673.

61. "Tilden to Be Entertainer," *New York Times*, December 5, 1929.

62. "Riviera Season Dominated by Tilden," *American Lawn Tennis* (April 20, 1930): 5; "The Riviera in Review," *American Lawn Tennis* (April 20, 1930): 8.

63. Laney, *Covering the Court*, 224.

64. "Tilden Defeats Borotra in 5 Sets in British Tennis," *Philadelphia Evening Bulletin*, July 2, 1930.

65. Laney, *Covering the Court*, 227.

66. "Bill Tilden Wins Net Title Beating Allison," *Philadelphia Evening Bulletin*, July 5, 1930.

67. S. Wallis Merrihew, "Intimate Talks with My Readers," *American Lawn Tennis* (July 20, 1930): 278.

68. S. Wallis Merrihew, "Intimate Talks with My Readers," *American Lawn Tennis* (July 5, 1930): 244.

69. "More about an Injured Leg," *American Lawn Tennis* (November 20, 1930): 598.

70. Allison Danzig, "Tilden Joins Movies, Quits as Amateur," *New York Times*, December 31, 1930.

13. "A BURNING AFFECTION FOR THE GAME"

1. Danzig, "Tilden Joins Movies."

2. Danzig, "Tilden Joins Movies."

3. Danzig, "Tilden Joins Movies."

4. Tilden, *My Story*, 111.

5. Tilden, *My Story*, 111.

6. "Tilden Will Not Seek Pro Crown," *Philadelphia Evening Bulletin*, January 1, 1931.

7. United Press Association, biographical material on William T. Tilden, New York, January 24, 1947.

8. "Editorial," *American Lawn Tennis* (January 20, 1931): 684.

9. Edward Stillman, "Tilden the Artist," *American Lawn Tennis* (January 20, 1931): 686.

10. According to Rich Hillway, Richards held the professional title in 1927, 1928, and 1930. Koželuh won the title in 1929. Just months before Bill signed a pro contract, however, Richards had expressed his disillusionment with the pro tour and said he was dropping the sport in order to make a more traditional living in the business world.

11. "Tilden Gets Offer of $50,000 for 2-Month Trip to Australia," *New York Times*, February 2, 1931.

12. "Australian Notes," *American Lawn Tennis* (March 20, 1931): 822.

13. Advertisements appeared in such publications as *American Lawn Tennis* (January 20, 1931): 699.

14. "Tilden and Koželuh Meet before 14,000," *American Lawn Tennis* (February 20, 1931): 723.

15. Allison Danzig, "Tilden Easy Victor in Pro Debut Here," *New York Times*, February 19, 1931.

16. "Tilden Again Wins in Straight Sets," *New York Times*, February 20, 1931.

17. Tilden, *My Story*, 113.

18. Tilden, *My Story*, 113.

19. Although they had played many times on their own tour, Richards believed his victory over Koželuh on September 20, 1930, at Forest Hills earned him the title as world professional champion for that year. Hence, he and not Koželuh should have been chosen to play Tilden on February 18, 1931, at Madison Square Garden and any matches that followed.

20. Brian I. C. Norton, "Norton on Tilden Today," *American Lawn Tennis* (July 20, 1931): 22.

21. Allison Danzig, "Tilden Will Play for Charity Today," *New York Times*, June 7, 1931.

22. Examples of Tilden's articles in the *New York Times* include "Shields and Woods Justified Choice," June 7, 1931; "England a Threat in Davis Cup Play," June 14, 1931; and "Borotra Favored to Win By Tilden," June 21, 1931.

23. Interview with Hillway.

24. Voss, *Tilden and Tennis*, 182.

25. "Vines Turns Pro; Signs with Tilden," *New York Times*, October 10, 1933.

26. "USLTA Opens Investigation into the Amateur Status of Vines," *New York Times*, September 9, 1933.

27. Ellsworth Vines, "Desire to Regain Davis Cup Kept Vines from Turning Pro Earlier," *New York Times*, October 11, 1933.

28. Vines, "Desire to Regain Davis Cup."

29. "Bill Is Host," *American Lawn Tennis* (January 20, 1934): 12.

30. Robert F. Kelley, "Sports of the Times," *New York Times*, January 6, 1934.

31. Tilden's top-ten list included the following: 1, Cochet; 2, Norman Brookes; 3, René Lacoste; 4, Hans Nusslein; 5, William Johnston; 6, Vincent Richards; 7, Jean Borotra; 8, Richard Norris Williams; 9, Bruce Barnes; 10, Karel Koželuh. Kelley, "Sports of the Times"; Allison Danzig, "Cochet Put First on Tilden's List," *New York Times*, January 6, 1934.

32. Due to their popular and financial success, additional Tilden-Vines matches were scheduled. According to Rich Hillway, of the seventy-three matches, Vines would win forty-seven.

33. "Vines Turns Pro; Signs with Tilden."

34. "Tilden Triumphs Twice at Tennis," *New York Times*, October 10, 1933.

35. "Tilden Conquers Richards Easily," *New York Times*, October 9, 1933.

36. "$12,000 Is Raised at Actors Benefit," *New York Times*, April 26, 1937.

37. Players like Lott and Stoefen did well on the tour. With their 12.5 percent portion of the gross, each player earned nineteen hundred dollars for their night's work at Madison Square Garden. After six nights and a total take of forty-nine thousand, Lott and Stoefen had each earned more than sixty-one hundred dollars. During the Depression, these were very rewarding figures.

38. As a businessman as well as a player now, Tilden would occasionally become the target of a lawsuit. In July 1934, for example, Bill was sued (along with Ellsworth Vines) for $250,000 for a breach of contract. Norman L. Sper claimed he had a contract with Vines to manage his career and publicize his matches. When those duties were given to William O'Brien, Sper filed suit. "Vines and Tilden Sued," *New York Times*, July 24, 1934.

39. Tilden, *My Story*, 116.

40. Rice, *Tumult and Shouting*, 160.

41. S. Wallis Merrihew, "The Editor's Talks with His Readers," *American Lawn Tennis* (January 20, 1934): 30.

42. E. C. Potter, "Potine de Paris," *American Lawn Tennis* (December 20, 1934): 12.

43. "Austin Writes for *L'Auto*," *American Lawn Tennis* (January 20, 1935): 11.

44. "Tilden and Vines Thrill Japanese," *American Lawn Tennis* (November 20, 1936): 8.

45. "Big Bill Tilden to Enter Films," *New York Times*, September 24, 1935.

46. Allison Danzig, "Vines Will Defeat Perry, Tilden Says," *New York Times*, December 19, 1936.

47. "Tilden Net Troupe Has Japanese Ace," *New York Times*, December 24, 1936.

48. "Perry and Tilden to Meet in Garden," *New York Times*, February 26, 1937.

49. Tilden, *My Story*, 117.

50. Tilden, *Me: The Handicap*, 123.

51. Tilden, *My Story*, 131.

52. "Tilden Picks France to Keep Davis Cup; His Offer to Aid U. S. Team Is Declined," *New York Times*, June 1, 1933.

53. "Tilden and Vines Ignored by Wear," *New York Times*, July 17, 1935.

54. Though the 1937 U.S. versus Germany Davis Cup match between Budge and von Cramm was indeed a good one, much of the hype surrounding the match centers on a supposed phone call made by the führer to von Cramm just before he stepped on the court. Many knowledgeable tennis authorities argue there is no such evidence to support such a claim. Rich Hillway, who has studied the issue thoroughly, argues there are no contemporaneous newspaper accounts of such a call, nor did Budge write of it two years later in his own book on the match. Moreover, von Cramm always denied the phone call ever occurred. In fact, it is not until 1969 that Budge mentions such an incident in another book of his, but even Budge's closest confidants were not persuaded. Hillway interviewed Gene Mako, Budge's doubles partner and close friend and someone who also observed the match. When Hillway asked Mako if his friend could have made up the Hitler incident, Mako nodded in the affirmative. The result, however, is that it is unlikely we will ever know for sure if the incident occurred.

55. Tilden, *My Story*, 297.

56. "Judgment against Tilden," *New York Times*, November 17, 1938.

57. Harry Harris, "Bill Tilden Again Stage Struck," *Philadelphia Evening Bulletin*, February 28, 1940.

58. "Tilden May Not Return to U.S.," *Philadelphia Evening Bulletin*, November 23, 1938.

59. Tilden, *My Story*, 233.

60. Tilden, *My Story*, 270.

61. Tilden's charge of $10 an hour would translate into approximately $170 per hour today. A package of ten lessons would then cost $1,700.

62. "Finnish Relief Fund," *American Lawn Tennis* (March 20, 1940): 12.

63. Dora Lurie, "Bill to Compete Here Today," *Philadelphia Inquirer*, July 1, 1944.

64. "Open Tennis Blocked," *New York Times*, March 24, 1942.

65. William T. Tilden 2nd, "Tilden's Passing Shots," *American Lawn Tennis* (August 1, 1945).

66. "Red Cross Matches Open Eastern Season," *American Lawn Tennis* (August 1, 1945): 6.

67. William T. Tilden 2nd, "Tilden's Passing Shots," *American Lawn Tennis* (August 1, 1945): 17.

68. Gertrude Moran was a top-ten player who became famous for wearing short tennis skirts that showed off her lace panties, and Gloria Butler was the daughter of plutocrat George Butler, who had hosted major prewar tennis events on the Riviera.

69. Gertrude "Gussie" Moran to Richard Hillway, November 5, 2011.

70. Tilden, *My Story*, 202.

71. Interview with Gardnar Mulloy.

14. "CONTRIBUTING TO THE DELINQUENCY"

1. "Tilden Will Visit 35 Camps," *New York Times*, May 11, 1945.

2. "Big Bill Tilden Is Still Swinging—This Time against Amateur-Pro Rule," *New York Times*, March 2, 1945.

3. "Tilden Inherits from Cousin," *New York Times*, May 12, 1945.

4. Art Anderson related account of accident to Richard Hillway. Additional information was attained through Tilden's own account in *My Story*, 306.

5. Tilden, *My Story*, 208.

6. "Pro Tennis Bodies Join to Aid Game," *New York Times*, May 19, 1946.

7. Tilden, *My Story*, 208.

8. "Tilden in Feature Match," *New York Times*, July 6, 1946.

9. Allison Danzig, "Budge, Perry, Riggs Pro Tennis Victors," *New York Times*, July 9, 1946.

10. Allison Danzig, "Sabin Rally Halts Tilden in Five Sets," *New York Times*, July 11, 1946.

11. Danzig, "Sabin Rally Halts Tilden."

12. "Bill Tilden Gets 9 Months in Jail for Sex Offense," *Philadelphia Inquirer*, January 17, 1947.

13. "Tilden Goes to Jail in Delinquency Case," *New York Times*, January 17, 1947.

14. "Tilden Gets 9 Mos. on Morals Charge," *New York Daily News*, January 16, 1947.

15. Alice Marble, "The King of Tennis," *American Lawn Tennis* (June 1947): 16.

16. Marble, "The King of Tennis."

17. Tilden, *My Story*, 309.

18. Rich Hillway interviewed Art Anderson about his mother's prison visits and her acceptance of Tilden's explanation about his arrest.

19. "Won't Release Tilden," *New York Sun*, July 11, 1947.
20. "Bill Tilden, Term Ended, in Doubt on Future," *Los Angeles Times*, September 1, 1947.
21. Tilden, *My Story*, 284.
22. Tilden, *My Story*, 288.
23. Tilden, *My Story*, 307.
24. Hebephilia is a sexual attraction to children (ages thirteen to fifteen) who have just entered puberty. Ephebophilia is a sexual attraction to children (ages sixteen to nineteen) who are in the final stages of puberty.
25. "Judge Refuses to Set Bail for Tilden, Named by Boy," *Los Angeles Times*, February 2, 1949.
26. "Tilden Gets Year on 56th Birthday," *New York Times*, February 11, 1949.
27. "Bill Tilden Goes to Jail on Delinquency Charge," *Los Angeles Times*, n.d.
28. Art Anderson communicated to Rich Hillway that he may well have been the boy that was present when the police came to arrest Tilden.
29. Hillway visited Art Anderson in Burbank, California, on twelve occasions in addition to scores of phone calls over the years prior to his death in 2011 at the age of seventy-nine.
30. John E. Stanchak, "Scandals in Hollywood," *Stars in World War II* (Fall 2015).
31. "Tilden Gets One-Year Road Camp Sentence," *Los Angeles Times*, February 11, 1949.
32. William T. Tilden to Arthur Anderson, May 11, 1949.
33. Gloria P. Butler to Mrs. Ada Philipps, February 15, 1949.
34. "Tilden Is Released from Jail," *New York Times*, December 19, 1949.

EPILOGUE

1. "Tilden Selected Greatest Netman," *New York Times*, February 4, 1950.
2. Tilden's stature among tennis savants would remain high long after his death. In many surveys among sports writers such as a *New York Times* poll in 1969 and a *Los Angeles Times* poll in 1976, Tilden remained ranked the number-one tennis player of all time. Though changes at the top occurred in such fields as boxing and football, tennis and baseball (Babe Ruth) remained the same.
3. Deford, *Big Bill Tilden*, 98.
4. "Big Bill Opens Tennis Clinic," *Salt Lake City Deseret News*, [date illegible], 1951, 1.
5. Information based on Richard Hillway's many interviews with Art Anderson.
6. Interview with Gardnar Mulloy.

7. Interview with Richard Savitt.

8. Interview with Victor Seixas.

9. Interviews with Angela Buxton.

10. Tennis historian Richard Hillway held many interviews with Art Anderson. His accounts of them, both in writing and orally, were passed on to the author.

11. Bion Abbott, "Big Bill Tilden, 60, Dies Alone in Apartment," *Los Angeles Times*, June 6, 1953.

12. "Bill Tilden Is Dead; Tennis Star Was 60," *New York Times*, June 6, 1953.

13. Arthur Daley, "Sports of the Times—He Was the Best," *New York Times*, June 9, 1953.

14. Al Laney, "Views of Sport," *New York Herald Tribune*, July 12, 1953.

15. Allison Danzig, "Greatest Tennis Player of All Time," *New York Times*, December 22, 1963.

16. Paul Gallico, "Doubled as Champion during Great Net Era," *Philadelphia Inquirer*, [date illegible], 1964.

17. Red Smith, "Views of Sport," *Philadelphia Inquirer*, June 6, 1953.

18. "Tilden Estate of Little Value," *New York Times*, July 25, 1953.

19. Hillway, "Tilden and His Protégé," 13.

20. Thirteenth annual Sports Collectors Convention Auction brochure, July 8–10, 1992.

21. "Last Rites Held for Bill Tilden," *Philadelphia Inquirer*, June 11, 1953.

22. The mortuary guest book is now in the possession of Richard Hillway.

23. According to Arthur Anderson, Tilden would have preferred a burial plot in California rather than his remains sent back to Philadelphia. Anderson told Rich Hillway that Tilden fell in love with a peaceful little cemetery in Los Angeles containing just forty-two plots. Marrion Anderson, however, whom Bill named the executrix of his will, felt it might be best if Bill's niece and nephew's wishes were granted and his ashes returned to the Tilden family plot at Ivy Hill in Philadelphia.

Bibliography

Alexander, George. *Wingfield, Edwardian Gentleman*. Portsmouth NH: Peter Randall, 1980.

Alotta, Robert I. *Mermaids, Monasteries, Cherokees, and Custer*. Chicago: Bonus Books, 1990.

Baker, Norman. "Whose Hegemony? The Origins of the Amateur Ethos in Nineteenth Century English Society." *Sport in History* 24, no. 1 (2004).

Baltzell, E. Digby. *Sporting Gentlemen: Men's Tennis from the Age of Honor to the Superstar*. New York: Free Press, 1995.

Benner, Ken. "Raised on Stories of Bill Tilden." *Journal of the Tennis Collectors of America*, no. 29 (2013).

Bodo, Peter. *The Courts of Babylon*. New York: Scribner, 1995.

Bollettieri, Nick, and Dick Schaap. *My Aces, My Faults*. New York: Avon, 1995.

Brenner, Don. "The Bill Tilden Tennis Auction: The Value of Tennis Memorabilia." *Journal of the Tennis Collectors of America*, no. 24 (2011–12).

Budge, Don. *Don Budge: A Tennis Memoir*. New York: Viking, 1969.

Burt, Nathaniel, and Wallace E. Davies. "The Iron Age, 1876–1905." In *Philadelphia: A 300-Year History*. New York: W. W. Norton, 1982.

Collins, Bud. "Big Bill Still Looms Large." *usOpen.org*, 2009.

———. *Bud Collins' Modern Encyclopedia of Tennis*. Detroit: Visible Ink Press, 1994.

———. *Bud Collins' Tennis Encyclopedia*. Detroit: Visible Ink Press, 1997.

———. *Tennis Encyclopedia*. New York: Visible Ink, 1980.

Conlon, Ben. "Big Bill Tilden: The Tennis Champ Talks Pictures." N.d.

Conners, Jimmy. *The Outsider: A Memoir*. New York: HarperCollins, 2013.

Crow, Randy. "Bill Tilden's Hall of Fame Partners." *Journal of the Tennis Collectors of America*, no. 16 (2010).

Cutler, Norman. *Inside Tennis*. London: Evans Bros., 1954.

Danzig, Allison, and Peter Schwed. *The Fireside Book of Tennis*. New York: Simon and Schuster, 1972.

Deford, Frank. *Big Bill Tilden*. New York: Simon and Schuster, 1975.

Fisher, Marshall Jon. *A Terrible Splendor*. New York: Three Rivers Press, 2009.

Gallico, Paul. *Farewell to Sport*. New York: International Polygonics, 1990.

Gleaves, John, and Mathew P. Llewellyn. "Charley Paddock and the Changing State of Olympic Amateurism." *Olympika* 21 (2012).

Gorn, Elliot, and Warren Goldstein. *A Brief History of American Sports*. New York: Hill and Wang, 1993.

Gwinn, Ralph W. "America's Stepchild?" *Charleston (sc) Daily Mail Magazine*, September 29, 1929.

Hart, B. H. Liddell. *The Lawn Tennis Masters Unveiled*. London: Arrowsmith, 1926.

Hart, Stan. *Once a Champion: Legendary Tennis Stars Revisited*. New York: Dodd, Mead, 1985.

Hassan, David. "What Makes a Sporting Icon?" *Sport in History* 33, no. 4 (2013).

Hillway, Richard. "Bill Tilden according to His First Protégé." *Tennis Collector* (Summer 2013).

———. "Bill Tilden and His Protégé, Art Anderson." *Tennis Collector* (Summer 2011).

Holt, Richard. *Sport and the British*. Oxford: Clarendon Press, 1989.

Jacobs, Helen. *Center Court*. New York: A. S. Boerner, 1950.

———. *Modern Tennis*. Indianapolis: Bobbs & Merrill, 1933.

Jennings, Jay, ed. *Tennis and the Meaning of Life*. New York: Harcourt, Brace, 1995.

Keyser, Nathan N., C. Henry Kain, John P. Garber, and Horace F. McCann. *History of Old Germantown*. Philadelphia: McCann, 1907.

Lacoste, René. *Lacoste on Tennis*. New York: William Morrow, 1928.

Laney, Al. *Covering the Court: A 50-Year Love Affair with the Game of Tennis*. New York: Simon and Schuster, 1968.

Marble, Alice. *The Road to Wimbledon*. New York: Scribners, 1946.

McFadden, John J. W. F. "The Peregrinations of Big Bill Tilden." Document in possession of the Germantown Cricket Club. February 1997.

McLoughlin, Maurice E. *Tennis as I Play It*. New York: Doran, 1915.

Myers, A. Wallis. *Twenty Years of Lawn Tennis*. London: Methuen, 1921.

Olliff, John. *The Romance of Wimbledon*. London: Hutchinson, 1946.

Patty, Budge. *Tennis My Way*. London: Hutchinson Library, 1951.

Perry, Fred J. *Perry on Tennis*. Philadelphia: Winston, 1937.

Potter, E. C., Jr. *Kings of the Court*. New York: A. S. Barnes, 1963.

Rice, Grantland. *The Tumult and the Shouting: My Life in Sport*. New York: A. S. Barnes, 1954.

Riessen, Marty, and Richard Evans. *Match Point*. Englewood Cliffs NJ: Prentice Hall, 1973.

Riggs, Bobby. *Tennis Is My Racket*. New York: Simon and Schuster, 1949.

Roberts, Randy. *Joe Louis*. New Haven CT: Yale University Press, 2010.

Sack, Allen J., and Ellen Staurowsky. *College Athletes for Hire*. Westport CT: Praeger, 1998.

Schuessler, Raymond. "Biggest Battles in Tennis History." *Modern Maturity*, August–September 1977.

Smith, Ronald A. *Sports & Freedom*. New York: Oxford University Press, 1988.

Smyth, John. *Behind the Scenes at Wimbledon*. London: Collins, 1965.

Stump, Al. "Big Bill Tilden: King of the Courts." *Sport Magazine*, February 1951.

Tilden, William T. *Aces, Places and Faults*. London: Robert Hale, 1938.

———. *The Art of Lawn Tennis*. London: Methuen, 1920.

———. *Better Tennis for the Club Players*. New York: American Sports, 1923.

———. *Glory's Net*. N.p.: New Lawn Tennis, 1930.

———. *It's All in the Game: Tennis Tales*. London: Methuen, 1922.

———. *Match Play and Spin of the Ball*. New York: Arno Press, 1925.

———. *Me: The Handicap*. London: Methuen, 1929.

———. *My Story: A Champion's Memoirs*. New York: Hellman, Williams, 1948.

———. *The Phantom Drive, and Other Tennis Stories*. New York: American Sports, 1924.

———. *The Pinch Quitter, and Other Tennis Stories for Junior Players*. N.p.: New Lawn Tennis, 1924.

———. *Singles and Doubles*. New York: George H. Doran, 1928.

———. *Tennis A to Z*. London: Victor Gollancz, 1950.

———. "Tennis Holds Court." *Mentor*, September 1929.

———. "Testimonial Dinner Speech." Document in the possession of the Union League of Philadelphia. January 25, 1915.

Tingay, Lance. *Tennis: A Pictorial History*. New York: G. P. Putnam, 1973.

Tinling, Ted. *Tinling: Sixty Years in Tennis*. London: Sidwick & Jackson, 1983.

Trevor, George, "The Greatest Tennis Player of All Time." *Munsey's Magazine*.

Tunis, John R. *Sports: Heroics and Hysterics*. New York: John Day, 1928.

Vaile, P. A. *Modern Tennis*. New York: Funk & Wagnalls, 1915.

Voss, Arthur. *Tilden and Tennis in the Twenties*. Troy NY: Whitston, 1985.

Walker, Randy. *On This Day in Tennis History*. N.p.: New Chapter Press, 2008.

Wiener, Alexander. "What I Learned from the Champion." *Youth's Companion*, May 13, 1926.

Wilder, Roy. *Friend of Tennis*. New York: Gladys Heldman, 1962.

Wilding, Anthony F. *On the Court and Off*. New York: Doubleday, 1913.

Wills, Helen. *Fifteen-Thirty*. New York: Scribners, 1937.

———. *Tennis*. New York: Scribners, 1928.

Index

acting by Bill Tilden, xviii, *fig. 13–15;* with Belfry Club, *fig. 13,* 138–39, 169–70; on Broadway, 238–40, 277–78; as a cabaret entertainer, 334; as a child, 7; in London theater, 332; in motion pictures, *fig. 15, fig. 20,* 223, 363; in New Haven CT, 241–42; in New Jersey theater, 330; in Philadelphia theater, 138–39, 169–70, 213, 309; in vaudeville monologue, 327. *See also* motion pictures

Actors Fund of America, 352–53

Adams, Maude, 6, 7

Adee, George T., 96

advertisements: athletes in, 61, 64–66, 99, 412–13n44; for Bill Tilden books, 176; commercialization and, 88, 99, 135, 215; for professional matches, 349–50, 436n13

airplane crash at National Championship, 94–95

Alexander, Ben, 214, 223

Alexander, Frederick B., 20, 22, 63

Alex Taylor Company, 64, 65

Algonquin Hotel, 223, 281, 344, 368

All England Croquet Club, 16

All England Lawn Tennis & Croquet Club, 16, 80. *See also* Wimbledon Championships

Allison, Wilmer, 337–38

Alonso, José, 144, 174

Alonso, Manuel, *fig. 16,* 135, 174, 254; Bill Tilden and, 118, 175, 176; National Championships and, 144, 178, 231; Wimbledon and, 119, 124

"The Amateur Racquet," 363

Amateur Rule Committee of USLTA, 184, 193–94, 195, 199, 205

amateur versus professional, 216; championships between, 358, 377; money and, 205, 248–49, 272; sporting goods affiliations and, 64–66, 412–13n44; Suzanne Lenglen and, 244–47. *See also* player-writer rule of USLTA

Ambassador Hotel, 371, 393

American Federation of Actors, 359

American Lawn Tennis: ads in, 175–76, 436n13; Bill Tilden and Harold Hackett feud and, 181; on Bill Tilden and motion pictures, 213; on Bill Tilden as a young player, 34–35, 49, 55; on Bill Tilden going pro, 348; on Bill Tilden sex crimes, 385–86; on Bill Tilden's public service, 233–34; on Bill Tilden's superior playing, 123, 133, 136, 168, 212, 244; Bill Tilden writings in, 61–63, 87–88, 99, 174, 279, 332–34; French team and, 240, 252, 331; on National Championships, 97, 133, 306–7; on player-writer rule, 190–91, 206, 217–18; on professional tennis, 274, 361; on tournaments of 1926, 267